English Reformers

General Editors

John Baillie (1886–1960) served as President of the World Council of Churches, a member of the British Council of Churches, Moderator of the General Assembly of the Church of Scotland, and Dean of the Faculty of Divinity at the University of Edinburgh.

John T. McNeill (1885–1975) was Professor of the History of European Christianity at the University of Chicago and then Auburn Professor of Church History at Union Theological Seminary in New York.

Henry P. Van Dusen (1897–1975) was an early and influential member of the World Council of Churches and served at Union Theological Seminary in New York as Roosevelt Professor of Systematic Theology and later as President.

THE LIBRARY OF CHRISTIAN CLASSICS

English Reformers

Edited by

T. H. L. PARKER
MA, DD

Westminster John Knox Press
LOUISVILLE • LONDON

© 1966 The Westminster Press

Paperback reissued 2006 by Westminster John Knox Press, Louisville, Kentucky

All rights reserved. No part of this book may be reproduced or transmitted in any form or by any means, electronic or mechanical, including photocopying, recording, or by any information storage or retrieval system, without permission in writing from the publisher. For information, address Westminster John Knox Press, 100 Witherspoon Street, Louisville, Kentucky 40202-1396.

Cover design by designpointinc.com

Published by Westminster John Knox Press
Louisville, Kentucky

This book is printed on acid-free paper that meets the American National Standards Institute Z39.48 standard.∞

PRINTED IN THE UNITED STATES OF AMERICA

Library of Congress Cataloging-in-Publication Data is on file at the Library of Congress, Washington, D.C.

ISBN-13: 978-0-664-23084-5
ISBN-10: 0-664-23084-9

GENERAL EDITORS' PREFACE

The Christian Church possesses in its literature an abundant and incomparable treasure. But it is an inheritance that must be reclaimed by each generation. THE LIBRARY OF CHRISTIAN CLASSICS is designed to present in the English language, and in twenty-six volumes of convenient size, a selection of the most indispensable Christian treatises written prior to the end of the sixteenth century.

The practice of giving circulation to writings selected for superior worth or special interest was adopted at the beginning of Christian history. The canonical Scriptures were themselves a selection from a much wider literature. In the patristic era there began to appear a class of works of compilation (often designed for ready reference in controversy) of the opinions of well-reputed predecessors, and in the Middle Ages many such works were produced. These medieval anthologies actually preserve some noteworthy materials from works otherwise lost.

In modern times, with the increasing inability even of those trained in universities and theological colleges to read Latin and Greek texts with ease and familiarity, the translation of selected portions of earlier Christian literature into modern languages has become more necessary than ever; while the wide range of distinguished books written in vernaculars such as English makes selection there also needful. The efforts that have been made to meet this need are too numerous to be noted here, but none of these collections serves the purpose of the reader who desires a library of representative treatises spanning the Christian centuries as a whole. Most of them embrace only the age of the church fathers, and some of them have long been out of print. A fresh translation of a work already translated may shed much new light upon its meaning.

This is true even of Bible translations despite the work of many experts through the centuries. In some instances old translations have been adopted in this series, but wherever necessary or desirable, new ones have been made. Notes have been supplied where these were needed to explain the author's meaning. The introductions provided for the several treatises and extracts will, we believe, furnish welcome guidance.

JOHN BAILLIE
JOHN T. MCNEILL
HENRY P. VAN DUSEN

CONTENTS

ABBREVIATIONS xiii
GENERAL INTRODUCTION xv
GENERAL BIBLIOGRAPHY xxiii
JOHN JEWEL: AN APOLOGIE OF THE CHURCH OF ENGLAND
    Introduction 3
    Bibliography 11
    Text 14
JOHN FOXE: TO THE TRUE AND FAITHFULL CONGREGATION
    OF CHRIST'S UNIVERSAL CHURCH
    Introduction 61
    Bibliography 69
    Text 72
WILLIAM TYNDALE: THE EXPOSITION OF THE FYRSTE
    EPISTLE OF SEYNT JHON
    Introduction 89
    Bibliography 97
    Text 100
JOHN PONET: A SHORT CATECHISME
    Introduction 147
    Bibliography 153
    Text 155
JOHN HOOPER: A DECLARACION OF CHRISTE AND OF HIS
    OFFYCE
    Introduction 185
    Bibliography 189
    Text 193

RICHARD TAVERNER: POSTILS ON EPISTLES AND
                             GOSPELS
    Introduction 221
    Bibliography 227
    Text 230

THOMAS CRANMER: CERTAIN SERMONS, OR HOMILIES
    Introduction 255
    Bibliography 260
    Text 262

NICHOLAS RIDLEY: A TREATISE AGAYNST THE ERROUR OF
                              TRANSUBSTANTIATION, AND EXTRACTS
                              FROM HIS EXAMINATIONS
    Introduction 289
    Bibliography 296
    Text 298

HUGH LATIMER: A SERMON ON THE LORD'S PRAYER
    Introduction 323
    Bibliography 329
    Text 331

INDEXES 349

ABBREVIATIONS

PS	The Parker Society.
PL	*Patrologiae Cursus Completus, Series Latina,* ed. by J. P. Migne. Paris, 1844 ff.
PG	*Patrologiae Cursus Completus, Series Graeca,* ed. by J. P. Migne. Paris, 1857 ff.
Mansi	*Sacrorum Conciliorum Nova, et Amplissima Collectio,* ed. by J. D. Mansi. Florence, 1759 ff.
Foxe	John Foxe, *Actes and Monuments.* Church Historians of England, 1853.
Corp. Iur. Can.	*Corpus Iuris Canonici . . . instruxit Aemilius Friedberg. Pars Prior Decretum Magistri Gratiani . . . Lipsiae.* 1879.
Corp. Iur. Civ.	*Corpus Iuris Civilis.* Berlin, 1895.
LXX	Septuagint.
Vulg.	Vulgate.
⟨ ⟩	indicate an editorial insertion in the text.
[ ]	indicate an editorial omission from the text.

General Introduction

WE MAY DEFINE THE ENGLISH REFORMERS AS THOSE ENGLISHmen who, in the half century that began about 1520, confessed that Jesus Christ is the complete and only mediator between God and men, and who therefore endeavored so to shape the doctrine and practice of the Church that her earthly existence should correspond to the truth of his existence. In this definition we place the Reformation within the sphere of faith in Jesus Christ, of repentance for sin, of love for the neighbor, of looking above the bewildering turmoils of sixteenth-century England to the eternal and unchanging Kingdom of Heaven; within the sphere of the Church and of assembling together to worship God, and therefore of the ministry and of reading and expounding the Bible and for this reason once again of faith, hope, and love; within the sphere of being baptized and of receiving the Holy Communion, of singing hymns and of praying in private and in public; within the sphere of obedience to God's demands and commands and of a rightly ordered moral life in private and in society. It is admittedly considerably easier to recognize (or think we recognize!) these elements in some events and writings than in others. There are also not a few occasions when we cannot see them at all, but only something that is their contradiction. If we can see the confession shining plain in the Book of Common Prayer or in some of the Homilies or in Tyndale's living sacrifice of himself to give England a Bible in her own tongue, we can see only *confusio hominum* in Henry's "divorce" proceedings or in the ambition of Northumberland. But *confusio hominum non tollit confessionem Dei,* to paraphrase an old saying. It serves to remind us once again that we men are *"eitel arme Sünder,"* as Matthias Claudius put it, "just poor sinners"; Thomas Cranmer, Nicholas Ridley, and John Foxe stand under the universal condemnation along with Henry VIII, Thomas More, and Edmund Bonner. The Reformation, in England as elsewhere, was no perfect and sinless work, but human, and therefore sinful. Yet in the midst of it all, sometimes blazing clearly, sometimes well-nigh obscured, the confession of Jesus Christ.

We find it difficult to recognize the Reformation in many of the books about it, where it is placed anywhere but in this sphere. Thus, to use the term to denote the whole history of *homo Europaeus* in this period is grossly to apply the particular to the general. The two volumes of the Cambridge Modern History (1903 and 1958) may call themselves *The Reformation,* but in this they are the Old and the Young Pretenders; *Europe in the Sixteenth Century* would better have described their substance. There is a danger in this misnaming. First, the whole age is called "The Reformation," and thus the word "Reformation" is drained of its own particular meaning. Then the Reformation itself, shorn of its title and lacking a clear shape, has to be fitted into the general pattern as a politico-, sociologico-, culturo-, scientifico-, etc., religious movement. In this operation it is the religious and theological element which comes off worst, being given only a walk-on part or even hissed off the stage as idiot controversies that must not be allowed to disturb our fantasy world of the sixteenth century.

That the story of the English Reformation was a part of the political history of England cannot be denied. Henry, Mary, and Elizabeth intended to call the religious tune, according to their own religious persuasions or to the demands of foreign or home affairs. They were often and largely successful. The Church achieved no such freedom here as in the cities of Switzerland. Government domination is a most important factor in the English Reformation, but is it the whole story or even the heart of the story? Has the historian done his duty when (like Dr. T. M. Parker: *The English Reformation to 1558*) he has described the changes that successive governments have made in the structure and worship of the Church of England and then has room for only a couple of paragraphs on what the Reformers believed? Or was Sir Maurice Powicke right to put it so baldly: "The one definite thing which can be said about the Reformation in England is that it was an act of State." [1] Or Prof. Owen Chadwick: "The English Reformation

---

[1] *The Reformation in England* (London, 1941), p. 1.

GENERAL INTRODUCTION xvii

was emphatically a political revolution." [2] Three considerations should show us that this interpretation is too naïve and partial. First, what Sir Maurice Powicke calls "the general acquiescence" of Englishmen in the religious changes and which he finds "one of the most mysterious things in our history." [3] If the Reformation was simply an act of state, this acquiescence is not just mysterious but so psychologically improbable as to be incredible. Might it not be that the Reformation also involved religious beliefs which, through books, preaching, private conversations, and multifarious means that Stephen Gardiner summed up as "printers, players, and preachers," [4] won credit for themselves? Secondly, how are we to explain the discrepancy between Professor Chadwick's "The English Reformation was emphatically a political revolution" and his later statement: "Seven years later [Elizabeth] told a Spaniard that the Protestants had driven her farther than she intended to go, and she was speaking truth as well as diplomacy. But she had no choice. If a Protestant, then despite her talk about the Lutheran Confession of Augsburg, despite her affirmation that she disagreed only with three or four things in the mass, she had no alternative to the Prayer Book hallowed by fire"? [5] Does this not mean that there was a struggle between the state and the representatives of the Reformation and that the state lost? And thirdly, the stubborn fact has to be explained that the Church which emerged was a Church of the Reformation, believing in justification by faith alone, holding to the Scriptures as the supreme authority in matters of faith, refusing the doctrine of transubstantiation. It was not inevitable that the Church should take this course; other possibilities were open, including the most probable one of "a Catholicism without the Pope," as Professor Chadwick calls it. If the Reformation is interpreted simply as an act of state, as emphatically a political revolution, this fact is inexplicable.

Or consider the view of the English Reformation as an anticlerical movement, a view that filled the gaze of the older liberal writers. For example, J. A. Froude: "The original Reformation was a revolt of the laity against the clergy, a revolt against a complicated and all-embracing practical tyranny, the most intolerable that the world has ever seen." [6] Even on the face of it, this concept

---

[2] *The Reformation* (London, 1964), p. 97.
[3] Powicke, *op. cit.*, p. 7.
[4] Foxe, 6.31.
[5] Chadwick, *op. cit.*, p. 131.
[6] *Lectures on the Council of Trent* (London, 1896), pp. 4-5. Cf. G. M. Trevelyan, *English Social History* (London, 1946), pp. 100-101.

should have been handled far more delicately and less generally. Does "anticlerical" mean against a separate ministerial order or against all clergy or only against a certain sort of clergy? Was it continued against the clergy of the Reformation? Were only laymen affected by it or did it touch some clergy too? Nevertheless, allow the expression as meaning a popular animosity against vices which were represented as involving so many of the clergy that all the clergy in general became tarred with the same brush. There was undoubtedly, even if we take Simon Fish and his like with a pinch of salt, a very strong anticlericalism in the first half of the sixteenth century. In some respects it accompanied the course of the Reformation. But it patently fails to account for all the elements that comprised the Reformation.

Or the Reformation is taken as the correction of ecclesiastical abuses—financial, administrative, and moral. The Church at the beginning of the century stood in sore need of reform. The house of God had to be purged of much filth and rubbish, that the beauty of its holiness might once more shine forth. We must admit at once that the correction of abuses constituted one of the most important parts of the Reformation. The *forma*, the comely appearance and shape, of the Church, has become *deformata;* the consequent restoration is a *reformatio*. But when the part is made into the whole and the Reformation is interpreted solely as a correction of abuses, misunderstanding has entered. Thus Edwyn Bevan's interpretation leaves us still on the threshold: The Reformers' "positive teaching consisted of parts of the Catholic tradition which they retained: their difference from the Roman Church was negative. A Protestant may admit this without prejudice to the Reformation. He may say that the work of clearing away all the false accretions which had gathered round the primitive Christian faith brought in fact a great positive gain, just as the cleaning of a picture or the freeing of a bronze statue from a crust, may allow a beauty to reappear which had become effaced." [7]

Moreover, the correction of abuses is usually interpreted too shallowly, as if it were merely a spring-clean in a village church that had been overlong neglected. The fabric and the furniture are left intact and clean; the dirt is swept outside. The shallow view receives a facile expression, whether in the passage from Bevan just quoted or in Maynard Smith's summary: "The storm in England had done good. It had destroyed a multitude of superstitions or at least condemned them. It had removed some, but

[7] *Christianity* (London, 1935), pp. 153–154.

not nearly all the abuses that existed in the Church. It had cleared the air and swept away the cobwebs spun by decadent schoolmen, and this had allowed the Church to enter into an alliance with sound learning. The storm had shaken the structure of the Church but not destroyed it, so that, when it had blown over, the Catholic creeds, orders and sacraments were intact." [8] It has stopped raining; we can all take our macks off. Was it coincidental, or not, rather, significant, that the man who spoke loudest and most wittily against abuses was the man who did not want to get involved, Erasmus of Rotterdam?

Or the Reformation may be understood as fundamentally a theological movement. Then will sound the cry, *"Ad fontes!"* The New Testament teaching, hidden almost completely for so long, is now at last recovered in its simplicity. Or if not that, at any rate late medieval theology (these "decadent schoolmen"!) is measured alongside the Word of God and corrected radically. Hence, the Reformation is given its theological platform from which it will attempt to carry out a program of reform, like a political movement. We may think here of F. D. Maurice, with his chapter on "Pure Protestantism" in *The Kingdom of Christ*. For him pure Protestantism is expressed in four leading principles: justification by faith, election, authority of Scripture, and the distinction of nations and the rights of kings. If we cannot accept such a view of the Reformation, it is because even theology, lying so near the center, is not the whole of the Reformation, but only a part. If we would do justice to this movement, it is necessary that we see it whole. And this is why, in our original definition, we placed it in the exclusive but so broad field of confession to Jesus Christ.

It remains to enter my apologia for the selection of English Reformation writings presented here. Perhaps no other volume in the series provided quite so much scope and therefore held quite so many pitfalls. It will be known from the prospectus that the original editors were Prof. Norman Sykes and Dr. R. D. Whitehorn. After the death of Professor Sykes, I was asked to take over the Anglican section of the book while Dr. Whitehorn continued with the Puritans. At a later date, Dr. Whitehorn found other commitments pressing upon him and I became myself responsible for the whole volume.

At the outset I was given some memoranda of advice that Professor Sykes had received from Reformation scholars. X suggested certain writings; Z suggested certain writings. These did not al-

---

[8] *Pre-Reformation England* (London, 1938), p. 525.

ways coincide. Nor did I find myself always in agreement with their choices. Therefore, I saw that I must be bold and resolute, make my own choice and stick to it. I am alone responsible for what is printed here. If any reader thinks (as I am sure many readers will think) that *this* ought to have been omitted in favor of *that*, let him be well assured that I sympathize. I too would like to have included *that*—indeed, it may be one of the unhappy typescripts now inhabiting a dismal envelope marked "Rejects."

Let me explain the principles on which I have made my choice. The series is called THE LIBRARY OF CHRISTIAN CLASSICS. This particular volume is *English Reformers*. I therefore regarded myself as limited to Christian classics by English Reformers. This last term was definite enough, save for dates. If *English* Reformers, then foreign Reformers were excluded, even if they lived and worked in England. The chief victims here were Bucer, Peter Martyr, and John Knox. By the same criterion, translations were excluded. I should have liked to include Tyndale's *Pathway to the Scriptures*, but it was too much of a translation from Luther, who had, moreover, been given some volumes in the series for himself alone. I did not see why these already pampered Continental lions should be yet further fattened with good English Christian meat. Next, if English *Reformers*, certain great figures would be excluded who demand sympathy or respect or who went some of the way with the Reformers (or at least some of the way in certain directions). I am thinking of Colet or More or Stephen Gardiner. As for dates, the *terminus a quo* was not difficult to determine, and in fact our earliest piece is by Tyndale in 1531. The *terminus ad quem* was less easy, but I have placed it in the mid fifteen sixties and the so-called Elizabethan Settlement, on the grounds that the rest of the century was mainly taken up with attacking and defending a position already occupied. The Puritans were not in the end included, and this for two reasons. A practical reason was that several Puritan works are being included in another series that is to be published in the United States. The other reason was that a Puritan movement had hardly emerged by the time of our *terminus ad quem*. The foreshadowings of it, however, can be seen in John Hooper.

But Christian *Classics* is a tall order. How many even excellent works deserve this ultimate honor? What may indisputably be called classics of the English Reformation? The Book of Common Prayer, certainly; the First Book of Homilies; the Thirty-nine Articles; the *Apologia Ecclesiae Anglicanae*, Tyndale's New Testament, and one or another of the English Bibles, some of Latimer's sermons and Foxe's *Actes and Monuments*. But many of these works were quite impracticable for our purposes: the Prayer Book because it is too easy to obtain and too well known, the Bible translations for the same cause, and Foxe because he is too bulky. Of those remaining, we have included some Homilies, the *Apologie*, and a sermon of Latimer's. Nevertheless, the English Reformation without Tyndale or Foxe would be unthinkable. I have therefore chosen Tyndale's *Exposition of I John* (which also contains a piece of Biblical translation hitherto neglected) and a preface from *Actes and Monuments*, which serves both as a summary of the whole work and also as an explanation of Foxe's purpose. I will confess that if anyone demands why the Thirty-nine Articles are not in, I shall be *anapologētos*—tongue-tied and ashamed—but alas! few are likely to ask for them.

For the rest, there were some Reformers, some subjects, and some forms that would need to be added if the volume was to make any claims to comprehensiveness. Ridley never wrote a classic; but he was himself a classic man. How could a book like this leave out Ridley? It was also necessary to have something on the Eucharistic controversy. Ridley and the Eucharistic controversy coincide in *A Treatise agaynst . . . Transubstantiation*. Hooper, not one of the pleasantest of characters but an unjustly neglected writer, stands out as a theologian above many whom one would rather have included. Concerning Hooper my conscience is clear. Taverner's Postils have also been too much overlooked, perhaps because they had such a short effective life. But it is surely impossible not to be delighted with these clear and fresh little expositions, nearly all pointing in exactly the right direction. And finally, I judged it good to have a catechism, since this form played such an important part in the Reformation. And of those available, *A Short Catechisme* picked itself: Cranmer's Catechism was a translation, Nowell's and Becon's both too long, the Prayer Book Catechism too well known.

A word about the editing. Precise bibliographical notes are given in the Bibliography sections preceding the individual pieces. It is necessary to mention that I have modernized the spelling in the texts. If anyone thinks this is a bowing down in the House of Rimmon, I for one will not disagree with him. But the case for it is that the other volumes have been translations from various languages into modern English, and this volume should conform. The punctuation and paragraphing have also been altered so as to accord as far as possible with modern English usage. This is really necessary, for sixteenth-century punctuation was often arbitrary or followed criteria other than grammatical. But I have left the punctuation fairly slack. I have tried above all to present a sound text, believing that this is the editor's first duty. The Parker Society is in many respects very good; its textual errors are not numerous; its notes contain a fund of information. The Jewel volumes, for example, are excellent. But not all the authors are treated so well, and the greatest weakness of the edition is that we do not always know what text is given and whether it is the earliest or the best text. With this in mind I have (except for the Homilies, where the earliest editions were not to hand and where I thought I could trust Griffiths' edition) collated every piece with the earliest edition known to me or with the final edition revised by the author. I have always made it clear what text I have followed.

Acknowledgments

A book of this sort cannot be compiled without the friendly help of others. I wish therefore to record my thanks for such aid. I am grateful to the Librarians of the British Museum and of St. Paul's Cathedral, and especially to those members of the staff of the Anderson Room of the Cambridge University Library who have continually assisted me in finding my way in the labyrinth of the sixteenth-century book world. Mr. H. M. Adams has been most kind in giving me information in the same field and has in particular allowed me to consult the manuscript of his bibliography of pre-1550 books in Cambridge libraries, which is now passing through the press and which will be of the greatest help to all students of sixteenth-century literature. My friends the Reverend Basil Hall and the Reverend George Yule have always been patient to talk about the work and to help with advice. I am also grateful to my son David for cheerfully lending a hand in such matters as dictating Richard Taverner to me while I typed. And I should like to add a sincere word of thanks for the very thorough and penetrating work on the typescript by the staff of The Westminster Press.

Books by husbands ought, by my way of thinking, to bear also their wife's name on the title page. Certainly this one should, for not only did my wife take upon her the wearisome burden of copying out notes and checking typescripts (thereby saving me much time), but continually and in divers manners she has helped the work along its course.

GENERAL BIBLIOGRAPHY

Since a bibliography is given for each separate piece, there is no need for an extended one here. The reader is referred to:
Conyers Read, ed., *Bibliography of British History: Tudor Period, 1485–1603.* 2d ed., Oxford, 1959.

GENERAL HISTORIES

Gilbert Burnet, *History of the Reformation of the Church of England,* ed. by N. Pocock. 7 vols. Oxford, 1865.
John Strype, *Ecclesiastical Memorials, relating chiefly to Religion, and the Reformation of it, and the emergencies of the Church of England, under King Henry VIII. King Edward VI. and Queen Mary I.* 6 vols. Oxford, 1822.
John Strype, *Annals of the Reformation and Establishment of Religion, and other various occurences in the Church of England, during Queen Elizabeth's happy reign.* 7 vols. Oxford, 1824.
A General Index to the Historical and Biographical Works of John Strype, A.M. 2 vols. Oxford, 1828.
R. W. Dixon, *History of the Church of England from the Abolition of the Roman Jurisdiction.* Vols. I–IV, London, 1878–1891; Vols. V–VI, ed. by H. Gee, Oxford, 1902.
A. G. Dickens, *The English Reformation.* London, 1964.
E. G. Rupp, *The English Protestant Tradition.* Cambridge, 1947.

COLLECTED WORKS OF THE REFORMERS

The Parker Society. Instituted A.D. M.DCCC.XL. For the Publication of the Works of the Fathers and Early Writers of the Reformed English Church.
Legh Richmond, ed., *The Fathers of the English Church; or a Selection from the Writings of the Reformers and Early Protestant Divines, of the Church of England.* 8 vols. London, 1807–1812.

(This edition, although inferior to that of the Parker Society in many respects, nevertheless contains some writings that are not in it—notably works by Frith, Joye, Barnes, and Laurence Saunders, as well as "Cranmer's" 1548 Catechism, the preface to and prayers from the Geneva Bible, the Duke of Somerset's *A spiritual and most precious pearl,* and works by Haddon and Foxe against Osorius.)

THEOLOGY

C. Hopf, *Martin Bucer and the English Reformation.* Oxford, 1946.

J. Hunt, *Religious Thought in England from the Reformation to the end of the last century.* 3 vols. London, 1870–1873.

H. E. Jacobs, *A Study in Comparative Symbolics; the Lutheran Movement in England during the reigns of Henry VIII and Edward VI, and its Literary Monuments.* Philadelphia, 1908. (I would not agree with Conyers Read that this book is "trustworthy." The author, himself a Lutheran, is too ready to find Lutheran influences everywhere.)

D. B. Knox, *The Doctrine of Faith in the Reign of Henry VIII.* London, 1961.

C. Hardwick, *A History of the Articles of Religion.* London, 1876.

William Beveridge, *Ecclesia Anglicana Ecclesia Catholica; or The Doctrine of the Church of England consonant to Scripture, Reason, and Fathers: in a Discourse upon the Thirty-nine Articles agreed upon in the Convocation held at London MDLXII.* 2 vols. Oxford, 1840.

E. H. Browne, *An Exposition of the Thirty-nine Articles, Historical and Doctrinal.* 13th ed., London, 1887.

John Jewel

AN APOLOGIE OF THE
CHURCH OF ENGLAND

John Jewel: An Apologie of the Church of England

INTRODUCTION

THE "APOLOGIA" WAS WRITTEN EARLY IN 1561 OR, MORE PROBably, in 1560; that is to say, soon after the settlement of religion in the Parliament of 1558–1559. The Church of England had only recently passed through its third violent revolution in ten years. The moderation observed under Henry VIII had been engulfed in the radical reforming activity of Edward's brief reign. The Church had then been in a moment swung completely round to the wholehearted Romanism of Mary Tudor. Now this in its turn had been reversed with the accession of Elizabeth and the zeal of her first Parliament. These facts of history alone demanded that the Church should give an account of herself and make her position clear. But added to this was the complexity of the religious position at home and abroad. What were the relationships between the Churches? How did Canterbury stand over against Germany, Geneva, Zurich, and Rome? What was going to be the outcome of the struggle for religious dominance in France? Hope was far from abandoned that England, allowed her portion of freedom, might even yet return to the Roman fold. Some events and dispositions were interpreted as straws which signalized that the wind was blowing in the right direction. Representatives from England were to be invited to the next session of the Council of Trent.[1] In England itself, there was apparently little doubt as to the true state of affairs. John Jewel might grumble about the crucifix in the Queen's Chapel and her slow-

---

[1] Cf. the title of 1617 edition, in which a further reason for the book is given: *& quod ad Concilium Tridentinum non accesserit* (in that the Church of England did not go to the Council of Trent) : in *Doctrina, et Politia Ecclesiae Anglicanae* . . . Londini, Apud Ioannem Billium. 1617.

ness in carrying through the reform of the Church, but he knew it was only slowness and not refusal, and that the crucifix was merely an inconsistency to be deplored and not a sign of a Romeward movement. They knew this in England. But the theologians of the Continent did not understand, and if Protestants, they were worried, hopeful if they were Romanists.

It was to put an end to all this uncertainty that William Cecil set Jewel to compose, in the name of the Church of England, a statement of her position. "Apology" does not, of course, bear its common modern meaning of the acknowledgment of error and of "begging someone's pardon." In Greek an *apologia* was the speech made in his own defense by an accused person. Thus, Paul, when he was arrested in Jerusalem, spoke to the crowd in Hebrew and said, "Brethren and fathers, hear the *apologia* which I now make before you" (Acts 22:1). The word is also used to powerful effect in Romans, where Paul speaks of the sinner before the judgment seat of God as being *anapologētos*, with nothing to say in his own defense. It is in this sense that the second-century writers such as Tertullian and Justin Martyr, declaring the faith and way of life of the Church and her place in God's purpose, received the name of "Apologists." Jewel had them in mind when he wrote the *Apologia*. He begins with a quotation from Tertullian's *Apologia* and later professes the same motive in writing as the Apologists had had: "And the ancient Christians, when they were slandered to the people . . . and did perceive that by such slanderous accusations, the religion which they professed might be brought in question, namely, if they should seem to hold their peace and in manner confess the fault; lest this might hinder the free course of the gospel, they made orations, they put up supplications, and made means to emperors and princes that they might defend themselves and their fellows in open audience" (PS, III. 55). Thus, before the Churches of the world, the Church of England makes her apologia. She speaks, not in her own mother tongue, but in Latin, the language that the foreign theologians will understand. Nevertheless, she almost at once translates her words into English, that her own people may know where they stand.

The argument runs as follows: All down the ages, Truth has been a persecuted foreigner in the world, and this is no less so today, when the Reformation truth is persecuted and quelled by Rome. But since our cause is that of Christ, the apostles and prophets, and the Church fathers, it is our duty to reply. In the first place, they accuse us of heresy. Here (Part II) is our confession of faith; read it and judge whether it is heretical. We believe in the Triune God, in the deity and humanity of Jesus Christ, our Redeemer, in the Holy Spirit, who is powerful to enlighten the hearts of men. We believe that there is one Church, dispersed throughout the world, and that Christ alone is its king and head. The ministry of the Church is threefold—bishops, priests, and deacons; their office is to teach and set forth the faith. Yet they are not in the place of Christ, who is ever present to help his Church. Christ has given his ministers "power to bind, to loose, to open, to shut." That is to say, by the preaching of the gospel the minister proclaims forgiveness to all who repent and believe, and, when any have sinned grievously and shut themselves off from the Church, restores them to the body of believers. In either case, these keys which open or shut God's Kingdom are "the word of the Gospel and the expounding of the law and Scriptures." It is lawful and honorable for the ministers to marry. We receive the canonical Scriptures gratefully, knowing that they are the foundation on which the Church is built and the criterion and norm of all doctrine. We accept the two Sacraments of Baptism and the Lord's Supper. Baptism is the Sacrament of forgiveness of sins by the death of Christ. In the Eucharist is set before our eyes the death of Christ for us and his resurrection, so that we may thank him for saving us and be reminded daily of his death. The bread and wine are holy and heavenly mysteries of Christ's body and blood and in them Christ, the true bread of eternal life, is so manifested (*exhiberi*) as present to us that by faith we truly receive his body and blood. Not that the bread and wine change their "nature" and are annihilated. On the contrary, they remain bread and wine. Yet this is not to say that the Lord's Supper is merely "a cold ceremony," for, as we have already said, Christ is really present and by faith we really take his body and blood. All the people receive both bread and wine. We do not reserve the Sacrament as something to be worshiped. Faith is necessary in those who use the Sacraments, for "the Sacraments of Christ without faith do not once profit these that be alive: a great deal less do they profit those that be dead." Purgatory is an old wives' tale. With regard to ceremonies in public worship, we are guided by the Pauline dictum that all things should "be done with comeliness, and in good order." We use the ceremonies handed down from the apostles, and also others that seem to be comely and orderly; but anything superstitious or contrary to Scripture we reject at once. Our common worship is conducted in English. All our worship also is through Christ alone, for it is he, and not his mother or his saints, by whom we have access to God. We are all sinners and are saved only by Jesus Christ, to whom we must turn for forgiveness. Once forgiven, our faith is lively and finds expression in good works. Finally, our human flesh shall rise again at the Last Day; Christ will wipe the tears from our faces and through him we shall enjoy everlasting life.

It is true (Part III [PS, III. 66 ff.]) that there have sprung up more or less contemporaneously with the Reformation certain heresies. But they are distinct from and opposed to the Reformation. In fact, they flourish wherever Roman error is taught. It is also true that there are topics of disagreement among the Reformers themselves, but these are nothing compared with the ancient controversies. And are there not disagreements within the Roman ranks, Thomists against Scotists, for example? In the Church of Rome (Part IV) immorality is rife. The same cannot be said of our Churches. Moreover, their accusation that we are seditious and that civil strife is engendered in our territories is not borne out by history, for we teach and practice civil obedience. They say (Part IV, §§ 15 ff. [PS, III. 76 ff.]) that we have left the unity of the Catholic Church. In fact, they themselves do not agree with the fathers on this and that. To be brief, they lack antiquity, universality, and the consent of all places and of all times, and we have only forsaken them that we might return to Christ and the apostles. If they say that these matters should have been determined only by a general council (Part VI), our reply is that this was in practice impossible, and the composition and procedure of the Council of Trent have merely confirmed the fact. The Christian prince has authority to call councils of the Church and to reform religion. This he has done in England, where, moreover, rather than wait forever for a general council, we set to work to reform our Church by a provincial synod.

Authorship

In his book on Jewel, Mr. J. E. Booty has misunderstood the part that Jewel played in the *Apologia:* "It seems that the *Apologia* was indeed a group project and therefore is more truly representative of the Church of England than has hitherto been thought." [2] He nevertheless admits that Jewel was the leading figure. In the Introduction to his edition of the *Apologie,* however, he apparently recedes from this position and merely says, "Jewel was the chief author, his name is therefore rightly attached

---

[2] *John Jewel as Apologist of the Church of England* (Church Historical Society [London, 1963]), p. 53.

to the work, but he did not bear the responsibility for it entirely alone." [3]

As, however, he does not explain why he no longer holds his earlier view, we had better give the evidence for the authorship here.

The title pages of the first Latin edition (1562) and of the first two English editions (1562 and 1564) do not bear an author's name. The collected *Workes* of John Jewel (1609 and 1611) do not contain the *Apologie* as a separate piece, though this seems to come from its being contained in *The Defense of the Apology*, which is printed in full, and not from doubts as to its authorship, for the life of Jewel which is given in this volume speaks of "his Apologie, begunne in the yeere 1561, and perfected in the yeere 1562." [4] The first edition in which the title page ascribes the work to Jewel seems to be 1626 (London, J. Boler).

In the second English edition, however, we have the principal clue to the authorship. The first English translation having proved unsatisfactory, the learned Lady Bacon, the mother of Francis, made another and submitted it to the archbishop for his approval. Parker and the author preferred it to the first, and it was therefore published in 1564. The archbishop wrote a graceful letter of thanks to the translator, in which he said that "both the chief author of the Latin work and I, severally perusing and conferring your whole translation, have without alteration allowed of it." [5] Mr. Booty takes "chief author" as implying that there was more than one author but that one of them took the leading part.[6] Jewel's adversary, Thomas Harding, also interprets it in this way: "Lastly, for commoditie as well of my utterance, as of my understanding, where neither he that penned the booke, who doubtless is the chief authour of it, who so ever he be, nor they that have holpe him with notes, counsels, and devises, have put their names." [7] Disregarding the last part of this sentence, which must be conjecture, or at best rumor, we may say that Harding is seizing on Parker's expression and using it to make it appear that there was something shady about the production of the *Apologie*. But I do not think that the rest of the evidence allows us to interpret "chief author" in precisely this way. In the same letter of Parker occurs another reference to the author (a reference that

---

[3] Booty, *An Apology*, p. xxxviii.
[4] *The Life of the Worthie Prelate* . . . (*Workes*, 1611 Sig.¶¶5ª).
[5] PS, III.51.
[6] Booty, *John Jewel*, p. 53.
[7] *Confutation* Sig.‡6ª.

Mr. Booty does not mention): "Ye have done pleasure to the author of the Latin book, in delivering him by your clear translation from the perils of ambiguous and doubtful constructions, and in making his good work more publicly beneficial." [8] Here the author, whoever he was, is put alone. The only other evidence with any color to suggest that others besides the "chief author" had a great hand in the book is the letter from Cox of Ely to Parker that Mr. Booty prints. After praising the *Apologia*, Cox congratulates Parker for getting this work done. "It is marvelouse well day to sett up men abowte such matters. . . . And for as muche as thei can do so excellently, it shall not be amisse, ye sett them styll aworke to make some brieffe and handsome confutation of the principall arguments that the papistes make and glory in." [9] But this is too vague. The plural seems to be a mere generalization, possibly because Cox did not know who the author was.

What, however, of the identification of the author with Jewel? Curiously enough, although the preparation and publication of the *Apologia* is mentioned in a number of letters, including one by Jewel himself, only once is he named as the author. This occurs in a letter by the ambassador at Paris, Throckmorton, who reports on January 24, 1562, to his master, Cecil, on the arrival of the book with the words, "I saw the bysshop of Saulsbery apology." [10] It is improbable that Throckmorton would write so definitely unless he had been told that Jewel was the author, although it is conceivable that he had misunderstood an earlier letter of Cecil's which told him: "I have caused the Bishop of Sarum to fayne an epistle [i.e., the *Epistola cuiusdam Angli* of 1561, which Mr. Booty prints as an Appendix]. . . . I have caused an apology to be wrytten but not prynted in the name of the whole clergy, which surely is wisely lernidly eloquently and gravely wrytten, but I staye the publishing of it, untill it may be furder pondered, for so is it requisite." [11]

Jewel mentioned the publication in a letter to his "father" Peter Martyr: "We have recently published an *Apologia* in regard to the change in religion and the separation from the Roman church. The book is not worth sending so far, but yet I send it to you. It is faulty in many places, like almost everything that is printed over here; our printers are very careless." [12] Whether the second sentence is an author's professional modesty or refers to the misprints,

[8] PS, III.51.
[9] *Calendar of State Papers Domestic*, 1547–80, Nr. 18. Quoted, pp. 52–3.
[10] *Calendar of State Papers Foreign*, 1561–2. N° 789, p. 481.
[11] *Public Records Office, State Papers*, 70/26, fol. 59^b.
[12] PS, IV.1245 f.

we cannot say. At any rate, when Peter Martyr wrote and thanked him for it, he spoke of *tuae Apologiae* [13] and not *vestrae Apologiae,* plainly regarding it as Jewel's own work.

There can be little, if any, doubt that the anonymity was a deliberate policy on the part of Cecil, Parker, and the author himself (whom we may, on the basis of the above-mentioned hints and the traditional ascription, take as Jewel). It was agreed that the book should speak for the whole Church of England, and that therefore no individual name should be affixed to it. Even the title page should proclaim this. Not *Apologia Joannis Juelli pro Ecclesia Anglicana* but *Apologia Ecclesiae Anglicanae,* the apologia which the Church of England herself makes. Jewel kept the secret well. Writing to Parker as late as 1568, he preserves the anonymity in his quietly amused way: "I am done to understand that Rainolde Woulfe is minded to print again the Latin Apology. I most humbly beseech your grace to stay him therefrom, until the said book be better perused either by your grace, or by some other. For in the first edition the author was many ways put to wrong: whereof these printers have small regard, as tendering only their private gain." [14] And a week later: "I beseech your grace to give strait order that the Latin Apology be not printed again in any case, before either your grace or some other have well perused it. I am afraid of printers: their tyranny is terrible." [15]

Thomas Harding tried to make of the anonymity a stick to beat the Church of England. The early Christian apologists, he said, wrote plainly and openly. But "ye set forth your Apology in the name of the Church of England, before any mean part of the church were privy to it, and so as though either ye were ashamed of it, or afraid to abide by it.... There is no man's name set to it." [16] But Jewel refuses to be drawn. Instead of acknowledging authorship, he explains in effect why the book has no man's name set to it. It is the *Apology of the Church of England;* but it would obviously be impracticable to print on the title page "the names of all the bishops, deans, archdeacons, parsons, vicars and curates of England." [17] Moreover, it is not "necessary, nor commonly used, to join private men's names to public matters." [18]

Mr. Booty's idea of a "group project," therefore seems to me a misreading of the evidence. I have no doubt that Strype's account is substantially correct: "This work was, as it seems, recommended to Bishop Jewel; and he performed it in a short time to a wonder. The copy was sent this year 1561 to Secretary Cecil, for his judg-

[13] PS, III.3.
[14] PS, IV.1274.
[15] PS, IV.1275.
[16] *Confutation* (PS, III.185).
[17] PS, III.185.
[18] PS, III.186.

ment, and the Queen's approbation. And in September the Archbishop put him in mind of reviewing and sending it back, in order to the publishing; giving him this hint in the close of a letter, that he hoped he forgot not the Apology." [19] If we say that Jewel wrote the *Apologia* at Cecil's command, that it was sent for comment to a few leading figures in Church and state, and that Jewel then revised it in the light of their criticisms and advice, we shall probably not be very far from the mark. But the secrecy that almost surrounds the authorship should be ascribed, not to any doubt that Jewel wrote it, but to its character as the *Apologia Ecclesiae Anglicanae*. The Church of England made this apologia with John Jewel, the chief author, as her mouthpiece.

John Jewel, a Devonshire man of the younger generation of English Reformers, was early moved toward the Reformation faith through his tutor at Oxford, John Parkhurst, and through Peter Martyr, then Professor of Divinity at Oxford. At the beginning of Mary's reign he recanted, but in the winter of 1554–1555, learning that he was still in danger, fled to the Continent, living in the house of Peter Martyr, first at Strasbourg and afterward at Zurich. On the accession of Elizabeth he returned to England and was soon afterward made Bishop of Salisbury. A few weeks later, on Passion Sunday, 1560, he preached his famous sermon at Paul's Cross, challenging the Romanists "to bring any one sufficient sentence out of any old Catholike Doctor, or Father; Or out of any old generall Councell; Or out of the holy Scriptures of God; Or any one example of the Primitive Church, whereby it may be cleerely and plainly proved that . . ." [20] and thereupon are enumerated twenty-seven points of difference between the Reformers and Rome. The challenge provoked a lengthy controversy with his old schoolfellow and colleague at Salisbury, Thomas Harding. In 1562 was published *Apologia Ecclesiae Anglicanae*, which again called forth a reply from Harding, *A Confutation of a Booke intituled an Apologie of the Church of England*. Jewel thereupon set out patiently to vindicate the book in detail with *A Defence of the Apologie of the Church of England*. This runs to 652 pages in the 1611 folio edition, and, as R. W. Dixon with gentle irony but complete truth says, "The reader who peruses all this may have a complete survey of the controversy between Rome and England in the sixteenth century." [21]

---
[19] *Life and Acts of Matthew Parker* (Oxford, 1821), I.197.
[20] *Workes*, 1611, p. 58 (PS, I.20 ff.).
[21] *History of the Church of England*, V.320.

BIBLIOGRAPHY

First Latin Edition:
Apologia Ec-/ clesiae Angli-/ canae./ Roma. I./ Non enim me pudet Euangelii Christi. Po-/ tentia siquidem est Dei, ad salutem omni credenti./ Londini/ Anno Domini/ M.D.LXII.
Colophon: Londini/ Apud Reginaldum vvolfium./ Anno Domini/ M.D.LXII.

First English Edition:
An Apologie;/ or aunswer in defence/ of the Church of England,/ concerninge the state of/ Religion used in the same./ Newly set forth in Latine, and nowe translated into Englishe./ Rom. 1./ I am not ashamed of the Gospell of/ Christ, for it is the power of God/ unto saluation to euery one that bele-/ueth./ Londini,/ Anno Domini M.D.LXII.
Colophon: Imprinted at London/ by Reginalde Wolfe./ Anno 1562.

Second English Translation:
An Apologie/ or answere in defence of the/ Churche of Englande,/ with a briefe and plaine/ declaration of the true/ Religion professed/ and used in/ the same./ Londini, Anno Domini/ M.D.LXIIII.
Colophon: Imprinted at London in Paules/ churche yard, at the signe/ of the Brasen serpent, by/ Reginalde Wolfe./ Anno Domini. M.D.LXIIII.

An Apologie did not appear in the collected works of Jewel in 1609 and 1611. It was translated many times subsequently. In one year, 1839, no less than three separate editions appeared, no doubt to counter the challenge of the Oxford Movement. Two collected editions of Jewel appeared in the nineteenth century, and the Latin original and the second English translation were given in both:

The Works of John Jewel, Bishop of Salisbury, edited for the Parker Society by the Rev. John Ayre, M.A. 4 vols. Cambridge, 1845–1850. The Latin and English come in Vol. 3.

The Works of John Jewel, D.D., Bishop of Salisbury, edited by R. W. Jelf, D.D. 8 vols. Oxford, 1848. The Latin comes in Vol. 4, the English in Vol. 8.

A new edition of Lady Bacon's translation has recently appeared:

An Apology of the Church of England by John Jewel, edited by J. E. Booty. Cornell University Press, 1963.

On the Controversy:
Thomas Harding, *A Confutation of a Booke intituled an Apologie of the Church of England.* Antwerpiae. M.D.LVI.

John Jewel, *A Defence of the Apologie of the Church of England.*

Works on Jewel:
Ioannis/ Ivelli Angli,/ Episcopi Sarisburiensis vita &/ mors . . . / Laurentio Humfredo . . ./ Autore/ . . . Londini/ Apud Iohannem Dayum Typo-/graphum. An. 1573.

The Life of the Worthie Prelate and Faithfull Servant of God Iohn Ievvel sometimes Bishop of Sarisburie. Prefaced to *The Workes of the very learned and Reuerend Father in God Iohn Iewell, not long since Bishop of Sarisburie* . . . London, Printed by Iohn Norton, Printer to the Kings most excellent Maiestie. 1609 and 1611.

The Apology of the Church of England; and an Epistle to one Seignior Scipio . . . written both in Latin, by . . . John Jewel . . . made English by a Person of Quality: To which is added the Life of the said Bishop, collected and written by the same hand. London . . . 1685. Reprinted in Christopher Wordsworth, *Ecclesiastical Biography.* London, 1853.

This life contains a long extract from Laurence Humphrey's *Iuelli vita et mors.* Of Humphrey the "Person of Quality" says that he "makes it his business to represent both the Church of England and Bishop *Jewel* as wondrous Friends to the Churches of *Switzerland,* that is, to the *Calvinists,* because he, Good Man, was one himself, tho not so mad as those that followed."

C. W. Le Bas, *The life of Bishop Jewel.* London, 1835.

Wyndham M. Southgate, *John Jewel and the Problem of Doctrinal Authority.* Harvard University Press, 1962.

John E. Booty, *John Jewel as Apologist of the Church of England.* (Church Historical Society [London, 1963]).

AN APOLOGIE OF THE CHURCH OF ENGLAND 13

Martin Schmidt, article "Jewel" in *Religion in Geschichte und Gegenwart*. Band III. Dritte Auslage, 1959.

The present text is the second English translation, checked against the first Latin edition. What is given is not a series of extracts, but an abridgment, with omissions indicated in the usual way by ellipses.

John Jewel: An Apologie of the Church of England

THE TEXT

Part I

It hath been an old complaint, even from the first time of the patriarchs and prophets, and confirmed by the writings and testimonies of every age, that the truth wandereth here and there as a stranger in the world, and doth readily find enemies and slanderers amongst those that know her not.[22] Albeit perchance this may seem unto some a thing hard to be believed, I mean to such as have scant well and narrowly taken heed thereunto, specially seeing all mankind of nature's very motion without a teacher doth covet the truth of their own accord; and seeing our Saviour Christ himself, when he was on earth, would be called the Truth, as by a name most fit to express all his divine power; yet we . . . do see, that this is not only no new thing, or hard to be believed, but that it is a thing already received, and commonly used from age to age. Nay truly, this might seem much rather a marvel, and beyond all belief, if the devil, who is the father of lies, and enemy to all truth, would now upon a sudden change his nature, and hope that truth might otherwise be suppressed than by belying it; or that he would begin to establish his own kingdom by using now any other practices than the same which he hath ever used from the beginning. For since any man's remembrance we can scant find one time, either when religion did first grow, or when it was settled, or when it did afresh spring up again, wherein truth and innocency were not by all unworthy means and most despitefully entreated. . . .

Wherefore we ought to bear it the more quietly, which have taken upon us to profess the gospel of Christ, if we for the same cause be handled after the same sort; and if we, as our forefathers

[22] Tertullian, *Apologeticus* I.2 (PL 1.260).

were long ago, be likewise at this day tormented and baited with railings, with spiteful dealings and with lies; and that for no desert of our own, but only because we teach and acknowledge the truth.

They cry out upon us at this present everywhere, that we are all heretics, and have forsaken the faith, and have with new persuasions and wicked learning utterly dissolved the concord of the Church; that we renew, and, as it were, fetch again from hell the old and many a day condemned heresies; that we sow abroad new sects, and such broils as never erst were heard of; also that we are already divided into contrary parts and opinions, and could yet by no means agree well among ourselves; that we be cursed creatures, and like the giants [23] do war against God himself, and live clean without any regard or worshipping of God; that we despise all good deeds; that we use no discipline of virtue, no laws, no customs; that we esteem neither right, nor order, nor equity, nor justice; that we give the bridle to all naughtiness, and provoke the people to all licentiousness and lust; that we labour and seek to overthrow the state of monarchies and kingdoms, and to bring all things under the rule of the rash inconstant people and unlearned multitude; that we have seditiously fallen from the Catholic Church, and by a wicked schism and division have shaken the whole world, and troubled the common peace and universal quiet of the Church; and that, as Dathan and Abiron conspired in times past against Moses and Aaron,[24] even so we at this day have renounced the Bishop of Rome, without any cause reasonable; that we set nought by the authority of the ancient fathers and councils of old time; that we have rashly and presumptuously disannulled the old ceremonies, which have been well allowed by our fathers and forefathers many hundred year past, both by good customs, and also in ages of more purity; and that we have by our own private head, without the authority of any sacred and general council, brought new traditions into the Church; and have done all these things not for religion's sake, but only upon a desire of contention and strife.

But that they for their part have changed no manner of thing, but have held and kept still such a number of years to this very day all things, as they were delivered from the apostles, and well approved by the most ancient fathers. . . .

Now therefore, if it be leefull [25] for these folks to be eloquent and fine-tongued in speaking evil, surely it becometh not us in our cause, being so very good, to be dumb in answering truly.

[23] Titans.   [24] Num., ch. 16.   [25] Permissible.

For men to be careless what is spoken by them and their own matter, be it never so falsely and slanderously spoken (especially when it is such that the majesty of God and the cause of religion may thereby be damaged), is the part doubtless of dissolute and wretchless [26] persons, and of them which wickedly wink at the injuries done unto the name of God. For, although other wrongs, yea oftentimes great, may be borne and dissembled of a mild and Christian man; yet he that goeth smoothly away and dissembleth the matter when he is noted of heresy, Ruffinus was wont to deny that man to be a Christian.[27] We therefore will do the same thing which all laws, which nature's own voice, doth command to be done, and which Christ himself did in like case, when he was checked and reviled;[28] to the intent we may put off from us these men's slanderous accusations, and may defend soberly and truly our own cause and innocency. . . .

If so be that Pope Pius [29] were the man (we say not, which he would so gladly be called) but if he were indeed a man that either would account us for his brethren, or at least would take us to be men, he would first diligently have examined our reasons, and would have seen what might be said with us, what against us, and would not in his Bull, whereby he lately pretended a Council,[30] so rashly have condemned so great a part of the world, so many learned and godly men, so many commonwealths, so many kings, and so many princes, only upon his own blind prejudices and foredeterminations, and that without hearing of them speak, or without shewing cause why.

But because he hath already so noted us openly, lest by holding our peace we should seem to grant a fault, and specially because we can by no mean have audience in the public assembly of the General Council, wherein he would no creature should have power to give his voice, or declare his opinion, except he were sworn and straitly bound to maintain his authority (for we have had good experience hereof in his last conference at the Council at Trident, where the ambassadors and divines of the princes of Germany, and of the free cities, were quite shut out from their company: nother [31] can we yet forget how Julius the Third, above

---

[26] Reckless.
[27] *In Hieron. invect.*, Lib. I (*PL* 21.541).
[28] John 8:49.
[29] Pius IV.
[30] The third part of the Council of Trent, summoned by Papal Bull of Nov. 29, 1560 (Mansi, XXXIII.112 ff.).
[31] Nor.

ten years past, provided warily [32] by his writ, that none of our sort should be suffered to speak in the Council,[33] except there were some peradventure that would recant and change his opinion), for this cause chiefly we thought it good to yield up an account of our faith in writing, and truly and openly to make answer to those things wherewith we have been openly charged; to the end the world may see the parts and foundations of that doctrine, in the behalf whereof so many good men have little regarded their own lives. And that all men may understand what manner of people they be, and what opinion they have of God and of religion, whom the Bishop of Rome, before they were called to tell their tale, hath condemned for heretics, without any good consideration, without any example, and utterly without law or right, only because he heard tell that they did dissent from him and his in some point of religion. . . .

Further, if we do shew it plain, that God's holy Gospel, the ancient bishops, and the primitive Church do make on our side, and that we have not without just cause left these men, and rather have returned to the apostles and old Catholic fathers; and if we shall be found to do the same not colourably or craftily, but in good faith, before God, truly, honestly, clearly, and plainly; and if they themselves which fly our doctrine, and would be called Catholics, shall manifestly see how all those titles of antiquity, whereof they boast so much, are quite shaken out of their hands, and that there is more pith in this our cause than they thought for; we then hope and trust, that none of them will be so negligent and careless of his own salvation, but he will at length study and bethink himself, to whether [34] part he were best to join him. Undoubtedly, except one will altogether harden his heart and refuse to hear, he shall not repent him to give good heed to this our defence and to mark well what we say, and how truly and justly it agreeth with Christian Religion.

For where they call us heretics, it is a crime so heinous, that, unless it may be seen, unless it may be felt, and in manner may be holden with hands and fingers, it ought not lightly to be

---

[32] *Diligenter:* carefully, deliberately. But the words ascribed to Julius III do not appear in his Bull of Nov. 14, 1548, resuming the Council, nor in that of his predecessor, Paul III, of May 22, 1542, summoning the Council. Jewel's own reference is to *Breve Julii III. citat a Calvino;* but a search in the Index of *Calvini Opera* (*Corpus Reformatorum*) has failed to discover it.
[33] See *Defence* (PS, III.207 f.).
[34] Which.

judged or believed, when it is laid to the charge of any Christian man. For heresy is a forsaking of salvation, a renouncing of God's grace, a departing from the body and Spirit of Christ. But this was ever an old and solemn property with them and their forefathers; if any did complain of their errors and faults, and desired to have true Religion restored, straightway to condemn such ones for heretics, as men newfangled and factious. . . .

Shortly to speak. This universal Religion, which Christian men profess at this day, was called first of the heathen people a sect and heresy. With these terms did they always fill princes' ears, to the intent when they had once hated us with a fore-determined opinion, and had counted all that we said to be faction and heresy, they might be so led away from the truth and right understanding of the cause. But the more sore and outrageous a crime heresy is, the more it ought to be proved by plain and strong arguments, especially in this time, when men begin to give less credit to their words, and to make more diligent search of their doctrine, than they were wont to do. For the people of God are otherwise instructed now than they were in times past, when all the bishops of Rome's sayings were allowed for Gospel, and when all Religion did depend only upon their authority. Nowadays the Holy Scripture is abroad, the writings of the apostles and prophets are in print, whereby all truth and Catholic doctrine may be proved, and all heresy may be disproved and confuted.

Sithence,[35] then, they bring forth none of these for themselves, and call us nevertheless heretics, which have neither fallen from Christ, nor from the apostles, nor yet from the prophets, this is an injurious and a very spiteful dealing. With this sword did Christ put off the devil when he was tempted of him: with these weapons ought all presumption, which doth avance itself against God, to be overthrown and conquered. "For all Scripture," saith St. Paul, "that cometh by the inspiration of God, is profitable to teach, to confute, to instruct, and to reprove; that the man of God may be perfect, and throughly framed to every good work." [36] Thus did the holy fathers alway fight against the heretics with none other force than with the Holy Scriptures. St. Augustine, when he disputed against Petilian, an heretic of the Donatists: "Let not these words," quoth he, "be heard between us, 'I say'; or, 'you say': let us rather speak in this wise: 'Thus saith the Lord.' There let us seek the Church: there let us boult out [37] our cause." [38] Likewise St. Jerome: "All those things," saith he, "which without the testi-

---

[35] Since.
[36] II Tim. 3:16–17.
[37] Sift out, examine.
[38] *De unitate ecclesiae* III.5 (*PL* 43.394).

mony of the Scriptures are holden as delivered from the apostles, be throughly smitten down by the sword of God's word." [39] St. Ambrose also, to Gratianus the Emperor: "Let the Scripture," saith he, "be asked the question; let the apostles be asked; let the prophets be asked; and let Christ be asked." [40] For at that time made the Catholic fathers and bishops no doubt but that our religion might be proved out of the Holy Scriptures. Neither were they ever so hardy to take any for an heretic, whose error they could not evidently and apparently reprove by the self-same Scriptures. And we verily do make answer on this wise, as St. Paul did, "According to this way which they call heresy we do worship God, and the Father of our Lord Jesus Christ, and do allow all things which have been written either in the law, or in the prophets," [41] or in the apostles' works.

Wherefore, if we be heretics, and they (as they would fain be called) be Catholics, why do they not as they see the fathers, which were Catholic men, have always done? Why do they not convince and master us by the divine Scriptures? Why do they not call us again to be tried by them? Why do they not lay before us how we have gone away from Christ, from the prophets, from the apostles, and from the holy fathers? Why stick they to do it? Why are they afraid of it? It is God's cause: why are they doubtful to commit it to the trial of God's Word? If we be heretics, which refer all our controversies unto the Holy Scriptures, and report us to the self-same words which we know were sealed by God himself, and in comparison of them set little by all other things, whatsoever may be devised by men, how shall we say to these folk, I pray you? what manner of men be they, and how is it meet to call them, which fear the judgment of the Holy Scriptures, that is to say, the judgment of God himself, and do prefer before them their own dreams, and full cold inventions; and, to maintain their own traditions, have defaced and corrupted now these many hundred years, the ordinances of Christ and of the apostles?

In like manner, because these men take us to be mad, and appeach us for heretics, as men which have nothing to do, neither with Christ, nor with the Church of God, we have judged it should be to good purpose and not unprofitable, if we do openly and frankly set forth our faith wherein we stand, and shew all that confidence which we have in Christ Jesu, to the intent all men

---

[39] *In Aggaeum proph.* I.11 (*PL* 25.1397 f.). Harding refused the application (PS, III.232 f.).
[40] *De fide*, Lib. I, cap. vi.43 (*PL* 16.537).
[41] Acts 24:14.

may see what is our judgment of every part of Christian Religion, and may resolve with themselves, whether the faith which they shall see confirmed by the words of Christ, by the writings of the apostles, by the testimonies of the Catholic fathers, and by the examples of many ages, be but a certain rage of furious and mad men, and a conspiracy of heretics. This therefore is our belief.

Part II

We believe that there is one certain nature and divine power, which we call God; and that the same is divided into three equal Persons, into the Father, into the Son, and into the Holy Ghost; and that they all be of one power, of one majesty, of one eternity, of one Godhead, and of one substance. And, although these three Persons be so divided; that neither the Father is the Son, nor the Son is the Holy Ghost or the Father; yet nevertheless we believe that there is but one very God; and that the same one God hath created heaven and earth, and all things contained under heaven.

We believe that Jesus Christ, the only Son of the eternal Father (as long before it was determined before all beginnings), when the fulness of time was come, did take of that blessed and pure Virgin both flesh and all the nature of man, that he might declare to the world the secret and hid will of his Father; which will had been laid up from before all ages and generations; and that he might full finish [42] in his human body the mystery of our redemption; and might fasten to the cross our sins and also that hand-writing which was made against us.

We believe that for our sake he died, and was buried, descended into hell, the third day by the power of his Godhead returned to life and rose again; and that the fortieth day after his resurrection, whiles his disciples beheld and looked upon him, he ascended into heaven, to fulfil all things, and did place in majesty and glory the self-same body wherewith he was born, wherein he lived on earth, wherein he was jested at, wherein he had suffered most painful torments and cruel kind of death, wherein he rose again, and wherein he ascended to the right hand of the Father, above all rule, above all power, all force, all dominion, and above every name which is named, not only in this world, but also in the world to come; [43] and that there he now sitteth, and shall sit, till all things be full perfected. And although the majesty and Godhead of Christ be everywhere abundantly dispersed, yet we believe that his body,

---

[42] Latin, *perageret:* completely accomplish.   [43] Eph. 1:21.

as St. Augustine saith, must needs be still in one place; [44] and that Christ hath given majesty unto his body, but yet hath not taken away from it the nature of a body; and that we must not so affirm Christ to be God, that we deny him to be man; and, as the martyr Vigilius saith, that Christ hath left us as touching his human nature, but hath not left us as touching his divine nature; [45] and that the same Christ, though he be absent from us concerning his manhood, yet is ever present with us concerning his Godhead.[46] From that place also we believe that Christ shall come again to execute that general judgment, as well of them whom he shall then find alive in the body, as of them that be already dead.

We believe that the Holy Ghost, who is the third Person in the Holy Trinity, is very God; not made, not create, not begotten, but proceeding from both the Father and the Son, by a certain mean unknown unto men, and unspeakable; and that it is his property to mollify and soften the hardness of man's heart, when he is once received thereunto, either by the wholesome preaching of the gospel, or by any other way; that he doth give men light, and guide them unto the knowledge of God, to all way of truth, to newness of the whole life, and to everlasting hope of salvation.

We believe that there is one Church of God, and that the same is not shut up (as in times past among the Jews) into some one corner or kingdom, but that it is catholic and universal, and dispersed throughout the whole world; so that there is now no nation which can truly complain that they be shut forth, and may not be one of the Church and people of God: And that this Church is the kingdom, the body, and the spouse of Christ; and that Christ alone is the prince of this kingdom; that Christ alone is the head of this body; and that Christ alone is the bridegroom of this spouse.

Furthermore, that there be divers degrees of ministers in the Church; whereof some be deacons, some priests, some bishops; to whom is committed the office to instruct the people, and the whole charge and setting forth of religion. Yet notwithstanding we say that there neither is, nor can be any one man, which may have

---

[44] *In Ioannis Evangelium,* Tract. XXX.1 (*PL* 35.1632). Also, *Ep.* CLXXXVII.iii.10 (*PL* 33.835–6). Harding objected that Augustine did not write *oportet* (must) but *potest* (can) (PS, III.254). Jewel replied that *oportet* occurred in Gratian's quotation of Augustine, in *Corp. Iur. Can.* (*De consecratione,* Dist. II, can. XLIV), I.1330.
[45] Not Vigilius, Bishop of Trent and martyr, but Vigilius Tapsensis, *Contra Eutychetem,* Lib. I (*PL* 62.98–9).
[46] Fulgentius, *Ad Trasim. Reg.,* Lib. II, cap. xvii (*PL* 62.264–5).

the whole superiority in this universal state; for that Christ is ever present to assist his Church, and needeth not any man to supply his room, as his only heir to all his substance; and that there can be no one mortal creature, which is able to comprehend or conceive in his mind the universal Church, that is to wit, all the parts of the world, much less able to put them in order, and to govern them rightly and duly. For all the apostles, as Cyprian saith, were of like power among themselves, and the rest were the same that Peter was; [47] and that it was said indifferently to them all, "Feed ye"; indifferently to them all, "Go into the whole world"; indifferently to them all, "Teach ye the gospel." And, as Jerome saith, "all bishops wheresoever they be, be they at Rome, be they at Eugubium, be they at Constantinople, be they at Rhegium, be all of like preeminence and of like priesthood." [48] And, as Cyprian saith, "there is but one bishoprick, and that a piece thereof is perfectly and wholly holden of every particular bishop." [49] And, according to the judgment of the Nicene Council, we say that the Bishop of Rome hath no more jurisdiction over the Church of God, than the rest of the patriarchs, either of Alexandria or Antiochia, have.[50] And as for the Bishop of Rome, who now calleth all matters before himself alone, except he do his duty as he ought to do, except he administer the sacraments, except he instruct the people, except he warn them and teach them, we say that he ought not of right once to be called a bishop, or so much as an elder. For a bishop, as saith Augustine, is a name of labour, and not of honour; because he would have that man to understand himself to be no bishop, which will seek to have preeminence, and not to profit others.[51] And that neither the Pope, nor any other worldly creature, can no more be head of the whole Church, or a bishop over all, than he can be the bridegroom, the light, the salvation, and life of the Church: for these privileges and names belong only to Christ, and be properly and only fit for him alone. And that no bishop of Rome did ever suffer himself to be called by such a proud name and title before Phocas the Emperor's time, who, as we know, by killing his own sovereign Maurice the Emperor, did by a traitorous villany aspire to the empire, which was about the six hundred and thirteenth year after Christ was born. Also, the Council of Carthage did circumspectly pro-

[47] *De unit. eccl.* (*PL* 4.502).
[48] *Ep.* CXLVI (*PL* 22.1194).
[49] *De unit. eccl.* (*PL* 4.501–2).
[50] For Harding's denial and Jewel's defense of Canon 6 of the first Nicene Council, see PS, III.305–6; Mansi, II.670–1.
[51] *De civitate Dei*, Lib. XIX, cap. xix (*PL* 41.647).

vide, that no bishop should be called either the highest bishop or chief priest.[52]

And therefore, sithence the Bishop of Rome will nowadays so be called, and challengeth unto himself an authority that is none of his; besides that he doth plainly contrary to the ancient councils and contrary to the old fathers, we believe that he doth give unto himself, as it is written by his own companion Gregory,[53] a presumptuous, a profane, a sacrilegious, and antichristian name; that he is also the king of pride; that he is Lucifer, which preferreth himself before his brethren; that he hath forsaken the faith, and is the forerunner of Antichrist.

Further, we say that the minister ought lawfully, duly, and orderly to be preferred to that office of the Church of God, and that no man hath power to wrest himself into the holy ministry at his own pleasure and list. Wherefore these persons do us the greater wrong, which have nothing so common in their mouth, as that we do nothing orderly and comely, but all things troublesomely, and without order; and that we allow every man to be a priest, to be a teacher, and to be an interpreter of the Scriptures.

Moreover, we say that Christ hath given to his ministers power to bind, to loose, to open, to shut; and that the office of loosing consisteth in this point, that the minister should either offer by the preaching of the gospel the merits of Christ and full pardon to such as have lowly and contrite hearts, and do unfeignedly repent them, pronouncing unto the same a sure and undoubted forgiveness of their sins, and hope of everlasting salvation; or else that the minister, when any have offended their brothers' minds with a great offence, and with a notable and open fault, whereby they have, as it were, banished and made themselves strangers from the common fellowship and from the body of Christ, then, after perfect amendment of such persons, doth reconcile them, and bring them home again, and restore them to the company and unity of the faithful. We say also, that the minister doth execute the authority of binding and shutting, as often as he shutteth up the gate of the Kingdom of Heaven against the unbelieving and stubborn persons, denouncing unto them God's vengeance and everlasting punishment; or else, when he doth quite shut them out from the bosom of the Church by open excommunication. Out of doubt, what sentence soever the minister of God shall give in this sort, God himself doth so well allow of it, that whatsoever here in earth by their means is loosed and bound, God himself will

[52] Third Council of Carthage, cap. 26 (Mansi, III.884).
[53] For these references to Gregory, see PS, I.344 f.

loose and bind and confirm the same in heaven.

And touching the keys, wherewith they may either shut or open the Kingdom of Heaven, we with Chrysostom say they be the knowledge of the Scriptures;[54] with Tertullian we say they be the interpretation of the law;[55] and with Eusebius we call them the Word of God.[56]

Moreover, that Christ's disciples did receive this authority, not that they should hear private confessions of the people, and listen to their whisperings, as the common massing priests do everywhere nowadays, and do it so, as though in that one point lay all the virtue and use of the keys; but to the end they should go, they should teach, they should publish abroad the Gospel, and be unto the believing a sweet savour of life unto life, and unto the unbelieving and unfaithful a savour of death unto death; and that the minds of godly persons, being brought low by the remorse of their former life and errors, after they once begun to look up unto the light of the Gospel and believe in Christ, might be opened with the Word of God, even as a door is opened with a key. Contrariwise, that the wicked and wilful folk, and such as would not believe nor return into the right way, should be left still as fast locked and shut up, and, as St. Paul saith, wax worse and worse.[57] This take we to be the meaning of the keys; and that after this fashion men's consciences either to be opened or shut. We say that the priest indeed is judge in this case, but yet hath no manner of right to challenge an authority, or power, as saith Ambrose.[58] And therefore our Saviour Jesu Christ, to reprove the negligence of the scribes and Pharisees in teaching, did with these words rebuke them, saying, "Woe unto you scribes and Pharisees, which have taken away the keys of knowledge, and have shut up the Kingdom of Heaven before men."[59] Seeing then the key, whereby the way and entry to the Kingdom of God is opened unto us, is the word of the Gospel and the expounding of the law and Scriptures, we say plainly, where the same word is not, there is not the key. And seeing one manner of word is given to all, and one only key belongeth to all, we say there is but one only power of all ministers, as concerning opening and shutting. And as touching the Bishop of Rome, for all his parasites flatteringly sing in his ears those words, "To thee will I give the keys of the King-

---

[54] *Op. imperf. in Matt.*, Hom. XLIX (*PG* 56.883).
[55] *Adversus Marcionem* IV.27.9 (*PL* 2.429).
[56] Neither Jewel nor any of his editors gives a reference for this.
[57] II Tim. 3:13.
[58] In *Corp. Iur. Can.* (*De Poenitentia*, Dist. I, can. LI), I.1170–1.
[59] Luke 11:52.

dom of Heaven" (as though those keys were fit for him alone, and for nobody else), except he go so to work, as men's consciences may be made pliant, and be subdued to the Word of God, we deny that he doth either open, or shut, or hath the keys at all. And, although he taught and instructed the people (as would to God he might once truly do, and persuade himself it were at the least some piece of his duty), yet we think his key to be never a whit better or of greater force than other men's. For who hath severed him from the rest? Who hath taught him more cunningly to open, or better to absolve than his brethren?

We say that matrimony is holy and honourable in all sorts and states of persons, in the patriarchs, in the prophets, in the apostles, in holy martyrs, in the ministers of the Church, and in bishops, and that it is an honest and lawful thing (as Chrysostom saith) [60] for a man living in matrimony to take upon him therewith the dignity of a bishop; and, as Sozomenus saith of Spiridion,[61] and as Nazianzene saith of his own father,[62] that a good and diligent bishop doth serve in the ministry never the worse for that he is married, but rather the better, and with more ableness to do good. Further we say that the same law, which by constraint taketh away this liberty from men, and compelleth them against their wills to live single, is the doctrine of devils, as Paul saith;[63] and that, ever since the time of this law, a wonderful uncleanness of life and manners in God's ministers, and sundry horrible enormities have followed, as the Bishop of Augusta,[64] as Faber,[65] as Abbas Panormitanus,[66] as Latomus,[67] as the Tripartite work,[68] which is annexed to the second tome of the Councils, and other champions of the Pope's band, yea, and as the matter itself and all histories do confess. For it was rightly said by Pius the Second, a bishop

[60] *Hom. II in Ep. ad Titum,* cap. I (*PG* 62.671).
[61] *Historia ecclesiastica,* Lib. i, cap. xi (*PG* 67.886 f.).
[62] *Orat.* xviii.8 (*PG* 35.994).
[63] I Tim. 4:1.
[64] A reference to Pseudo-Udalrichus, *Epistola de continentia clericorum* (*edidit* L. de Heinemann) in *Monumenta Germaniae Historica; libelli de lite Imperatorum et Pontificum Saeculis XI et XII,* Tomus I (Hannoverae. MDCCCXCVII), pp. 254–260.
[65] *Epistolae Divi Pauli Apostoli, cum commentariis . . . Iacobi Fabri Stapulensis* (1531), fol. 160.
[66] *Panormitani super Tertio Decretalium* (1534), fol. 16.
[67] No less than four theologians called Latomus were writing in the middle of the sixteenth century. This is presumably a reference to Luther's opponent, Jacobus Latomus, *Opera, quae praecipue adversus horum temporum haereses . . .* (Lovanii . . . Anno M.D.L.).
[68] *Opusculum tripartitum,* Lib. III, cap. vii, in P. Crabbe, *Secundus Tomus Conciliorum Omnium . . .* (Coloniae Agrippinae . . . M.D.LI), p. 1002.

of Rome, that he saw many causes why wives should be taken away from priests, but that he saw many more and more weighty causes why they ought to be restored them again.[69]

We receive and embrace all the Canonical Scriptures, both of the Old and New Testaments, giving thanks to our God, who hath raised up unto us that light which we might ever have before our eyes, lest, either by the subtlety of man, or by the snares of the devil, we should be carried away to errors and lies. Also, that these be the heavenly voices, whereby God hath opened unto us his will; and that only in them man's heart can have settled rest; that in them be abundantly and fully comprehended all things, whatsoever be needful for our salvation, as Origen, Augustine, Chrysostom, and Cyrillus have taught;[70] that they be the very might and strength of God to attain to salvation; that they be the foundations of the prophets and apostles, whereupon is built the Church of God; that they be the very sure and infallible rule, whereby may be tried, whether the Church doth stagger or err, and whereunto all ecclesiastical doctrine ought to be called to account; and that against these Scriptures neither law nor ordinance, nor any custom ought to be heard; no, though Paul his own self, or an angel from heaven, should come and teach the contrary.

Moreover, we allow the sacraments of the Church, that is to say, certain holy signs and ceremonies, which Christ would we should use, that by them he might set before our eyes the mysteries of our salvation, and might more strongly confirm our faith which we have in his blood, and might seal his grace in our hearts. And those sacraments, together with Tertullian, Origen, Ambrose, Augustine, Jerome, Chrysostom, Basil, Dionysius, and other Catholic fathers, do we call figures, signs, marks or badges, prints, copies, forms, seals, signets, similitudes, patterns, representations, remembrances, and memories. And we make no doubt, together with the same doctors, to say that those be certain visible words, seals of righteousness, tokens of grace; and do expressly pronounce that in the Lord's Supper there is truly given unto the believing the body and blood of the Lord, the flesh of the Son of God, which quickeneth our souls, the meat that cometh from above, the food of immortality, grace, truth, and life; and the Supper to be the communion of the body and blood of Christ, by the partaking whereof we be revived, we be strengthened, and be fed unto immortality, and whereby we are joined, united, and incorporate

---

[69] *Bap. Platinae . . . de vitis ac gestis summorum Pontificum . . .* (1551), p. 295.
[70] For references, see PS, II.688, 696.

unto Christ, that we may abide in him, and he in us.

Besides, we acknowledge there be two sacraments, which we judge properly ought to be called by this name; that is to say, Baptism, and the sacraments [71] of thanksgiving. For thus many we see were delivered and sanctified by Christ, and well allowed of the old fathers, Ambrose and Augustine.

We say that Baptism is a sacrament of the remission of sins, and of that washing, which we have in the blood of Christ; and that no person, which will profess Christ's name, ought to be restrained or kept back therefrom; no, not the very babes of Christians; forsomuch as they be born in sin, and do pertain unto the people of God.

We say that Eucharistia, the Supper of the Lord, is a sacrament, that is to wit, an evident token [72] of the body and blood of Christ, wherein is set as it were before our eyes the death of Christ, and his resurrection, and what act soever he did whilst he was in his mortal body; to the end we may give him thanks for his death, and for our deliverance; and that, by the often receiving of this sacrament, we may daily renew the remembrance of that matter, to the intent we, being fed with the body and blood of Christ, may be brought into the hope of the resurrection and of everlasting life, and may most assuredly believe that the body and blood of Christ doth in like manner feed our souls, as bread and wine doth feed our bodies. To this banquet we think the people of God ought to be earnestly bidden, that they may all communicate among themselves, and openly declare and testify both the godly society which is among them, and also the hope which they have in Christ Jesu. For this cause, if there had been any which would be but a looker-on, and abstain from the Holy Communion, him did the old fathers and bishops of Rome in the primitive Church, before private mass came up, excommunicate as a wicked person and as a pagan. Neither was there any Christian at that time which did communicate alone, whiles other looked on. For so did Calixtus in times past decree that, after the consecration was finished, all should communicate, except they had rather stand without the Church doors; "because thus," saith he, "did the apostles appoint, and the same the holy Church of Rome keepeth still." [73]

Moreover, when the people cometh to the Holy Communion, the sacrament ought to be given them in both kinds; for so both Christ hath commanded, and the apostles in every place have

---

[71] Jewel frequently uses sacrament to mean either part of the Eucharist.
[72] In *Defence:* representation; in Latin *Apologia: symbolum.*
[73] Anacletus, *Ep.* i in *Corp. Iur. Can.* (*De consecr.,* Dist. II, can. X), I.1317.

ordained, and all the ancient fathers and Catholic bishops have followed the same. And whoso doth contrary to this, he (as Gelasius saith) committeth sacrilege.[74] And therefore we say that our adversaries at this day, who, having violently thrust out and quite forbidden the Holy Communion, do, without the word of God, without the authority of any ancient council, without any Catholic father, without any example of the primitive Church, yea, and without reason also, defend and maintain their private masses and the mangling of the sacraments, and do this not only against the plain express commandment and bidding of Christ, but also against all antiquity, do wickedly therein, and are very Church-robbers (*sacrilegos*).

We affirm that bread and wine are holy and heavenly mysteries of the body and blood of Christ, and that by them Christ himself, being the true bread of eternal life, is so presently given unto us, as that by faith we verily receive his body and his blood. Yet say we not this so, as though we thought that the nature of bread and wine is clearly changed and goeth to nothing; as many have dreamed in these later times, which yet could never agree among themself of this their dream. For that was not Christ's meaning, that the wheaten bread should lay apart his own nature, and receive a certain new divinity; but that he might rather change us, and (to use Theophylactus' words) [75] might transform us into his body. For what can be said more plainly than that which Ambrose saith, "Bread and wine remain still the same they were before, and yet are changed into another thing"? [76] or that which Gelasius saith, "The substance of the bread, or the nature of the wine, ceaseth not so to be"? [77] or that which Theodoret saith, "After the consecration the mystical signs do not cast off their own proper nature; for they remain still in their former substance, form, and kind"? [78] or that which Augustine saith, "That which ye see is the bread and cup, and so our eyes tell us; but that which your faith requireth to be taught is this: The bread is the body of Christ, and the cup is his blood"? [79] or that which Origen saith, "Bread which is sanctified by the word of God, as touching the material substance thereof, goeth into the belly, and is cast out

---

[74] In *Corp. Iur. Can.* (De consecr., Dist. II, can. XII), I.1318.
[75] *Enarratio in Euangelium Ioannis*, cap. vi, v. 53, seq. (PG 123.1310).
[76] *De Sacramentis*, Lib. IV, cap. iv (PL 16.440–1).
[77] The work, *De duabus naturis in Christo, adversus Eutychem et Nestorium*, was in the sixteenth century ascribed to Gelasius. Jewel probably quoted it from *Haereseologia* (Basileae 1556), p. 689.
[78] *Eranistes seu Polymorphus. Dialogus II. Inconfusus* (PG 83.167).
[79] *Serm. CCLXXII ad Infant.* (PL 38.1246).

into the privy"? [80] or that which Christ himself said, not only after the blessing of the cup, but after he had ministered the Communion: "I will drink no more of this fruit of the vine"? [81] It is well known that the fruit of the vine is wine, and not blood.

And in speaking thus we mean not to abase the Lord's Supper, or to teach that it is but a cold ceremony only, and nothing to be wrought therein (as many falsely slander us we teach). For we affirm that Christ doth truly and presently give his own self in his Sacraments; in Baptism, that we may put him on; and in his Supper, that we may eat him by faith and spirit, and may have everlasting life by his cross and blood. And we say not, this is done slightly and coldly, but effectually and truly. For, although we do not touch the body of Christ with teeth and mouth, yet we hold him fast, and eat him by faith, by understanding, and by the spirit. And this is no vain faith which doth comprehend Christ; and that is not received with cold devotion, which is received with understanding, with faith, and with spirit. For Christ himself altogether is so offered and given us in these mysteries, that we may certainly know we be flesh of his flesh, and bone of his bones; and that Christ continueth in us, and we in him. And therefore in celebrating these mysteries, the people are to good purpose exhorted, before they come to receive the Holy Communion, to lift up their hearts, and to direct their minds to heaven-ward; because he is there, by whom we must be full fed, and live.[82] Cyril saith, when we come to receive these mysteries, all gross imaginations must quite be banished.[83] The Council of Nice, as is alleged by some in Greek, plainly forbiddeth us to be basely affectioned, or bent toward the bread and wine, which are set before us.[84] And, as Chrysostom very aptly writeth, we say that the body of Christ is the dead carcase, and we ourselves must be the eagles: [85] meaning thereby, that we must fly high, if we will come unto the body of Christ. "For this table," as Chrysostom saith, "is a table of eagles, and not of jays." [86] Cyprian also, "This bread," saith he, "is the food of the soul, and not the meat of the belly." [87] And Augustine,

---

[80] *Comm. in Matt. xi.14* (PG 13.950).
[81] Mark 14:25 and par.
[82] I.e., Lift up your hearts. Answer: We lift them up unto the Lord.
[83] *Apologeticus pro duodecim capitibus adversus Orientales Episcopos* (PG 76.374–5[?]).
[84] Gelasius, *Hist. Conc. Nic.*, cap. xxx (Mansi, II.887).
[85] *In Ep. I ad Corinthios*, Hom. XXIV (PG 61.203).
[86] *Ibid.* (PG 61.203).
[87] Ascribed to Cyprian in sixteenth century, but in fact by the twelfth-century Arnoldus Carnotensis, Abbot of Bonneval, *De cardinalibus Christi operibus* —*De coena Domini* (PL 189.1643 ff.).

"How shall I hold him," saith he, "which is absent? How shall I reach my hand up to heaven, to lay hold upon him that sitteth there?" He answereth, "Reach thither thy faith, and then thou hast laid hold on him." [88]

We cannot also away in our churches with the shews, and sales, and buying and selling of masses, nor the carrying about and worshipping of bread; nor such other idolatrous and blasphemous fondness; which none of them can prove that Christ or his apostles did ever ordain or left unto us. And we justly blame the bishops of Rome, who, without the word of God, without the authority of the holy fathers, without any example of antiquity, after a new guise, do not only set before the people the sacramental bread to be worshipped as God, but do also carry the same about upon an ambling horse, whithersoever themselves journey; as in old time the Persians' fire, and the reliques of the goddess Isis, were solemnly carried about in procession; [89] and have brought the sacraments of Christ to be used now as a stage-play, and a solemn sight; to the end that men's eyes should be fed with nothing else but with mad gazings, and foolish gauds, in the self-same matter, wherein the death of Christ ought diligently to be beaten into our hearts, and wherein also the mysteries of our redemption ought with all holiness and reverence to be executed.

Besides, where they say, and sometime do persuade fools, that they are able by their masses to distribute and apply unto men's commodity all the merits of Christ's death, yea, although many times the parties think nothing of the matter, and understand full little what is done, this is a mockery, a heathenish fancy, and a very toy. For it is our faith that applieth the death and cross of Christ to our benefit, and not the act of the massing priest. "Faith had in the sacraments," [90] saith Augustine, "doth justify, and not the sacraments." [91] And Origen saith, "Christ is the priest, the propitiation, and sacrifice; which propitiation cometh to every one by mean of faith." [92] So that by this reckoning we say that the sacraments of Christ without faith do not once profit these that be alive: a great deal less do they profit those that be dead.

And as for their brags they are wont to make of their purgatory, though we know it is not a thing so very late risen amongst them, yet is it no better than a blockish and an old wives' device.

[88] *In Ioan. Ev.*, Tract. I.4 (*PL* 35.1759).
[89] Not Nicolaus Leonicenus (as PS) but Nicolaus Leonicus, *De varia historia libri tres* . . . (Basileae 1531), p. 145.
[90] Latin: *Fides sacramentorum.*
[91] *In Ioan. Ev.*, Tract. LXXX.3 (*PL* 35.1840).
[92] *In Ep. ad Rom.*, Lib. III.8 (*PG* 14.950–2).

Augustine indeed sometime saith, there is such a certain place: sometime he denieth not but there may be such a one: [93] sometime he doubteth: sometime again he utterly denieth it to be, and thinketh that men are therein deceived by a certain natural goodwill they bear their friends departed.[94] But yet of this one error hath there grown up such a harvest of these mass-mongers, the masses being sold abroad commonly in every corner, the temples of God became shops, to get money; and silly [95] souls were persuaded that nothing was more necessary to be bought. Indeed there was nothing more gainful for these men to sell.

As touching the multitude of vain and superfluous ceremonies, we know that Augustine did grievously complain of them in his own time; [96] and therefore have we cut off a great number of them, because we know that men's consciences were cumbered about them, and the Churches of God overladen with them. Nevertheless we keep still and esteem, not only those ceremonies which we are sure were delivered us from the apostles, but some others too besides, which we thought might be suffered without hurt to the Church of God; because we had a desire that all things in the holy congregation might (as Paul commandeth) be done with comeliness, and in good order; [97] but, as for all those things which we saw were either very superstitious, or unprofitable, or noisome, or mockeries, or contrary to the Holy Scriptures, or else unseemly for honest or discreet folks, as there be an infinite number nowadays where papistry is used, these, I say, we have utterly refused without all manner exception, because we would not have the right worshipping of God any longer defiled with such follies.

We make our prayers in that tongue which all our people, as meet is, may understand, to the end they may (as Paul counselleth us) take common commodity by common prayer; [98] even as all the holy fathers and Catholic bishops, both in the Old and New Testament, did use to pray themselves, and taught the people to pray too; lest, as Augustine saith, "like parrots and ousels we should seem to speak that we understand not." [99]

Neither have we any other mediator and intercessor, by whom we may have access to God the Father, than Jesus Christ, in whose only name all things are obtained at his Father's hand. But it is a

---

[93] *Enarratio in Ps. LXXXV* (PL 37.1093-4).
[94] Pseudo-Augustine, *Hypomnesticon* V.v (PL 45.1654).
[95] Poor, helpless.
[96] *Ep.* LV.xix.35 (PL 33.221-2).
[97] Cf. Preface "Of Ceremonies" to the *Book of Common Prayer*.
[98] I Cor. 14:12 ff.
[99] *Enarr. in Ps. XVIII.* ii.1 (PL 36.157). Ousel = Merula = blackbird.

shameful part, and full of infidelity, that we see everywhere used in the Churches of our adversaries, not only in that they will have innumerable sorts of mediators, and that utterly without the authority of God's Word; so that, as Jeremy saith,[1] the saints be now as many in number, or rather above the number of the cities; and poor men cannot tell to which saint it were best to turn them first. And, though there be so many as they cannot be told, yet every one of them hath his peculiar duty and office assigned unto him of these folks, what thing they ought to ask, what to give, and what to bring to pass—but besides this also, in that they do not only wickedly, but also shamelessly, call upon the blessed Virgin, Christ's mother, to have her remember that she is a mother, and to command her Son, and to use a mother's authority over him.

We say also, that every person is born in sin, and leadeth his life in sin; that nobody is able truly to say his heart is clean; that the most righteous person is but an unprofitable servant; that the law of God is perfect, and requireth of us perfect and full obedience; that we are able by no means to fulfil that law in this worldly life; that there is no one mortal creature which can be justified by his own deserts in God's sight; and therefore that our only succour and refuge is to fly to the mercy of our Father by Jesu Christ, and assuredly to persuade our minds that he is the obtainer of forgiveness for our sins, and that by his blood all our spots of sin be washed clean; that he hath pacified and set at one all things by the blood of his cross; that he by the same one only sacrifice, which he once offered upon the cross, hath brought to effect and fulfilled all things, and that for that cause he said, when he gave up the ghost, "It is finished"; [2] as though he would signify that the price and ransom was now full paid for the sin of all mankind. If there be any then that think this sacrifice not sufficient, let them go in God's name, and seek another that is better. We verily, because we know this to be the only sacrifice, are well content with it alone, and look for none other; and, forasmuch as it was to be offered but once, we command it not to be renewed again. And, because it was full and perfect in all points and parts, we do not ordain in place thereof any continual succession of offerings.

Besides, though we say we have no meed [3] at all by our own works and deeds, but appoint all the mean of our salvation to be in Christ alone, yet say we not that for this cause men ought to live loosely and dissolutely; nor that it is enough for a Christian to be baptized only and to believe; as though there were nothing else required at his hand. For true faith is lively, and can in no wise be

[1] Jer. 2:28; 11:13.   [2] John 19:30.   [3] Deserving.

idle. Thus therefore teach we the people, that God hath called us, not to follow riot and wantonness, but, as Paul saith, "unto good works, to walk in them"; [4] that God hath plucked us out "from the power of darkness, to serve the living God," [5] to cut away all the remnants of sin, and "to work our salvation in fear and trembling"; [6] that it may appear how that the Spirit of sanctification is in our bodies, and that Christ himself doth dwell in our hearts.

To conclude: we believe that this our self-same flesh wherein we live, although it die, and come to dust, yet at the last day it shall return again to life by the means of Christ's Spirit which dwelleth in us; and that then verily, whatsoever we suffer here in the meanwhile for his sake, Christ will wipe from off our eyes all tears and lamentation; and that we through him shall enjoy everlasting life, and shall for ever be with him in glory. So be it.

Part IV

On this fashion likewise do these men slander us as heretics, and say that we have left the Church and fellowship of Christ; not because they think it is true (for they do not much force of that [7]), but because to ignorant folk it might perhaps some way appear true. We have indeed put ourselves apart, not as heretics are wont from the Church of Christ, but, as all good men ought to do, from the infection of naughty persons and hypocrites.

Nevertheless, in this point they triumph marvellously, that they be the Church, that their Church is Christ's spouse, the pillar of truth, the ark of Noe; and that without it there is no hope of salvation. Contrariwise they say that we be runagates; [8] that we have torn Christ's seat; that we are plucked quite off from the body of Christ, and have forsaken the Catholic faith. And, when they leave nothing unspoken that may never so falsely and maliciously be said against us, yet this one thing are they never able truly to say, that we have swerved either from the Word of God, or from the apostles of Christ, or from the primitive Church. Surely we have ever judged the primitive Church of Christ's time, of the apostles, and of the holy fathers, to be the Catholic Church; neither make we doubt to name it Noe's ark, Christ's spouse, the pillar and upholder of all truth, nor yet to fix therein the whole mean of our salvation. It is doubtless an odious matter for one to leave the fellowship whereunto he hath been accustomed, and specially of

[4] I Thess. 4:7 and Eph. 2:10.
[5] Col. 1:13 and I Thess. 1:9.
[6] Phil. 2:12.
[7] They are not interested in that.
[8] Renegades.

those men, who, though they be not, yet at least seem and be called Christians. And to say truly, we do not despise the Church of these men (howsoever it be ordered by them nowadays), partly for the name sake itself, and partly for that the gospel of Jesu Christ hath once been therein truly and purely set forth. Neither had we departed therefrom, but of very necessity and much against our wills. But I put case, an idol be set up in the Church of God, and the same desolation, which Christ prophesied to come,[9] stood openly in the holy place. What if some thief or pirate invade and possess Noe's ark? These folks, as often as they tell us of the Church, mean thereby themselves alone, and attribute all these titles to their own selves, boasting as they did in times past, which cried, "The temple of the Lord, the temple of the Lord";[10] or as the Pharisees and scribes did, which cracked [11] they were "Abraham's children." [12] Thus with a gay and jolly shew deceive they the simple, and seek to choke us with the very name of the Church. Much like as if a thief, when he hath gotten into another man's house, and by violence either hath thrust out or slain the owner, should afterward assign the same house to himself, casting forth of possession the right inheritor; or if Antichrist, after he hath once entered into the temple of God, should afterward say, This house is mine own; and Christ hath nothing to do withal. For these men now, after they have left nothing remaining in the Church of God that hath any likeness of this Church, yet will they seem the patrons and the valiant maintainers of the Church; very like as Gracchus, amongst the Romans, stood in defence of the treasury, notwithstanding with his prodigality and fond expenses he had utterly wasted the whole stock of the treasury. And yet was there never any thing so wicked, or so far out of reason, but lightly it might be covered, and defended by the name of the Church. For the wasps also make honey-combs as well as bees; and wicked men have companies like to the Church of God: yet, for all that, they be not straightway the people of God, which are called the people of God; neither be they all Israelites, as many as are come of Israel the father. . . .

So that these men's part had been, first to have clearly and truly proved that the Romish Church is the true and right-instructed Church of God; and that the same, as they do order it at this day, doth agree with the primitive Church of Christ, of the apostles, and of the holy fathers, which we doubt not but was indeed the true Catholic Church. For our parts, if we could have judged ignorance, error, superstition, idolatry, men's inventions, and the same commonly disagreeing with the Holy Scriptures, either

[9] Mark 13:14 and par.
[10] Jer. 7:4.
[11] Boasted.
[12] John 8:34, 39, etc.

pleased God, or to be sufficient for the obtaining everlasting salvation; or if we could ascertain ourselves, that the Word of God was written but for a time only, and afterward again ought to be abrogated and put away; or else that the sayings and commandments of God ought to be subject to man's will, that whatsoever God saith and commandeth, except the Bishop of Rome willeth and commandeth the same, it must be taken as void and unspoken; if we could have brought ourselves to believe these things, we grant there had been no cause at all why we should have left these men's company. As touching that we have now done, to depart from that Church, whose errors were proved and made manifest to the world, which Church also had already evidently departed from God's Word; and yet not to depart so much from itself, as from the errors thereof; and not to do this disorderly or wickedly, but quietly and soberly, we have done nothing herein against the doctrine either of Christ, or of his apostles. For neither is the Church of God such as it may not be dusked with some spot, or asketh not sometime reparation. Else what needeth there so many assemblies and councils, without the which, as saith Egidius, the Christian faith is not able to stand? "For look," saith he, "how often councils are discontinued, so often is the Church destitute of Christ." [13] Or if there be no peril that harm may come to the Church, what need is there to retain to no purpose the names of bishops, as is now commonly used among them? For if there be no sheep that may stray, why be they called shepherds? If there be no city that may be betrayed, why be they called watchmen? If there be nothing that may run to ruin, why be they called pillars? Anon after the first creation of the world, the Church of God began to spread abroad, and the same was instructed with the heavenly word which God himself pronounced with his own mouth. It was also furnished with divine ceremonies. It was taught by the Spirit of God, by the patriarchs and prophets, and continued so even till the time that Christ shewed himself to us in the flesh. This notwithstanding, how often, O good God, in the mean while, and how horribly was the same Church darkened and decayed! Where was that Church then, when all flesh upon earth had defiled their own way? [14] Where was it, when amongst the number of the whole world there were only eight persons (and they neither all chaste and good) whom God's will was should be saved alive from that universal destruction and mortality? [15] when Eli the prophet so lamentably and bitterly made moan, that only him-

---

[13] Egidius Viterbiensis, *Orat. Syn. Later.* (Mansi, XXXII.670).
[14] Gen. 6:12.
[15] Gen., chs. 6 and 7.

self was left of all the whole world, which did truly and duly worship God? [16] and when Esay said, "The silver of God's people (that is, of the Church) was become dross; [17] and that the same city, which aforetime had been faithful, was now become an harlot; [18] and that in the same was no part sound throughout the whole body, from the head to the foot"? [19] or else, when Christ himself said, that the house of God was made by the Pharisees and priests "a den of thieves"? [20] Of a truth, the Church, even as a corn-field, except it be eared,[21] manured, tilled and trimmed, instead of wheat it will bring forth thistles, darnel, and nettles. For this cause did God send ever among [22] both prophets and apostles and last of all his own Son, who might bring home the people into the right way, and repair anew the tottering Church after she had erred. . . .

But, forsomuch as these men avouch the universal possession of the Catholic Church to be their own, and call us heretics, because we agree not in judgment with them, let us know, I beseech you, what proper mark and badge hath that Church of theirs, whereby it may be known to be the Church of God. I wis,[23] it is not so hard a matter to find out God's Church, if a man will seek it earnestly and diligently. For the Church of God is set upon a high and glistering place, in the top of an hill, and built upon the foundation of the apostles and prophets.[24] "There," saith Augustine, "let us seek the Church; there let us try our matter." [25] And as he saith again in another place, "The Church must be shewed out of the holy and Canonical Scriptures; and that which cannot be shewed out of them is not the Church." [26] Yet, for all this, I wot not how, whether it be for fear, or for conscience, or despairing of victory, these men alway abhor and fly the word of God, even as the thief fleeth the gallows. And no wonder truly, for, like as men say the cantharus [27] by and by perisheth and dieth as soon as it is laid in balm; notwithstanding balm be otherwise a most sweet-smelling ointment; even so these men well see their own matter is damped and destroyed in the Word of God, as if it were in poison. There-

---

[16] I Kings 19:10.
[17] Isa. 1:22.
[18] Isa. 1:21.
[19] Isa. 1:6.
[20] Matt. 21:13.
[21] Plowed.
[22] Latin, *subinde:* "from time to time" or "one after another."
[23] I wis = certainly.
[24] Eph. 2:20.
[25] *De unit. eccl.* III.5 (*PL* 43.394).
[26] *De unit. eccl.* III.6 and IV.7 (*PL* 43.395–6).
[27] Fly.

fore the Holy Scriptures, which our Saviour Jesu Christ did not only use for authority in all his speech, but did also at last seal up the same with his own blood, these men, to the intent they might with less business drive the people from the same, as from a thing dangerous and deadly, have used to call them a bare letter, uncertain, unprofitable, dumb, killing, and dead: which seemeth to us all one as if they should say, "The Scriptures are to no purpose, or as good as none." Hereunto they add also a similitude not very agreeable, how the Scriptures be like to a nose of wax; [28] how they may be fashioned and plied all manner of ways, and serve all men's turns. Wotteth not the Bishop of Rome that these things are spoken by his own minions? Or understandeth he not he hath such champions to fight for him? Let him hearken then how holily and how godly one Hosius writeth of this matter, a bishop in Polonia, as he testifieth of himself; a man doubtless well spoken and not unlearned, and a very sharp and stout maintainer of that side. One will marvel, I suppose, how a good man could either conceive so wickedly, or write so despitefully of those words which he knew proceeded from God's mouth, and specially in such sort as he would not have it seem his own private opinion alone, but the common opinion of all that band. He disembleth, I grant you indeed, and hideth what he is, and setteth forth the matter so, as though it were not he and his side, but the Zuenckfeldian heretics that so did speak.[29] "We," saith he, "will bid away the same Scriptures, whereof we see brought not only divers, but also contrary interpretations; and we will hear God speak, rather than we will resort to these naked elements, and appoint our salvation to rest in them. It behoveth not a man to be expert in the law and Scripture, but to be taught of God. It is but lost labour that a man bestoweth in the Scriptures, for the Scripture is a creature, and a certain bare letter." [30] This is Hosius' saying, uttered altogether with the same spirit and the same mind wherewith in times past Montane and Marcion were moved, who, as men report, used to say, when with a contempt they rejected the Holy Scriptures, that themselves knew many more and better things than either Christ or the apostles ever knew.

[28] *Explicationes Catholicae praecipuarum controversiarum* . . . *per Albertum Pighium* (Parisiis M.D.LXXXVI), fol. 90.
[29] This sentence did not appear in the first Latin edition, but was inserted in 1581 to meet the charge of misrepresenting Hosius. For Jewel's excuse that several others had misunderstood Hosius similarly, see *Defence, ad loc.* (PS, IV.757 f.).
[30] *De expresso Dei verbo* in *D. Stanislai Hosii* . . . *Opera omnia* . . . (Coloniae . . . M.D.LXXIIII), I.624.

As for us, we run not for succour to the fire,[31] as these men's guise is, but we run to the Scriptures; neither do we reason with the sword, but with the Word of God: and therewith, as saith Tertullian, "do we feed our faith; by it do we stir up our hope, and strengthen our confidence." [32] For we know that the gospel of Jesu Christ is the power of God unto salvation; [33] and that therein consisteth eternal life. And, as Paul warneth us, we do not hear, no not an angel of God coming from heaven, if he go about to pull us from any part of this doctrine. [34] Yea, more than this, as the holy martyr Justin speaketh of himself, we would give no credence to God himself, if he should teach us any other gospel.[35]

For where these men bid the Holy Scriptures away, as dumb and fruitless, and procure us to come to God himself rather, who speaketh in the Church and in Councils, which is to say, to believe their fancies and opinions; this way of finding out the truth is very uncertain, and exceeding dangerous, and in manner a fantastical and a mad way, and by no means allowed of the holy fathers. Chrysostom saith: "There be many oftentimes which boast themselves of the Holy Ghost; but truly whoso speak of their own head do falsely boast they have the Spirit of God. For, like as (saith he) Christ denied he spake of himself, when he spake out of the Law and Prophets; even so now, if any thing be pressed upon us in the name of the Holy Ghost, save the Gospel, we ought not to believe it. For, as Christ is the fulfilling of the Law and the Prophets, so is the Holy Ghost the fulfilling of the Gospel." [36] Thus far goeth Chrysostom. . . .

Part V

But here I look they will say, though they have not the Scriptures, yet may chance they have the ancient doctors and the holy fathers with them. For this is a high brag they have ever made, how that all antiquity and a continual consent of all ages doth make on their side; and that all our cases be but new and yesterday's work, and until these few last years never heard of. Questionless, there can nothing be more spitefully spoken against the religion of God than to accuse it of novelty, as a new comen up

---

[31] I.e., we do not use the threat of the stake as an argument.
[32] *Apol.* XXXIX.3 (*PL* I.468 f.).
[33] Rom. 1:16.
[34] Gal. 1:8.
[35] This sentence omitted from second edition of *Defence*. Jelf suggests that Jewel was doubtful, on second thoughts, of its authenticity.
[36] Pseudo-Chrysostom, *De Spir. Sancto Hom.* (*PG* 52.824–5).

matter. For as there can be no change in God himself, no more ought there to be in his religion.

... As for our doctrine, which we may rightlier call Christ's Catholic doctrine, it is so far off from new, that God, who is above all most ancient, and the Father of our Lord Jesus Christ, hath left the same unto us in the Gospel, in the prophets' and apostles' works, being monuments of greatest age. So that no man can now think our doctrine to be new, unless the same think either the prophets' faith, or the Gospel, or else Christ himself to be new.

And as for their religion, if it be of so long continuance as they would have men ween it is, why do they not prove it so by the examples of the primitive Church, and by the fathers and councils of old times? Why lieth so ancient a cause thus long in the dust destitute of an advocate? Fire and sword they have had always ready at hand; but as for the old councils and the fathers, all mum, not a word. ...

It is a world to see how well-favouredly and how towardly [37] touching religion these men agree with the fathers, of whom they use to vaunt that they be their own good.[38] The old council Eliberine made a decree, that nothing that is honoured of the people should be painted in the churches.[39] The old father Epiphanius saith: "It is an horrible wickedness, and a sin not to be suffered, for any man to set up any picture in the churches of the Christians, yea, though it were the picture of Christ himself." [40] Yet these men store all their temples and each corner of them with painted and carved images, as though without them religion were nothing worth.

The old fathers Origen and Chrysostom exhort the people to read the Scriptures, to buy them books, to reason at home betwixt themselves of divine matters; wives with their husbands, and parents with their children.[41] These men condemn the Scriptures as dead elements, and, as much as ever they may, bar the people from them. The ancient fathers Cyprian, Epiphanius, and Jerome say, "It is better for one who perchance hath made a vow to lead a sole life, and afterward liveth unchastely, and cannot quench the flames of lust, to marry a wife and to live honestly in wedlock." [42]

[37] Dutifully.
[38] Possession.
[39] Council of Elvira, Canon 36 (Mansi, II.11).
[40] See *Ep.* LI in Jerome (*PL* 22.526).
[41] Origen, *Hom. ix.5 in Levit.* (*PG* 12.515); Chrysostom, *In Matt.*, Hom. II. (*PG* 57.28) and *In Ioan.*, Hom. XXXII (*PG* 59.187 f.).
[42] Cyprian, *Ep.* IV (*PL* 4.366–7); Epiphanius, *Adversus Haereses*, Lib. ii, tom. 1, *Haer.* lxi (*PG* 41.1050); Jerome, *Ad Demetr., Ep.* XCVII (*PL* 22.1123).

And the old father Augustine judgeth the self-same marriage to be good and perfect, and ought not to be broken again.[43] These men, if a man have once bound himself by a vow, though afterward he burn, keep queans, and defile himself with never so sinful and desperate a life, yet they suffer not that person to marry a wife; or, if he chance to marry, they allow it not for marriage. And they commonly teach it is much better and more godly to keep a concubine and harlot, than to live in that kind of marriage.

The old father Augustine complained of the multitude of vain ceremonies wherewith he even then saw men's minds and consciences overcharged.[44] These men, as though God regarded nothing else but their ceremonies, have so out of measure increased them, that there is now almost none other thing left in their churches and places of prayer.

Again, that old father Augustine denieth it to be leeful for a monk to spend his time slothfully and idly, and under a pretensed and counterfeit holiness to live all upon others.[45] And whoso thus liveth, an old father Apollonius likeneth him to a thief.[46] These men have (I wot not whether to name them) droves or herds of monks, who for all they do nothing, nor yet once intend to bear any shew of holiness, yet live they not only upon others, but also riot lavishly of other folks' labours.

The old council at Rome decreed that no man should come to the service said by a priest well known to keep a concubine.[47] These men let to farm concubines to their priests, and yet constrain men by force against their will to hear their cursed paltry service.

The old canons of the apostles command that bishop to be removed from his office, which will both supply the place of a civil magistrate, and also of an ecclesiastical person.[48] These men, for all that, both do and will needs serve both places. Nay rather, the one office which they ought chiefly to execute they once touch not, and yet nobody commandeth them to be displaced.

The old council Gangrense commandeth that none should make such difference between an unmarried priest and a married

[43] *De bono viduitatis* X.13 (*PL* 40.438).
[44] *Ep.* LV.xix.35 (*PL* 33.221-2).
[45] See PS, IV.798, notes 9-14.
[46] From Sozomen as quoted in *Cassiodori-Epiphanii Historia ecclesiastica tripartita* (ed. by W. Jacob and R. Hanslik; *Corpus scriptorum ecclesiasticorum Latinorum*, Vol. LXXI [1952], p. 463).
[47] Synod of Rome, under Nicolas I (Mansi, V.521-2).
[48] *Canones Apostolorum*, LXXXII (Mansi, I.45-6).

priest, as he ought to think the one more holy than the other, for single life sake.⁴⁹ These men put such a difference between them, that they straightway think all their holy service to be defiled, if it be done by a good and honest man that hath a wife.

The ancient Emperor Justinian commanded that in the holy administration all things should be pronounced with a clear, loud, and treatable voice, that the people might receive some fruit thereby.⁵⁰ These men, lest the people should understand them, mumble up all their service, not only with a drowned and hollow voice, but also in a strange and barbarous ⁵¹ tongue.

The old council at Carthage commanded nothing to be read in Christ's congregation but the Canonical Scriptures: ⁵² these men read such things in their churches as themselves know for a truth to be stark lies and fond fables.

But, if there be any that think that these above rehearsed authorities be but weak and slender, because they were decreed by emperors and certain petty bishops, and not by so full and perfect councils, taking pleasure rather in the authority and name of the Pope; let such a one know that Pope Julius doth evidently forbid that a priest in ministering the Communion should dip the bread in the cup.⁵³ These men, contrary to Pope Julius' decree, divide the bread, and dip it in the wine.

Pope Clement saith it is not lawful for a bishop to deal with both swords; "For if thou wilt have both," saith he, "thou shalt deceive both thyself and those that obey thee." ⁵⁴ Nowadays the Pope challengeth to himself both swords, and useth both.⁵⁵ Wherefore it ought to seem less marvel, if that have followed which Clement saith, that is, "that he hath deceived both his own self, and those which have given ear unto him."

Pope Leo saith, upon one day it is lawful to say but one mass in one church.⁵⁶ These men say daily in one church commonly ten masses, twenty, thirty, yea, oftentimes more: so that the poor gazer on can scant tell which way he were best to turn him.

---

⁴⁹ Council of Gangra, Canon 4 (Mansi, II.1105–6).
⁵⁰ *Corp. Iur. Civ.* III.699.
⁵¹ I.e., alien.
⁵² Third Council of Carthage, cap. 47 (Mansi, III.891). Harding objected that this was a misrepresentation (PS, IV.815), but Jewel replied that he had quoted from the *Abbreviations* of the Council of Hippo, which were presented at Carthage (*Abbrev.* 38 in Mansi, III.896; PS, IV.815).
⁵³ In *Corp. Iur. Can.* (*De consecr.*, Dist. II, can. VII), I.1316.
⁵⁴ In error for Bernard *De consideratione* II, cap. 6, 10 and 11 (*PL* 182.748). See *Defence* (PS, IV.819).
⁵⁵ See PS, IV.820 on Pope Boniface VIII.
⁵⁶ *Ep.* ix.2 (*PL* 54.627).

Pope Gelasius saith it is a wicked deed and sibb [57] to sacrilege in any man to divide the Communion, and when he received one kind, to abstain from the other.[58] These men, contrary to God's Word, and contrary to Pope Gelasius, command that one kind only of the Holy Communion be given to the people, and by so doing they make their priests guilty of sacrilege.

But if they will say that all these things are worn now out of ure [59] and nigh dead, and pertain nothing to these present times; yet, to the end all folk may understand what faith is to be given to these men, and upon what hope they call together their general councils, let us see in few words what good heed they take to the self-same things, which they themselves these very last years (and the remembrance thereof is yet new and fresh), in their own general council that they had by order called, decreed and commanded to be devoutly kept. In the last council at Trident, scant fourteen years past, it was ordained by the common consent of all degrees, that one man should not have two benefices at one time.[60] What is become now of that ordinance? Is the same too so soon [61] worn out of mind and clean consumed? For these men, ye see, give to one man not two benefices only, but sundry abbeys many times, sometime also two bishopricks, sometime three, sometime four, and that not only to an unlearned man, but oftentimes even to a man of war.

In the said council a decree was made, that all bishops should preach the gospel.[62] These men neither preach nor once go up into the pulpit, neither think they it any part of their office. What great pomp and crake then is this they make of antiquity? Why brag they so of the names of the ancient fathers, and of the new and old councils? Why will they seem to trust to their authority, whom when they list they despise at their own pleasure?

But I have a special fancy to common [63] a word or two rather with the Pope's good holiness, and to say these things to his own face. Tell us, I pray you, good holy father, seeing ye do crake so much of all antiquity, and boast yourself that all men are bound

---

[57] Akin.
[58] In *Corp. Iur. Can.* (*De consecr.*, Dist. II, can. XII), I.1318.
[59] Use.
[60] This cannot possibly be *Sessio* XXIV, cap. xvii (as PS, IV.821), which did not take place until 1563, a year after the *Apologia* was written. It refers rather to *Sessio* VII, cap. iv, seq. (Mansi, XXXIII.48 ff.). This was held in 1547, and therefore fits well enough Jewel's dating of it as "scant fourteen years past."
[61] I.e., also so soon.
[62] *Sessio* V, cap. ii (Mansi, XXXIII.30 f.).
[63] Exchange.

to you alone, which of all the fathers have at any time called you by the name of the highest prelate, the universal bishop, or the head of the Church? [64] Which of them ever said that both the swords were committed to you? Which of them ever said that you have authority and a right to call councils? Which of them ever said that the whole world is but your diocese? Which of them, that all bishops have received of your fulness? Which of them, that all power is given to you as well in heaven as in earth? Which of them, that neither kings, nor the whole clergy, nor yet all people together, are able to be judges over you? Which of them, that kings and emperors by Christ's commandment and will do receive authority at your hand? Which of them with so precise and mathematical limitation hath surveyed and determined you to be seventy and seven times greater than the mightiest kings? Which of them, that more ample authority is given to you than to the residue of the patriarchs? Which of them, that you are the Lord God? or that you are not a mere natural man, but a certain substance made and grown together of God and man? Which of them, that you are the only head-spring of all law? Which of them, that you have power over purgatories? Which of them, that you are able to command the angels of God as you list yourself? Which of them that ever said, that you are Lord of Lords, and the King of Kings? We can also go further with you in like sort. What one amongst the whole number of the old bishops and fathers ever taught you, either to say private mass whiles the people stared on, or to lift up the sacrament over your head (in which point consisteth now all your religion), or else to mangle Christ's sacraments, and to bereave the people of the one part, contrary to Christ's institution and plain expressed words? But, that we may once come to an end, what one is there of all the fathers which hath taught you to distribute Christ's blood and the holy martyrs' merits, and to sell openly as merchandises your pardons and all the rooms and lodgings of purgatory? These men are wont to speak much of a certain secret doctrine of theirs, and manifold and sundry readings. Then let them bring forth somewhat now, if they can, that it may appear they have at least read or do know somewhat. They have often stoutly noised in all corners where they went, how all the parts of their religion be very old, and have been approved not only by the multitude, but also by the consent and continual observation of all nations and times. Let them therefore once in their life shew this their antiquity: let them make appear at eye, that the things whereof they make such ado have taken so long

[64] For all these references, see PS, IV.822 ff.

and large increase: let them declare that all Christian nations have agreed by consent to this their religion.

Nay, nay, they turn their backs, as we have said already, and flee from their own decrees, and have cut off and abolished again within a short space the same things which but a few years before themselves had established for evermore, forsooth, to continue. How should one then trust them in the fathers, in the old councils, and in the words spoken by God? They have not, good Lord, they have not (I say) those things which they boast they have: they have not that antiquity, they have not that universality, they have not that consent of all places nor of all times.[65] And though they have a desire rather to dissemble, yet they themselves are not ignorant hereof: yea, and sometime also they let not to confess it openly. And for this cause they say that the ordinances of the old councils and fathers be such as may now and then be altered, and that sundry and divers decrees serve for sundry and divers times of the Church. Thus lurk they under the name of the Church, and beguile silly creatures with their vain glozing.[66] It is to be marvelled that either men be so blind as they cannot see this, or, if they see it, to be so patient as they can so lightly and quietly bear it. . . .

But, say they, ye have been once of our fellowship, but now ye are become forsakers of your profession, and have departed from us. It is true we have departed from them, and for so doing we both give thanks to Almighty God, and greatly rejoice on our own behalf. But yet for all this, from the primitive Church, from the apostles, and from Christ, we have not departed. True it is, we were brought up with these men in darkness, and in the lack of knowledge of God, as Moses was taught up in the learning and the bosom of the Egyptians. "We have been of your company," saith Tertullian, "I confess it, and no marvel at all; for," saith he, "men be made and not born Christians."[67] But wherefore, I pray you, have they themself, the citizens and dwellers of Rome, removed and come down from those seven hills, whereupon Rome sometime stood, to dwell rather in the plain called Mars his field? They will say peradventure, because the conducts of water, wherewithout men cannot commodiously live, have now failed and are dried up in those hills. Well then, let them give us like leave in seeking the water of eternal life, that they give themselves in seeking the water of the well. For the water verily failed amongst them. . . . With great distress went men scattering about, seeking some spark

---

[65] I.e., the Vincentian Canon. [67] *Apol.* XVIII.4 (*PL* 1.378).
[66] Deceit.

of heavenly light to refresh their consciences withal; but that light was already thoroughly quenched out, so that they could find none. This was a rueful state: this was a lamentable form of God's Church. It was a misery to live therein without the Gospel, without light, and without all comfort.

Wherefore, though our departing were a trouble to them, yet ought they to consider withal how just cause we had of our departure. For if they will say, it is in no wise lawful for one to leave the fellowship wherein he hath been brought up, they may as well in our names, or upon our heads, condemn both the prophets, the apostles, and Christ himself. For why complain they not also of this, that Lot went quit his way out of Sodom, Abraham out of Chaldee, the Israelites out of Egypt, Christ from the Jews, and Paul from the Pharisees? For, except it be possible there may be a lawful cause of departing, we see no reason why Lot, Abraham, the Israelites, Christ, and Paul may not be accused of sects and sedition, as well as others.

And, if these men will needs condemn us for heretics, because we do not all things at their commandment, whom (in God's name) or what kind of men ought they themselves to be taken for, which despise the commandment of Christ and of the apostles? If we be schismatics because we have left them, by what name shall they be called themselves, which have forsaken the Greeks,[68] from whom they first received their faith, forsaken the primitive Church, forsaken Christ himself and the apostles, even as children should forsake their parents? For though those Greeks, who at this day profess religion and Christ's name, have many things corrupted amongst them, yet hold they still a great number of those things which they received from the apostles. They have neither private masses, nor mangled sacraments, nor purgatories, nor pardons. And as for the titles of high bishops, and those glorious names, they esteem them so as, whosoever he were that would take upon him the same, and would be called either universal bishop, or the head of the universal Church, they make no doubt to call such a one both a passing proud man, a man that worketh despite against all the other bishops his brethren, and a plain heretic. . . .

We truly have renounced that Church, wherein we could neither have the Word of God sincerely taught, nor the sacraments rightly administered, nor the name of God duly called upon; which Church also themselves confess to be faulty in many points; and wherein was nothing able to stay [69] any wise man, or one that hath consideration of his own safety. To conclude, we have forsaken

[68] I.e., in the schism of 1054 ff.   [69] Keep.

the Church, as it is now, not as it was in old time, and have so gone from it, as Daniel went out of the lions' den, and the three children out of the furnace; and to say truth, we have been cast out by these men (being cursed of them, as they use to say, with book, bell, and candle), rather than have gone away from them of ourselves.

And we are come to that Church, wherein they themselves cannot deny (if they will say truly, and as they think in their own conscience) but all things be governed purely and reverently, and, as much as we possibly could, very near to the order used in the old time.

Let them compare our churches and theirs together, and they shall see that themselves have most shamefully gone from the apostles, and we most justly have gone from them. For we, following the example of Christ, of the apostles, and the holy fathers, give the people the Holy Communion whole and perfect. But these men, contrary to all the fathers, to all the apostles, and contrary to Christ himself, do sever the sacraments, and pluck away the one part from the people, and that with most notorious sacrilege, as Gelasius termeth it.[70]

We have brought again the Lord's Supper unto Christ's institution, and will have it to be a Communion in very deed, common and indifferent to a great number, according to the name. But these men have changed all things, contrary to Christ's institution, and have made a private mass of the Holy Communion. And so it cometh to pass, that we give the Lord's Supper unto the people, and they give them a vain pageant to gaze on.

We affirm, together with the ancient fathers, that the body of Christ is not eaten but of the good and faithful, and of those that are endued with the Spirit of Christ. Their doctrine is, that Christ's very body effectually, and, as they speak, really and substantially, may not only be eaten of the wicked and unfaithful men, but also (which is monstrous to be spoken) of mice and dogs.

We use to pray in churches after that fashion, as, according to Paul's lesson, the people may know what we pray, and may answer Amen with a general consent.[71] These men, like sounding metal, yell out in the churches unknown and strange words without understanding, without knowledge, and without devotion; yea, and do it of purpose, because [72] the people should understand nothing at all.

---

[70] In *Corp. Iur. Can.* (*De consecr.*, Dist. II, can. XII), I.1318.
[71] I Cor. 14:16.
[72] Latin, *ne:* in order that.

But, not to tarry about rehearsing all points wherein we and they differ (for they have well nigh no end), we turn the Scriptures into all tongues: they scant suffer them to be had abroad in any tongue. We allure the people to read and to hear God's Word: they drive the people from it. We desire to have our cause known to all the world: they flee to come to any trial. We lean unto knowledge: they unto ignorance. We trust unto light: they unto darkness. We reverence, as it becometh us, the writings of the apostles and prophets: and they burn them. Finally, we in God's cause desire to stand to God's only judgment: they will stand only to their own. Wherefore, if they will weigh all these things with a quiet mind, and fully bent to hear and to learn, they will not only allow this determination of ours, who have forsaken errors, and followed Christ and his apostles, but themselves also will forsake their own selves, and join of their own accord to our side.

Part VI

But peradventure they will say, it was treason to attempt these matters without a sacred general council; for in that consisteth the whole force of the Church: there Christ hath promised he will ever be a present assistant. Yet they themselves, without tarrying for any general council, have broken the commandments of God and the decrees of the apostles; and as we said a little above, they have spoiled and disannulled almost all, not only ordinances, but even the doctrine of the primitive Church. And where they say it is not lawful to make a change without a council, what was he that made us these laws, or from whence had they this injunction? . . .

Yet truly we do not despise councils, assemblies, and conferences of bishops and learned men; neither have we done that we have done altogether without bishops or without a council. The matter hath been treated in open parliament, with long consultation, and before a notable synod and convocation. . . .

But these men will neither have the case to be freely disputed, nor yet, how many errors soever there be, suffer they any to be changed. For it is a common custom of theirs, often and shamelessly to boast that their Church cannot err, that in it there is no fault, and that they must give place to us in nothing. Or if there be any fault, yet must it be tried by bishops and abbots only, because they be the directors and rulers of matters; and they be the Church of God. . . .

But I put case, these abbots and bishops have no knowledge:

what if they understand nothing what religion is, nor how we ought to think of God? I put case, the pronouncing and ministering of the law be decayed in priests, and good counsel fail in the elders, and, as the prophet Micah saith, "the night be unto them instead of a vision, and darkness instead of prophesying"; [73] or, as Esaias saith, what if all the watchmen of the city are become blind? [74] What if the salt have lost his proper strength and savouriness, and, as Christ saith, be good for no use, scant worth the casting on the dunghill? [75]

Well, yet then, they will bring all matters before the Pope, who cannot err. To this I say, first, it is a madness to think that the Holy Ghost taketh his flight from a general council to run to Rome, to the end, if he doubt or stick in any matter, and cannot expound it of himself, he may take counsel of some other spirit, I wot not what, that is better learned than himself. For, if this be true, what needed so many bishops, with so great charges and so far journeys, have assembled their convocation at this present at Trident? It had been more wisdom and better, at least it had been a much nearer way and handsomer, to have brought all things rather before the Pope, and to have come straight forth, and have asked counsel at his divine breast. Secondly, it is also an unlawful dealing to toss our matter from so many bishops and abbots, and to bring it at last to the trial of one only man, specially of him who himself is appeached by us of heinous and foul enormities, and hath not yet put in his answer; who hath also aforehand condemned us without judgment by order pronounced, and or ever we were called to be judged. . . .

What will ye say, if the Pope's advocates, abbots and bishops, dissemble not the matter, but shew themselves open enemies to the Gospel, and though they see, yet they will not see, but wry [76] the Scriptures, and wittingly and knowingly corrupt and counterfeit the Word of God, and foully and wickedly apply to the Pope all the same things which evidently and properly be spoken of the person of Christ only, nor by no means can be applied to any other? And what though they say "the Pope is all and above all"? or that "he can do as much as Christ can"? and that "one judgment-place and one council-house serve for the Pope and for Christ both together"? or "that the Pope is the same light which should come into the world," which words Christ spake of himself alone; and that "whoso is an evil-doer hateth and flieth from that light"? or that "all the other bishops have received of the

---

[73] Micah 3:6.
[74] Isa. 56:10.
[75] Matt. 5:13.
[76] I.e., twist.

Pope's fulness"? [77] Shortly, what though they make decrees expressly against God's Word, and that not in hucker-mucker [78] or covertly, but openly and in the face of the world; must it needs yet be gospel straight whatsoever these men say? Shall these be God's holy army? or will Christ be at hand among them there? Shall the Holy Ghost flow in their tongues, or can they with truth say, We and the Holy Ghost have thought good [79] so? . . .

But will these men (I say) reform us the Church, being themselves both the persons guilty and the judges too? Will they abate their own ambition and pride? Will they overthrow their own matter, and give sentence against themselves that they must leave off to be unlearned bishops, slow bellies, heapers together of benefices, takers upon them as princes and men of war? Will the abbots, the Pope's dear darlings, judge that monk for a thief which laboureth not for his living? and that it is against all law to suffer such a one to live and to be found either in city or in country, or yet of other men's charges? or else, that a monk ought to lie on the ground, to live hardly with herbs and peason,[80] to study earnestly, to argue, to pray, to work with hand, and fully to bend himself to come to the ministry of the Church? In faith, as soon will the Pharisees and scribes repair again the temple of God, and restore it unto us a house of prayer instead of a thievish den. . . .

Nevertheless, we can bear patiently and quietly our own private wrongs. But wherefore do they shut out Christian kings and good princes from their convocation? Why do they so uncourteously, or with such spite, leave them out, and, as though they were not either Christian men, or else could not judge, will not have them made acquainted with the cause of Christian Religion, nor understand the state of their own churches? . . .

They will say to this, I guess, "Civil princes have learned to govern a commonwealth, and to order matters of war; but they understand not the secret mysteries of religion." If that be so, what is the Pope, I pray you, at this day other than a monarch or a prince? Or what be the cardinals, who must be no nother nowadays but princes and kings' sons? What else be the patriarchs, and, for the most part, the archbishops, the bishops, the abbots? What be they else at this present in the Pope's kingdom but worldly

---

[77] Hostiens, *Lectura in quinque Decretalium Gregorianarum libros* (1512), fol. 75ᵇ. *Panormitani super Tertio Decretalium* (1534), fol. 156.
[78] Hugger-mugger, secrecy.
[79] 1564 omits *good*.
[80] Plural of "pease."

princes, but dukes and earls, gorgeously accompanied with bands of men whithersoever they go; oftentimes also gaily arrayed with chains and collars of gold? They have at times, too, certain ornaments by themselves, as crosses, pillars, hats, mitres, and palls; which pomp the ancient bishops, Chrysostom, Augustine, and Ambrose, never had. Setting these things aside, what teach they? what say they? what do they? how live they? I say not, as may become a bishop, but as may become even a Christian man. Is it so great a matter to have a vain title, and by changing a garment only to have the name of a bishop?

Surely to have the principal stay and effect of all matters committed wholly to these men's hands, who neither know nor will know these things, nor yet set a jot by any point of religion, save that which concerns their belly and riot; and to have them alone sit as judges, and to be set up as overseers in the watch-tower, being no better than blind spies; of the other side, to have a Christian prince of good understanding and of a right judgment to stand still like a block or a stake, not to be suffered nother to give his voice nor to shew his judgment, but only to wait what these men shall will and command, as one which had neither ears, nor eyes, nor wit, nor heart; and, whatsoever they give in charge, to allow it without exception, blindly fulfilling their commandments, be they never so blasphemous and wicked, yea, although they command him quite to destroy all religion, and to crucify again Christ himself, this surely, besides that it is proud and spiteful, is also beyond all right and reason, and not to be endured of Christian and wise princes. Why, I pray you, may Caiaphas and Annas understand these matters, and may not David and Ezechias do the same? Is it lawful for a cardinal, being a man of war, and delightious in blood, to have place in a council, and is it not lawful for a Christian emperor or a king? We truly grant no further liberty to our magistrates than that we know hath both been given them by the Word of God, and also confirmed by the examples of the very best-governed commonwealths. For, besides that a Christian prince hath the charge of both tables committed to him by God, to the end he may understand that not temporal matters only, but also religious and ecclesiastical causes, pertain to his office; besides also that God by his prophets often and earnestly commandeth the king to cut down the groves, to break down the images and altars of idols, and to write out the Book of the Law for himself; and besides that the prophet Esaias saith, "A king ought to be a patron and nurse of the church"; [81] I say, besides all

[81] Isa. 49:23.

these things, we see by histories and by examples of the best times, that good princes ever took the administration of ecclesiastical matters to pertain to their duty. . . .

And, to rehearse no more examples out of the old law, let us rather consider, since the birth of Christ, how the Church hath been governed in the Gospel's time. The Christian emperors in old time appointed the councils of the bishops. Constantine called the council at Nice; Theodosius the First called the council at Constantinople; Theodosius the Second, the council at Ephesus; Martian, the council at Chalcedon. And, when Ruffinus the heretic had alleged for authority a council, which, as he thought, should make for him, Jerome his adversary, to confute him, "Tell us," quoth he, "what emperor commanded that council to be called?" [82] The same Jerome again, in his epitaph upon Paula, maketh mention of the emperor's letters, which gave commandment to call the bishops of Italy and Grecia to Rome to a council.[83] Continually, for the space of five hundred years, the emperor alone appointed the ecclesiastical assemblies, and called the councils of the bishops together. . . .

Let us see then, such men as have authority over the bishops (such men as receive from God commandments concerning religion, such as bring home again the Ark of God, make holy hymns, oversee the priests, build the temple, make orations touching divine service, cleanse the temples, destroy the hill-altars,[84] burn the idols' groves, teach the priests their duty, write them out precepts how they should live, kill the wicked prophets, displace the high priests) call together the councils of bishops, sit together with the bishops, instructing them what they ought to do, condemn and punish an heretical bishop, be made acquainted with matters of religion, which subscribe and give sentence, and do all these things not by another man's commission, but in their own name, and that both uprightly and godly. Shall we say it pertaineth not to such men to have to do with religion? Or shall we say, a Christian magistrate, which dealeth amongst others in these matters, doth either naughtily, or presumptuously, or wickedly? The most ancient and Christian emperors and kings that ever were did busy themselves with these matters, and yet were they never for this cause noted either of wickedness or of presumption. And what is he, that can find out either more catholic princes, or more notable examples? . . .

We truly for our parts, as we have said, have done nothing in

---

[82] *Apol. adv. Ruff.*, Lib. II (*PL* 23.443).
[83] *Ep.* LXXXVI (*PL* 22.881).
[84] Latin, *excelsa:* high places.

altering religion, either upon rashness or arrogancy, nor nothing but with good leisure and great consideration. Neither had we ever intended to do it, except both the manifest and most assured will of God, opened to us in his Holy Scriptures, and the regard of our own salvation, had even constrained us thereunto. For, though we have departed from that Church which these men call catholic, and by that means get us envy [85] amongst them that want skill to judge, yet is this enough for us, and it ought to be enough for every wise and good man, and one that maketh account of everlasting life, that we have gone from that Church which had power to err; which Christ, who cannot err, told so long before it should err; and which we ourselves did evidently see with our eyes to have gone both from the holy fathers, and from the apostles, and from Christ his own self, and from the primitive and catholic Church; and we are come, as near as we possibly could, to the Church of the apostles and of the old catholic bishops and fathers; which Church we know hath hitherunto been sound and perfect, and, as Tertullian termeth it, a pure virgin spotted as yet with no idolatry, nor with any foul or shameful fault; [86] and have directed according to their customs and ordinances not only our doctrine, but also the sacraments and the form of common prayer. . . .

And forsomuch as we heard God himself speaking unto us in his Word, and saw also the notable examples of the old and primitive Church, again, how uncertain a matter it was to wait for a general council, and that the success thereof would be much more uncertain; but specially, forsomuch as we were most ascertained of God's will, and counted it a wickedness to be too careful and over-cumbered about the judgments of mortal men, we could no longer stand taking advice with flesh and blood, but rather thought good to do the same thing that both might rightly be done, and hath also many a time been done, as well of good men, as of many catholic bishops; that is, to remedy our own churches by a provincial synod. For thus know we the old fathers used to put in experience, before they came to the public universal council. There remain yet at this day canons, written in councils of free cities, as of Carthage under Cyprian, as of Ancyra, of Neocaesarea, and of Gangra, which is in Paphlagonia, as some think, before that the name of the general council at Nice was ever heard

---

[85] Latin, *invidia:* ill will.
[86] Jewel gives no reference, and there seems to be an error here. If Migne's Index *(PL* Index, Vol. II, cols. 671-2) is complete, this comparison is not found in Tertullian.

of. After this fashion in old time did they speedily meet with and cut short those heretics the Pelagians, and the Donatists, at home, with private disputation, without any general council. Thus also, when the Emperor Constantius evidently and earnestly took part with Auxentius the bishop of the Arians' faction, Ambrose [87] the bishop of the Christians, appealed not unto a general council, where he saw no good could be done by reason of the Emperor's might and great labour; but appealed to his own clergy and people, that is to say, to a provincial synod. And thus it was decreed in the council at Nice, that the bishops should assemble twice every year.[88] And in the council at Carthage it was decreed that the bishops should meet together in each of their provinces, at least once in the year: [89] which was done, as saith the council at Chalcedon, of purpose that, if any errors and abuses had happened to spring up any where, they might immediately at the first entry be destroyed where they first begun.[90] So likewise, when Secundus and Palladius rejected the council at Aquila, because it was not a general and a common council, Ambrose, bishop of Milan, made answer that no man ought to take it for a new or strange matter, that the bishops of the west part of the world did call together synods, and make private assemblies in their provinces, for that it was a thing before then used by the west bishops no few times, and by the bishops of Grecia used oftentimes and commonly to be done.[91] And so Charles the Great, being Emperor, held a provincial council in Germany for putting away images, contrary to the second council at Nice.[92] Neither pardy even amongst us is this so very a strange and new a trade. For we have had ere now in England provincial synods, and governed our churches by homemade laws. What should one say more? Of a truth, even those greatest councils, and where most assembly of people ever was (whereof these men use to make such an exceeding reckoning), compare them with all the churches which throughout the world acknowledge and profess the name of Christ, and what else, I pray you, can they seem to be but certain private councils of bishops and provincial synods? For admit peradventure Italy, France, Spain, England, Germany, Denmark, and Scotland meet togethers; if there want Asia, Grecia, Armenia, Persia, Media, Mesopotamia, Egypt, Ethiopia, India, and Mauritania, in all which places there

[87] For "Ambrose," 1581, 1591, and 1599 read "Athanasius."
[88] Council of Nicaea, Canon 5 (Mansi, II.679).
[89] Third Council of Carthage, cap. 2 (Mansi, III.880).
[90] Council of Chalcedon, *Actio* XV, Canon 19 (Mansi, VII.365-6).
[91] Mansi, III.602.
[92] At Frankfurt in 794 (Mansi, XIII.907 ff.).

be both many Christian men, and also bishops, how can any man, being in his right mind, think such a council to be a general council? Or, where so many parts of the world do lack, how can they truly say they have the consent of the whole world? Or what manner of council, ween you, was the same last at Trident? Or how might it be termed a general council, when out of all Christian kingdoms and nations there came unto it but only forty bishops,[93] and of those some so cunning,[94] that they might be thought meet to be sent home again to learn their grammar, and so well learned, that they had never studied divinity?

Whatsoever it be, the truth of the gospel of Jesus Christ dependeth not upon the councils, nor, as St. Paul saith, upon mortal creatures' judgments.[95] And if they which ought to be careful for God's Church will not be wise, but slack their duty, and harden their hearts against God and his Christ, going on still to pervert the right ways of the Lord, God will stir up the very stones, and make children and babes cunning, whereby there may ever be some to confute these men's lies. For God is able (not only without councils, but also, will the councils nill the councils) to maintain and advance his own kingdom. "Full many be the thoughts of man's heart," saith Salomon; "but the counsel of the Lord abideth stedfast."[96] "There is no wisdom, there is no knowledge, there is no counsel against the Lord."[97] "Things endure not," saith Hilarius, "that be set up with men's workmanship. By another manner of means must the Church of God be builded and preserved; for that Church is grounded upon the foundation of the apostles and prophets, and is holden fast together by one corner-stone, which is Christ Jesu."[98] . . .

But by your favour, some will say, these things ought not to have been attempted without the Bishop of Rome's commandment, forsomuch as he only is the knot and band of Christian society. He only is that priest of Levi's order, whom God signified in the Deuteronomy, from whom counsel in matters of weight and true judgment ought to be fetched; and whoso obeyeth not his judgment, the same man ought to be killed in the sight of his

---

[93] Not so, says Harding, nearer 200 (PS, IV.1051). If by "same last" Jewel means (as p. 42) 1547, the numbers were as follows: Session VI, about 70; Session VII, about 75; Session VIII, 43 plus certain cardinals (Mansi, XXXIII.46,49,61). But if he means 1551, there were about 60 present, of whom some 50 were bishops (Mansi, XXXIII.90).
[94] Learned.
[95] I Cor. 4:3.
[96] Prov. 19:21.
[97] Prov. 21:30.
[98] *Tract. in Ps. CXXVI* (PL 9.696).

brethren; and that no mortal creature hath authority to be judge over him, whatsoever he do; that Christ reigneth in heaven, and he in earth; that he alone can do as much as Christ or God himself can do, because Christ and he have but one council-house; that without him is no faith, no hope, no church; and whoso goeth from him quite casteth away and renounceth his own salvation. Such talk have the canonists, the Pope's parasites surely, but with small discretion or soberness; for they could scant say more, at least they could not speak more highly, of Christ himself.

As for us, truly, we have fallen from the Bishop of Rome upon no manner of worldly respect or commodity. And would to Christ he so behaved himself, as this falling away needed not; but so the case stood that, unless we left him, we could not come to Christ. Neither will he now make any other league with us, than such a one as Nahas the king of the Ammonites would have made in times past with them of the city of Jabes, which was to put out the right eye of each one of the inhabitants.[99] Even so will the Pope pluck from us the Holy Scripture, the gospel of our salvation, and all the confidence which we have in Christ Jesu: and upon other condition can he not agree upon peace with us.

For whereas some use to make so great a vaunt, that the Pope is only [1] Peter's successor, as though thereby he carried the Holy Ghost in his bosom, and cannot err, this is but a matter of nothing, and a very trifling tale. God's grace is promised to a good mind, and to one that feareth God, not unto sees and successions. "Riches," saith Jerome, "may make a bishop to be of more might than the rest; but all the bishops, whosoever they be, are the successors of the apostles." [2] If so be the place and consecrating only be sufficient, why then Manasses succeeded David, and Caiaphas succeeded Aaron. And it hath been often seen, that an idol hath stand in the temple of God. In old time Archidamus the Lacedaemonian boasted much of himself, how he came of the blood of Hercules: but one Nicostratus in this wise abated his pride: "Nay," quoth he, "thou seemest not to descend from Hercules, for Hercules destroyed ill men, but thou makest good men evil." And when the Pharisees bragged of their lineage, how they were of the kindred and blood of Abraham, "Ye," saith Christ, "seek to kill me, a man which have told you the truth, as I heard it from God. Thus Abraham never did. Ye are of your father the devil, and will needs obey his will." [3]

Yet notwithstanding, because we will grant somewhat to suc-

---

[99] I Sam. 11:1 ff.
[1] I.e., that the Pope alone is.
[2] *Ep.* CXLVI (*PL* 22.1194).
[3] John 8:40 f.

cession, tell us, hath the Pope alone succeeded Peter? and wherein, I pray you? In what religion? in what office? in what piece of his life hath he succeded him? What one thing (tell me) had Peter ever like unto the Pope, or the Pope like unto Peter? Except peradventure they will say thus; that Peter, when he was at Rome, never taught the gospel, never fed the flock, took away the keys of the Kingdom of Heaven, hid the treasures of his Lord, sat him down only in his castle in St. John Lateran, and pointed out with his finger all the places of purgatory and kinds of punishments, committing some poor souls to be tormented, and other some again suddenly releasing thence at his own pleasure, taking money for so doing; or that he gave order to say private masses in every corner; or that he mumbled up the holy service with a low voice, and in an unknown language; or that he hanged up the Sacrament in every temple and on every altar, and carried the same about before him whithersoever he went, upon an ambling jennet, with lights and bells; or that he consecrated with his holy breath oil, wax, wool, bells, chalices, churches, and altars; or that he sold jubilees, graces, liberties, advowsons, preventions, first-fruits, palls, the wearing of palls, bulls, indulgences, and pardons; or that he called himself by the name of the head of the church, the highest bishop, bishop of bishops, alone most holy; or that by usurping he took upon himself the right and authority over other folk's churches; or that he exempted himself from the power of any civil government; or that he maintained wars, set princes together at variance; or that he, sitting in his chair, with his triple crown full of labels, with sumptuous and Persian-like gorgeousness, with his royal sceptre, with his diadem of gold, and glittering with stones, was carried about, not upon palfrey, but upon the shoulders of noblemen. These things, no doubt, did Peter at Rome in times past, and left them in charge to his successors, as you would say, from hand to hand; for these things be nowadays done at Rome by the Popes, and be so done, as though nothing else ought to be done.

Or contrariwise peradventure they had rather say thus: that the Pope doth now all the same things, which we know Peter did many a day ago: that is, that he runneth up and down into every country to preach the gospel, not only openly abroad, but also privately from house to house; that he is diligent, and applieth that business in season and out of season, in due time and out of due time; that he doth the part of an Evangelist, that he fulfilleth the work and ministry of Christ, that he is the watchman of the house of Israel, receiveth answers and words at God's mouth, and, even as he receiveth them, so delivereth them over to the people; that he is the salt of the earth; that he is the light of the world; that he doth not feed his own self, but his flock; that he doth not entangle himself with the worldly cares of this life; that he doth not use a sovereignty over the Lord's people; that he seeketh not to have other men minister to him, but himself rather to minister unto others; that he taketh all bishops as his fellows and equals; that he is subject to princes, as to persons sent from God; that he giveth to Caesar that which is Caesar's; and that he, as the old bishops of Rome did (without any question), calleth the emperor his lord. Unless therefore the Popes do the like nowadays, and Peter did the things aforesaid, there is no cause at all why they should glory so of Peter's name and of his succession. . . .

For of very truth we have departed from him, whom we saw had blinded the whole world this many an hundred year; from him, who too far presumptuously was wont to say he could not err, and, whatsoever he did, no mortal man had power to condemn him, neither kings, nor emperors, nor the whole clergy, nor yet all the people in the world together, no, and though he should carry away with him to hell a thousand souls; from him who took upon him power to command, not only men, but even God's angels, to go, to return, to lead souls into purgatory, and to bring them back again when he list himself; whom Gregory said, without all doubt, is the very forerunner and standard-bearer of Antichrist, and hath utterly forsaken the catholic faith;[4] from whom also those ringleaders of ours, who now with might and main resist the gospel, and the truth, which they know to be the truth, have or[5] this departed every one of their own accord and good will, and would even now also gladly depart from him, if the note of inconstancy and shame, and their own estimation among the people, were not a let unto them. In conclusion, we have departed from him, to whom we were not bound, and who had nothing to say for himself, but only I know not what virtue or power of the place where he dwelleth, and a continuance of succession.

[4] *Ep.* XXXIII (*PL* 77.891).   [5] Ere.

John Foxe

TO THE TRUE AND FAITHFULL CONGREGATION OF CHRIST'S UNIVERSAL CHURCH

John Foxe: To the True and Faithfull Congregation of Christ's Universal Church

INTRODUCTION

THE SIXTEENTH CENTURY WAS ACUTELY CONSCIOUS OF THE PAST, both out of an antiquarian interest and also as a pressure on the present. Attention had been fastened on the culture of Greece and Rome, brought to light by discoveries of statuary, by laborious lexicography, by the learned editions of the classics. The Christian renaissance entered into the Hebrew world of the Old Testament, the Greek world of the New, and of the Church fathers. Accused of innovating and novelty, the Reformers were driven back to a study of the past, which could alone disprove the charge. The general history of the Church, of liturgy, of doctrines, was investigated widely and intensively. Vast compilations of histories began to make their appearance, the Magdeburg "Centuries," for example, or Jean Crispin's Martyrology,[1] or John Foxe's *Actes and Monuments of these latter and perilous dayes, touching matters of the Church,* but better known as Foxe's Book of Martyrs.

To explain his purpose and methods, Foxe made extensive use of prefaces. Eight are collected in the 1841 ff. editions, though they are not all from the same original edition. The first is in the form of a thanksgiving to Christ: *Ad Dominum Iesum Christum Servatorem Clementissimum Eucharisticon*—a thanksgiving that the work is done, an acknowledgment that this is only through the strength given to him, and a prayer that the work will be useful. The second is addressed *To the right virtuous, most excel-*

---

[1] *Actiones et monimenta martyrum eorum qui a Wicleffo et Husso ad nostram hanc aetatem in Germania, Gallia, Britannia, Flandria, Italia, et . . . Hispania, veritatem evangelicam sanguine suo constanter obsignaverunt* (Genevae. 1560).

lent, and noble Princess, Queen Elizabeth, "our peaceful Salome." With indignation he speaks of the stir that the first edition has created and of the minute scrutiny and consequent criticisms it has received at the hands of enemies. He apologizes to the Queen that he has written in English, but explains that he has not had her and other learned people in mind but the unlearned. For they have lived in ignorance, especially of God's Word, but also of Church history, with the result that they have in the past been imposed upon by the Papists with their biased and fraudulent histories. The knowledge of the gospel is necessary to any nation, and this is why he has written his Church history, which is, after all, not something separate from the gospel.

The third preface, *Ad Doctum Lectorem,* throws more light on Foxe's methods than on his intentions, save that he repeats that the Church needs true accounts of the past in place of invented "Golden legends."

In *To the Persecutors of God's Truth* he denounces the judgment of God. They must not imagine that they will escape his judgment at the Last Day: "In that day, when you shall be charged with the blood of so many martyrs, what will ye, or can you say? How think ye to excuse yourselves? Or what can you for yourselves allege? Will ye deny to have murdered them? This book will testify and denounce against you."

The next preface is *To the True and Faithfull Congregation.* Here he explains his purpose in writing the *Actes and Monuments:* "For first, to see the simple flock of Christ, especially the unlearned sort, so miserably abused, and all for ignorance of history, not knowing the course of times and true descent of the Church, it pitied me that part of diligence so long to have been unsupplied in this my-country Church of England." What makes it worse is that "the multitude of chronicles and story-writers" have been monks, or at least Papists, and have handled their stories partially. "This partial dealing and corrupt handling of histories, when I considered, I thought with myself nothing more lacking in the Church than a full and a complete story ... whereby all studious readers, beholding as in a glass the state, course, and alteration of religion, decay of doctrine, and the controversies of the Church, might discern the better between antiquity and novelty." But this history cannot be treated in a secular fashion; it must be viewed eschatologically. In 1501 "the Lord began to show in the parts of Germany wonderful tokens, and bloody marks of his Passion." This was the beginning of the final seventy years of the Babylonish captivity, which (at the date of

TO THE TRUE AND FAITHFULL CONGREGATION 63

the second edition, 1570) is now drawing to an end, unless we reckon from 1517, the year of the Ninety-five Theses, when there will be sixteen years still to pass.

The Utility of this Story follows, and contains another important statement of purpose. Although there are far too many books in the world, the martyrs deserve to be remembered. What is more, there is great usefulness in reading about them, for they not only serve as examples and encouragements, but their history shows God at work: "By reading thereof we may learn a lively testimony of God's mighty working in the life of man, contrary to the opinion of Atheists, and all the whole nest of Epicures." Then again, the deaths of the saints teach us *contemptus mundi* and the fear of God.

In *To all the Professed Friends and Followers of the Pope's Proceedings* he propounds four questions: (1) If Isa. 11:9 and 65:25, with their promises of peace among men and among animals, are true, how can the Church of Rome, which has spilt so much blood, be Sion? (2) Why do you hate Protestants so much that you will not live with them? (3) What does Rev., ch. 13, the prophecy of the two beasts, mean? (4) Is the religion of Christ spiritual or corporal (i.e., consisting, as in the Old Testament, of rites, sacrifices, and ceremonies)?

He balances this preface with the naïve *Four Considerations given out to Christian Protestants.* (1) What wonderful prosperity the land has enjoyed under Elizabeth! (2) Compare this with times past. (3) How happy would the martyrs be to be living in such times! (4) Therefore, let us reform our lives and make good use of our blessings.

Foxe himself asserts that his intention in writing was simple (i.e., single). He was mistaken, however, for many motives and elements emerge, some quite plain but others only latent. Thus who can doubt that he was impelled by a desire to write the history of the English Reformation, a story noble and thrilling in itself and containing a diversity of characters and richness of incident? Again, he wanted to honor and commemorate the martyrs themselves. It was not seemly that those who had died for the Lord should be forgotten like common criminals. Again, "The blood of the martyrs is the seed of the Church." Foxe's Book of Martyrs was intended to serve as an inspiration, example, and so to say, gospel call for his own and future generations. Mozley also draws attention to Foxe's humanitarianism. His horror of capital punishment and especially of burning alive is seen in his endeavors to save Joan Boucher, the Anabaptist, in 1550, and the

Flemish Anabaptists in 1575. When he wrote to the queen on their behalf, he told her that even to pass a butcher's slaughterhouse upset him. We shall not be fanciful if we see the *Actes and Monuments* incidentally as a manifesto directed against brutal forms of punishment.

We have not yet said everything about the significance of the *Actes and Monuments,* however. The most important elements, which provide the clue to the understanding of the work, are four in number and are to be found in the prefaces.

1. *The value of Church history.* It was a belief common to the Reformers that they had on their side not only the Bible but also, on the major dogmas at issue, the Church fathers. It was not they who were the innovators; it was the Romanists. Unfortunately, they had a difficult battle to fight here, for all the evidence seemed to the contrary. And in England they had the stubborn conservatism of the countryman to contend against (and that meant the majority of Englishmen). Innovation covered anything that had not been done "in my time or my father's time or my grandfather's time"—in other words since about 1490. For the learned Reformers, however, "modern" meant the Lateran Council of 1215. It was precisely this problem that Foxe had in mind. The "ignorant folk" had been accustomed to late medieval Christianity. No one could point to a great upheaval when this brand of religion had come in, because it had very slowly evolved. They had been taught that this was Christianity and they could imagine no other sort. The history books had themselves sprung from this religion and naturally enough treated it as the true faith. Foxe knew that the first need was for Bibles; but he believed that the second need was for history books that would put a different slant on things. To the queen he speaks of "the ignorant flock of Christ committed to your government in this realm of England; who, as they have been long led in ignorance, and wrapped in blindness, for lack especially of God's word, and partly also for wanting the light of history, I thought pity but that such should be helped, their ignorance relieved, and simplicity instructed." In *To the True and Faithfull Congregation* he speaks more fully and bluntly. "The unlearned sort" among the simple flock of Christ have been abused "all for ignorance of history." What was needed was "a full and a complete story. . . . Whereby all studious readers, beholding as in a glass the state, course, and alteration of religion, decay of doctrine, and the controversies of the Church, might discern the better between antiquity and novelty." Thus the *Actes and*

Monuments is to serve as an adjunct to the Gospel in enlightening the eyes of Englishmen.

2. *The pedigree of the Church of England.* The Reformation Church was no newfangled invention; nor was it simply the resurrection of the Church of the fathers after many centuries in the grave. God had never left himself without a Church in the world, though very often this Church was hard to discern. There was a Church before 1517. Foxe is concerned to show the continuity of the Reformed Church with the past, and to this end he provides a pedigree for the Church of England. This pedigree he traces back by way of "faithful witnesses" in the fifteenth century (Hoccleve, Wycliffe, Thorp, White, Purvey, Pateshul, Pain, Gower, Chaucer, . . . Lord Cobham, Sir Roger Acton, John Beverley, etc.), through the fourteenth century, away to Bede and the saints who figure in Bede's history, and the saints of Roman Britain, "in whose time the doctrine of faith without men's traditions was sincerely preached," right to the apostles and Christ. The "Kalender" which Foxe provided, and which provoked such misunderstanding and opposition that he had to withdraw it, associates the English martyrs of the sixteenth century with the Catholic saints, in whose line Foxe saw them standing. The juxtaposition makes moving reading: "Robert Barnes, Thomas Garrard, William Hierome, William Wolsey, Robert Pigot, Luke Evangelist, Nicholas Ridley, Hugh Latimer, John Web." Or: "Thomas Dungate, John Foreman, Anne Tree, Simon Miller, Eliza Coper, Mary Magdalene." Foxe proclaimed to the Church of England that she was in the line of apostolic succession that was joined, not by manual ordination, but by the transmission of the apostolic doctrine.

3. *The mighty works of God.* History, for Foxe, is not only the record "of the life of societies of men, of the changes which those societies have gone through, of the ideas which have determined the actions of those societies, and of the material conditions which have helped or hindered their development" (Firth). It is also "a lively testimony of God's mighty working in the life of man, contrary to the opinion of the Atheists, and all the whole nest of Epicures." Here even his champion J. F. Mozley fails to appreciate him: "Nor does Foxe escape the snare of credulity when he comes down to the events of his own time. The men of his age believed fervently in miracles and in the constant and direct intervention of God in human affairs by way of reward and punishment. Any misfortune that befel a man, ill health, accident, loss

of repute or money, and above all, death, might be interpreted by his enemies as a judgment from heaven." The Reformers were faced by the practical atheism of the neo-Epicureanism that accompanied the Renaissance. God is not concerned with the affairs of men. To it they opposed the Biblical doctrine of the Providence of God, that God continues to work in the world with the same purpose and in the same spirit as he created the world, preserving, upholding, guiding, overruling in the lives of men and of nations. Where Foxe, like most others in his day, went astray was in believing that he could, with the eyes of faith, directly discern the working of God and therefore deduce his particular purposes. And yet, when Foxe comes to specific cases, he is usually remarkably reticent. He plainly believes that God is present at the burnings, upholding the victims, giving them strength and constancy, and putting words of witness in their mouths. But he very rarely speaks of this in narrating martyrdoms. More often he will utter the prayer that God will give us a like constancy in life and in death, or he will break out into praise: "Such a Lord is God, glorious and wonderful in all his saints!" or: "For whose joyful constancy the Lord be praised!" Often when recounting an escape from death or prison, he will attribute it to the secret working of God: "Many other like examples of God's helping hand have been declared upon his elect saints and children, in delivering them out of danger by wonderful and miraculous ways, some by one means, some by another." "Wonderful and miraculous" does not mean a divine interference in the affairs of men but the steady and continuous, though unseen, working of God through natural means.

4. *The apocalyptic.* Providence must not be viewed fragmentarily, as if neither the workings nor the plans of God were related. God works providentially according to his one purpose of creation and recreation, his one purpose in Jesus Christ: "to gather together all things in Christ" (Eph. 1:10). This purpose Foxe believes not only to be worked out in history, but also to be discernible in history. For him this involves interpreting history in the light of the Biblical apocalyptic. Here he was on familiar ground, for he wrote a commentary on the Revelation of St. John.[2] The *Actes and Monuments* divides Church history into five periods: The age of persecution, lasting for about three hundred years, was followed by "the flourishing time of the church" for another three hundred years. Then came "the declining or backsliding time of the church" over yet another three hundred years.

[2] *Eicasmi, seu meditationes, in sacram Apocalypsin* (1587).

"Fourthly, followed the time of Antichrist, and loosing of Satan, or desolation of the church," which occupied four hundred years—and this brings us to the fourteenth century and Wycliffe. Finally, there has come the time of reformation and purging, when Antichrist has been unmasked and has steadily lost ground to the true Church. So far this age has lasted around two hundred and eighty years, "and how long it shall continue more, the Lord and Governor of all times, he alone knoweth."

The apocalyptic understanding of the age was not, of course, peculiar to Foxe. Luther himself can say: "The world has come to its end; the Roman Empire is almost gone and torn to bits. . . . Now that the Roman Empire is almost gone, Christ's coming is at the door, and the Turk is the Empire's token of farewell, a parting gift to the Roman Empire." This may happen even before he has time to finish his translation of the Bible into German.

If we turn for a moment to another and very different Reformer, John Bale, a friend of Foxe, we shall find the same outlook. Like Foxe, he wrote a commentary on Revelation, *The Image of bothe churches*. Here he continually describes the conflict between the Church of Jesus Christ and the synagogue of Satan throughout history. And this he does, not as a theologian so much as a historian (or perhaps it would be safer to say, a chronicler). The Revelation itself he regards as the key to the interpretation of history: "It is a full clearance to all the chronicles and most notable histories which hath been wrote since Christ's ascension, opening the true natures of their ages, times and seasons. . . . In the text are they only proposed in effect, and promised to follow in their seasons, and so ratified with the other scriptures; but in the chronicles they are evidently seen by all ages fulfilled. Yet is the text a light to the chronicles, and not the chronicles to the text." He therefore found it necessary in composing his book to consult not only commentaries (of which he give a long but inaccurate list) but also history books: "What chronographers and historians I have herein followed for the times and ages of the christian church, besides the scriptures, it will evidently appear hereafter in the margin of this volume." Using this method of interpretation, he cannot fail to understand his own age as the outworking of the Apocalypse. But the particular interest of his commentary lies in the pinpointing and localizing of the Apocalypse. That Gog and Magog should be the Pope and Mohammed will surprise no one who knows the period. But where do Master Packington and Alexander Seyton and "poor Master Tolwyn" fit into the Revelation of St. John the Divine? They come in ch. 13, v. 13, which speaks of a deceiving beast that "doeth great signs, that he should even make fire come down out of heaven upon the earth in the sight of men." For Bale, this verse is describing the England that he knows. The deceiving beast can succeed only by muzzling the truth, God's Word, and then letting loose his own familiars; he must also destroy the champions of the truth, great and small: "Already have they taken in England from the Bibles the annotations, tables and prefaces to perform their damnable enterprises. They have straitly forbidden the reading thereof for time of their Romish service. Some have they burned and put to silence, and all in the face of the people. Yea, they raise the maids of Ipswich and of Kent, to work wonders and marvels, and now of late the foolish northern men to fight for their church. . . . The discreet citizen of London, Master Packington, was slain with a gun at St. Thomas of Acre (as they call it) . . . . It is not long ago also, since Alexander Seyton, an excellent learned man, with poor Master Tolwyn, recanted at Paul's Cross."

Foxe, with far greater sublimity and breadth of mind than Bale, produced one of the most influential history books ever written. He bids his fellow countrymen, who are nearly all at least nominal members of the Church of England, to be aware of and live up to their inheritance. They are living in a glorious age. The Bible is open. The gospel is preached. God is worshiped purely and obediently (*pace* the Puritans and the Romanists!). A word in passing may be said against Professor Haller's thesis that the *Actes and Monuments* is a religionationalistic book designed to give Englishmen the belief that England was a nation chosen by God above all others to do his will. Foxe was no Rosenberg, with his Nazi blood and folk ideology. There is this much truth in it, that he was influenced by the nationalistic surges of his age and by the relative prosperity and popular pride that marked Elizabeth's reign. But he knew very well that the Kingdom of God was not to be equated with the realm ruled by Queen Elizabeth. The kingdom to which his book bears witness is the Kingdom of Christ. The Reformation that he recounts is a step, probably the final step, on the course of God's plan from the Creation to the Second Coming. It was this robust and joyful hope that provided the sinews in the faith of the "Gospellers" and imparted such an urgency to their lives.

BIBLIOGRAPHY

The forerunner of the *Actes and Monuments,* a short book of only 212 folios, appeared in 1554:
Commentarii/ rervm in ecclesia ge-/starum; maximarumque, per/ totam Europam, persecutio-/num, a Vvicleui temporibus/ ad hanc usque aetatem descriptio./ Liber primus./ Autore Ioanne Foxo Anglo./ . . ./ Argentorati/ Excudebat Vuendelinus Rihelius/ Anno M.D.LIIII.

The first edition proper dates from 1563:
Actes/ and Monuments/ of these latter and perillous dayes,/ touching matters of the Church, wherein/ ar comprehended and described the great persecu-/tions & horrible troubles, that haue bene wrought/ and practised by the Romishe Prelates, special-/lye in this Realme of England and Scot-/lande, from the yeare of our Lorde a/ thousande, unto the tyme/ nowe present./ Gathered and collected according to the/ true copies & wrytinges certificatorie, as wel/ of the parties them selues that suffered, as/ also out of the Bishops Registers,/ which wer the doers therof,/ by Iohn Foxe./ Imprinted at London by Iohn Day,/ dwellyng ouer Aldersgate./ Cum priuilegio Regiae Maiestatis. (N.D. but:)
Colophon: Imprinted at London/ by Iohn Day dwelling ouer Alders-/gate, beneth saynt Martins, Anno./ 1563. the .20. of March./ Cum gratia & priuilegio Regiae/ maiestatis./ These bookes are to be sold at his shop/ under the gate.

The Preface here printed was first published in the next edition of 1570, but the present text comes from the two-volume edition of 1583, the last to be published in the author's lifetime and to be revised by him:
Actes/ and Monuments of matters most/ speciall and memorable, happenyng in the/ Church, with an Vniuersal history of the same,/ wherein is set forth at large the whole race and course/

of the Church, from the primitiue age to these lat-/ter tymes of ours, with the bloudy times, horrible trou-/bles, and great persecutions agaynst the true Martyrs/ of Christ, sought and wrought as well by Heathen/ Emperours, as nowe lately practised/ by Romish Prelates, especially in this/ Realme of England and/ Scotland./ Newly reuised and recognised, partly also/ augmented, and now the fourth time agayne/ published and recommended to the studious/ Reader, by the Authour (through the Helpe of/ Christ our Lord) Iohn Foxe, which/ desireth thee good Reader to helpe him/ with thy Prayer./ Apoc. VII./ Salus sedenti super thronum & agno./ An. 1583. Mens Octobr.

Colophon: At London./ Printed by Iohn Daye, dwelling ouer/ Aldersgate beneath Sainct Martins./ Anno. 1583./ Cum gratia & Priuilegio Regiae Maiestatis.

The/ seconde Volume/ of the Eccle-/siasticall Historie, conteining the/ Acts and Monvments/ of Martyrs, with a Generall discourse of these/ latter Persecutions, horrible troubles and tumultes, stirred vp/ by Romish Prelates in the Church, with diuers other things/ incident, especially to this Realme of Englande and/ Scotland, as partly also to all other forreine na-/tions appertaining, from the time of King/ Henry the VIII. to Queene/ Elizabeth our gra-/cious Ladie nowe/ raigning. /Newly recognised and inlarged by the Authour/ Iohn Foxe. 1583/ At London/ Printed by Iohn Day, dwelling ouer Aldersgate./ Cum gratia & priuilegio Regiae Maiestatis.

Colophon: Imprinted at London by Iohn Daye,/ dwellyng ouer Aldersgate beneath/ S. Martins./ Cum Gratia & Priuilegio Regiae Maiestatis./ An. Dom. 1583.

The first of the nineteenth-century complete editions of Foxe was edited by S. R. Cattley (8 vols.; London, 1841). This is the edition that was the object of S. R. Maitland's immoderate and unbalanced attacks.[8] In a later edition many of the worst editing errors were corrected:

The Acts and Monuments of John Foxe. Carefully Revised, With Notes and Appendices. (The Church Historians of England. Reformation Period. London, 1853.)

The editors, or revisers, of this edition were R. R. Mendham

---

[8] *Notes on the contributions of the Rev. G. Townsend . . . to the new edition of Fox's Martyrology* (London, 1841–1842).
Remarks on the Rev. S. R. Cattley's defence of his edition of Fox's Martyrology (London, 1842).

and J. Pratt. It was printed by the Religious Tract Society (without date) in 8 volumes.

Foxe has found a strong and learned defender in J. F. Mozley, in whose biography the controversy between Maitland and Cattley may be studied:

J. F. Mozley, *John Foxe and His Book*. London, 1940.

Recently there have appeared:

W. Haller, *Foxe's Book of Martyrs and the Elect Nation*. London, 1963.

H. C. White, *Tudor Books of Saints and Martyrs*. University of Wisconsin Press, 1963.

John Foxe: To the True and Faithfull Congregation of Christ's Universal Church

THE TEXT

Solomon, the peaceable prince of Israel, as we read in the first of Kings, after he had finished the building of the Lord's Temple (which he had seven years in hand), made his petition to the Lord for all that should pray in the said Temple, or turn their face toward it. And his request was granted, the Lord answering him, as we read in the said book (cap. 6). "I have heard," saith he, "thy prayer, and have sanctified this place," etc.[4] Albeit the infinite majesty of God is not to be compassed in any material walls, yet it so pleased his goodness to respect this prayer of the king, that not only he promised to hear them which there prayed, but also replenished the same with his own glory. For so we read again in the book aforesaid, *"Et non poterant ministrare propter nebulam, quia replevit gloria Domini domum Domini."* [5]

Upon like trust in God's gracious goodness, if I, sinful wretch, not comparing with the building of that Temple, but following the zeal of the builder, might either be so bold to ask, or so happy to speed, after my seven years' travail about this Ecclesiastical History, most humbly would crave of Almighty God to bestow his blessing upon the same; that as the prayers of them which prayed in the outward Temple were heard, so all true disposed minds which shall resort to the reading of this present History, containing the Acts of God's holy Martyrs, and monuments of his Church, may, by example of their life, faith, and doctrine, receive some such spiritual fruit to their souls, through the operation of his grace; that it may be to the advancement of his glory, and profit of his

---

[4] Not cap. 6, but I Kings 9:3.
[5] I Kings 8:11: "And they could not minister, because of the cloud; for the glory of the Lord filled the house of the Lord."

TO THE TRUE AND FAITHFULL CONGREGATION 73

Church, through Christ Jesus our Lord. *Amen.*

But, as it happened in that Temple of Solomon, that all which came thither came not to pray, but many to prate, some to gaze and see news, other to talk and walk, some to buy and sell, some to carp and find fault, and, finally, some also at the last to destroy and pluck down, as they did indeed (for what is in this world so strong, but it will be impugned? what so perfect, but it will be abused? so true, that will not be contraried? or so circumspectly done, wherein wrangling Theon [6] will not set in his tooth?); even so neither do I look for any other in this present History, but that, amongst many well-disposed readers, some wasp's nest or other will be stirred up to buzz about mine ears. Such a dangerous thing it is nowadays to write or do any good, but either by flattering a man must offend the godly, or by true speaking procure hatred with the wicked. Of such stinging wasps and buzzing drones I had sufficient trial in my former edition before, who if they had found in my book any just cause to carp, or upon any true zeal of truth had proceeded against the untruths of my story and had brought just proofs for the same, I could have right well abide it. For God forbid but that faults, wheresoever they be, should be detected and accused. And therefore accusers in a commonwealth after my mind do serve to no small stead.

But then such accusers must beware they play not the dog, of whom Cicero in his Oration speaketh, which, being set in Capitolio to fray away thieves by night, left the thieves, and fell to bark at true men walking in the day.[7] Where true faults be, there to bay and bark is not amiss. But to carp where no cause is; to spy in other straws, and to leap over their own blocks; to swallow camels, and to strain gnats; to oppress truth with lies, and to set up lies for truth; to blaspheme the dear martyrs of Christ, and to canonize for saints whom Scripture would scarce allow for good subjects, that is intolerable. Such barking curs, if they were well served, would be made a while to stoop. But with these brawling spirits I intend not at this time much to wrestle.

Wherefore to leave them a while, till further leisure serve me to attend upon them, thus much I thought in the mean season, by way of protestation or petition, to write unto you both in general and particular the true members and faithful Congregation of Christ's Church, wheresoever either congregated together, or dispersed through the whole Realm of England, that forsomuch as all the seeking of these adversaries is to do what they can, by discrediting of this History with slanders and sinister surmises,

[6] Horace, *Epistola* 1.18.   [7] Cicero, *Orat.* 2; *pro Roscio*, cap. XX.

how to withdraw the readers from it, this, therefore, shall be in few words to premonish and desire of all and singular of you (all well-minded lovers and partakers of Christ's gospel), not to suffer yourselves to be deceived with the big brags and hyperbolical speeches of those slandering tongues, whatsoever they have or shall hereafter exclaim against the same. But indifferently staying your judgment till truth be tried, you will first peruse, and then refuse; measuring the untruths of this History, not by the scoring up of their hundreds and thousands of lies which they give out, but wisely weighing the purpose of their doings according as you find; and so to judge of the matter.

To read my books I allure neither one nor other. Every man as he seeth cause to like as he list. If any shall think his labour too much in reading this story, his choice is free either to read this, or any other which he more mindeth. But if the fruit thereof shall recompence the reader's travail, then would I wish no man so light eared, to be carried away for any sinister clamour of adversaries, who many times deprave good doings, not for the faults they find, but therefore find faults because they would deprave. As for me and my History, as my will was to profit all and displease none, so if skill in any part wanted to will, yet hath my purpose been simple; and certes the cause no less urgent also, which moved me to take this enterprise in hand.

For first, to see the simple flock of Christ, especially the unlearned sort, so miserably abused, and all for ignorance of history, not knowing the course of times and true descent of the Church, it pitied me that part of diligence so long to have been unsupplied in this my-country Church of England. Again, considering the multitude of chronicles and story writers,[8] both in England and out of England, of whom the most part have been either monks, or clients to the See of Rome, it grieved me to behold how partially they handled their stories. Whose painful travail albeit I cannot but commend, in committing divers things to writing, not unfruitful to be known or unpleasant to be read; yet it lamented me to see in their Monuments the principal points, which chiefly concerned the state of Christ's Church, and were most necessary of all Christian people to be known, either altogether pretermitted, or if any mention thereof were inserted, yet were all things drawn to the honour specially of the Church of Rome, or else to the favour of their own sect of religion. Whereby the vulgar sort, hearing and reading in their writings no other Church mentioned or magnified but only that Church which here flourished in this world in riches

[8] Historians.

and jollity, were drawn also to the same persuasion, to think no other Church to have stood in all the earth but only the Church of Rome.

In the number of this sort of writers, besides our monks of England (for every monastery almost had his chronicler) I might also recite both Italian and other country authors, as Platina, Sabellicus, Nauclerus, Martinus, Antoninus, Vincentius, Onuphrius, Laziardus, Georgius Lilius, Pollid. Virgilius,[9] with many more, who, taking upon them to intermeddle with matters of the Church, although in part they express some truth in matters concerning the bishops and See of Rome, yet, in suppressing another part, they play with us, as Ananias and Sapphira did with their money,[10] or as Apelles did in Pliny,[11] who, painting the one half of Venus coming out of the sea, left the other half unperfect. So these writers, while they show us one half of the Bishop of Rome, the other half of him they leave unperfect, and utterly untold. For as they paint him out on the one part glistering in wealth and glory, in shewing what succession the Popes had from the chair of S. Peter, when they first began, and how long they sat, what churches and what famous buildings they erected, how far their possessions reached, what laws they made, what councils they called, what honour they received of kings and emperors, what princes and countries they brought under their authority, with other like stratagems of great pomp and royalty; so, on the other side, what vices these Popes brought with them to their seat, what abominations they practised, what superstition they maintained, what idolatry they procured, what wicked doctrine they defended contrary to the express Word of God, to what heresies they fell, into what divisions of sects they cut the unity of Christian religion, how some practised by simony, some by necromancy and sorcery, some by poisoning, some indenting with the devil to come by their papacy, what hypocrisy was in their lives, what corruption in their doctrine, what wars they raised, what bloodshed they caused, what treachery they traversed against their lords and emperors, im-

[9] B. Platina, *Liber de vita Christi ac de vitis summorum pontificum omnium* (Venice, 1479); Sabellicus, *Exempla virtutum et vitiorum* (Basel, 1555); J. Nauclerus, *Chronica . . . usque ad 1564* (Cologne, 1564—first ed., 1544); P. Martinus, *Chronicon expeditissimum* (Antwerp, 1574); Antoninus, *Prima [-tertia] pars historialis* (Basel, 1502); Vincentius, *Speculum historiale* (1474); O. Panvinius, *Chronicon ecclesiasticum*, (Cologne, 1568); Laziardus, *Epitomata a primaeva mundi origine* (Paris, 1521); G. Lily, *Chronicon . . . in quos . . . Britanniae Imperium diversis temporibus translatum est* (Frankfurt, 1565). P. Vergilius, *Anglicae historicae* (1534).
[10] Acts 5:1-11.
[11] Pliny, *Historia naturalis*, Lib. XXXV, cap. X.

prisoning some, betraying some to the Templars and Saracens, in bringing other under their feet, also in beheading some, as they did with Fredericus and Conradinus, the heirs and offspring of the house of Fredericus Barbarossa, anno 1268; [12] furthermore, how mightily Almighty God hath stood against them, how their wars never prospered against the Turk, how the judgments of the godly learned from time to time have ever repugned against their errors, etc.—of these and a thousand other more not one word hath been touched, but all kept as under Benedicite, in auricular confession.[13]

This partial dealing and corrupt handling of histories when I considered, I thought with myself nothing more lacking in the Church than a full and a complete story; which, being faithfully collected out of all our monastical writers and written Monuments, should contain neither every vain written fable, for that would be too much, not yet leave out any thing necessary, for that would be too little; but, with a moderate discretion taking the best of every one, should both ease the labour of the reader from turning over such a number of writers, and also should open the plain truth of times lying long hid in obscure darkness of antiquity. Whereby all studious readers, beholding as in a glass the state, course, and alteration of religion, decay of doctrine, and the controversies of the Church, might discern the better between antiquity and novelty. For if the things which be first, after the rule of Tertullian,[14] are to be preferred before those that be latter, then is the reading of histories much necessary in the Church, to know what went before, and what followed after. And therefore not without cause *historia,* in old authors, is called the witness of times, the light of verity, the life of memory, teacher of life, and shewer of antiquity, etc. Without the knowledge whereof, man's life is blind, and soon may fall into any kind of error; as by manifest experience we have to see in these desolate latter times of the Church, when the Bishops of Rome, under colour of antiquity, have turned truth into heresy, and brought such new found devices of strange doctrine and religion, as in the former age of the Church were never heard of before, and all through the ignorance of times and for lack of true history.

[12] See Foxe, 2.455 ff., 472; 4.143,144.
[13] The particulars of this sentence are obscure, but the general meaning is clear: These episodes have been kept secret, just as what is confessed to the priest is kept secret.
[14] *"Primum quodque verissimum est."* This marginal note by Foxe suggests *Adversus Marcionem* IV.5: *si constat id verius quod prius, id prius quod ab initio."* (*PL* 2.366).

TO THE TRUE AND FAITHFULL CONGREGATION 77

For to say the truth, if times had been well searched, or if they which wrote histories had, without partiality, gone upright between God and Baal, halting on neither side, it might well have been found, the most part of all this catholic corruption [15] intruded into the Church by the bishops of Rome, as transubstantiation, elevation and adoration of the Sacrament, auricular confession, forced vows of priests not to marry, veneration of images, private and satisfactory masses, the order of Gregory's mass now used,[16] the usurped authority and *summa potestas* of the See of Rome, with all the rout of their ceremonies and weeds of superstition overgrowing now the Church; all these, I say, to be new nothings lately coined in the mint of Rome without any stamp of antiquity, as by reading of this present History shall sufficiently, I trust, appear. Which history therefore I have here taken in hand, that as other story writers heretofore have employed their travail to magnify the Church of Rome, so in this History might appear to all Christian readers the image of both churches,[17] as well of the one as of the other; especially of the poor oppressed and persecuted Church of Christ. Which persecuted Church, though it hath been of long season trodden under foot by enemies, neglected in the world, not regarded in histories, and almost scarce visible or known to worldly eyes, yet hath it been the true Church only of God, wherein he hath mightily wrought hitherto, in preserving the same in all extreme distresses, continually stirring up from time to time faithful ministers, by whom always hath been kept some sparks of his true doctrine and religion.

Now forasmuch as the true Church of God goeth not lightly alone, but is accompanied with some other church or chapel of the devil to deface and malign the same, necessary it is therefore the difference between them to be seen, and the descent of the right Church to be described from the Apostles' time: which, hitherto, in most part of histories hath been lacking, partly for fear, that men durst not, partly for ignorance, that men could not, discern rightly between the one and the other. Who, beholding the Church of Rome to be so visible and glorious in the eyes of the world, so shining in outward beauty, to bear such a port, to carry such a train and multitude, and to stand in such high authority, supposed the same to be the only right Catholic mother. The other, because it was not so visibly known in the world, they

---
[15] Either corruption of catholicity, or universal corruption, or corruption by the so-called catholics.
[16] I.e., the Gregorian Sacramentary.
[17] An expression probably borrowed from the title of John Bale's book, *The Image of bothe churches,* an exposition of Revelation.

thought therefore it could not be the true Church of Christ. Wherein they were far deceived. For although the right Church of God be not so invisible in the world that none can see it, yet neither is it so visible again that every worldly eye may perceive it. For like as is the nature of truth, so is the proper condition of the true Church, that commonly none seeth it, but such only as be the members and partakers thereof. And, therefore, they which require that God's holy Church should be evident and visible to the whole world, seem to define the great synagogue of the world, rather than the true spiritual Church of God.

In Christ's time who would have thought but the congregations and councils of the Pharisees had been the right Church? and yet had Christ another Church in earth besides that; which, albeit it was not so manifest in the sight of the world, yet was it the only true Church in the sight of God. Of this Church meant Christ, speaking of the Temple which he would raise again the third day. And yet after that the Lord was risen, he showed not himself to the world, but only to his elect, which were but few. The same Church after that increased and multiplied mightily among the Jews; yet had not the Jews eyes to see God's Church, but did persecute it, till at length all their whole nation was destroyed.

After the Jews, then came the heathen emperors of Rome, who having the whole power of the world in their hands, did what the world could do, to extinguish the name and Church of Christ. Whose violence continued the space of three hundred years. All which while the true Church of Christ was not greatly in sight of the world, but rather was abhorred everywhere, and yet notwithstanding the same small silly [18] flock, so despised in the world, the Lord highly regarded and mightily preserved. For although many then of the Christians did suffer death, yet was their death neither loss to them, nor detriment to the Church; but the more they suffered, the more of their blood increased.

In the time of these emperors God raised up then in this realm of Britain divers worthy preachers and witnesses, as Elvanus, Meduinus, Meltivianus, Amphibalus, Albanus, Aaron, Julius, and other more: in whose time the doctrine of faith without men's traditions was sincerely preached. After their death and martyrdom it pleased the Lord to provide a general quietness to his Church, whereby the number of his flock began more to increase.

In this age then followed here in the said land of Britain Fastidius, Ninianus, Patricius, Bacchiarius, Dubricius, Congellus, Kentigernus, Helmotus, David, Daniel, Sampson, Elvodugus, Asaphus,

[18] Weak.

Gildas, Henlanus, Elbodus, Dinothus, Samuel, Nivius, and a great sort more, which governed the Church of Britain by Christian doctrine a long season; albeit the civil governors for the time were then dissolute and careless (as Gildas very sharply doth lay to their charge [19]), and so at length were subdued by the Saxons.

All this while, about the space of four hundred years, religion remained in Britain uncorrupt, and the Word of Christ truly preached, till, about the coming of Austen and of his companions from Rome, many of the same Britain preachers were slain by the Saxons. After that began Christian faith to enter and spring among the Saxons, after a certain romish sort, yet notwithstanding somewhat more tolerable than were the times which after followed, through the diligent industry of some godly teachers which then lived amongst them; as Aidanus, Finianus, Coleman Archbishop of York, Beda, John of Beverly, Alcuinus, Noetus, Hucharius, Serlo, Achardus, Ealredus, Alexander, Neckam, Negellus, Fenallus, Ælfricus, Sygeferthus, and such other; who, though they erred in some few things, yet neither so grossly nor so greatly to be complained of in respect of the abuses that followed. For as yet, all this while, the error of transubstantiation and elevation, with auricular confession, was not crept in for a public doctrine in Christ's Church, as, by their own Saxon sermon made by Ælfric,[20] and set out in the volumes of this present History, may appear. During the which mean time, although the Bishops of Rome were had here in some reverence with the clergy, yet had they nothing as yet to do in setting laws touching matters of the Church of England: but that only appertained to the kings and governors of the land, as is in this story to be seen.

And thus the Church of Rome, albeit it began then to decline apace from God, yet, during all this while, it remained hitherto in some reasonable order, till at length after that, the said bishops began to shoot up in the world through the liberality of good princes, and especially by Matilda, a noble duchess of Italy, who at her death made the Pope heir of all her lands, and endued his see with great revenues.[21] Then riches begot ambition, ambition destroyed religion, so that all came to ruin. Out of this corruption sprang forth here in England, as did in other places more, another

---

[19] "Britain has kings, but they are tyrants; she has judges, but unrighteous ones" (*The Works of Gildas*, tr. by J. A. Giles [London, 1841], p. 24; *Epistola Gildae* in Gildas, *De Excidio Britanniae*, ed. J. Stevenson [English Historical Society, 1838], p. 36).
[20] For text and translation, see Foxe, 5.280-289.
[21] Aeneas Sylvius, *Historia Bohemica*, cap. XXI (in *Opera* [Basel, 1551], p. 96).

romish kind of monkery, worse than the other before, being much more drowned in superstition and ceremonies, which was about the year of our Lord, 980. Of this swarm was Egbert, Agilbert, Egwin, Boniface, Wilfrid, Agatho, James, Romain, Cedda, Dunstan, Oswald, Athelwold; Athelwin, duke of East-Angles; Lanfranc, Anselm, and such others.[22]

And yet in this time also, through God's providence, the Church lacked not some of better knowledge and judgment, to weigh with the darkness of those days. For although King Edgar, with Edward his base [23] son, being seduced by Dunstan, Oswald, and other monkish clerks, was then a great author and fautor [24] of much superstition, erecting as many monasteries as were Sundays in the year, yet, notwithstanding, this continued not long. For, eftsoons after the death of Edgar, came King Ethelred and Queen Alfrida his mother, with Alferus duke of Merceland,[25] and other peers and nobles of the realm, who displaced the monks again, and restored the married priests to their old possessions and livings. Moreover, after that, followed also the Danes, which overthrew those monkish foundations, as fast as King Edgar had set them up before.

And thus hitherto stood the condition of the true Church of Christ, albeit not without some repugnance and difficulty, yet in some mean state of the truth and verity, till the time of Pope Hildebrand, called Gregory VII, which was near about the year 1080, and of Pope Innocentius III in the year 1215: by whom altogether was turned upside down, all order broken, discipline dissolved, true doctrine defaced, Christian faith extinguished. Instead whereof was set up preaching of men's decrees, dreams, and idle traditions. And whereas, before, truth was free to be disputed amongst learned men, now, liberty was turned into law, argument into authority. Whatsoever the Bishop of Rome denounced, that stood for an oracle of all men to be received without opposition or contradiction; whatsoever was contrary, *ipso facto* it was heresy, to be punished with faggot and flaming fire. Then began the sincere faith of this English Church, which held out so long, to quail. Then was the clear sunshine of God's Word overshadowed with mists and darkness, appearing like sackcloth to the people, who neither could understand what they read, nor yet permitted to read what they could understand. In these miserable days, as the true visible Church began now to shrink and keep in for fear, so upstart a new sort of players to furnish the stage, as school doctors, canonists, and four orders of friars; be-

[22] Foxe, 1.350 ff., 363, 364, 376; 2.30.
[23] Illegitimate.
[24] Supporter.
[25] Mercia (Foxe, 2.67, 68).

TO THE TRUE AND FAITHFULL CONGREGATION 81

sides other monastical sects and fraternities of infinite variety; which, ever since, have kept such a stir in the Church, that none for them almost durst rout,[26] neither Caesar,[27] king, nor subject. What they defined, stood. What they approved, was catholic. What they condemned, was heresy. Whomsoever they accused, none almost could save. And thus have these hitherto continued, or reigned rather, in the Church, the space now of four hundred years and odd. During which space the true Church of Christ, although it durst not openly appear in the face of the world, was oppressed by tyranny; yet neither was it so invisible or unknown, but by the providence of the Lord some remnant always remained from time to time, which not only showed secret good affection to sincere doctrine, but also stood in open defence of truth against the disordered Church of Rome.

In which catalogue, first, to pretermit Berthramus and Berengarius,[28] who were before Pope Innocent III, a learned multitude of sufficient witnesses here might be produced, whose names neither are obscure nor doctrine unknown; as Joachim, Abbot of Calabria, and Almericus,[29] a learned bishop, who was judged an heretic for holding against images in the time of the said Innocentius. Besides the martyrs of Alsace, of whom we read an hundred to be burned by the said Innocentius in one day, as writeth Ulric Mutius.[30] Add likewise to these the Waldenses or Albigenses,[31] which, to a great number, segregated themselves from the Church of Rome. To this number also belonged Reymundus, Earl of Tholose, Marsilius, Patavius, Gulielmus de Sancto Amore, Simon Tornacensis, Arnoldus de Nova Villa, Johannes Semeca, besides divers other preachers in Suabia standing against the Pope, anno 1240; Laurentius Anglicus, a master of Paris, anno 1260; Petrus Johannes, a Minorite, who was burned after his death, anno 1290; Robertus Gallus, a Dominic friar, anno 1292; Robert Grosthead, Bishop of Lincoln, who was called "Malleus Romanorum," anno 1250; Lord Peter of Cugnieres, anno 1329. To these we may add, moreover, Gulielmus Ockam, Bongratius

[26] Snore.
[27] Emperor.
[28] Ratramnus (i.e., Berthramus) and Berengarius were both condemned for their Eucharistic doctrine at the Synod of Vercelli, 1050.
[29] For the condemnation of Joachim of Fiore and Almericus, see *Decretalium Collectiones* (Lipsiae, 1881), col. 6–7.
[30] Hulderichus Mutius, *De Germanorum prima origine, moribus*, etc. (Basel, 1539), p. 196.
[31] For the supposed relationship between the Waldenses and Albigenses, see articles in Hastings' *Encyclopedia of Religion and Ethics*, and bibliographies there.

Bergomensis, Luitpoldus Andreas Laudensis, Ulricus Hangenor, treasurer to the emperor, Joannes de Ganduno, anno 1330, mentioned in the *Extravagantes;* [32] Andreas de Castro, Buridianus, Euda, Duke of Burgundy, who counselled the French king not to receive the new found constitutions and Extravagantes of the Pope into his realm; Dantes Alligerius, an Italian, who wrote against the Pope, monks, and friars, and against the Donation of Constantine, anno 1330; Taulerus, a German preacher; Conradus Hager, imprisoned for preaching against the mass, anno 1339; the author of the book called *Pœnitentiarius Asini*,[33] compiled about the year 1343; Michael Cesenas, a gray friar; Petrus de Corbaria, with Johannes de Poliaco, mentioned in the Extravagantes, and condemned by the Pope; Johannes de Castilione, with Franciscus de Arcatara, who were burned about the year of our Lord, 1322; Johannes Rochtaylada, otherwise called Haybalus, with another friar martyred about the year 1346; Franciscus Petrarcha, who called Rome the whore of Babylon, etc., anno 1350; Georgius Ariminensis, anno 1350; Joannes de Rupe Scissa, imprisoned for certain prophesies against the Pope, anno 1340; Gerhardus Ridder, who also wrote against monks and friars a book called *Lacrymæ Ecclesiæ*,[34] anno 1350; Godfridus de Fontanis, Gulielmus de Landuno, Joannes Monachus Cardinalis Armachanus, Nicolaus Orem, preacher, anno 1364; Militzius, a Bohemian, who then preached that Antichrist was come, and was excommunicate for the same, anno 1366; Jacobus Misnensis, Matthias Parisiensis, a Bohemian born, and a writer against the Pope, anno 1370; Joannes Montziger, Rector of the University of Ulm, anno 1384; Nilus, Archbishop of Thessalonica, Henricus de Iota, Henricus de Hassia, etc.

I do but recite the principal writers and preachers in those days. How many thousands there were which never bowed their knees to Baal, that is known to God alone. Of whom we find in the writings of one Bruschius,[35] that xxxvi citizens of Mentz were burned, anno 1390; who, following the doctrine of the Waldenses, affirmed the Pope to be the great Antichrist. Also Massæus [36] re-

---

[32] The *Extravagantes* were Papal decretals not included in Gratian. The present reference is to the *Extravagantes communes* in *Corp. Iur. Can.* II.1201 ff.

[33] A fourteenth-century verse satire mentioned and quoted in part by M. Flacius Illyricus, *Catalogus testium veritatis, qui ante nostram aetatem Pontifici Romano, eiusque erroribus reclamarunt* (Strasbourg, 1562), p. 522. See also Foxe, 2.708–9.

[34] Flacius Illyricus, *op. cit.,* p. 519.

[35] *De omnibus Germaniae Episcopatibus Epitomes. Authore Gaspare Bruschio Poeta Laureato* (1549), fol. 17ᵃ.

[36] *Chroniconum multiplicis historiae . . . libri viginti* (Antwerp, 1540), p. 235.

cordeth of one hundred and forty, which in the province of Narbonne were put to the fire for not receiving the decretals of Rome; besides them that suffered at Paris to the number of xxiiii at one time, anno 1210; and the next year after there were four hundred brent under the name of heretics; besides also a certain good eremite, an Englishman, of whom mention is made in John Bacon, Dist. 2, Quest. 1, who was committed for disputing in Paul's Church against certain Sacraments of the Church of Rome, anno 1306.

To descend now somewhat lower in drawing out the descent of the Church. What a multitude here cometh of faithful witnesses in the time of John Wickliff, as Ocliff, Wickliff, anno 1379, W. Thorp, White, Purvey, Patshall, Payne, Gower, Chaucer, Gascoyne, William Swinderby, Walter Brute, Roger Dexter, William Sautry, about the year 1400; John Badby, anno 1410; Nicholas Tayler, Rich. Wagstaffe, Mich. Scrivener, William Smith, John Henry, Wm. Parchmenar, Roger Goldsmith, with an anchoress called Matilda, in the city of Leicester; Lord Cobham; Sir Roger Acton, knight; John Beverley, preacher; John Huss, Jerome of Prague, a schoolmaster, with a number of faithful Bohemians and Thaborites not to be told; with whom I might also adjoin Laurentius Valla, and Joannes Picus, the learned Earl of Mirandula. But what do I stand upon recital of names, which almost are infinite?

Wherefore, if any be so far beguiled in his opinion to think the doctrine of the Church of Rome (as it now standeth) to be of such antiquity, and that the same was never impugned before the time of Luther and Zuinglius now of late, let them read these histories: or if he think the said history not to be of sufficient credit to alter his persuasion, let him peruse the Acts and Statutes of Parliaments, passed in this realm of ancient time, and therein consider and confer the course of times; where he may find and read, An. 5 Regis Richardi 2 in the year of our Lord 1380, of a great number (which there be called evil persons) *going about from town to town in frieze gowns, preaching unto the people, etc.*[37] Which preachers, although the words of the Statute do term there to be dissembling persons, preaching divers sermons containing heresies and notorious errors, to the emblemishment of Christian faith, and of holy Church, etc., as the words do there pretend; yet notwithstanding, every true Christian reader may conceive of those preachers to teach no other doctrine, than now they hear their own preachers in pulpits preach against the Bishop of Rome, and the corrupt heresies of his Church.

[37] 5 Rich. II, Stat. 2., c.5, in *Statutes of the Realm*, Vol. II (1826), pp. 25 f.

Furthermore, he shall find likewise in the statutes, An. 2 Henry 4, Cap. 15, in the year of our Lord 1402,[38] another like company of good preachers and faithful defenders of true doctrine against blind heresy and error. Whom, albeit the words of the statute there, through corruption of that time, do falsely term to be false *and perverse preachers, under dissembled holiness, teaching in those days openly and privily new doctrines and heretical opinions, contrary to the faith and determination of holy Church, etc.*, yet notwithstanding whosoever readeth histories, and conferreth the order and descent of times, shall understand these to be no false teachers, but faithful witnesses of the truth; not teaching any new doctrines contrary to the determination of holy Church; but rather shall find that Church to be unholy which they preached against, teaching rather itself heretical opinions, contrary both to antiquity and verity of Christ's true Catholic Church.

Of the like number also, or greater, of like faithful favourers and followers of God's holy Word, we find in the year of our Lord 1422, specified in a letter sent from Henry Chichesly, Archbishop of Canterbury, to Pope Martin V, in the fifth year of his popedom, where mention is made *of so many here in England, infected* (as he said) *with the heresies of Wickliff and Huss, that without force of any army, they could not be suppressed, etc.*[39] Whereupon the Pope sent two cardinals to the archbishop, to cause a tenth to be gathered of all spiritual and religious men,[40] and the money to be laid in the chamber apostolic; and if that were not sufficient, the residue to be made up of chalices, candlesticks, and other implements of the church, etc.

What shall need then any more witness to prove this matter, when you see, so many years ago, whole armies and multitudes thus standing against the Pope? who, though they be termed here for heretics and schismatics, yet in that which they call heresy served they the living Lord within the ark of his true spiritual and visible Church.

And where is then the frivolous brag of the Papists, who make so much of their painted sheath; and would needs bear us down, that this government of the Church of Rome, which now is, hath been of such an old standing, time out of mind, even from the primitive antiquity; and that there never was any other church

---

[38] 2 Henr. IV, c.15, in *Statutes* . . . , Vol. II, pp. 125 ff.
[39] See Mandell Creighton, *A History of the Papacy* (1897), Vol. II, pp. 156 ff.
[40] Spiritual men = clergy in general; religious men = members of one of the religious orders.

demonstrable here in earth for men to follow, besides the said only catholic mother Church of Rome? when as we have sufficiently proved before, by the continual descent of the Church till this present time, that the said Church, after the doctrine which is now reformed, is no new begun matter, but even the old continued Church by the providence and promise of Christ still standing; which, albeit it hath been of late years repressed by the tyranny of Roman bishops more than before, yet notwithstanding it was never so oppressed, but God hath ever maintained in it the truth of his Gospel, against heresies and errors of the Church of Rome, as in this History more at full is to be seen.

Let us now proceed farther as we began, deducing this descent of the Church unto the year 1501. In which year the Lord began to show in the parts of Germany wonderful tokens, and bloody marks of his Passion; as the bloody cross, his nails, spear, and crown of thorns, which fell from heaven upon the garments and caps of men, and rocks [41] of women; as you may farther read in this book.[42] By the which tokens almighty God, no doubt, presignified what grievous afflictions and bloody persecutions should then begin to ensue upon his Church for his Gospel's sake, according as in this History is described; wherein is to be seen what Christian blood hath been spilt, what persecutions raised, what tyranny exercised, what torments devised, what treachery used, against the poor flock and Church of Christ; in such sort as since Christ's time greater hath not been seen.

And now by revolution of years we are come from the time of 1501, to that year now present 1570. In which the full seventy years of the Babylonical captivity draweth now well to an end, if we count from the first appearing of these bloody marks above mentioned. Or if we reckon from the beginning of Luther and his persecutions, then lacketh yet xvi years. Now what the Lord will do with this wicked world, or what rest he will give to his Church after these long sorrows, he is our Father in heaven, his will be done in earth as seemeth best to his divine Majesty.

In the mean time let us for our parts with all patient obedience wait upon his gracious leisure, and glorify his holy name, and edify one another with all humility. And if there cannot be an end of our disputing and contending one against an other, yet let there be a moderation in our affections. And forasmuch as it is the good will of our God, that Satan thus should be let loose amongst us for a short time; yet let us strive in the mean while, what we can, to amend the malice of the time, with mutual hu-

[41] Distaffs.   [42] Foxe, 4.257.

manity. They that be in error, let them not disdain to learn. They which have greater talents of knowledge committed instruct in simplicity them that be simple. No man liveth in that commonwealth where nothing is amiss. But yet because God hath so placed us Englishmen here in one commonwealth, also in one Church, as in one ship together, let us not mangle or divide the ship, which, being divided, perisheth; but every man serve in his order with diligence, wherein he is called. They that sit at the helm, keep well the point of the needle, to know how the ship goeth, and whither it should; whatsoever weather betideth, the needle, well touched with the stone of God's Word, will never fail. Such as labour at the oars, start for no tempest, but do what they can to keep from the rocks. Likewise they which be in inferior rooms, take heed they move no sedition nor disturbance against the rowers and mariners. No storm so dangerous to a ship on the sea, as is discord and disorder in a weal public. What countries and nations, what kingdoms and empires, what cities, towns, and houses, discord hath dissolved, in stories is manifest; I need not spend time in rehearsing examples.

The God of peace, who hath power both of land and sea, reach forth his merciful hand to help them up that sink, to keep up them that stand, to still these winds and surging seas of discord and contention among us; that we, professing one Christ, may, in one unity of doctrine, gather ourselves into one ark of the true Church together; where we, continuing stedfast in faith, may at the last luckily [43] be conducted to the joyful port of our desired landing-place by his heavenly grace. To whom, both in heaven and earth, be all power and glory, with his Father and the Holy Spirit, for ever. Amen.

[43] Prosperously.

William Tyndale

THE EXPOSITION OF THE FYRSTE EPISTLE OF SEYNT JHON

William Tyndale: The Exposition of the Fyrste Epistle of Seynt Jhon

INTRODUCTION

ON THE CONTINENT A SCORE OF PRESSES COULD BARELY KEEP pace with the theologians' supply of Bible commentaries and presumably the public demand for them. Zwingli, Melanchthon, Oecolampadius, Calvin, Brentius, Bucer, Musculus, Münster, Vatablus, Pellicanus, Bullinger—the roll call is well-nigh infinite —all had commentaries on several books to their credit. Their works, highly professional products making use of the latest scholarship, fill many vast folios. Cross the Channel, and the difference is startling and bewildering. We are hard put to it to think of any commentators. There was John Colet, of course, making history in the early years of the century with his commentaries on Romans and I Corinthians. But what else? Bale's commentary on Revelation, *The Image of bothe churches;* Hooper's Annotations on Rom., ch. 13, and expositions of four psalms (though not, it seems, published at the time); John Foxe's commentary on Revelation; Pilkington's commentaries on Obadiah and Haggai, though these came only in Elizabeth's reign. None of these works receives a mention in the relevant chapter of *The Cambridge History of the Bible,* and the author says: "It is significant that no English names appear." [1]

There is, however, one little regarded man who deserves a paragraph or two to himself; not so much, perhaps, for his achievement as for his intentions. Lancelot Ridley was first cousin to the famous Nicholas, was, like him, a Cambridge man (B.A. 1523 or 1524, D.D. 1540 or 1541) and also, like him, an adherent of the Reformation. He never rose to any eminence in the Church of England, apart from being a prebendary of Canterbury, but spent

[1] *Cambridge History of the Bible,* p. 92.

his working life as incumbent of two Cambridgeshire villages, first as Rector of Willingham (1545 to 1554, when he was deprived) and in Elizabeth's days as Rector of Stretham (1560 to 1576). He was, according to Bale, "a Christian man endued with learning and in the times of the illustrious English Kings Henry and Edward was a notable proclaimer *(buccinator)* of the divine Word."[2] And Tanner tells us that he knew Hebrew, Greek, and Latin.[3] They both ascribe to him several commentaries. Bale: Ephesians, Philippians, Colossians, Joshua, Matthew, the last epistles of John, and Jude.[4] Tanner: Ephesians, Philippians, Colossians, Joshua, Matthew, the last epistles of John, Jude, the last two epistles of John in Latin, and either both epistles to the Thessalonians or only the second.[5] The only commentaries of his known to me are those on Ephesians, Philippians, Colossians, and Jude.[6] I have not seen Colossians. It is conceivable, but to my mind improbable on stylistic grounds, that the expositions on II and III John in St. Paul's Cathedral Library and bound up with Tyndale's I John and Ridley's Jude may be by Ridley.

His preface to Ephesians, revised for Philippians, illuminates not only the Biblical scene in England about the fifteen forties, but also his own clear view of the need for commentaries. We will quote it at length:

"Many and dyvers causes moved me to wryte this Commentary in Englyshe, O gentyle reader for theyr sakes whiche do nat understande Latyn but onely rede Englysshe, to helpe the rude and ignoraunte people to more knowlege of God and of his holy worde. Because I perceyve fewe or none to go about to open by commentaries or exposicions in Englyshe to the unlearned to declare the holy Scriptures nowe suffered to all people of this realme to rede & to study at their pleasure to their edifyenge and comforte in god by the kynges gracyous lycence; for the whiche thi⟨n⟩g hye thankes is to be gyven to God and laud & praise to the kinges highnes that so tendereth the helth & salvacyon of his subiectes, that wylleth they shal lacke nothyng that may be to their comforte and soules helth and specyally that they shall nat lacke the worde of God. . . . Because I could percayve fewe or none to go aboute to open and declare thys worde of lyfe to the Englysshe people unlearned in tonges that it myghte be lyfe in dede, whyche nowe undeclared to

---

[2] *Scriptorum illustrium maioris Brytannie* (Basileae. M.D.LIX), p. 714.
[3] *Bibliotheca Britannico-Hibernica* (London. MDCCXLVIII), p. 631.
[4] Bale, *Scriptorum illustrium,* p. 714.
[5] Tanner, *op. cit.,* p. 631.
[6] See Bibliography.

them but onelye had in the bare Lettre do appere to many rather deathe then lyfe, rather to brynge men in to errours and heresyes then into the truethe and veryte of Goddes worde, whiche nowe undeclared bryngeth not so muche the symple, rude, and ignoraunte people from theyr ignoraunte blyndnes, corrupte and backewarde iudgementes, false trustes, evyll beleves, vayne superstycyousnes and fayned holynes, in the whyche the people have bene in blyndnes longe tyme for lacke of knowledge of holye Scripture. which the man of Rome kepte under the hatche & wolde nat suffer to com to lyght . . . therefore I as one of the least lerned of al hath set forth an[d] exposicion to this Epystel of Saynt Paule to the Ephesyans as afore this in the Epystel of Jude the Apostle of Chrest, that the people that can but onely rede Englishe may the better know part of the holsome doctryne of saynt Paule. . . . And in this thynge to be done I have used the helpe of tonges, as of the Greke, Hebrewe and the Latyne tonges, and the helpe of the olde Catholyke Doctours approved by the Churche and also of the beste authors that in these dayes nowe do wryte . . ."

The second cause is that he must use such talents as God has given him and not be idle.

"The thyrde cause was to exhorte other that be muche better learned than I, that can do muche better to set fourth some parte of the holy Scripture in Englyshe or in Latyne to shewe the goodnes of God to us Englyshemen, to shewe that God is the God of Englande as well as of Fraunce, Italye, Germanye, or other countrees. . . . Ye, I doubte not but Englyshe men shulde gyve as greate lighte to the worde of God as ever dyd these countres, yf they wolde applye theyr studye, wyttes and myndes to wryte upon the holy Scrypture. . . . Which thynge many learned men wolde do, yf hye rulers . . . wolde excyte and provoke learned men ther unto. And when a Commentary of the holy scrypture were wryten approved of learned men worthye ⟨or worth ye?⟩ pryntynge, it myghte be prynted and set fourth with pryvelege."

He puts this more strongly in the preface to Philippians: "I mervell there is so fewe (of so many great lerned men in this Realme) that setteth fourth the holy scryptures by some commentary or expositions"; and "so I wolde wyshe that hye Ruelers and bysshoppes wolde set lerned men on worke, and cause them to set forth some godly expositions upon the holy scriptures."

The reader will long since have perceived, not only Ridley's failure to come to the point, but also his sense and good intentions. "Scripture alone is not sufficient. If commentaries do not come spontaneously, the civil and Church government should remedy the matter. Commentaries must be based on the original languages, the great commentators of the past and the best moderns." All that Ridley lacked was the ability to write good commentaries. Yet his attempts seem to have met a need. Ephesians was printed twice in 1540, Philippians twice in the year it came out, and Jude twice in 1538 and then again after a space of eleven years.[7]

One thing we may certainly share with Ridley: surprise that "fewe or none" were writing commentaries. Why was this? The reasons are complex, not simple as Mr. Basil Hall suggests: "The reason for this should be obvious. Trilingual studies at Oxford and Cambridge, in comparison with the continental achievement, were almost stillborn, and the energies of English scholars were absorbed in the intense controversial and political struggle between Catholic and Protestant."[8] The comparative backwardness of "trilingual studies" is undoubtedly a contributory factor. It was not that many Englishmen did not know their languages, but that there was not a sufficiently strong climate of opinion at the universities. English Reformers were also absorbed in the great controversy; but this can hardly be taken seriously as a bar to writing commentaries when we consider the time devoted to polemics on the Continent, or even more, when we reflect on Calvin, busy and distracted beyond the worst fears of any English Reformer, nevertheless writing so many commentaries. There are other factors. In the Continental Protestant countries, the battle for vernacular Bibles was won early and comparatively easily. For German readers, Luther's New Testament appeared in 1522 and the "Zurich" Bible by 1530. France and French-speaking Switzerland had the Colinaeus New Testament of 1523, the so-called "Antwerp" Bible in 1530, and Olivétan in 1535. In England, on the contrary, New Testaments, with or without annotations, were forbidden. Not until 1535 was a breakthrough achieved. The English Reformers may therefore have felt that the first need was for an English Bible and that commentaries could come later. Unfortunately, however, they did not come at all. Then again, if marginal annotations were pinpricks to the old guard, what would commentaries be? It is significant that the only commentaries before 1535 were written from abroad, and that Ridley's expositions came after the Bible was "suffered to all people of this realme to rede & to study at their pleasure." I should regard this as the major cause but for the fact that when the Scriptures were allowed, commentaries did not follow. Should we perhaps connect this phenomenon with the relative scarcity of preaching in England and with the fear of anything

[7] See Bibliography.   [8] *Cambridge History of the Bible*, pp. 92–93.

that was not official or authorized? Whatever the causes, the melancholy fact remains that the land of Colet, which had sheltered Erasmus, which was to produce a J. B. Lightfoot, could, during the Reformation, offer no commentator of anything like the stature of those on the Continent.

William Tyndale did what he could. He not only devoted his existence to Biblical translation, but also wrote expositions of two parts of the New Testament—the Sermon on the Mount and the first Epistle of St. John. In his purpose he is of Lancelot Ridley's mind. The English Bible must come first, but we should not be content with this. The Bible has to be explained to people who have for long been taught a perversion of the Bible: "As it is not enough that the father and mother have both begotten the child and brought it into this world, except they care for it and bring it up, till it can help the self; even so it is not enough to have translated, though it were the whole scripture into the vulgar and common tongue, except we also brought again the light to understand it by, and expel that dark cloud which the hypocrites have spread over the face of the scripture, to blind the right sense and true meaning thereof. . . . And for the same cause have I taken in hand to interpret this epistle of St. John the evangelist to edify the layman, and to teach him how to read the scripture, and what to seek therein; and that he may have to answer the hypocrites, and to stop their mouths withal." [9]

This statement of purpose warns the reader what he should not look for. If he has read any of the better sort of foreign sixteenth-century commentary, with its interest in philological and historical questions, he will know that already the commentary is beginning to take on a specialized and highly academic form. Even those writers who have a practical aim, and disclaim any desire to show their learning, cannot go far without revealing what a lot they are hiding. But Tyndale keeps himself very severely to his purpose. Here are no discussions of authorship or date and place of writing. The few philological investigations are of the most rudimentary and direct kind and are dealt with in a sentence or two. He does not mention and treat of other men's exegesis. He wants only to explain what the epistle means and to explain it to Christians untrained in any of the theological disciplines. When "the boy that driveth the plough" has learned to read, he will have at hand the New Testament in his mother tongue and such a small commentary as the Exposition on I John.

[9] See p. 106.

The New Testament Text of I John

We possess four different versions by Tyndale of this epistle; those contained in the three editions of his New Testament (1525/26; 1534; and 1535) and also the one used in his Exposition. This last has not been taken into account in the history of the English Bible, though it is, as I shall show, a separate revision. Westcott supplied a collation of the three New Testament versions of I John, but made no mention of the Exposition.[10] J. F. Mozley noted that it differed from the New Testament texts, but gave no details.[11] Francis Fry does not notice it at all, as he is concerned exclusively with the New Testaments.[12] In fact, it deserves better treatment than this, not only in its own right, as containing some improvements, but also as occupying a place in the history of Tyndale's New Testament and therefore of the English Bible.

This is not the place to give the complete collation of the texts that I have made between the 1531 copy of the Exposition in the British Museum and the three copies of the New Testament in the Cambridge University Library. We must be content with conclusions, and I must ask the reader to trust my figures until he can at last see it all set out in some learned periodical or other.

General analysis:

Exp. has about 260 independent readings against A (1525/26), B (1534) and C (1535) when they agree among themselves.

Exp. has 15 independent readings against A, B, and C when they disagree among themselves.

Exp. agrees with A against B and C 12 times.

Exp. agrees with B and C against A 14 times.

Exp. agrees with B against A and C once.

Exp. agrees with C against A and B 4 times.

Exp. agrees with A and B against C 3 times.

Exp. agrees with A and C against B once.

We may draw the following inferences from these statistics:

1. There are some 275 independent readings in a document of about 2,400 words. This means that, on the one hand, the body of the text is constant, and that therefore Tyndale (despite the Par-

---

[10] *History of the English Bible*, pp. 295–297. His collation is accurate but incomplete. He omits the following: I John 2:26: 1525—*as concerning;* 1534 f. —*concerning;* ch. 3:16: 1525—*for;* 1534 f.—*that;* ch. 3:16: 1525—*our brethren;* 1534 f.—*the brethren;* ch. 4:17: 1525—*judgment, that;* 1534 f.; *judgment. For.*
[11] *William Tyndale*, p. 203.
[12] *A Bibliographical Description.*

ker Society assertion to the contrary [13]) had the first edition before him as he prepared the text for the Exposition. But on the other hand, such a large number of variants [14] shows that the Exposition text represents a thorough revision and hence is a version that can stand on its own.

2. It is significant that where the Exposition agrees with one or more of the New Testament texts against the others, this agreement is most often with the first edition against the two later, or with them against the first. This fits in with its intermediate position between the editions. In other words, some readings are retained that were to be discarded later; others are anticipated.

3. From this we may further infer that Tyndale, when he came to revise the New Testament for the 1534 edition, used not only the 1525/26 edition but also his intermediate revision, the Exposition text.

4. When we examine the independent readings more closely, we find that although many are purely stylistic, not a few have the authority of Tyndale's usual originals. (It is generally agreed that he based his text on Erasmus' Greek New Testament and 1527 Latin version, on the Vulgate, and on Luther's 1522 German New Testament.) For example:

2:7: Exp. *ye had* (found in all four) for *ye heard*
3:12: *righteous* (found in all four) for *good*

On the other hand, there is often a conflict of authorities—though this also confirms the care that he took. For example:

2:18: Exp. *hour* (Greek, Vulg., Luther) for *time* (Erasmus, Latin)

5. Among the independent variants are not a few that have passed into the Authorized Version. Where either the New Testaments or the Exposition have the AV reading, the former predominate by about 90 to 50. Examples of AV in the editions against the Exposition are:

1:2; 2:25; and 5:13: *eternal* for Exp. *everlasting*
3:4, 6, 9, 10, 15; and 5:1, 18: *whosoever* for *all that*
3:17: *this world's good* for *the substance of the world* (Erasmus: *substantiam mundi;* Vulg.: *subst. huius mundi*)

But, on the other hand, the Exposition foreshadows the AV with the following readings:

---

[13] *Expositions . . . by William Tyndale,* p. 153, n. 3.
[14] Westcott finds only 45 variants between the three New Testament texts of I John (*op. cit.,* pp. 295–297). Add the four I have noted and we have 49 —about one sixth of the number of independent readings in the Exposition.

2:4; 3:18, 19; and 4:6: *truth* for *verity*
2:12, 28; 3:7, 18; and 5:21: *little children* for *babes*
3:15: *murderers* for *a man-slayer*
     murderer for *man-slayer*
5:6: *This is* . . . *Jesus Christ* for *This Jesus Christ* . . . *is*

I do not know whether these readings passed directly into the AV from the Exposition or whether they occur in one or more of the intervening Bibles.

We may end this section with an uncertainty. It is surprising that, having in many places improved on 1525/26, Tyndale does not make use of all the better readings in 1534 but reverts to the first attempt. Why, for example, does he keep to *heard* in ch. 2:7 when Erasmus' Greek and Latin, the Vulgate, and Luther all give *had?* Why, again, persist in following Luther with *cometh* in ch. 2:21 when the others have *is?* There is no easy answer to such questions, for like so much Biblical work in the sixteenth century, complications and confusions abound.

BIBLIOGRAPHY

Parker Society prints what, with its customary imprecision in matters bibliographical, it calls "an ancient edition . . . in the library of St. Paul's Cathedral." [14a] There is, however, a yet more ancient edition in the British Museum. This is our present text—its first reprinting since the first edition.

The exposi-/tion of the fyrste Epistle of seynt/ Jhon with a Prologge be-/fore it: by W.T.
Colophon: The yere of our lorde. 1531. in September.
This volume (which is ascribed by Short-Title Catalogue to the printer Martin de Kayser of Antwerp, I do not know on what evidence) is printed in black letter, and consists of 62 folios.

The next edition that I have seen is the one in St. Paul's Cathedral Library. Unfortunately, the title page is missing. Inside the cover has been written "1539," and this date has also been printed on the spine; but this, of course, is not evidence. It is to be presumed that this is the 1538 edition printed by J. Nicolson at Southwark. All I can say with certainty is that it is not the same edition as the 1531 in the British Museum. It is in black letter and occupies 86 folios. On fol.lxxxvii[a] a new work starts: "Here begyn-/neth the .ii. Epistle/ of S.Jhon." This ends fol.xcii[b]: "The ende of the .ii. epistle/ of S.Jhon." Then on fol.xciii[a]: "Here begyn/neth the .iii. Epistle/ of S.Jhon." And fol.xcvii[b]: "The ende of the/ iii. Epistle." The last part of the volume consists of Lancelot Ridley's Exposition in the epistell of Jude (1538). This is not the time to engage in a discussion on the authorship of the expositions on II and III John. [Since preparing this edition, I have established that they are translations of Bullinger.]

The Exposition was next printed in Day's collected volume:
*The Whole/ workes of W. Tyndall, Iohn/ Frith, and Doct. Barnes
. . ./ . . . At London/ Printed by Iohn Daye,/ . . ./ An.1573.*
(But colophon 1572.)

[14a] *Expositions*, p. 134.

98 WILLIAM TYNDALE

In the Parker Society:
  Expositions and Notes on Sundry Portions of the Holy Scriptures . . . by William Tyndale, Martyr, 1536. Edited for the Parker Society by the Rev. Henry Walter, B.D., F.R.S. Cambridge. 1849.

Tyndale's New Testaments:
The first edition I have used in Fry's facsimile:
  The First New Testament Printed in the English Language (1525 or 1526). Translated from the Greek by William Tyndale. Reproduced in Facsimile with an Introduction by Francis Fry F.S.A. (Bristol. Printed for the Editor. MDCCCLXII.)
  The ne-/we Testament, dyly/gently corrected and/ compared with the/ Greke by Willyam/ Tindale: and fynes-/shed in the yere of ou/re Lorde God/ A. M.D. & xxxiiij./in the moneth of/ Nouember. (Camb. Univ. Lib. Young 152.)
  The newe/ Testament, dylygent-/ly corrected and/ compared with/ the Greke by/ Willyam/ Tindale: and fynesshed/ in the yere of oure/ Lorde God A./ M.D. and./ xxxv. (This is second title page of Camb. Univ. Lib. Syn.8.53.91; the first is missing.)

Lancelot Ridley's Works:
  An exposition in/ the epistell of Jude/ the apostel of Christ/ wherein he setteth/ playnly before eue-/ry mans eyes false/ apostels, and theyr/ craftes, by y̆ which/ they haue longe de-/ceyued symple chri-/stian people./ 1538.
  A commenta-/ry in Englyshe upon/ Sayncte Paules Epystle/ to the Ephesyans for the/ instruccyon of them that/ be unlearned in tonges, ga/thered out of the holy Scry/ptures and of the olde ca/tholyke Doctours of the/ Chyrche, and of the/ best authors that/ nowe a dayes/ do wryte/ Anno .D. 1540/ Per Lancelotum Ridleum/ Cantabrigensem./ Cvm privilegio/ Ad imprimendum solum.
  Colophon: Imprinted at london/ by me Robert Redman./ Cum preuilegeo ad im-/primendum solum.
  An exposytion/ in Englyshe upon the Epi/styll of saynt Paule to the/ Philippians, for the instruc/tion of them that be unler-/ned in tonges: gathered out/ of holy scriptures, & of the/ olde catholike doctours of/ the church, & of the best au-/thors that now adayes do/ write. By Lancelot/ Rydley of Can-/torbury. N.D.
  Colophon: Prynted at Cantorbury in/ Saynt Paules paryshe/ by John Mychell.

Ephesians, Philippians, and part of Jude reprinted in *Fathers of English Church* II.7–300.

Secondary Works:
R. Demaus, *William Tyndale. A Biography.* New ed. revised by Richard Lovett. London, 1886.
J. F. Mozley, *William Tyndale.* London, 1937.
W. E. Campbell, *Erasmus, Tyndale and More.* London, 1949.
W. A. Clebsch, *England's Earliest Protestants. 1520–1535.* Yale University Press, 1964.
Francis Fry, *A Bibliographical Description of the Editions of the New Testament. Tyndale's Version in English.* London, 1878.
W. F. Moulton, *The History of the English Bible.* 5th ed. revised and enlarged by J. H. Moulton and W. F. Moulton. London, 1911.
B. F. Westcott, *A General View of the History of the English Bible.* 3d ed. revised by W. A. Wright. London, 1905.
A. W. Pollard, ed., *Records of the English Bible.* Oxford, 1911. (This contains the best short account of the translations in its introduction.)
C. C. Butterworth, *The Literary Lineage of the King James Bible 1340–1611.* Philadelphia, 1941.
S. L. Greenslade, ed., *The Cambridge History of the Bible: The West from the Reformation to the Present Day.* Cambridge, 1963.
Historical Catalogue of the Printed Editions of Holy Scripture in the Library of the British and Foreign Bible Society, compiled by T. H. Darlow and H. F. Moule. Vol. 1, English. London, 1903.

William Tyndale: The Exposition of the Fyrste Epistle of Seynt Jhon

THE TEXT

THE PROLOGUE

Except a man have the profession of his baptism in his heart, he cannot understand the scripture.

As a man can by no means read, except he be first taught the letters of the crossrow,[15] even so it is unpossible for a man, of whatsoever degree or name he be of, to understand aught in the scripture unto the honour of God and health of his soul, except he be first taught the profession of his baptism, and have it also written in his heart.

Which profession standeth in two things. The one is the knowledge of the law of God, understanding it spiritually, as Christ expoundeth it, Matthew in the v., vi., and vii., so that the root and life of all laws is this: "Love thy Lord God with all thine heart, all thy soul, and all thy might"; [16] and thy neighbour as thyself for his sake: and that love only be the fulfilling of the law (as Paul teacheth [17]); and that whatsoever deed we do and not of that love, that same fulfilleth no law in the sight of God.

And the other is to know the promises of mercy which are in our Saviour Christ; understanding them also purely without all leaven, after the mercifullest fashion as scripture soundeth [18] them, and after all fatherly love and kindness of God, unto all that repent toward the law, and believe in Christ. . . .

Notwithstanding we, being all sons of one God, and servants of one Christ, must agree among ourselves; and he that hath offended must meekly knowledge his fault, and offer himself to make amends unto the utmost of his power; and if he have not wherewith, ask forgiveness for Christ's sake; the other is bound to for-

---

[15] Alphabet.
[16] Matt. 22:37 ff.
[17] Rom. 13:10.
[18] Expresses.

give him. Neither, without reconciling himself unto his brother, may any man be at the first received unto the profession of Christ's faith, nor continue therein, nor be received in again, if he be for his open offences put thereout. For how can a man love his neighbour as well as himself, and be sorry that he hath hurt him, except he should offer himself to make amends?

And we must from henceforth walk in the life of penance, (if ye will have it so called,) and after the doctrine of Christ every man tame his flesh with prayer, fasting, and the continual meditations of Christ's penance and passions for us, and of the holy saints, and with such abstinence, and kind of living, as every man thinketh most meet for his complexion; [19] the younger confessing their infirmities to the elder, discreeter, and better learned, and asking their advice and wholesome counsel for the repressing of their diseases; but all to tame the flesh, and to serve thy neighbour, without any superstitious mind.

But to God-ward is there no satisfaction, save faith in Christ's blood out of a repenting heart. For our outward deeds cannot be referred unto God, to do him service in his own person, and to help him, or make him better therewith. We can do no more with them, were they never so perfect, and done with all love, than satisfy the law for the present time, and do our duty unto our neighbours, and tame our own flesh; but not to make satisfaction to God for sin that is once past. The sin that is once committed must God forgive freely, of a fatherly love, for Christ's sake.

When God visiteth us with sickness, poverty, or whatsoever adversity it be, he doth it not of a tyrannous mind, to satisfy his lust in our suffering of evil to make satisfaction for the sin that is past, of which we repent and be sorry; but of a fatherly love, to make us know ourselves and feel his mercy, and to tame our flesh, and to keep us from sinning again. . . .

Even so is it of God. If any of his children, that have professed his law and the faith of our Saviour, be negligent to tame his flesh with prayer, fasting, and good deeds after the doctrine of Christ, he will surely scourge him, to bring him into the right way again, and to keep that the doctrine of his soul's health perish not in him. But he taketh not his mercy from us, nor thinketh on the sin that is past, after that we repent and be full converted, but absolveth us both *a poena et culpa* [20] for Christ's sake. . . .

The knowledge of our baptism is the key and the light of the scripture.

[19] Constitution.   [20] I.e., not only remits punishment but also pardons guilt.

And again, as he which knoweth his letters well and can spell perfectly, cannot but read if he be diligent; and as he which hath clear eyes without impediment or let, and walketh thereto in the light and open day, cannot but see, if he attend and take heed; even so whosoever hath the profession of baptism written in his heart, cannot but understand the scripture, if he exercise himself therein, and compare one place to another, and mark the manner of speech, and ask here and there the meaning of a sentence of them that be better exercised.

For as the doctrine which we should be taught before we were baptized, and for lack of age is deferred unto the years of discretion, is the key that bindeth and looseth, locketh and unlocketh, the conscience of all sinners; even so that lesson, where it is understood, is only the key that openeth all the scripture, and even the whole scripture in itself, gathered together in a narrow compass, and brought into a compendiousness. And till thou be taught that lesson, that thine heart feel the sweetness of it, the scripture is locked and shut up from thee, and so dark that thou couldest not understand it, though Peter, Paul, or Christ himself did expound it unto thee; no more than a blind man can see, though thou set a candle before him, or shewedst him the sun, or pointedst with thy finger unto that thou wouldest have him look upon.

Now we be all baptized. But, alas! not one, from the highest to the lowest, ever taught the profession or meaning thereof. And therefore we remain all blind generally, as well our great Rabbins for all their high learning which they seem to have, as the lay people. Yea, and so much the more blind are our great clerks, that where the lay people, [f]or a great number of them, are taught nought at all, they be all wrong taught, and the doctrine of their baptism is all corrupt unto them with the leaven of false glosses, ere they come to read the scripture. So that the light which they bring with them, to understand the scripture withal, is utter darkness, and as contrary unto the scripture as the devil unto Christ. By reason whereof the scripture is locked up and become so dark unto them, that they grope for the door, and can find no way in; and is become a maze unto them, in which they wander as in a mist, or (as we say) led of Robin Goodfellow,[21] that they cannot come to the right way, no, though they turn their caps; and the brightness thereof hath blinded their eyes with malice, so that though they believe not the scripture to be false, yet they persecute the right understanding thereof, and cannot believe it true in the plain sense, which it speaketh to them in. It is become a turn-

[21] Puck—e.g., as in *Midsummer Night's Dream*.

again lane [22] unto them, which they cannot go through, nor make iii. lines agree together. And finally, the sentences of the scripture are nothing but very riddles unto them, at the which they cast as the blind man doth at the crow,[23] and expound by guess, an hundred doctors an hundred ways; and one man in xx. sermons alleging one text after xx. fashions, having no sure doctrine to cleave unto; and all for lack of the right knowledge of the profession of our baptism.

He that hath the profession of his baptism written in ⟨his⟩ heart can be no heretic.
Another conclusion is this: As he which ever creepeth along by the ground, and never climbeth, cannot fall from on high, even so no man that hath the profession of his baptism written in his heart, can stumble in the scripture and fall unto heresies, or become a maker of division and sects and a defender of wild and vain opinions. For the whole and only cause of heresies and sects is pride. Now the law of God, truly interpreted, robbeth all them in whose hearts it is written, and maketh them as bare as Job, of all things whereof a man can be moved to pride. And on the other side, they have utterly forsaken themselves, with all their high learning and wisdom, and are become the servants of Christ only, which hath bought them with his blood, and have promised in their hearts unfeignedly to follow him, and to take him only for the author of their religion, and his doctrine only for their wisdom and learning, and to maintain it in word and deed, and to keep it pure, and to build no strange doctrine thereupon, and to be at the highest never, but fellow with their brethren, and in that fellowship to wax ever lower and lower, and every day more servant than other unto his weaker brethren, after the example and image of Christ, and after his commandment and ordinance, and not in feigned words of the pope.

This be said because of them that say that the scripture maketh men heretics, and corrupteth with false opinions, contrary unto

[22] "This, in old records, is called Wind-again Lane, and lieth in the parish of St. Sepulchre's, going down to Fleet-dike [in the City of London]; which men must turn again the same way they came, for there it is stopped. The proverb is applied to those who . . . must seasonably alter their manners." (T. Fuller, *Worthies of England* [London, 1840], 2.348.) But here it means that they are baffled at Scripture—"and evermore come out at that same door," etc.

[23] Cf. "Ye cast and conjecture this much like in show,
As the blind man casts his staff, or shootes the crow."

(J. Heywood, *A dialogue conteinyng the number in effect of all the proverbs in the english tongue.* 1546. Pt. 2, ch. 9.)

the profession of their baptism; and the light wherewith they should expound the scripture is turned into darkness in their hearts, and the door of the scripture locked, and the wells stopped up ere they come at it.

And therefore, because their darkness cannot comprehend the light of scripture, as it is written, "The light shined in darkness, but the darkness could not comprehend it"; [24] they turn it into blind riddles, and read it without understanding, as lay-men do our lady matins, or as it were Merlin's prophecies, ever their minds upon their heresies. And when they come to a place that soundeth like, there they rest, and wring out wonderful expositions, to stablish their heresies withal; after the tale of the boy that would fain have eaten of the pasty of lampreys, but durst not unto [25] the bells sang unto him, "Sit down, Jack boy, and eat of the lamprey," to stablish his wavering conscience withal. Is it not a great blindness to say in the beginning of all together, that the whole scripture is false in the literal sense, and killeth the soul? Which pestilent heresy to prove, they abuse the text of Paul saying, "The letter killeth"; [26] because that text was become a riddle unto them, and they understood it not: when Paul by this word *letter* understood the law given by Moses to condemn all conscience, and to rob them of all righteousness, to compel them unto the promises of mercy that are in Christ.

Heresy springeth not of the scripture, no more than darkness of the sun, but is a dark cloud that springeth out of the blind hearts of hypocrites, and covereth the face of the scripture, and blindeth their eyes, that they cannot behold the bright beams of the scripture.

The whole and sum then of all together is this: If our hearts were taught the appointment made between God and us in Christ's blood, when we were baptized, we had the key to open the scripture, and light to see and perceive the true meaning of it, and the scripture should be easy to understand. And because we be not taught that profession, is the cause why the scripture is so dark, and so far passing our capacity. And the cause why our expositions are heresies, is because we be wrong taught, and corrupt with false opinions beforehand, and made heretics ere we come at the scripture, and have corrupt it, and it not us; as the taste of the sick maketh wholesome and well-seasoned meat bitter, wearish,[27] and unsavoury. Nevertheless yet the scripture abideth pure in herself and bright, so that he which is sound in the faith shall at once perceive that the judgment of the heretics is corrupt

---

[24] John 1:5.
[25] Until.
[26] II Cor. 3:6.
[27] Insipid.

in their expositions, as an whole man doth feel at once, even with smelling to the meat, that the taste of the sick is infected. And with the scripture shall they ever improve heresies and false expositions: for the scripture purgeth herself, even as the water once in the year casteth all filthiness unto the sides. Which to be true ye see by the authority of Paul, saying, "All the scripture was given of God by inspiration, and is good to teach withal, to improve," [28] and so forth; and by the ensample of Christ and the apostles, how they counfounded the Jews with the same scripture which they had corrupt, and understood them amiss after their own darkness; and as ye see by the ensample of us now also, how we have manifestly improved [29] the hypocrites in an hundred texts which they had corrupt to prove their false opinions brought in besides the scripture, and have driven them off. . . .

Finally then, forasmuch as the scripture is the light and life of God's elect, and that mighty power wherewith God createth them and shapeth them after the similitude, likeness, and very fashion of Christ; and therefore sustenance, comfort, and strength to courage them, that they may stand fast, and endure, and merrily bear [30] their souls' health, wherewith the lusts of the flesh subdued and killed, and the spirit mollified and made soft, to receive the print of the image of our Saviour Jesu: and asmuch as the scripture is so pure of itself, that it can corrupt no man, but the wicked only, which are infect beforehand, and, ere they come at it, corrupt it with the heresies that they bring with them: and forasmuch as the complaint of the hypocrites, that the scripture maketh heretics, is vain and feigned; and the reasons wherewith they would prove that the lay people ought not to read the scripture, false, wicked, and the fruit of rotten trees. Therefore are they faithful servants of Christ, and faithful ministers and dispensers of his doctrine, and true-hearted toward their brethren, which have given themselves up into the hand of God, and put themselves in jeopardy of all persecution, their very life despised, and have translated the scripture purely and with good conscience, submitting themselves, and desiring them that can to amend their translation, or (if it please them) to translate it theirselves after their best manner, yea, and let them sew to their glosses, as many as they think they can make cleave thereto, and then put other men's translation out of the way.[31]

[28] II Tim. 3:16.
[29] Proved wrong.
[30] Bear up.
[31] *Therefore . . . way.* An autobiographical passage. He refers in particular to his frequently repeated challenge that his opponents shall cease to attack him and instead undertake to translate the Bible themselves.

Howbeit, though God hath so wrought with them that a great part is translated; yet, as it is not enough that the father and the mother have both begotten the child and brought it into this world, except they care for it and bring it up, till it can help the self; even so it is not enough to have translated, though it were the whole scripture into the vulgar and common tongue, except we also brought again the light to understand it by, and expel that dark cloud which the hypocrites have spread over the face of the scripture, to blind the right sense and true meaning thereof. And therefore are there divers introductions ordained for you, to teach you the profession of your baptism, the only light of the scripture; one upon the epistle of Paul to the Romans, and another called "The Pathway into the Scripture." And for the same cause have I taken in hand to interpret this epistle of St. John the evangelist to edify the layman, and to teach him how to read the scripture, and what to seek therein; and that he may have to answer the hypocrites, and to stop their mouths withal.

And first, understand that all the epistles that the apostles wrote are the Gospel of Christ, though all that is the Gospel be not an epistle. It is called a Gospel, that is to say, glad tidings, because it is an open preaching of Christ; and an epistle, because it is sent as a letter, or a bill, to them that are absent.

Here beginneth the first epistle of St. John

CHAPTER I

1. That which was from the beginning declare we unto you, which we have heard, which we have seen with our eyes, which we looked upon, and our hands have handled of the word of life. 2. For the life appeared, and we have seen, and bear witness, and shew unto you that everlasting life,[82] *which was with the Father, and appeared unto us.*

In that St. John saith, *The thing which was from the beginning,* and *the everlasting life that was with the Father,* he witnesseth that Christ is very God; as he doth in the beginning of his Gospel, saying: "The word," or the thing, "was at the beginning, and the

---

[82] 1534 Note: John here, as in his Gospel, and as Paul and Peter in their epistles, teacheth first the justifying of faith and that all mercy cometh by Christ only, without all other respects and then what
This note is incomplete; it should not be joined to "John viii," as Fry (*A Bibliographical Description,* p. 54), for this is a separate note.

thing was with God, and that thing was God, and all things were made by it." [33]

And when he saith, *Which we heard, and saw with our eyes, and our hands handled* him; he testifieth that Christ is very man also; as he doth in the beginning of his Gospel, saying: "The word," or that thing, "was made flesh," [34] that is, became man. And thus we have in plain and open words a manifest article of our faith, that our Saviour Christ is very God and very man.

Which article whosoever not only believeth, but also believeth in it, the same is the son of God, and hath everlasting life in him, and shall never come into condemnation. . . . And to believe in the words of this article is that eating of Christ's flesh, and drinking his blood, of which is spoken John vi.: "The words which I speak are spirit and life, and the flesh profiteth not at all"; [35] meaning of the fleshly eating of his body, and fleshly drinking of his blood. There is therefore great difference between believing that there is a God and that Christ is God and man, and to believe in God and Christ, God and man, and in the promises of mercy that are in him. The first is common to good and bad, and unto the devils thereto, and is called the faith and believe of the history. The second is proper unto the sons of God, and is their life, as it is written, "The righteous liveth by faith"; [36] that is, in putting his trust, confidence, and whole hope in the goodness, mercy, and help of God, in all adversities, bodily and ghostly, and all temptations, and even in sin and hell, how deep soever he be fallen therein.

But as he which feeleth not his disease can long for no health, even so it is impossible for any man to believe in Christ's blood, except Moses have had him first in cure,[37] and with his law have robbed him of his righteousness, and condemned him unto everlasting death, and have shewed him under what damnation they are in by birth in Adam, and how all their deeds (appear they never so holy) are yet but damnable sin, because they can refer nothing unto the glory of God, but seek themselves, their own profit, honour and glory. So that repentance toward the law must go before this belief; and he which repenteth not, but consenteth unto the life of sin, hath no part in this faith.

And when John calleth Christ the everlasting life that was with the Father, he signifieth that Christ is our life; as after in the Epistle, and in the first also of his Gospel, saying, "In him was life." [38] For until we receive life of Christ by faith, we are dead,

[33] John 1:1.
[34] John 1:14.
[35] John 6:63.
[36] Gal. 3:11.
[37] Under his charge.
[38] John 1:4.

and can be but dead, as saith John in the iii.: "He that believeth not in the Son, can see no life, but the wrath of God abideth upon him." [39] Of which wrath we are heirs by birth, saith Paul, Eph. ii.[40] Of which wrath we are ignorant, until the law be published; and walk quietly after our lusts, and love God wickedly, that he should be content therewith, and maintain us therein, contrary unto his godly and righteous nature. But as soon as the law (whose nature is to utter sin, Rom. iii.,[41] and to set man at variance with God) is preached; then we first awake out of our dream, and see our damnation, and hath the law which is so contrary unto our nature, and grudge against God thereto, as young children do against their elders when they first command, and count God a cruel tyrant because of his law, in that he condemneth us for that thing which we cannot love, nor of love fulfil.

But when Christ is preached, how that God for his sake receiveth us to mercy, and forgiveth us all that is past, and henceforth reckoneth not unto us our corrupt and poisoned nature, and taketh us as his sons, and putteth us under grace and mercy, and promiseth that he will not judge us by the rigorousness of the law, but nurture us with all mercy and patience, as a father most merciful, only if we will submit ourselves unto his doctrine and learn to keep his laws; yea, and he will thereto consider our weakness, and, whatsoever chanceth, never taketh away his mercy, till we cast off the yoke of our profession first, and run away with utter defiance, that we will never come more at school; then our stubborn and hard hearts mollify and wax soft; and in the confidence and hope that we have in Christ, and his kindness, we go to God boldly as unto our father, and receive life, that is to say, love unto God and unto the law also.

3. *That which we have seen and heard we declare unto you, that ye may have fellowship with us, and that our fellowship may be with the Father, and with his Son Jesus Christ. 4. And these things we write unto you, that your joy may be full.*

To bring unto the fellowship of God and Christ, and of them that believe in Christ, is the final intent of all the scripture, why it was given of God unto man, and the only thing which all true preachers seek; and whereby ye shall ever know and discern the true word of God from all false and counterfeited doctrine of vain traditions, and the true preacher from the wily hypocrite. "We preach unto you," saith St. John, "that everlasting life which we have heard, and in hearing received through faith, and are sure of

---

[39] John 3:36.   [40] Eph. 2:3.   [41] Rom. 3:20.

it, to draw you to us out of the fellowship that ye have with the damned devils in sinful lusts and ignorance of God"; for we "seek you and not yours," as saith Paul, ii. Cor. xii.[42] We love you as ourselves in God, and therefore would have you fellows and equal with us, and build you upon the foundation laid of the apostles and prophets, which is Christ Jesus, and make you of the household of God for ever; that ye and we, fellows and brethren, and coupled together in one spirit, in one faith, and in one hope, might have our fellowship thereby with God, and become his sons and heirs, and with Jesus Christ, being his brethren and co-heirs, and to make your joy full through that glad tidings, as the angel said unto the shepherds, Luke ii.: "Behold, I shew you great joy that shall be unto all the people, how that there is a Saviour born unto you this day, which is Christ the Lord." [43] And these tidings we bring you with the word of God only, which we received of his Spirit, and out of the mouth of his Son, as true messengers. . . .

5. *And this is the tidings which we have heard of him, and declare unto you, that God is light,[44] and in him is no darkness at all. 6. If we say that we have fellowship with him, and yet walk in darkness, we lie, and do not the truth. 7. But and if we walk in light,[45] as he is in light, then have we fellowship together, and the blood of Christ his Son cleanseth us from all sin.*

As the devil is darkness and lies, so is God light and truth only; and there is no darkness of falsehead and consenting to wickedness in him. And the brightness of his light is his word and doctrine, as the c. and xix. Psalm saith, "Thy word is a lantern unto my feet, and a light to my paths." [46] And Christ is "the light that lighteneth all men." [47] And the apostles are called "the light of the world," [48] because of the doctrine. And all that know truth are light: "Ye were once darkness," saith Paul, Eph. v., "but now light in the Lord; walk therefore as the children of light." [49] And good works are called the fruits of light. And all that live in ignorance are called darkness; as he saith afterwards, "He that hateth his brother walketh in darkness." For if the light of the glorious Gospel of Christ did shine in his heart, he could not hate his brother.

By "walking," understand consenting, doing, and working. If then we walk in darkness, that is, consent and work wickedness, and say we have fellowship with God, we lie. For to have fellow-

[42] II Cor. 12:14.
[43] Luke 2:10.
[44] 1534 Note: John viii.
[45] 1534 Note: (Light) is the doctrine of Christ.

[46] Ps. 119:105.
[47] John 1:9.
[48] Matt. 5:14.
[49] Eph. 5:8.

ship with him is to know, and consent, and profess his doctrine in our hearts. Now if the commandments of God be written in our hearts, our members cannot but practise them, and shew the fruit. So whether light or darkness be in the heart, it will appear in the walking. For though our members be never so dead unto virtue, yet if our souls knowledge the truth, and consent unto righteousness, we have the spirit of life in us. . . . And then, finally, if we have the light in our hearts, and walk therein, then we have fellowship with God, and are his sons and heirs, and are purged from all sin through Christ's blood.

8. If we say we have no sin, we deceive ourselves, and truth is not in us.

If we think there is no sin in us, we are beguiled and blind, and the light of God's word is not in us, and either follow sin as beasts without conscience at all, or if we see the gross sins, as murder, theft, and adultery, yet we have hanged a vail of false glosses upon Moses's face, and see not the brightness of the law, how that it requireth of us as pure an heart to God, and as great love unto our neighbours, as was in our Saviour Jesus, and ceaseth not before to condemn us as sinners.

9. If we knowledge [50] our sins, he is faithful and just to forgive us our sins, and to cleanse us from all unrighteousness.

If we confess our sins, not in the priest's ear (though that tradition, restored unto the right use, were not damnable), but in our hearts to God, with true repentance and fast [51] belief; then is he faithful to forgive and to purge us, because of his merciful truth and promise. For he promised Abraham, that in his seed all the world should be blessed from the curse of sin; and hath abundantly renewed his everlasting mercy unto us in the new testament, promising that our sins shall be forgiven us in Christ's blood, if we repent, and trust thereto.

10. If we say we have not sinned, we make him a liar, and his word is not in us.

For his word testifieth against us, that we are all sinners; yea, and else Christ died in vain. . . . And the scripture witnesseth that we are damnable sinners, and that our nature is to sin. Which corrupt and poisoned nature, though it be begun to be healed, yet

---

[50] 1534 Note: If we confess our sins, God, which cannot lie, hath promised to forgive them.
[51] Steadfast, firm.

it is never thorough whole until the hour of death. For the which cause, with all our best fruits there grow weeds among. Neither can there be any deed so perfect that could not be amended. When a blind bungler wondereth at his glorious works, a cunning workman, that hath a clear judgment, perceiveth that it is impossible to make a work that could not be made better. Now the law requireth works of us in the highest degree of perfection, and ceaseth not to accuse us, until our works flow naturally as glorious in perfection as the works of Christ. And Christ teacheth us to pray in our pater-noster, "Forgive us our trespasses as we forgive our trespassers." Whereby ye may easily understand, that we sin daily one against another, and all against God. Christ taught also to pray, that our Father should not let us slip into temptation; signifying that our nature cannot but sin, if occasions be given, except that God of his especial grace keep us back: which pronity [52] to sin is damnable sin in the law of God. . . . Which impotency and feebleness is damnable in the law of God, except that we saw it and repented, and were fled to Christ for mercy.

Chapter II

1. My little children, I write these things unto you, that ye sin not. And though any man sin, yet we have an advocate with the Father, even Jesus Christ, which is righteous.

I write unto you on the one side, that God is light; and therefore that no man, which willingly walketh in the unfruitful works of darkness, hath any fellowship with that light, or part in the blood of his Son. And this I write and testify unto you, my dear children, that ye sin not: that is, that ye consent not unto sin and should sin of lust and purpose maliciously, but contrariwise that ye fear God, and resist sin with all your might and power according as ye have promised. For whosoever sinneth of purpose after the knowledge of truth, the same sinneth against the Holy Ghost remediless. Hebrews vi. and also x.[53]

And on the other side, I testify unto you, that we be all way [54] sinners, though not of purpose and malice after the nature of damned devils, but of infirmity and frailty of our flesh; which flesh not only letteth us, that our works cannot be perfect, but also now and then, through manifold occasions and temptations, carrieth us clean out of the right way, spite of our hearts. Howbeit (I say) if, when the rage is past, we turn unto the right way again, and confess our sins unto our Father with a repenting heart, he hath

[52] Inclination.   [53] Heb. 6:4 ff. and 10:26 ff.   [54] In every respect.

promised us mercy, and is true to fulfil it. So that if we sin not devilishly against the Holy Ghost, refusing the doctrine which we cannot improve that it should not be true but after the frailty of man, there is no cause to despair: for we have an advocate and an intercessor with the Father, even Jesus Christ that is righteous.

The name of our advocate is *Jesus,* that is to say, a Saviour. . . . And this advocate and our Jesus, to save us from our sins, continueth ever, as it is written, Hebre. vii., and hath *sempiternum Sacerdotium,*[55] an everlasting office, to make an atonement for sin: by the reason whereof, saith the text, "he is able ever to save them that come to God through him" [56] with repentance and faith, and liveth ever to speak for us. And beside that our Jesus is God, and almighty, he [57] took our nature upon him, and felt all our infirmities and sicknesses, and in feeling learned to have compassion on us, and for compassion cried mightily in prayers to God the Father for us, and was heard. And the voice of the same blood that once cried, not for vengeance as Abel's, but for mercy only, and was heard, crieth now and ever, and is ever heard, as oft as we call unto remembrance with repenting faith, how that it was shed for our sins. He is also called *Christus,* that is to say, king anointed with all might and power over sin, death and hell, and over all sins; so that none that flieth unto him shall ever come into judgment of damnation. He is anointed with all fulness of grace, and hath all the treasure and riches of the Spirit of God in his hand, with which he blesseth all men, according to the promise made to Abraham; and is thereto merciful, to give unto all that call on him. And how much he loveth us, I report me unto the ensample of his deeds.

And he is *righteous,* both toward God, in that he never sinned, and therefore hath obtained all his favour and grace; and also toward us, in that he is true to fulfil all the mercy that he hath promised us, even unto the uttermost jot.

2. *And he is the satisfaction for our sins; and not for ours only, but also for all the world's.*

That I call *satisfaction,* the Greek calleth *Ilasmos,* and the Hebrew *Copar:* [58] and it is first taken for the suaging of wounds,

---

[55] An eternal priesthood.
[56] Heb. 7:25.
[57] 1531: *almighty. He* . . . If we accept that reading, we need a comma after *that.*
[58] I.e., ἱλασμός and כֹּפֶר. In the three editions of his New Testament he translates it by the clumsy "he it is that obtaineth grace" (as also in *The Obedience of a Christian Man,* PS, I.285).

sores, and swellings, and the taking away of pain and smart of them; and thence is borrowed for the pacifying and suaging of wrath and anger, and for an amends-making, a contenting, satisfaction, a ransom, and making at one, as it is to see abundantly in the Bible. So that Christ is a full contenting, satisfaction and ransom for our sins: and not for ours only, which are apostles and disciples of Christ while he was yet here; or for ours which are Jews, or Israelites, and the seed of Abraham; or for ours that now believe at this present time, but for all men's sins, both for their sins which went before and believed the promises to come, and for ours which have seen them fulfilled, and also for all them which shall afterward believe unto the world's end, of whatsoever nation or degree they be. . . .

Let this therefore be an undoubted article of thy faith: not of an history faith, as thou believest a gest [59] of Alexander, or of the old Romans, but of a lively faith and belief, to put thy trust and confidence in, and to buy and sell thereon, as we say; and to have thy sins taken away, and thy soul saved thereby, if thou hold it fast; and to continue ever in sin, and to have thy soul damned, if thou let it slip; that our Jesus, our Saviour that saveth his people from their sins, and our Christ, that is our king over all sin, death and hell, anointed with fulness of all grace and with the Spirit of God, to distribute unto all men, hath, according unto the Epistle to the Hebrews and all the scripture, in the days of his mortal flesh, with fasting, praying, suffering, and crying to God mightily for us, and with shedding his blood, made full satisfaction both *a pœna* and *a culpa* (with our holy father's leave) for all the sins of the world; both of theirs that went before, and of theirs that come after in the faith; whether it be original sin or actual: and not only the sins committed with consent to evil in time of ignorance, before the knowledge of the truth, but also the sins done of frailty after we have forsaken evil and consented to the laws of God in our hearts, promising to follow Christ and walk in the light of his doctrine. . . .

[*3. And hereby are we sure that we know him, if we keep his commandments.*[60]] *4. He that saith, I know him, and yet keepeth not his commandments, is a liar, and the truth is not in him.*

When our Pharisees say, "Do as we bid you, and not as we do": they testify that they keep not God's commandments: unto which

---

[59] Story.
[60] 1534 Note: He that keepeth the commandments knoweth God; and he that keepeth it not, knoweth not God.

testimony our eyes also bear record. And they that keep not God's commandments be liars and have no truth in them: and then, when they preach, they cannot but preach lies. And then, though they preach Christ, they preach him falsely, unto their fleshly vantage, and not our souls' health. And forasmuch as we may have no fellowship with them that keep not God's commandments, i. Cor. v.,[61] and inasmuch as all such are false prophets, void of all truth, it followeth that we ought to give our doctors none audience, though their defenders stood by them with their swords drawn; but rather to lay down our heads, and stretch forth our necks to be slain.

5. *He that keepeth his word,*[62] *in him verily is the love of God perfect, and hereby know we that we are in him.*

That is, "he that keepeth his commandments, loveth unfeignedly"; and is thereby sure that he is in God. For to be in God is to believe in the mercy of God; and to believe in mercy is cause of love, and love cause of working. And therefore he that worketh for God's sake, is sure that he loveth and that he trusteth in God; which is to be in God or in Christ. And as by wilful keeping of the commandments we be sure that we love God, and believe in God; even so through wilful breaking of them, we may be sure that we neither love nor believe in him, and therefore that we be not in him.

6. *He that saith he abideth in him, ought to walk as he walked.*

All that be baptized in Christ are washed in him, to put off pride, wrath, hate and envy, with all their old conversation, by which they oppressed their neighbours; and have promised to become, every man even as Christ himself unto his brethren, in love and kindness both in word and deed. . . .

7. *Brethren, I write no new commandment unto you, but an old commandment which ye had at the beginning: for an old commandment is the word which ye heard from the beginning.*

I write no new precept, but only put you in remembrance of that old which was taught you when ye were first baptized in Christ, to love each other as he did you: which is an old commandment, and was given at the beginning of the world, and hath ever since been written in the heart of all that put their hope in God.

[61] I Cor. 5:9 ff.
[62] 1534 Note: He that keepeth God's Word loveth God and is in God and walketh as Christ did.

8. *Again, a new commandment I write unto you, which is true in him, and also in you; for the darkness is past, and the true light now shineth.*

The devil hath sown his darkness in the field where this commandment should grow; and the weeds of men's traditions had overgrown the corn of this old commandment; so that it was antiquate, and clean out of knowledge. But Christ, the light of all true doctrine, now shineth and hath scattered the darkness, and plucked up the weeds by the roots, and restored this old commandment again. And in him it is a true commandment, for he loved truly. And in you it is a true commandment, for ye, for his sake, love one another truly also. And by the reason of this renewing it is called a new commandment, as it is now called a new learning, and may well so be; for it hath lien long in darkness, and that in such darkness, that many be shrined for holy saints, whose deeds and living (when thou lookest upon them in the light of this old doctrine that now shineth again out of darkness) are more abominable than the deeds and living of him [63] which of late, for all his exalting his throne and swearing by his high honour, and for all the worships of his hat and glory of his precious shoes, when he was pained with the colic of an evil conscience, having no nother shift, because his soul could find in nother issue, took himself a medicine, *ut emitteret spiritum per posteriora.*

9. *He that saith he is in the light, and yet hateth his brother, is in darkness.*

For whosoever feeleth his own damnation under the law, and believeth in the mercy that is in Christ, the same cannot but love Christ, and his neighbour for his sake. And therefore he that hateth his brother for any offence done to him, the same seeth not what Christ hath done for him, but is in darkness still.

10. *He that loveth his brother, abideth in the light, and there is none offending in him.*

Abideth in the light; that is, continueth in the knowledge of Christ. *And there is none offending in him;* that is, first, he will willingly do nothing, either in word or in deed, that shall offend his brother: for love will not let him. And secondarily, if aught be done or said, that may be well done or said, he taketh it to the best, and is not offended. And thus ye see that the knowledge of Christ is cause of all goodness, and the ignorance of Christ cause of all evil. And so the doctrine of them is not false, which say that

[63] Cardinal Wolsey.

faith in Christ is root of all godly virtue and the cause of keeping the commandments; and where faith is, there to be no sin nor damnation; and that say unbelief to be the mother of all vice, and cause of breaking the commandments, and to keep men in sin and damnation only, as faith only looseth us thence.

11. And he that hateth [64] his brother is in darkness; and walketh in darkness, and knoweth not whither he goeth: for darkness hath blinded his eyes.

He that hateth his brother is in the ignorance of Christ and of his own sin, and without repentance and faith that his sins be forgiven him in Christ; and therefore is merciless unto his brother, whom Christ commandeth him to pity and love.

And in that ignorance *he walketh,* that is, worketh evil, and loveth the things of the world, and seeketh in them the lusts of the flesh, which are the quenching of the Spirit and death of the soul, and for love of them hateth his brother. And this ignorance of Christ, which is unbelief, is the cause of all the wickedness that we do unto our brethren.

12. I write unto you, little children, that your sins are forgiven you for his name's sake. I write unto you, fathers, that ye know him that was from the beginning. I write unto you, young men, how that ye have overcome the wicked.

I write unto you, that are young in the faith and yet weak, and therefore fall now and then, *how that your sins are forgiven you,* as soon as ye repent and reconcile yourselves unto your brethren whom ye have offended, even for his name's sake only, and not for our own deeds, whether afore or after, or for any other man's deeds or satisfaction, save for his only.

I write unto you, that are fathers in the doctrine of God, to teach other *how that ye know him that was from the beginning,* and is no new thing, though he newly received our nature. And through knowledge of him which is the only light, and the door unto the knowledge of God, ye are become fathers in the scriptures. . . .

I write unto you, young men, that are strong in suffering persecutions, and fight for your profession, not with the sword, but with suffering, *how that ye have overcome that wicked* which poisoned the world at the beginning, and yet worketh in the children of

---

[64] 1534 Note: He that hateth is in darkness and knoweth not what Christ hath done for him; but he that loveth is in light and wotteth what Christ hath done.

darkness and unbelief; and that in believing the word of truth, as it followeth anon after.

13. I write unto you, young children, how that ye know the Father. 14. I write unto you, fathers, how that ye know him that was from the beginning. I write unto you, young men, that ye be strong, and the word of God dwelleth in you, and that ye have overcome the wicked.

I write unto you, young children, how that ye know the Father, whom ye love through knowledge of the Son; or else ye had never known him as a Father, but as a judge and a tyrant, and had hated him.

I write unto you, fathers, as before, how ye are fathers of all truth, in knowing the Son: or else ye had ever continued in darkness remediless.

I write unto you, young men, how that ye are strong, and that your strength is the word of God, which dwelleth in your breast through faith, in which ye have overcome the wicked devil, and all his pomps; as it followeth in the v. chapter: "This is the victory that overcometh the world, even our faith." [65]

15. Love not the world, nor the things that are in the world. If a man love the world, the love of the Father is not in him.[66] *16. For all that is in the world, as the lust of the flesh, the lust of the eyes, and the pride of good, are not of the Father, but are of the world. 17. And the world vanisheth away, and the lust thereof: but he that doeth the will of God abideth ever.*

The love of the world quencheth the love of God. Balaam,[67] for the love of the world, closed his eyes at the clear light which he well saw. For love of the world the old Pharisees blasphemed the Holy Ghost, and persecuted the manifest truth, which they could not improve. For love of the world many are this day fallen away; and many which stood on the truth's side, and defended it awhile, for love of the world have gotten them unto the contrary part, and are become the pope's mamelukes,[68] and are waxed the most wicked enemies unto the truth, and most cruel against it. . . .

By the lust of the flesh is understood lechery, which maketh a man altogether a swine. And by the lust of the eyes is understood covetousness, which is the root of all evil, and maketh to err from

---

[65] I John 5:4.
[66] 1534 Note: He that loveth the world loveth not God.
[67] Num., chs. 22 f.
[68] Fighting slaves.

the faith, i. Timoth. the last.[69] And then followeth *pride*. Which iii. are the world, and captains over all other vices, and occasions of all mischief. . . .

18. Little children, it is now the last hour: and as ye have heard that antichrist should come, even so now are many antichrists come already; whereby we know that it is the last hour. 19. They went out of us, but were none of us; for had they been of us, they had continued with us. But that fortuned that it might appear, how they were not all of us.

Hour is here taken for time; *the last hour* is as much to say as "the last time." Though the apostles might not know when the last day shall be, and how long the world should endure, yet this was shewed them, and us by them, that antichrist should first come; and not only come, but also prevail, and be received after a worldly manner, and reign over all; and set up a long-continuing kingdom, with damnable sects and wonderful kinds of hypocrisy, that is to say, falsehood cloaked under a contrary pretence, as testifieth Paul and also Peter. Which antichrist began with the apostles, and sue [70] his doctrine among the doctrine of the apostles; preaching many things as the apostles did, and adding ever somewhat of his own, that the weeds might ever grow up together with the corn. Of which John gathered a sign, that the last day drew nigh; though he could not be sure how long it were thereto.

Antichrist is one of the first that seeth the light, and cometh and preacheth Christ awhile, and seeketh his glory in Christ's Gospel. But when he espieth that there will be no glory cleave unto that preaching, then he getteth him to the contrary party, and professeth himself an open enemy, if he cannot disguise himself, and hide the angle [71] of his poisoned heresy under a bait of true doctrine.

The apostles were clear-eyed, and espied antichrist at once, and put him to flight, and weeded out his doctrine quickly. But when charity waxed cold, and the preachers began to seek themselves, and to admit glory and honour of riches; then antichrist disguised himself after the fashion of a true apostle, and preached Christ wilily, bringing in now this tradition, and now that, to darken the doctrine of Christ; and set up innumerable ceremonies, and sacraments, and imagery, giving them significations at the first; but at the last, the significations laid apart, preached the work as an holy deed, to justify and to put away sin, and to save the soul, that men should put their trust in works, and in whatsoever was unto his glory and profit; and under the name of Christ ministered Christ

[69] I Tim. 6:10.   [70] Sowed.   [71] Fishhook.

out of altogether,[72] and became head of the congregation himself. . . .

20. *But ye have ⟨an⟩ anointing*[73] *of that holy, and know all thing. 21. I write not unto you as though he knew not the truth, but as unto them that know it, and how that no lie is of truth.*

Christ in the scripture is called *The Holy;* because he only sanctifieth and halloweth us. And he is called "Christ," that is to say, anointed; because he anointeth our souls with the Holy Ghost, and with all the gifts of the same. Ye are not anointed with oil in your bodies, but with the Spirit of Christ in your souls: which Spirit teacheth you all truth in Christ, and maketh you to judge what is a lie, and what truth, and to know Christ from antichrist. For except he taught your souls within, the pouring in of words at your ears were in vain. For "they must be all taught of God," John vi.,[74] and, "the things of God no man knoweth, save the Spirit of God; and the carnal man knoweth not the things of the Spirit of God";[75] when contrary, "the spiritual (that is anointed with the Spirit) judgeth all things," i. Cor. i.[76] And therefore we are forboden to call us any master upon earth. Matt. xxiii.,[77] seeing we have all one master now in heaven, which only teacheth us with his Spirit, though by the administration and office of a faithful preacher: which preacher yet cannot make his preaching spring in the heart, no more than a sower can make his corn grow, nor can say, "This man shall receive, and this not"; but soweth the word only, and committeth the growing to God, whose Spirit breatheth where he listeth, and maketh the ground of whose heart he lusteth fruitful, and chooseth whom he will at his own pleasure, and for no other cause known unto any man.

22. *Who is a liar, but he that denieth that Jesus is Christ? The same is antichrist, that denieth the Father and the Son.*

"Forasmuch as antichrist and Christ are two contraries, and the study of antichrist is to quench the name of Christ, how can the pope and his sects be antichrist, when they all preach Christ?" "How was," say I again to thee, "Pelagius, whose doctrine the

---

[72] Completely engineered Christ out of the Church.
[73] 1531: *an oynting.*
  1534 Note: Oyntment: that is, knowledge of the truth and all the gifts of the spirit.
[74] John 6:45.
[75] I Cor. 2:11.
[76] I Cor. 2:15.
[77] Matt. 23:8 ff.

pope defendeth in the highest degree, antichrist, and all other heretics?" Verily, sir, the pope seeketh himself, as all heretics did; and abuseth the name of Christ, to gather offerings, tithes and rents in his name, to bestow them unto his own honour and not Christ's, and to bring the conscience of the people into captivity under him through superstitious fear, as though he had such authority given him of Christ. And every syllable, that hath a sound as though it made for his purpose, that he expoundeth falsely and fleshly; and therewith juggleth and bewitcheth the ears of the people, and maketh them his own possession, to believe what him listeth, as though it made no matter to them whether he preached true or false, so they believe and do as he biddeth them. But all the texts that shew his duty to do, he putteth out of the way; and all the texts thereto, that set the consciences at liberty in Christ, and prove our salvation to be in Christ only. And, with Pelagius, he preacheth the justifying of works; which is the denying of Christ. He preacheth a false binding and loosing with ear-confession, which is not in the trust and confidence of Christ's blood-shedding. He preacheth the false penance of deeds; not to tame the flesh that we sin no more, but to make satisfaction, and to redeem the sin that is past: which what other can it be, save the denying of Christ, which is ⟨the⟩ only redemption of sin? He maketh of the works of the ceremonies, which were wont to be signs and remembrances of things to be believed or done, image-service unto God and his saints which are spirits, to purchase with the merits of them whatsoever the blind soul imagineth; which all are the denying of Christ. For if thou wilt receive any anointing of grace or mercy any whence, save of him, he is no longer Christ unto thee. Christ is called Jesus, a Saviour; he is called Christus, king anointed over all men, of whom they must hold, and whose benefit must all they have be.[78] He is called Emmanuel, God is with us: for he only maketh God our God, our strength, power, sword and shield, and, shortly, our Father. He is called Sanctus, that is, holy, that halloweth, sanctifieth and blesseth all nations. And these be his names for ever, and be no names of hypocrisy. . . .

Nay, Christ is no hypocrite, or disguised, that playeth a part in a play, and representeth a person, or state, which he is not; but is alway that his name signifieth. He is ever a Saver, and ever anointeth with grace, and ever maketh God with us, and ever sanctifieth. Neither is there any other to save and sanctify from sin, or anoint with grace, or to set God at one with men. And these things, which his name signify, doth he ever unto all that have trust and confi-

[78] All they have is of his benefit or blessing.

dence in his blood, as soon as they repent of the sin which they desire to be saved and sanctified from.

Now though the pope and his sects give Christ these names, yet in that they rob him of the effect, and take the significations of his names unto themselves, and make of him but an hypocrite, as they themselves be, they be right antichrists, and deny both the Father and Son. For they deny the witness that the Father bare unto his Son, and deprive the Son of all the power and glory that his Father gave him.

23. Whosoever denieth the Son, the same hath not the Father. "For no man knoweth the Father, but the Son, and to whom the Son sheweth him," Matt. xi.[79] Moreover, if thou know not the mercy that God hath shewed thee in Christ, thou canst not know him as a Father. Thou mayest well, besides [80] Christ, know him as a tyrant. And thou mayest know him by his works, as the old philosophers did, that there is a God; but thou canst neither believe in his mercy, nor love his laws, which is his only worship in the spirit, save by Christ.

24. Let therefore abide in you that which ye heard at the beginning. If that which ye heard at the beginning shall remain in you, then shall ye continue in the Son, and in the Father. 25. And this is the promise that he hath promised us, everlasting life.

If we abide in the old doctrine which the apostles taught, and hearken to no new, then abide we in the Son (for upon the Son build they us), and in the Father through confidence in the Son; and are heirs of everlasting life.

26. These things have I written unto you, because of them that deceive you. 27. And the anointing that ye received of him dwelleth in you, and ye need not that any man teach you; but as that anointing teacheth you of all things and is true, and is no lie, even as it hath taught you, so abide therein.

When a true preacher preacheth, the Spirit entereth the hearts of the elect, and maketh them feel the righteousness of the law of God, and by the law the poison of their corrupt nature; and thence leadeth them, through repentance, unto the mercy that is in Christ's blood; and as an ointment healeth the body, even so the Spirit, through confidence and trust in Christ's blood, healeth the soul, and maketh her [81] love the law of God; and therefore is it

---

[79] Matt. 11:27.
[80] Apart from.
[81] *Her* because *soul* is feminine in Latin.

called anointing or an ointment, and may well be signified by the oil of our sacrament.[82] But outward oil can neither heal the soul, nor make her feel, save as a sign, or as a bush at a tavern door quencheth a man's thirst, neither is it a thing to put trust in. Let us therefore follow the teaching of the Spirit; which we have received (as Paul saith [83]) in earnest, to certify our hearts, and to make us feel the things of God, and not cleave unto the traditions of men; in which is no feeling, but that one saith so, and another thus, confirming their assertions with glorious persuasions of wisdom, but not after the wisdom of God: which reasons another denieth with contrary sophisms; and so riseth brawling about vain words, without all [84] certainty.

28. And now, little children, abide in him, that when he shall appear, we may have confidence, and not be made ashamed of him at his coming.[85]

Here are ii. things to be marked: one, if we cleave unto Christ after the doctrine of the apostles, and as they built us upon him, we shall be bold and sure of ourselves at his coming; as a servant, which in his master's absence doth only his master's commandments, cannot be confounded at his coming home again. But and if we follow men's doctrine, how can we be bold, yea, how should we not be ashamed with our teachers, unto whom then he shall say (when they boast themselves how that they have been his vicars), "I know you not; depart from me, ye that have wrought wickedness, and under my name have brought in damnable sects, and have taught your disciples to believe in other things than in me."

Now the sum of all that the apostles taught, and how they built us upon Christ, is the New Testament. But the pope's doctrine is not there found, but improved. Confounded therefore shall he be, which, witting and willing, shutteth his eyes at the true light, and openeth them to believe his lies.

Another thing is this: all the scripture maketh mention of the resurrection and coming again of Christ, and that all men, both they that go before, and they that come after, shall then receive their rewards together; and we are commanded to look every hour for that day. And what is done with the souls from the departing their bodies unto that day, doth the scripture make no mention,

[82] I.e., the subsidiary rite of anointing in baptism.
[83] II Cor. 1:22.
[84] Any.
[85] 1534 Note: Here ye see that Christ and sin cannot dwell together, for Christ's Spirit fighteth against sin.

save only that they rest in the Lord, and in their faith. Wherefore he that determineth aught of the state of them that be departed, doth but teach the presumptuous imaginations of his own brain; neither can his doctrine be any article of our faith. What God doth with them is a secret laid up in the treasury of God: and we ought to be patient, being certified of the scripture, that they which die in the faith are at rest, and ought no more to search that secret, than to search the hour of the resurrection, which God hath put only in his own power. But this remember, that the whole nature of man is poisoned and infect with sin. And the whole life of sin must be mortified. And the root of all sin, and first vice that we were infect with, is, that we would be wise where God hath not taught us; as ye see how Eve would have been as God, in the knowledge of good and bad. And therefore hath God hid many things in his power; and commanded that we shall search none of his secrets further than he hath opened them in his scripture, to mortify this poison of all poisons, the desire to appear wise, and that we be ashamed to be ignorant in any thing at all. Wherefore they that violently make articles of the faith, without God's word, are yet alive in the root of all sin and vice, and grow out of the devil, and not out of Christ. And their articles are of the blindness of the devil, and not of the light of Christ; for Christ's light hath testimony of the scripture everywhere.

29. If ye know that he is righteous, know that all that work righteousness are born of him.

Our nature is to work wickedness, and so blind thereto that it can see no righteousness. And then it followeth that we must be born anew in Christ, ere we can either do or yet know what is righteous. And in him we must first be made righteous ourselves, ere we can work righteous works; which conclusion is contrary unto the pope: for he saith, that the works do make the man righteous; and Christ's doctrine saith, that the man maketh the works righteous. A righteous man springeth out of righteous works, saith the pope's doctrine. Righteous works spring out of a righteous man, and a righteous man springeth out of Christ, saith Christ's doctrine. The works make the man righteous, which before was wicked, saith the pope. The works declare that the man is righteous, saith Christ's doctrine; but the man was first made righteous in Christ; and the Spirit of Christ taught him what righteousness was, and healed his heart, and made him consent thereto, and to have his lust in righteousness, and to work righteously.

Chapter III

1. Behold what love the Father hath shewed us, that we should be called the sons of God. For this cause the world knoweth you not, because it knoweth not him. 2. Dearly beloved, now we are the sons of God, though yet it appeareth not what we shall be: but we know that when he shall appear we shall be like him; for we shall see him as he is.

The love of God to us-ward is exceeding great, in that he hath made us his sons, without all deserving of us; and hath given us his Spirit through Christ, to certify our hearts thereof, in that we feel that our trust is in God, and that our souls have received health and power to love the law of God; which is a sure testimony that we are sons, and under no damnation. Neither ought it to discourage us, or to make us think we were less beloved, because the world hateth us, and persecuteth us; for the world knoweth us not. Neither any marvel; for the world could not know Christ himself, for all his glorious coming with miracles and benefits, in healing the sick and raising the dead. But for all the oppression of the world, we are yet sure that we are God's sons. And in like manner, though the glory that we shall be in, appear not, yet we are sure that we shall be like him, when he appeareth. As darkness vanisheth away at the coming of the sun, and the world receiveth a new fashion, and is turned into light, and suddenly made glorious; even so when he appeareth, and we shall see him as he is, we shall, with the sight of him, be changed into the glory of his image, and made like him. And then shall the world know both him and us, unto their shame and confusion.

3. And all that have this hope in him purge themselves as he is pure.

The faith and hope of a christian man are no dead, idle, or barren things; but lively, working, and fruitful. For when the law through conscience of sin hath slain the soul, then hope and trust in Christ's blood, through certifying of the conscience that the damnation of the law is taken away, quickeneth her again; and make her to love the law, which is the purifying of the soul, and her life, and serving the law in the inner man. And then the said gifts of hope and faith, stretch themselves forth unto the members, dead with natural lust, consent, and custom to sin; and quicken them, and purgeth them with the wholesome penance of Christ's doctrine; and make them serve the law outward, and bear wholesome fruit of love unto the profit of their neighbours, according to Christ's love unto us. For if the Spirit of Christ, with which God anointeth us and maketh us kings, and sealeth us and maketh us his sure and several kingdom, and which he giveth us in earnest, ii. Cor. i.,[86] and with which he changeth us into the image of Christ, ii. Cor. iii.,[87] dwell in our souls through faith, the same Spirit cannot but quicken the members also, and make them fruitful, Rom. viii.[88]. . .

4. All that commit sin commit unrighteousness; for sin is unrighteousness.[89]

That the English calleth here *unrighteousness*, the Greek calleth *anomia*, unlawfulness or breaking the law. So that all sin is breaking of God's law, and only the transgression of God's law is sin. Now all God's laws are contained in these two points; believe in Christ, and love thy neighbour. And these two points are the interpreting and expounding of all laws: so that whatsoever edifieth in faith and love, is to be kept as long as it so doth; and whatsoever hurteth faith or love, is to be broken immediately, though king, emperor, pope, or an angel command it. And all indifferent things, that neither help nor hurt faith and love, are whole [90] in the hands of father, mother, master, lord and prince. So that if they will sin against God, and overlade our backs, we may well run away, if we can escape; but not avenge ourselves. But and if they will break into thy conscience, as the pope doth with his dumb traditions, and saith, "To do this saveth thy soul, and to leave it undone loseth thy soul"; then defy them as the works of antichrist, for they make thee sin against the faith that is in Christ's blood, by which only thy soul is saved, and for lack of that only damned.

And how love breaketh the law, take an ensample. It is a good law that men come to the church on the Sundays, to hear God's word, and to receive the sacrament of the body and blood of Christ, in remembrance of his benefits, and so to strengthen thy soul for to walk in his love, and in the love of our neighbour for his sake, &c.; yet if my father, mother, or any other that requireth my help be sick, I break that good commandment, to do my duty to my elders or my neighbour. And thus all laws are under love, and give

---
[86] II Cor. 1:22.
[87] II Cor. 3:18.
[88] Rom. 8:12 ff.
[89] 1534 Note: He that worketh righteousness is born of God and taught of his Spirit.
[90] Completely.

room to love. And love interpreteth them, yea and breaketh them at a time, though God himself command them. For love is lord over all laws.

5. *And ye know that he appeared to take away our sins; and there is no sin in him.*

Christ died not alone to purchase pardon for our fore-sins, but also to slay all sin and the life of sin in our members. For all we that are baptized in the name of Christ, saith Paul,[91] Rom. vi., are baptized to die with him concerning sin; and that as he after his resurrection dieth no more, so we after our baptism should walk in a new life, and sin no more. Our members are crucified with him, in all that pertaineth unto the life of sin. And if in Christ be no sin, then how can there be wilful sin in the faith that is in him, or in the quick members, that through faith grow out of him? Every man therefore that hath the true faith of Christ, purgeth himself, as he is pure.

6. *All that abide in him sin not. And all that sin have neither seen him nor known him.*

As there is no sin in Christ the stock, so can there be none in the quick members, that live and grow in him by faith. And they that give themselves to sin, have neither seen, known, or felt by faith, the mercy that is in him. . . .

7. *Little children, let no man beguile you. He that worketh righteousness is righteous, as he is righteous.*

Judge men by their deeds. For whosoever hath the light of God in his soul, he will let his light shine, that men shall see his good works. And therefore where ye see not the righteousness of works in the members outward, there, be sure, is no righteousness of faith in the heart inward. Let no man mock you with vain words. Whosoever preacheth the Christ in word and deed, him take for Christ's vicar. . . .

8. *He that sinneth is of the devil, for the devil sinneth from the beginning.*[92] *But for this cause appeared the Son of God, even to destroy the works of the devil. 9. All that are born of God do no sin, for his seed abideth in them* [93] *and they cannot sin, because they be born of God. 10. And hereby are the sons of God known, and also the sons of the devil.*

[91] Rom. 6:3 f.
[92] 1534 Note: Joh. 8 f.
[93] 1534 Note: Seed, that is, the holy Ghost.

God and the devil are two contrary fathers, two contrary fountains, and two contrary causes; the one of all goodness, the other of all evil. And they that do evil are born of the devil, and first evil by that birth ere they do evil. . . .

And on the other side, they that do good are first born of God, and receive of his nature and seed; and, by the reason of that nature and seed, are first good ere they do good, by the same rule. And Christ, which is contrary to the devil, came to destroy the works of the devil in us, and to give us a new birth, a new nature, and to sow new seed in us, that we should, by the reason of that birth, sin no more. For the seed of that birth, that is to wit the Spirit of God and the lively seed of his word sown in our hearts, keepeth our hearts, that we cannot consent to sin; as the seed of the devil holdeth the hearts of his, that they cannot consent to good. . . .

And finally, there is great difference between the sin of them that believe in Christ unfeignedly and the sin of them that believe not. For they that believe not, sin [94] of purpose and of consent to wickedness, that it is good, casting and compassing aforehand without grudge of conscience, to bring their purpose about—as ye see our hypocrites have vexed all Christendom this xx. years to bring a little lust to effect. Their fathers conceived mischieve viii. hundred years ago; and the sons consent unto the same and have no power to depart therefrom. And therefore their sin is devilish and under the damnation of the law. But if he that believeth sin, he doth it not of purpose or that he consenteth unto the life of sin, but of infirmity, chance, and some great temptation that hath overcome him. And therefore his sin is venial, and under mercy and grace, though it be murder, theft, or adultery; and not under the damnation of the law. So that his Father shall scourge him, but not cast him away, or damn him. . . .

10. All that work not righteousness are not of God; nor he that loveth not his brother. 11. For this is the tidings which ye heard at the beginning, that we should love [95] one another, 12. and not be as Cain, which was of the devil and slew his brother. And wherefore slew he him? For his deeds were evil, and his brother's righteous. 13. Marvel not my brethren though the world hate you.

The law of righteousness is, that we love one another as Christ loved us; and he that hath not this love living in his heart, and,

---

[94] 1531: *believe, sin not of purpose . . .* But the sense of the whole sentence demands a correction.
[95] 1534 Note: Love is the first precept, and cause of all other.

when the time is, bringeth not forth the fruits thereof, the same is not of God, but of the devil; whose birth and properties of the same ye see described in Cain, how he resisted God, and persecuted the children of God for their belief and works thereof. And as ye see in Cain and his brother Abel, so shall it ever continue, between the children of God and of the devil, unto the world's end. Wonder not therefore, though the world hate you.

14. We know that we are translated from death [96] to life, because we love the brethren. He that loveth not his brother abideth in death. 15. All that hate their brethren are murderers; and ye know that no murderer hath eternal life abiding in him.

If thou love thy brother in Christ, and art ready to do and to suffer for him, as Christ did for thee, then thou art sure thereby, that thou art the son of God, and heir of life, and delivered from death and damnation. So have Christian men signs, to know whether they be in the state of grace or no. And on the other side, he that hath no power to love his brethren, may be sure that he is in the state of death and damnation. Another is this: let every man look upon his heart, and be sure that he which hateth his brother hath slain him before God, and is a murderer. And murderers shall not obtain the kingdom of God, Gala. v.,[97] but are Cain's brethren and the devil's children, and are heirs of death, and ever under damnation. Compare the regiment of the spiritualty, which have had the temporal sword in their hands now above viii. hundred years, unto this doctrine of John, and judge whether they have led us truly after the steps of Christ's doctrine, or no.

16. Hereby we are assured of love, because he left his life for us; and therefore ought we to leave our lives for our brethren. 17. He then that hath the substance of the world, and seeth his brother have need, and shutteth up his compassion [98] from him, how dwelleth the love of God in him?

If we felt the love of Christ's death, it would sure set our heart on fire to love him again, and our brethren for his sake, and should never cease to slay our resisting members, until we could not only be well content that our brethren were in a more prosperous state than we, but also until we could bless them when they curse us, and pray for them when they persecute us, and to suffer death for

---

[96] 1534 Note: He that loveth is escaped death. He that loveth not is in death and a murtherer and hath not eternal life.
[97] Gal. 5:19–21, where, however, murder is not explicitly named.
[98] 1534 Note: He that hath no compassion loveth not God.

them, to testify the word of their soul's health unto them, and with love to overcome them, and to win them unto Christ. If now every christian man ought to have this rule of his profession before his eyes to learn it, that he should love his brother as Christ did him, to depart with his life for his brother's ensample, how far are they off from good scholars, that cannot find in their hearts to depart with a little of the abundance and superfluity of their temporal goods, to help their neighbour's need?

18. My little children, let us not love in word, nor with the tongue; but with the deed, and of a truth. 19. For thereby[99] *we know that we be of the truth, and so shall we certify our hearts in his sight.*

If we have power to work, then doth the work certify our hearts that our faith in Christ, and love to God and our neighbour for his sake, are unfeigned; and that we are true children, and no hypocrites. And then are we bold in our conscience before God. . . . For the sight of the work doth certify us that God hath called us and chosen us unto grace and mercy.

But and if, when the time of working is come, I flee and have no power to work, then will our conscience accuse us of sin and transgression within the heart before God; and so, for fear of the rod, we dare not be bold, but draw back and stand aloof. . . .

20. But if our hearts condemn us, God is greater than our heart, and knoweth all thing.

If our conscience accuse us of sin, God is so great and so mighty that it cannot be hid.

21. Dearly beloved, if our hearts condemn us not, then we trust to God-ward. 22. And whatsoever we ask, that shall we receive of him;[1] *because we keep his commandments, and do the things which are pleasant in his sight.*

Keeping of the commandments maketh a man see his faith, and to be bold therein. And faith, when it is without conscience of sin, goeth in to God boldly; and is strong and mighty in prayer to conjure God by all his mercies, and therewith obtaineth whatsoever he asketh of all his promises. And the text saith, because we keep his commandments. Yea, verily his commandments make us bold. But

---

[99] 1534 Note: By love we know that we are in the truth and have quiet consciences to Godward.

[1] 1534 Note: He that keepeth himself from sin is strong in the faith and obtaineth all that he prayeth for.

the keeping of men's traditions and dumb ceremonies make us not bold before God, nor certify our conscience that our faith is unfeigned. . . .

23. And this is his commandment, That we believe [2] in his Son Jesus Christ, and love one another, as he gave commandment.

Faith is the first, and also the root, of all commandments: and out of faith springeth love; and out of love, works. And when I break any commandment, I sin against love. For had I loved, I had not done it. And when I sin against love, I sin against faith. For had I earnestly, and with a full trust, remembered the mercy that Christ hath shewed me, I must have loved. Wherefore when we have broken any commandment, there is no other way to be restored again, than to go through repentance unto our faith again, and ask mercy for Christ's sake. And as soon as we have received faith that our sin is forgiven, we shall immediately love the commandment again, and through love receive power to work.

24. And he that keepeth his commandments abideth in him, and he in him. And hereby we know that there dwelleth in us of his Spirit which he gave us.

Through the works we are sure that we continue in Christ, and Christ in us; and that his Spirit dwelleth in us. For his Spirit it is that keepeth us in faith, and through faith in love, and through love in works.

Chapter IV

1. Dearly beloved, believe not every spirit, but prove the spirits whether they be of God. For many false prophets are gone out in the world.

Spirits are taken here for preachers, because of the preaching or doctrine, which, if it be good, is of the Spirit of God; and if it be evil, of the spirit of the devil. Now ought we not to believe every man's doctrine unadvisedly, or condemn any man's preaching ere it be heard and seen what it is. But a Christian man's part is to examine, judge and try it, whether it be true or no. "Quench not the Spirit," saith Paul, i. Thessalo. the last,[3] "neither despise prophesyings; but prove all things, and keep that which is good." De-

---

[2] 1534 Note: Faith is the first commandment, and love the second, and he that hath them is in God and hath his Spirit.
[3] I Thess. 5:19.

stroy not the gifts of the Spirit of God; but try whether they be of God, and good for the edifying of his congregation: and keep that which is good, and refuse that which is evil. And suffer every person that hath any gift of God to serve God therein, in his degree and estate, after a Christian manner and a due order. Why shall we try the doctrines? Verily, for there be many false prophets abroad already. . . . Wherewith shall we try it? With the doctrine of the apostles, and with the scripture, which is the twitchstone: [4] yea, and because ye love compendiousness, ye shall have a short rule to try them withal.

2. *Hereby know ye the Spirit of God. Every spirit that confesseth that Jesus Christ is come in the flesh, is of God. 3. And every spirit that confesseth not that Jesus Christ is come in the flesh, is not of God.*[5] *And the same is that spirit of antichrist, of whom ye have heard that he should come; and even now he is in the world already.*

Whatsoever opinion any member of antichrist holdeth, the ground of all his doctrine is, to destroy this article of our faith, that Christ is come in the flesh. For though the most part of all heretics confess that Christ is come in the flesh, after their manner, yet they deny that he is come as the scripture testifieth, and the apostles preached him to be come. The whole study of the devil and all his members is to destroy the hope and trust that we should have in Christ's flesh, and in those things which he suffered for us in his flesh, and in the testament and promises of mercy which are made us in his flesh. For the scripture testifieth that Christ hath taken away the sin of the world in his flesh; and that the same hour that he yielded up his spirit into the hands of his Father, he had full purged, and made full satisfaction for all the sins of the world: so that all the sin of the world, both before his passion and after, must be put away through repentance toward the law, and faith and trust in his blood, without respect of any other satisfaction, sacrifice, or work. For if I once sin, the law rebuketh my conscience, and setteth variance between God and me: and I shall never be at peace with God again, until I have heard the voice of his mouth, how that my sin is forgiven me for Christ's blood sake. And as soon as I that believe, I am at peace with God, Roma. v.,[6] and love his law again, and of love work. . . .

---

[4] Touchstone.
[5] 1534 Note: They that say works justify from sin are they that deny Christ to be come in the flesh.
[6] Rom. 5:1.

4. Ye are of God, little children, and have overcome them. For greater is he that is in you than he that is in the world.

He that dwelleth in you, and worketh in you through faith, is greater than he which dwelleth and worketh in them through unbelief. And in his strength ye abide by your profession, and confess your Lord Jesus, how that he is come in the flesh and hath purged the sin of all that believe in his flesh. . . .

5. They be of the world, and therefore they speak of the world, and the world attendeth unto them. 6. We be of God, and he that knoweth God heareth us; and he that is not of God heareth us not. And hereby we know the spirit of truth, and the spirit of error.

There be, and ever shall be, ii. generations in the world: one of the devil, which naturally hearken unto the false apostles of the devil, because they speak so agreeable unto their natural complexion; and another of God, which hearken unto the true apostles of God, and consent unto their doctrine. And this is a sure rule to judge spirits withal; that we judge them to have the spirit of truth which hearken unto the true doctrine of Christ's apostles, and them to have the spirit of error, which hearken unto worldly and devilish doctrine, abhorring the preaching of the apostles. . . .

7. Dearly beloved, let us love one another; for love is of God: and all that love are born of God, and know God. 8. And he that loveth not, knoweth not God; for God is love.

John singeth his old song again, and teacheth an infallible and sure token, which we may see and feel at our fingers' ends, and thereby be out of all doubt, that our faith is unfeigned, and that we know God, and be born of God, and that we hearken unto the doctrine of the apostles purely and godly, and not of any curiosity, to seek glory and honour therein unto ourselves, and to make a cloak thereof to cover our covetousness and filthy lusts. Which token is, if we love one another. For the love of a man's neighbour unfeignedly springeth out of the unfeigned knowledge of God in Christ's blood: by which knowledge we be born of God, and love God and our neighbours for his sake. And so he that loveth his neighbour unfeignedly is sure of himself, that he knoweth God, and is of God unfeignedly: and contrariwise, he that loveth not, knoweth not God. For God in Christ's blood is such a love, that if a man saw it, it were impossible that he should not break out into the love of God again, and of his neighbour for his sake.

9. Herein appeared the love of God unto us-ward, because God sent his only Son into the world, that we should live through him. 10. Herein is love, not that we loved God, but that he loved us, and sent his Son a satisfaction for our sins.[7]

If a man had once felt within in his conscience the fierce wrath of God toward sinners, and the terrible and most cruel damnation that the law threateneth; and then beheld with the eyes of a strong faith the mercy, favour and grace, the taking away of the damnation of the law, and restoring again of life, freely offered us in Christ's blood, he should perceive love, and so much the more, that it was shewed us when we were sinners and enemies to God, Roma. v.,[8] and that without all deservings, without our endeavouring, enforcing and preparing ourselves, and without all good motions, qualities and properties of our freewill; but when our hearts were as dead unto all good working as the members of him whose soul is departed. . . . The text is plain: we were stone dead, and without life or power to do or consent to good. The whole nature of us was captive under the devil, and led at his will. And we were as wicked as the devil now is (except that he now sinneth against the Holy Ghost), and we consented unto sin with soul and body, and hated the law of God. But God, of his grace only, quickened us in Christ; and raised us out of that death, and made us sit with Christ in heavenly things: that is, he set our hearts at rest, and made us sit fast in the life of Christ's doctrine, and unmoveable from the love of Christ. And finally we are, in this our second birth, God's workmanship and creation in Christ; so that, as he which is yet unmade hath no life nor power to work, no more had we, till we were made again in Christ.[9] The preaching of mercy in Christ quickened our hearts through faith wrought by the Spirit of Christ, which God poured into our hearts, ere we wist.

11. Dearly beloved, if God so loved us, then ought we to love one another.[10]

If we felt the love of God in Christ's blood, we could not but love again, not only God and Christ, but also all that are bought with Christ's blood. If we love God for the pleasures that we receive, then love we ourselves. But if we love him to do him pleasure again, that can we no otherwise do, than in loving our neigh-

---

[7] 1534 Note: God hath shewed us a token of love.
[8] Rom. 5:8 ff.
[9] Eph. 2:4 ff.
[10] 1534 Note: Love is commanded.

bours for his sake: them that are good, to continue them in their goodness, and them that are evil, to draw them to good. Love is the instrument wherewith faith maketh us God's sons, and fashioneth us like the image of God, and certifieth us that we so are. . . .

12. No man hath at any time seen God. If we love one another, God dwelleth in us, and his love is perfect in us.

Though we cannot see God, yet if we love one another, we be sure that he abideth in us, and that his love is perfect in us; that is, that we love him unfeignedly. For to love God truly, and to give him thanks, is only to love our neighbour for his sake: for upon his person thou canst bestow no benefit. And forasmuch as we never saw God, let us make no image of him, nor do him any image-service after our own imagination; but let us go to the scripture, that hath seen him, and there wete what fashion he is of, and what service he will be served with. Blind reason saith God is a carved post, and will be served with a candle: but scripture saith God is love, and will be served with love. If thou love thy neighbour, then art thou the image of God thyself; and he dwelleth in the living temple of thine heart. And thy loving of thy neighbour for his sake is his service and worship in the spirit, and a candle that burneth before him in thine heart, and casteth out the light of good works before the world, and draweth all to God, and maketh his enemies leave their evil and come and worship him also.

13. Hereby we know that we abide in him, and he in us. For he hath given us of his Spirit.

He that hath not Christ's Spirit, the same is none of his, Roma. viii.[10a] If we have the Spirit of God, then are we sure. But how shall we know whether we have the Spirit? Ask John, and he will say, "If we love one another."

14. And we have seen and do testify, that the Father hath sent his Son, the Saviour of the world. 15. Whosoever confesseth that Jesus is the Son of God, in him dwelleth God, and he in God. 16. And we have known and believed the love that God hath to us.

First, the apostles taught no fables, but that they saw and received of God by the witness of his Spirit. Secondarily, John ascendeth up one step higher, from love to faith; and saith, "He that believeth that Jesus is God's Son, hath God in him." And I doubt not but the pope and his defenders will answer John, and say, "Then the devil hath God in him, and is also in God": for

[10a] Rom. 8:9.

other faith, than such as the devil hath, felt they never any. But John preventeth them: "We have known and believed the love that God hath to us": that is, we believe not only with story faith, as men believe old chronicles, but we believe the love and mercy that God shewed us, and put our trust and confidence therein (and so taketh scripture belief) : we believe that Jesus is the Son of God, made man and slain for our sins, which is a token of great love. And that love believe we, and trust thereto. Where Paul saith, i. Corinth. xii., "No man can call Jesus Lord except the Holy Ghost had taught him." [11] " But through the Holy Ghost" he meaneth, not with the mouth only, but in the heart, with unfeigned faith, putting his hope and trust in the lordship which he hath over sin, damnation, hell, and death. For so could no man call Jesus lord, except the Holy Ghost had taught him; as Christ saith, Matt. xvi., "Flesh and blood shewed thee not that." [12]

But yet how shall I see my faith? I must come down to love again, and thence to the works of love, ere I can see my faith. Not alway, but sometime, thou shalt feel thy faith without the outward deed; as in great adversity and persecution, when the devil assaulteth thee with desperation, and layeth thy sins before thee, and would bear thee in hand that God had cast thee away, and left thee succourless, for thy sins' sake: then cometh faith forth with her shield, and turneth back again the darts of the devil, and answereth: "Nay; for Jesus is the Son of God, yea, and my very God and my very lord, and hath taken away my sins and all damnation. And this trouble and adversity which is come upon me, by setting on of thee and of thy limbs, is only to make me feel the mercy of my Father, and his power and help within in my soul, and to slay the rest of the poison which remaineth in the flesh." . . .

[*16. God is love, and he that abideth in love, abideth in God and God in him.*] *17. Herefore is love perfect with us, that we should have confidence in the day of judgment, (that as he is, even so are we in this world).*

Howsoever this text doth sound, this methinketh should be the meaning: that we should provoke each other to love, and ever have those ensamples of edifying before our eyes that should most move us to love. For perfect love serveth to make a man bold, because it is the keeping of the commandments. And therefore he that is perfect in love, when he seeth himself, yet in this world, to be unto his neighbour as God is unto him, and to be like his heavenly Father in all ensample of kindness, is bold in the presence of God;

---

[11] I Cor. 12:3.   [12] Matt. 16:17.

yea, though he come to judge sinners. When, on the other side, they that continue ever in their wickedness, and grow not in love, fall often; and therefore their conscience ever accuseth them, and putteth them in fear, by the reason of the fresh memory of the offence, that they cannot at once be bold, though they have never so great promises of mercy.

18. There is no fear in love; but perfect love casteth out fear: for fear hath painfulness. He therefore that feareth, is not perfect in love.

Love is not painful; [13] but maketh all things easy and pleasant: fear of punishment, for the trespass newly committed, is painful: therefore, where love is perfect, there is no such fear. Love is the fulfilling of all commandments: and therefore, where love is perfect, there is no sin; and where the conscience doth not accuse of sin, there is faith bold to go in to God and to stand before him and look him in the face, and to conjure [14] him by all his mercies, and to ask the petitions of his desire. Lack of love is the breaking of the commandments, and cause of sin; and where the conscience accuseth of sin, there faith is abashed, dismayed, ashamed and afraid to go in, for fear of rebuke. Love therefore serveth to make a man bold in the day of judgment, and in all temptations. . . .

19. We love him, because he loved us first.

We deserve not the love of God first; but he deserveth our love, and loveth us first, to win us, and to make us his friends of his enemies; and as soon as we believe his love we love again. And so faith is mother of all love: and as great as my faith is, so great is love, though faith cannot be perfectly seen, but through the works of love and in the fire of temptation.

20. If a man say, I love God, and hateth his brother, he is a liar.[15] *For how can he, that loveth not his brother whom he seeth, love God whom he seeth not? 21. And this commandment have we of him, that he which loveth God, love his brother also.*

To love a man's neighbour in God is a sure rule to know that we love God: and not to love him is a sure token that we love not God; and to hate our neighbour is to hate God. For to love God is to do his commandments; as Christ saith, John xv.: "Ye are my lovers, if ye do those things which I have commanded you." [16]

[13] Difficult.
[14] Implore.
[15] 1534 Note: He that loveth not his brother, loveth not God.
[16] John 15:14.

And [17] the commandment is, to love our neighbours: then he that loveth not his neighbour loveth not God. And [18] likewise to hate the commandment is to hate God that commanded it: and the commandment is to love our neighbours: he then that hateth his brother, whom God biddeth him love, hateth God.

Chapter V

1. All that believe that Jesus is Christ are born of God. And all that love him which begat, love him that is begotten of him. 2. In this we know that we love the sons of God, when we love God and keep his commandments. 3. For this is the love of God, that we keep his commandments.

This is a sure conclusion, that we be born of God through faith. And that faith maketh us God's sons, in that we believe that Jesus is Christ: as the first chapter of John also testifieth, "He gave them power to be the sons of God, in that they believed in his name." [19]

What it is to believe that Jesus is Christ, may be understood by that which is above rehearsed. It is a far other thing than as the devil believed it, against his will and to his great pain; or as they believe it, which, to fulfil their sin, envy the glory of Christ, and persecute his Gospel, forbidding to preach it or to read in it. To believe that Jesus is Christ, is to believe in Christ: that is, to believe earnestly, and to put all thy trust therein, and to lay the price of thy soul thereupon; that the son of Mary, whom the angel commanded to be called Jesus, because he should save his people from their sins, is that Christ, that Messias, and that anointed, which God promised the fathers should come and bless all nations, and anoint them with the oil of his Spirit and with mercy and grace, and to deliver them from death of their souls, which is the consenting to sin, and to make them alive with consenting unto the law of God, and in certifying them that they be the sons of God; and to put thy whole trust in all that he suffered in his flesh for thy sake, and in all promises of mercy that are in him; and that thou be full persuaded that there is no nother name under heaven, given unto men to be saved from sin by, or to purchase forgiveness of the least sin that ever was committed.

Another conclusion is this: Whosoever loveth God loveth all that believe in God. For all that love him that begetteth, love them that are begotten of him: and all that believe in God are begotten of God through that belief, and made his sons: then all that love God love all that believe in God.

[17] If. [18] If. [19] John 1:12.

Another conclusion is this: When we love God and his law, then we love the sons of God. Which is this-wise proved: The love of God is to keep the law of God; by the text, before and after, the law of God is to love our neighbours; and therefore if we love God, in keeping his laws, we must needs love the sons of God.

But John should seem to be a very negligent disputer to many men, in that he here certifieth us of the love of our neighbours by the love of God, when above he certifieth us that we love God because we love our neighbours. . . . Which kind of disputing schoolmen call *petitio principii,* the proving of ii. certain things, each by the other; and is no proving at all. . . .

But it is not so here: for both the demonstrations are certain, both the proof of the love of God and his law by the love of my neighbour, and the proof of the love of my neighbour by the love of God and his law. For when ii. things are so joined together that they cannot be separated, then the presence of the one uttereth the presence of the other, whethersoever thou first seest. As, if I see fire, I am sure that something doth burn; and if I smell burning, I am certified of fire. Even so the love of God is the cause why I love my neighbour; and my love toward my neighbour is the effect of the love of God. And these ii. loves are ever inseparable; so that whethersoever I feel first, the same certifieth me of the other.

John calleth the love of a man's neighbour the deeds of love, after the Hebrew speech, as to help at need. For the deed declareth what the man is within: neither can my love to God, and faith, be seen to the world, save through the works: and by the works doth Christ command us to judge. So that, if a man have evil works, and continueth therein, he loveth not God, nor knoweth God, no, though he call himself master doctor or God's vicar; neither understandeth he God's word, for all his high divinity, but is in all his preaching an hypocrite, a false prophet, and a liar, though his preaching please the world never so well. Nevertheless, a man is certified that he loveth God, ere he come at the work, by the testimony of the Spirit, which is given him in earnest. " The Spirit," saith Paul, Ro. viii., "testifieth unto our spirit, that we be the sons of God": [20] and then it testifieth that we believe in God; for through faith are we sons. And then it certifieth me that I love God; for faith and love are inseparable. The Spirit through faith certifieth my conscience that my sins are forgiven, and I received under grace and made the very son of God and beloved of God; and then naturally mine heart breaketh out into the love of God again, and I seek how to utter my love, and to do God some plea-

---

[20] Rom. 8:16.

sure; and because I can neither do service or pleasure unto his own person, my neighbour is set before me, to do God service and pleasure in him, and to be to him as Christ is to me, because he is my brother, bought with Christ's blood as I am. And I consent unto that law, and love it, ere I come at the deed, and long after the deed. And then, when I love my neighbour in the deed, according to this law, I am sure that I love him truly. Or else, if I examined not my love by this law, I might be deceived. . . .

3. And his commandments are not grievous. 4. For all that is born of God overcometh the world: and this is the victory that overcometh the world, even our faith.[21]

To love is not painful. The commandments are but love; therefore they be not grievous, because love maketh the commandments easy. The service that a mother doth unto her child is not grievous, because she loveth it; but if she should do the tenth part unto one that she loved not, her heart would brast [22] for impatience. Unto a man that feeleth not the love of Christ it is as impossible to keep the commandments, as for a camel to enter through the eye of a needle. But impossible is possible, and easy too, where the love of Christ is believed.

For it followeth: All that are born of God overcome the world; that is to wit, the devil, which is the ruler of the world, and his disciples, which have their lust in his governance, and consent to sin both in body and soul, and give themselves to follow their lusts without resistance; and their own flesh, which also consenteth to sin, do they overcome, with all that moveth to sin. By what victory? Verily, through faith. For if our souls be truly underset with sure hope and trust, and continual meditations of Christ's love, shewed already, and of succour, help and adsistence [23] that is promised in his name, and with the continual memory of their ensamples which in times past have fought through faith and overcome, then were it impossible for the world, with all his chivalry, to overthrow us with any assault, or with any ordinance that he could shoot against us. For if that faith and meditation were ever present in us, then love through that faith should easily overcome whatsoever peril thou couldest imagine. Read in the Bible, and see what conquests faith hath made, both in doing and also suffering. . . .

[*5. Who is it that overcometh the world, but he that believeth that Jesus is the Son of God?*] *6. This is he that came by water*

[21] 1534 Note: Faith is our victory.   [22] Burst.   [23] Assistance.

and blood, Jesus Christ; not by water only, but by water and blood. And it is the Spirit that testifieth, because the Spirit is truth. 7. For there are iii. that bear witness in heaven, the Father, the Word, and the Holy Ghost; and these iii. are one.[24] *8. And there are iii. which bear record in earth, the Spirit, water, and blood; and these three are one.*

Christ came with three witnesses, water, blood, and Spirit. He ordained the sacrament of baptism to be his witness unto us; and he ordained the sacrament of his blood to be his witness unto us. And he poureth his Spirit into the hearts of his, to testify and to make them feel that the testimony of those ii. sacraments are true. And the testimony of these three is, as it after followeth, that we have everlasting life in the Son of God. And these iii. are one full witness; sufficient at the most that the law requireth, which saith ii., or iii. at the most, is one full sufficient witness. . . .

9. If we receive the witness of men, the witness of God is greater. For this is the witness that God hath borne of his Son.

If the witness of men, so they be iii., is to be received; much more is the witness of God to be received. Now the witness that these iii., water, blood, and Spirit, bear, is the witness of God, and therefore the more to be believed.

10. He that believeth in the Son of God, hath witness in himself. And he that believeth not God, maketh him a liar, because he doth not believe the witness that God hath testified of his Son. 11. And this is the witness, that God hath given us eternal life, and this life is in his Son.[25] *12. He that hath the Son hath life: and he that hath not the Son of God hath not life.*

The true believers have the testimony of God in their hearts, and they glorify God, witnessing that he is true. They have the kingdom of God within them; and the temple of God within them; and God in that temple; and have the Son of God, and life through him. And in that temple they seek God, and offer for their sins the sacrifice of Christ's blood, and the fat of his mercies in the fire of their prayers; and in the confidence of that sacrifice go in boldly to God their Father.

But the unbelievers blaspheme God, and make him false, describing him after the complexion of their lying nature. And be-

---

[24] We may note that although he includes this famous interpolation, Tyndale does not comment on it. In his 1534 New Testament he printed it in small type and in parentheses.

[25] 1534 Note: In Christ is the life eternal.

cause they be so full stuffed with lies that they can receive nothing else, they look for the kingdom of God in outward things, and seek God in a temple of stone, where they offer their image-service and the fat of their holy deeds; in confidence whereof they go in to God, and trust to have everlasting life. . . .

13. These things have I written unto you that believe in the name of the Son of God, that ye may know that ye have everlasting life, and that ye may believe in the Son of God.
They that have the faith of Christ's apostles know that they have eternal life. For the Spirit testifieth unto their spirits that they are the sons of God, Ro. viii.,[26] and received under grace. Our doctors say they cannot know whether they be in the state of grace; therefore they have not the faith of the apostles. And that they know it not is the cause why they rail on it.

14. This is the confidence that we have in him, that if we ask aught according to his will, he heareth us. 15. And if we know that he heareth us, whatsoever we ask, we know that we have the petitions that we ask of him.
Christ saith, Matt. vii., "Ask and it shall be given you";[27] and John, in the xvi. chapter, "Whatsoever ye ask in my name, he shall give it you."[28] To ask in the name of Jesu Christ, and according to his will, be both one; and are nothing else but to ask the things contained in the promises and testament of God to us-ward, that God will be our Father, and care for us both in body and in soul; and, if we sin of frailty, and repent, forgive us; and minister all things necessary unto this life, and keep us that we be not overcome of evil, &c. Now if they which believe in Christ are bold with God that he heareth them, and sure that he granteth their petitions, it followeth that they which are not bold that he heareth them, nor sure that he granteth their petitions, do not believe in Christ. . . .

16. If a man see his brother sin a sin not unto death, let him ask; and he shall give him life for them that sin not unto death. There is a sin unto death; and for it say I not that thou shouldest pray. 17. All unrighteousness is sin: and there is a sin not to death.
Whatsoever sin we see in the world, let us pray, and not despair. For God is the God of mercy. But for the sin to death, which is resisting grace, and fighting against mercy, and open blaspheming of the Holy Ghost, affirming that Christ's miracles are done in Beelze-

---

[26] Rom. 8:16.   [27] Matt. 7:7.   [28] John 16:23.

bub, and his doctrine to be of the devil, I think that no Christian man, if he perceive it, can otherwise pray than as Paul prayed for Alexander the coppersmith (the ii. Tim. the last,) "that God would reward him according unto his works." [29] They that go back again after they know the truth, and give themselves willingly to sin for to follow it, and persecute the doctrine of truth by profession to maintain falsehood for their glory and vantage, are remediless: as ye may see Heb. vi. and x. . . .[30]

18. We know that all that are born of God, sin not; [31] *but he that is born of God keepeth himself; and the wicked twitcheth him not.*

As thou readest in the third chapter, they that are born of God cannot sin; for the seed of God keepeth them.[32] They cannot cast off the yoke of Christ, and consent to continue in sin, nor defy his doctrine, nor persecute it, for to quench it, or to maintain any thing contrary unto it. But in whatsoever captivity they be in the flesh, their hearts yield not; but imagine to break loose, and to escape, and fly away, unto the party and standart of their Lord Christ. And as men of war they ever keep watch and prepare themselves unto war, and put on the armour of God, the which is God's word, the shield of faith, the helmet of hope, and harness themselves with the meditation of those things which Christ suffered for us, and with the ensamples of all the saints that followed him, and think earnestly that it is their part to live as purely as the best, and come after as fast as they can. And yet, in all their works, they knowledge themselves sinners unfeignedly, as long as one jot of the perfectness, that was in the deeds of Christ, is lacking in theirs: so that the devil cannot twyche the hearts of them, neither with a pride, or vain glory of pure living, neither to make them consenting unto the flesh in gross sins, if at a time they be taken tardy, and catch a fall. Whatsoever chance them, the devil can catch no hold of them, to keep them still in captivity; but they will break loose again, and repent and do penance, to chaste [33] their flesh, that they come no more under the devil's claws.

19. We know that we be of God, and that the whole world is set on mischief.

[29] II Tim. 4:14.
[30] Heb. 6:4 ff. and 10:26 ff.
[31] 1534 Note: He that is born of God sinneth not.
[32] I John 3:9.
[33] Discipline.

They that believe, that is to say, put their trust in Christ, see both their own glorious state in God, and also the wretched estate of the world in their wickedness. But the world, as they know not God, nor the glory of the sons of God, even so they see not their own miserable estate in wickedness, and damnation under the law of God; but the worse they are, the bolder they be, and the surer of themselves, the further from repentance, and the more standing in their own conceits, for the darkness that is in them. And therefore, say our doctors, a man cannot know whether he be in the state of grace or no; nor needeth to care therefore. And they be therefore the blind leaders of the blind.

20. We know that the son of God is come, and hath given us understanding to know him that is true: and we be in the truth through Jesus Christ. He is very God, and eternal life.

Christ is all, and the fountain of all; and of his fulness receive we all. And as he poureth the gifts of his grace upon them that believe in him, so he giveth them understanding to know the very God, and that they be in the very God, and that they have obtained that through his purchasing; and leaveth not his sheep in darkness. And the same Jesus Christ is very God and eternal life: God and eternal life was he from the beginning, and became man for the great love he had to us, for to bring us unto his eternal life. And he that hath any other way thither, whether his own works, or other men's, or works of ceremonies, or sacraments, or merits of saints, or of aught save Jesu Christ only, shall never come thither. The world seeth the pope, and seeth that they which be in the pope be lords in this world: and therefore they care to be in the pope; but whether they be in God or not, they say, it is not necessary to know.

21. Little children, beware of images.

Serve none image in your hearts. Idolatry is Greek, and the English is image-service: and an idolater is also Greek, and the English an image-servant. Be not idolaters nor commit idolatry; that is, be none image-servants, nor do any image-service, but beware of serving all manner images. And think it not enough to have put all the images of false gods out of the way, if ye now set up the image of very God and of his true saints in their rooms, to do the same service unto them which ye did unto the other. For ye may do as strong image-service unto the image of God and of his saints, as unto the images of false Gods: yea, thou mayest commit as great idolatry to God, and yet before none outward image, but before the image which thou hast feigned of God in thine heart, as thou mayest before an outward image of the devil. . . .

This much I have said because of them that deceive you, to give you an occasion to judge the spirits.

John Ponet

A SHORT CATECHISME

John Ponet: A Short Catechisme

INTRODUCTION

THE WORD "CATECHISM" WAS IN ENGLISH USE BY THE BEGINNING of the sixteenth century. The first instance recorded by the Oxford English Dictionary occurs in 1502, where it refers, not to the instruction of children by set question and answer, but to *catechesis*, the act of instructing. In 1509 John Colet, drawing up the statutes for his new school, specifies, "I will that the children learne first above all the catechyzon in Englishe." It is a matter of conjecture what he meant by "the catechyzon." The form of the word gives point to Becon's definition in *A new Catechisme*, when the child, asked what he means by the word, replies, "As I remember, I heard our schoolmaster say, that it is a Greek word." [1] The cognate word "catechize" appears in the middle of the fifteenth century, or possibly as early as 1425.[2] Here again it bears the meaning of instructing in the faith.

Originally, *catechesis* was the instruction of candidates for Baptism. According to Father J. P. Christopher, "Augustine was the first to appreciate the value of question and answer in instructing the candidate." [3] But straightforward teaching held its place alongside the dialogue form.[4]

The earliest Reformation catechism is said to have been Luther's *Kurze Form der 10 Geboten, des Glaubens, des Vater-*

---

[1] *The Catechism of Thomas Becon*, PS, p. 9.
[2] See *Middle English Dictionary*, ed. by Hans Kurath and S. M. Kuhn (University of Michigan Press, 1956).
[3] St. Augustine, *The First Catechetical Instruction* (London, 1946), p. 6.
[4] See, for a full account, the article in *Dictionnaire de Théologie Catholique* II, cols. 1877–1968. It is not correct to say that "Catechising is instruction by means of question and answer," as *Prayer Book Dictionary*, ed. by G. Harford and M. Stevenson, p. 156.

unsers of 1520. This was followed by very many others, as the Reformers saw both the need for the instruction of children and also the chance of spreading their teaching. In England, catechisms were not uncommon from at least the fifteen thirties onward. It had been traditional for primers to include some teaching, perhaps for children, among their assortments. Thus, William Marshall's *A goodly prymer in englyshe* (1534–1535) includes a short catechism in dialogue (apparently taken from George Joye's *Ortulus animae,* 1530) between a father and a son. In the first edition the father asks the questions and the son answers. In the second, however, it is the child who asks and the father who replies. This gives a certain freshness and charm at the first, though one soon wonders why the father did not react in the manner of Father William in similar circumstances. There are only twenty-two questions and answers; after an initial perambulation on the topic of God, the dialogue deals wth the Creed and the Ten Commandments. Not every primer, however, contained a catechism. There is none, for example, in Hilsey's *Manual* or in the so-called "King Henry's Primer." In 1548 was published *Catechismus, That is to say, a shorte Instruction into Christian Religion for the singuler commoditie and profyte of children and yong people. Set forth by the mooste reverende father in god Thomas Archbyshop of Canterbury.* This is the English translation, by Cranmer or one of his associates, of the catechism of Justus Jonas. Although it is intended "for the behove of yong children, whiche muste be brought up with playne and shorte lessons," as Cranmer's Preface puts it, it is not in dialogue form, but consists of twenty-three brief sermons. It follows the familiar pattern of the Ten Commandments, the Creed, and the Lord's Prayer, with further material on Baptism, the authority of the keys, and the Lord's Supper. The Church Catechism in the Book of Common Prayer that followed the next year, was in dialogue.

The catechism with which we are now concerned, *A Short Catechisme* (1553; Latin, 1552), came on the scene, therefore, when the form had already established itself as a part of Reformation literature. Its origins and authorship are uncertain, not only from lack of evidence, but also from conflicting evidence and from the confusion caused by the work's being printed together with the 1553 Articles. The Articles had been agreed upon by the Convocation of March, 1553. After a separate publication they were printed after the Catechism, which, on account of its size, claimed the senior position. So much so, that not only was the whole book referred to sometimes *tout court* as "The Catechism," but the official character of the Forty-two Articles was sometimes transferred to the Catechism. On account of its Reformed teaching, it provided a valuable piece of evidence against certain of the Reformers at their trials, and it is here that the confusion comes clearly to light. It was insisted by the Romanists that the Catechism was set forth deceitfully, as bearing the authority of Convocation. At Philpot's Disputation in October, 1553, Weston said, "There is a book of late set forth, called the catechism, bearing the name of this honourable synod, and yet put forth without your consents, I learned." [5] When Philpot replied, two days later, he said that he thought they were mistaken about the circumstances and that what in fact had happened was that the "synod of London" had given "the authority to make ecclesiastical laws" to "certain persons" who would be appointed by the king. This was why many members of the Convocation had no cognizance of the authorization of the Catechism.[6] When the same Weston accused Cranmer the next year that "you have set forth a catechism in the name of the Synod of London and yet there be fifty who, witnessing that they were of the number of the convocation, never heard one word of this catechism," Cranmer advanced a different reason, that he had been ignorant of the title, did not like it when he heard of it, and complained to the Council, who had excused it as meaning that the Catechism was published at the same time as the Convocation.[7] It is rather hard both to see what the fuss is about, and also why the Reformers did not reply straight out that the title page of *Catechismus brevis* and of *A short Catechisme* did not claim authority of Convocation for it, but only for the Articles. Since they did not do so, we should perhaps infer that they had intended the title pages to be more ambiguous than in fact they are. As they stand, the only real suggestion that the Catechism is put forth with authority is the reference to the King: *authoritate Regia commendatus*—"sett fourth by the Kings majesties authoritie." This is more ambiguous in English than in Latin, where the phrase clearly relates to the teaching of the Catechism in schools: *omnibus Ludimagistris authoritate Regia commendatus*. The unfortunate imprecision of the sixteenth century in translating led to *commendatus* becoming "sett fourth." Sir John Cheke, in the letter soon to be quoted, translates it accurately.

The authorship is also somewhat uncertain, though perhaps more mystery has been made of the matter than necessary. When

[5] *The Examinations and Writings of John Philpot*, PS, pp. 179–180.
[6] *Ibid.*, PS, p. 181.
[7] Foxe, 6.468.

one or other of the judges at Ridley's Disputation said that Cranmer had ascribed the Catechism to Ridley the day before, they were (if the records are correct) quite definitely mistaken; and Ridley's reply, "I think surely, that he would not say so" [8] removes any doubt. The true authorship seems to be established by a letter from Sir John Cheke to Bullinger in June, 1553. Praising King Edward, he says, "Besides this, he has lately recommended to the schools by his authority the catechism of John, bishop of Winchester, and has published the articles of the synod of London." [9] An entry in *State Papers Domestic* also ascribes the Catechism to him: "Bishop Poynet has set forth a catechism in Latin and English; begs that the bearer may have license for the sole printing thereof." [10]

John Ponet was one of the leading English Reformers, yet he is also one of the lesser known, and we should, therefore, say a word about his life. A Cambridge man of about the same generation as Ascham, Cecil, Cox, and Grindal, he became a fellow of Queens' and a lecturer in Greek before being taken up by Cranmer and made his chaplain in the mid fifteen forties. He was consecrated Bishop of Rochester in 1550, but held this see for less than a year; for, when Gardiner was deprived of his bishopric, Ponet was translated to Winchester. It was while he was here that the *Catechismus brevis* was published. On Mary's accession in 1553, however, Gardiner was restored and Ponet ejected. It is possible that he took some part in Wyatt's rebellion of 1554. However that may be, he escaped to the Continent in 1554 and lived in Strasbourg, where he wrote *A Short Treatise of politike power* (1556) and where he died in 1556.

This somewhat shadowy figure ought perhaps to be regarded, not so much as the author of the Catechism as the mouthpiece of Cranmer's group of Reformers. The King's prefatory injunction speaks of its being examined by "certain bishops and other learned men." It is, indeed, a typical piece of Renaissance-Reformation writing in its purpose as well as in its execution, with its dual purpose of serving education as well as religion. The scene is no longer the home, with the child learning the Lord's Prayer from a primer before the fire, nor the church, with the children and

---

[8] *The Works of Nicholas Ridley*, PS, p. 227.
[9] *Original Letters*, PS, I.142.
[10] 1547–80, p. 44—Sept. 7, 1552. Cranmer's admission, "As for the Catechism, the book of Articles, with the other book against Winchester, he granted the same to be his doings" (PS, II.220), will therefore mean that he sponsored the Catechism.

"yong people" being catechized during the service, but the grammar school, with lessons to be learned and a master to be reckoned with; for the Catechism was deliberately intended as a schoolbook, a Latin reader. It is, therefore, not only written in careful classical Latin, but the author takes pains to vary his words and phrases so as to give as wide a vocabulary and syntax as he can. As we have seen, the book was authorized for the use of schools; in the words of the Injunction it was appointed "out for all schoolmasters to teach, that the yet unskilful and young age, having the foundations laid, both of religion and good letters, may learn godliness together with wisdom." [11] Religion and good letters are married immediately in the introduction, when the dialogue form is defended as the form used by Socrates in philosophy as well as by Apollinarius in theology.

He makes his starting point the profession of the Christian religion, which he summarizes as faith in God and love toward God and the neighbor. It is, he explains, from the Bible that he learns that there is a God, as also that he learns of God's demands in the law and of his promises in the Gospel; and all that is learned in the Bible is summed up in the Creed.

The consideration of the Creed is deferred, however, until the Ten Commandments have been dealt with, though no reason is given for this. He expounds the commandments (giving far more time to the second Table than to the first, incidentally) and then goes on to explain the office of the law. The "law of nature" which was "engraffed by God in the nature of man, while nature was yet sound and uncorrupted," [12] has been hidden from men by the entrance of sin—though he makes a somewhat gnostic distinction between "the wise" who are "somewhat after a sort not utterly [13] ignorant" of the law of nature, and the "greatest part of men" who see hardly anything at all. But because the *lex naturae* is a broken reed, God has given men the commandments to make them aware of their sin and to drive them to seek forgiveness in Christ.

He goes on to the Creed; and his exposition of it takes up the greater part of the book. What is chiefly of interest is his overriding emphasis on the ascension and session of Christ, which alone occupies almost six pages in Parker Society. (The importance of establishing this doctrine lies, of course, in the use made of it in the Reformed Eucharistic teaching, that the body of Christ is in heaven and not on earth, and that this nevertheless does not constitute a bar to the power of Christ coming to men on earth.

[11] PS, p. 492.   [12] PS, p. 499.   [13] All this to translate *utcunque!*

The point will be taken up in the trials of certain of the Reformers.) The section on the Holy Spirit leads in to a discussion of the Sacraments.

The Catechism ends with an exposition of the Lord's Prayer.

It will be seen, therefore, that it follows the general pattern of the Reformation Catechism: Ten Commandments, Creed, Lord's Prayer. *A Catechisme, or first Instruction and Learning of Christian Religion* (1570) of Alexander Nowell, which superseded our present Catechism and perhaps made use of it, follows almost the same course, though at greater length: the first part is on the Law and Obedience, the second on the Gospel and faith, and the third on Prayer and Thanksgiving. The section on the Sacraments, however, as with Luther and with the Church Catechism, are placed in a fourth part, instead of being treated as part of the Creed.

A Short Catechisme shared the fate of so many others of the more or less official formularies of King Edward's reign. When he died, they were discarded (at least, in England) and when the Reformation returned with Elizabeth, it was preferred to write new works rather than revise old ones.

BIBLIOGRAPHY

Catechismus/ Brevis, Christi-/anae Disciplinae/ summam continens, omnibus/ Ludimagistris authoritate/ Regia/ commendatus./ [Also Articles of 1552.]/ Londini,/ Cum priuilegio Sereniss. Regis./ Anno Do. M.D.LIII.
Colophon: Excusum Londini apud Reginaldum/ Wolfium, Regiae Maiestatis/ in Latinis Typo-/graphum./ Anno Domini. M.D.LIII.

Another edition in Cambridge University Library has an identical title page with the above, and the text follows the same pages. But a side is left blank after the *Catechismus* and therefore the *Articuli* begin on recto instead of verso. This means that the colophon also has to be printed on recto. This may explain Hudson's statement that "One Latin edition is without colophon; the other was printed by Reginald Wolf." The copy he saw may have lacked the (separately printed)
Colophon: Excusum Londini, apud Reginal-/dum Wolfium, Regiae Ma-/iestatis in Latinis/ Typographum./ Anno Domini. M.D.LIII.

A Short/ Catechisme, or playne in-/struction, conteynynge the/ summe of Christian learninge, sett/ fourth by the Kings maiesties/ authoritie, for all Schole-/maisters to teache./ [Also Articles.]/ 1553./ Imprinted at London by Jhon/ Day with the kings most gracious licence/ and priviledge forbidding all other/ to prynt thys Catechisme.
Colophon: Impryn-/ted at London by Jhon Day/ dwelling ouer Aldersgate beneth/ Saynct Martyns./ These Cathechismes are to bee/ solde at hys shop, by the litle Coun-/duit in Chepesyde at the/ sygne of the Resur-/reccion./ Cum priuilegio ad impri-/mendum solum.

Our text is, except where otherwise stated, a reprint of this edition.

The Two Liturgies, A.D. 1549, and A.D. 1552: with other Docu-

ments set forth by authority in the reign of King Edward VI. Edited for the Parker Society by the Rev. Joseph Ketley, M.A. Cambridge. 1844.

Winthrop S. Hudson, *John Ponet (1516?–1556) Advocate of Limited Monarchy.* University of Chicago Press, 1942.

Other Catechisms:

A Dialogue between the Father, & the Son asking certain questions, & the Father answering. In *Three Primers put forth in the Reign of Henry VIII* (ed. by Edward Burton, Oxford, 1834).

Catechismvs,/ That is to say,/ a shorte Instruction/ into Christian Reli-/gion for the synguler/ commoditie and profyte of/ children and yong people. Set/ forth by the mooste reuerende/ father in God Thomas Arch/ byshop of Canterbury, Pri-/mate of all England and/ Metropolitane./ Gualterus Lynne/ excudebat./ 1548.[14]

This, with the Latin original, was edited by E. Burton (Oxford, 1829).

A new Ca-/techisme sette forth Dialoge/ wise in familiare talke betwene/ the father and the son, lately made/ and now fyrst of all published by/ Thomas Becon.

Catechismvs,/ siue prima Institutio, Disci-/plinaque Pietatis/ Christianae, Latine explicata . . . Londini,/ In Officina Reginaldi/ Wolfii . . ./ Anno Dom. M.D.LXX./ XVI.Calend. IVL.

A Catechisme,/ or first Instruction and Learn-/ing of Christian/ Religion./ Translated out of Latine into/ Englishe./ At London./ Printed by Iohn Daye/ dwelling ouer Aldersgate./ . . . An. 1570.

(These last two are Nowell's Catechism).

See also:

Charles C. Butterworth, *The English Primers (1529–1545): Their Publication and Connection with the English Bible and the Reformation in England.* University of Pennsylvania Press, 1953.

C. H. Garrett, "John Ponet and the Confession of the Banished Ministers" in *Church Quarterly Review,* 1943 f., pp. 47–74, 181–204.

[14] See D. G. Selwyn, "A Neglected Edition of Cranmer's Catechism," in *Journal of Theological Studies,* April, 1964, pp. 76–91.

John Ponet: A Short Catechisme

THE TEXT

It is the duty of them all, whom Christ hath redeemed by his death, that they not only be servants to obey, but also children to inherit: so to know which is the true trade of life, and that God liketh, that they may be able to answer to every demand of religion, and to render account of their faith and profession.

And this is the plainest way of teaching, which not only in philosophy Socrates, but also in our religion Apollinarius, hath used; that both by certain questions, as it were by pointing, the ignorant might be instructed, and the skilful put in remembrance, that they forget not what they have learned. We therefore having regard to the profit, which we ought to seek in teaching of youth, and also to shortness, that in our whole schooling there should be nothing either overflowing or wanting, have conveyed the whole sum into a dialogue, that the matter itself might be the plainer to perceive, and we the less stray in other matters beside the purpose. Thus then beginneth the Master to appose his Scholar.

Master. Sith I know, dear son, that it is a great part of my duty, not only to see that thou be instructed in good letters, but also earnestly and diligently to examine what sort of religion thou followest, in this thy tender age; I thought it best to oppose thee by certain questions, to the intent I may perfectly know whether thou hast well or ill travailed therein. Now therefore tell me, my son, what religion that is which thou professest.

Scholar. That, good master, do I profess, which is the religion of the Lord Christ; which in the xi. of the Acts is called the Christian religion.

Master. Dost thou then confess thyself to be a follower of Christian godliness and religion, and a scholar of our Lord Christ?

Scholar. That forsooth do I confess, and plainly and boldly profess; yea, therein I account the whole sum of all my glory, as in the thing which is both of more honour, than that the slenderness of my wit may attain unto it; and also more approaching to God's majesty, than that I, by any feat of utterance, may easily express it.

Master. Tell me then, dear son, as exactly as thou canst, in what points thou thinkest that the sum of Christian religion standeth.

Scholar. In two points; that is to say, true faith in God, and assured persuasion conceived of all those things which are contained in the holy scriptures; and in charity, which belongeth both to God and to our neighbour.

Master. That faith which is conceived by hearing and reading of the word, what doth it teach thee concerning God?

Scholar. This doth it principally teach: that there is one certain nature, one substance, one ghost and heavenly mind, or rather an everlasting Spirit, without beginning or ending, which we call God: whom all the people of the world ought to worship with sovereign honour and the highest kind of reverence. Moreover out of the holy words of God, which by the prophets and the beloved of almighty God are in the holy books published, to the eternal glory of his name, I learn the law and the threatenings thereof; then the promises and the gospel of God. These things, first written by Moses and other men of God, have been preserved whole and uncorrupted, even to our age. And since that, the chief articles of our faith have been gathered into a short abridgement, which is commonly called the Creed, or Symbol, of the Apostles.

Master. Why is this abridgement of the faith termed with the name of a symbol?

Scholar. A symbol is as much to say, as a sign, mark, privy token, or watchword, whereby the soldiers of one camp are known from their enemies. For this reason the abridgement of the faith, whereby the Christians are known from them that be no Christians, is rightly named a Symbol.

Master. First tell me somewhat, what thou thinkest of the law: and then afterward of the Creed or Symbol.

Scholar. I shall do, good master, with a good will as you command me. The Lord God hath charged us by Moses, that we have none other God at all, but him; that is to say, that we take him alone for our one only God, our Maker and Saviour: that we reverence not, nor worship any portraiture or any image whatsoever, whether it be painted, carved, graven, or by any mean fashioned howsoever it be: that we take not the name of our Lord God in vain; that is, either in a matter of no weight or of no truth. Last of all this ought we to hold stedfastly and with devout conscience, that we keep holily and religiously the Sabbath day, which was appointed out from the other for rest and service of God.

Master. Very well. Now hast thou rehearsed unto me the laws of the first table, wherein is, in a sum, contained the knowledge and true service of God. Go forward and tell me, which be the duties of charity, and our love toward men.

Scholar. Do you ask me, master, what I think of the other part of the law, which is commonly called the second table?

Master. Thou sayest true, my son; that is it indeed that I would fain hear of.

Scholar. I will in few words dispatch it, as my simple wit will serve me. Moses hath knit it up in a short sum: that is, that with all loving affection we honour and reverence our father and mother; that we kill no man; that we commit no advoutry; [15] that we steal nothing; that we bear false witness against none: last of all, that we covet nothing that is our neighbour's.

Master. How is that commandment of the honouring father and mother, to be understanded?

Scholar. Honour of father and mother containeth love, fear, and reverence, yea, and it further standeth in obeying, succouring, defending, and nourishing them, if need require. It bindeth us also most humbly, and with most natural affection, to obey the magistrate, to reverence the ministers of the Church, our schoolmasters, with all our elders, and betters.

Master. What is contained in that commandment, Do not kill?

Scholar. That we hate, wrong, or revile no man. Moreover it commandeth us, that we love even our foes, do good to them that hate us, and that we pray for all prosperity and good hap to our very mortal enemies.

Master. The commandment of not committing advoutry, what thinkest thou it containeth?

Scholar. Forsooth this commandment containeth many things; for it forbiddeth, not only to talk with another man's wife, or any other woman, unchastely, but also to touch her, yea, or to cast an eye at her wantonly; or with lustful look to behold her; or by any unhonest mean to woo her; either ourselves, or any other in our behalf; finally, herein is debarred all kind of filthy and straying lust.

Master. What thinkest thou of the commandment, not to steal?

Scholar. I shall shew you, as briefly as I have done the rest, if it please you to hear me. It commandeth us to beguile no man; to

[15] Adultery.

occupy no unlawful wares; to envy no man his wealth; and to think nothing profitable, that either is not just, or differeth from right and honesty: briefly, rather willingly lese [16] that is thine own, than thou wrongfully take that is another's, and turn it to thine own commodity.

Master. How may that commandment be kept, of bearing no false witness?

Scholar. If we neither ourselves speak any false or vain lie, nor allow it in other, either by speech or silence, or by our present company. But we ought always to maintain truth, as place and time serveth.

Master. Now remaineth the last commandment, of not coveting any thing that is our neighbour's: what meaneth that?

Scholar. This law doth generally forbid all sorts of evil lusts, and commandeth us to bridle and restrain all greedy unsatiable desire of our will, which holdeth not itself within the bonds of right and reason; and it willeth that each man be content with his estate. But whosoever coveteth more than right, with the loss of his neighbour, and wrong to another, he breaketh and utterly looseth the bond of charity, and fellowship among men. Yea, and upon him (unless he amend) the Lord God, the most stern revenger of the breaking his law, shall execute most grievous punishment. On the other side, he that liveth according to the rule of these laws, shall find both praise and bliss, and God also his merciful and bountiful good Lord.

Master. Thou hast shortly set out the x. commandments. Now, then, tell me how all these things, that thou hast particularly declared, Christ hath in few words contained, setting forth unto us in a sum the whole pith of the law?

Scholar. Will you that I knit up in a brief abridgment all that belongeth both to God and to men?

Master. Yea.

Scholar. Christ saith thus: "Thou shalt love the Lord thy God with all thy heart, with all thy soul, with all thy mind, and with all thy strength. This is the greatest commandment in the law. The other is like unto this: Thou shalt love thy neighbour as thyself. Upon these two commandments hang the whole law, and the prophets." [17]

Master. I will now that thou tell me further, what law is that which thou speakest of? that which we call the law of nature? or some other besides?

Scholar. I remember, master, that I learned that of you long

---

[16] Lose.   [17] Mark 12:30 and par.

ago: that it was ingraffed by God in the nature of man while nature was yet sound and uncorrupted. But after the entrance of sin, although the wise were somewhat after a sort not utterly ignorant of that light of nature; yet was it by that time so hid from the greatest part of men that they scant perceived any shadow thereof.

Master. What it the cause that God willed it to be written out in tables, and that it should be privately appointed to one people alone?

Scholar. I will shew you. By original sin and evil custom the image of God in man was so at the beginning darkened, and the judgment of nature so corrupted, that man himself doth not sufficiently understand what difference is between honesty and dishonesty, right and wrong. The bountiful God therefore, minding to renew that image in us, first wrought this by the law written in tables, that we might know ourselves, and therein, as it were in a glass, behold the filth and spots of our soul, and stubborn hardness of a corrupted heart; that by this mean yet, acknowledging our sin, and perceiving the weakness of our flesh, and the wrath of God fiercely bent against us for sin, we might the more fervently long for our Saviour Christ Jesus, which by his death and precious sprinkling of his blood hath cleansed and washed away our sins, pacified the wrath of the almighty Father, by the holy breath of his Spirit createth new hearts in us, and reneweth our minds after the image and likeness of their Creator, in true righteousness and holiness. Which thing neither the justice of the law, nor any sacrifices of Moses were able to perform. And that no man is made righteous by the law, it is evident: not only thereby, that the righteous liveth by faith; but also hereby, that no mortal man is able to fulfil all that the law of both the tables commandeth. For we have hindrances that strive against the law: as the weakness of the flesh, froward appetite, and lust naturally engendered. As for sacrifice, cleansings, washings, and other ceremonies of the law, they were but shadows, likenesses, images and figures of the true and everlasting sacrifice of Jesus Christ, done upon the cross. By the benefit whereof alone all the sins of all believers, even from the beginning of the world, are pardoned, by the only mercy of God, and by no desert of ours.

Master. I hear not yet, why Almighty God's will was to declare his secret pleasure to one people alone, which was the Israelites.

Scholar. Forsooth, that had I almost forgotten. I suppose it was not done for this intent, as though the law of the x. commandments did not belong generally to all men: forasmuch as the Lord our God is not only the God of the Jews, but also of the Gentiles: but rather this was meant thereby, that the true Messias, which is our Christ, might be known at his coming into the world: who must needs have been born of that nation, and none other, for true performance of the promise. For the which cause, God's pleasure was to appoint out for himself one certain people, holy, sundered from the rest, and as it were peculiarly his own; that by this mean his divine Word might be continually kept holy, pure, and uncorrupted.

Master. Hitherto thou hast well satisfied me, dear son. Now let us come to the Christian confession, which I will that thou plainly rehearse unto me.

Scholar. It shall be done. I believe in God, the Father almighty, maker of heaven and earth. And in Jesu Christ, his only Son, our Lord; which was conceived by the Holy Ghost; born of the virgin Mary; suffered under Ponce Pilate; was crucified, dead, and buried. He went down to hell. The third day he rose again from the dead. He went up to heaven; sitteth on the right hand of God the Father almighty; from thence shall he come, to judge the quick and the dead. I believe in the Holy Ghost. I believe the holy universal church, the communion of saints, the forgiveness of sins, the rising again of the flesh, and the life everlasting.

Master. All these, my son, thou hast rehearsed generally and shortly. Therefore thou shalt do well to set out largely all that thou hast spoken particularly; that I may plainly perceive what thy belief is concerning each of them. And first I would hear of the knowledge of God, afterward of the right serving of him.

Scholar. I will with a good will obey your pleasure, dear master, as far as my simple wit will suffer me. Above all things we must stedfastly believe and hold that God almighty, the Father, in the beginning, and of nothing, made and fashioned this whole frame of the world and all things whatsoever are contained therein, and that they all are made by the power of his word, that is of Jesu Christ the Son of God. Which thing is sufficiently approved by witness of scriptures. Moreover that, when he had thus shapen all creatures, he ruled, governed and saved them by his bounty and liberal hand, hath ministered, and yet also ministereth, most largely all that is needful for maintenance and preserving of our life; that we should so use them, as behoveth mindful and godly children.

Master. Why dost thou call God Father?

Scholar. For two causes: the one, for that he made us all at the beginning, and gave life unto us all. The other is more weighty, for that by his Holy Spirit and by faith he hath begotten us again, making us his children, giving us his kingdom and the inheritance of life everlasting, with Jesu Christ his own, true, and natural Son.

Master. Seeing then God hath created all other things to serve man, and made man to obey, honour, and glorify him, what canst thou say more of the beginning and making of man?

Scholar. Even that which Moses wrote: that God shaped the first man of clay, and put into him soul and life; then, that he cast Adam in a dead sleep, and brought forth a woman, whom he drew out of his side, to make her a companion with him of all his life and wealth. And therefore was man called Adam, because he took his beginning of the earth, and the woman called Eve, because she was appointed to be the mother of all living.

Master. What image is that, after the likeness whereof thou sayest that man was made?

Scholar. That is most absolute righteousness and perfect holiness: which most nearly belongeth to the very nature of God, and most clearly appeared in Christ, our new Adam. Of the which in us there scant are to be seen any sparkles.

Master. What! are there scant to be seen?

Scholar. It is true, forsooth. For they do not now so shine, as they did in the beginning, before man's fall, forasmuch as man by the darkness of sins, and mist of errors, hath corrupted the brightness of this image. In such sort hath God in his wrath wreaked him [18] upon the sinful man.

Master. But I pray thee tell me, wherefore came it thus to pass?

Scholar. I will shew you. When the Lord God had made the frame of this world, he himself planted a garden, full of delight and pleasure, in a certain place eastward, and called it Eden; wherein, beside other passing fair trees, not far from the midst of the garden was there one specially called the tree of life, and another called the tree of knowledge of good and evil. Herein the Lord of his singular love placed man, and committed unto him the garden to dress, and look unto, giving him liberty to eat of the fruits of all the trees of paradise, except the fruit of the tree of knowledge of good and evil. The fruit of this tree if ever he tasted, he should without fail die for it. But Eve, deceived by the devil counterfeiting the shape of a serpent, gathered of the forbidden fruit, which was for the fairness to the eye to be desired, for the sweetness in taste to be reached at, and pleasant for the knowledge of good and evil. And she eat thereof, and gave unto her husband to eat of the same. For which doing they both im-

[18] Avenged himself.

mediately died; that is to say, were not only subject to the death of the body, but also lost the life of the soul, which is righteousness. And forthwith the image of God was defaced in them, and the most beautiful proportion of righteousness, holiness, truth, and knowledge of God, was confounded and in a manner utterly blotted out. There remained the earthly image, joined with unrighteousness, guile, fleshly mind, and deep ignorance of godly and heavenly things. Hereof grew the weakness of our flesh; hereof came this corruption, and disorder of lusts and affections; hereof came that pestilence; hereof came that seed and nourishment of sins wherewith mankind is infected, and it is called sin original. Moreover thereby nature was so corrupted and overthrown, that unless the goodness and mercy of almighty God had holpen us by the medicine of grace, even as in body we are thrust down into all wretchedness of death, so must it needs have been, that all men of all sorts should be thrown into everlasting punishment and fire unquenchable.

Master. Oh the unthankfulness of men! But what hope had our first parents, and from thenceforth the rest, whereby they were relieved?

Scholar. When the Lord God had both with words and deeds chastised Adam and Eve (for he thrust them both out of the garden with a most grievous reproach), he then cursed the serpent, threatening him that the time should one day come, when the Seed of the woman should break his head. Afterward the Lord God stablished that same glorious and most bountiful promise; first with a covenant made between him and Abraham, by circumcision, and in Isaac his son; then again by Moses; last of all by the oracles of the noble prophets.

Master. What meaneth the serpent's head, and that Seed that God speaketh of?

Scholar. In the serpent's head lieth all his venom, and the whole pith of his life and force. Therefore do I take the serpent's head to betoken the whole power and kingdom, or more truly the tyranny, of the old serpent the devil. The Seed (as saint Paul doth plainly teach [19]) is Jesus Christ, the Son of God, very God and very man, conceived of the Holy Ghost, engendered of the womb and substance of Mary, the blessed pure and undefiled maid; and was so born and fostered by her as other babes be, saving that he was most far from all infection of sin.

Master. All these foundations that thou hast laid are most true. Now therefore let us go forward to those his doings, wherein lieth

[19] Gal. 3:16.

our salvation and conquest against that old serpent.

Scholar. It shall be done, good master. After that Christ Jesus had delivered in charge to his apostles that most joyful and in all points heavenly doctrine, the Gospel, which in Greek is called Euangelion, in English good tidings, and had as by sealing stablished the same with tokens and miracles innumerable, whereof all his life was full, at length was he sore scourged, mocked with potting,[20] scorning, and spitting in his face, last of all his hands and feet bored through with nails, and he fastened to a cross. Then he truly died, and was truly buried, that by his most sweet sacrifice he might pacify his Father's wrath against mankind, and subdue him by his death, who had the authority of death, which was the devil; forasmuch not only the living, but also the dead, were they in hell, or elsewhere, they all felt the power and force of this death. To whom lying in prison (as Peter saith) Christ preached, though dead in body, yet relived [21] in Spirit.[22] The third day after he uprose again, alive in body also; and with many notable proofs, the space of xl. days, he abode among his disciples, eating and drinking with them. In whose sight he was conveyed away in a cloud, up into heaven, or rather above all heavens, where he now sitteth at the right hand of God the Father, being made Lord of all things, be they in heaven, or in earth, King of all kings, our everlasting and only high Bishop, our only attorney, only mediator, only peace-maker between God and men. Now sithens that he is entered into his glorious majesty, by sending down his Holy Spirit unto us (as he promised) he lighteneth our dark blindness, moveth, ruleth, teacheth, cleanseth, comforteth, and rejoiceth our minds; and so will he still continually do, till the end of the world.

Master. Well, I see thou hast touched the chief Articles of our religion, and hast set out, as in a short abridgment, the Creed that thou didst rehearse. Now therefore I will demand thee questions of certain points.

Scholar. Do as shall please you, master: for ye may more perfectly instruct me in those things that I do not throughly understand, and put me in remembrance of that I have forgotten, and print in my mind deeper such things, as have not taken stedfast hold therein.

Master. Tell me then. If by his death we get pardon of our sins, was not that enough, but that he must also rise again from the dead?

Scholar. It was not enough, if ye have a respect either to him, or

---

[20] Mocking. [21] Latin, *vivificatus*. AV, "quickened." [22] I Peter 3:18-19.

to us. For unless he had risen again, he should not be taken for the Son of God. For which cause also, while he hung upon the cross, they that saw him upbraided him and said: "He hath saved other, but can not save himself. Let him now come down from the cross, and we will believe him." [23] But now uprising from the dead to everlasting continuance of life, he hath shewed a much greater power of his Godhead, than if by coming down from the cross he had fled from the terrible pains of death. For to die is common to all men; but to loose the bonds of death, and by his own power to rise again, that properly belongeth to Jesus Christ, the only-begotten Son of God, the only author of life. Moreover it was necessary that he should rise again with glory, that the sayings of David and other prophets of God might be fulfilled, which told before that neither his body should see corruption, nor his soul be left in hell.[24] As for us, we neither had been justified, nor had had any hope left to rise again, had not he risen again, as Paul doth in divers places plainly shew.[25] For if he had remained in the prison of death, in grave, and been holden in corruption, as all men beside, how could we have hoped for safety by him which saved not himself? It was meet therefore, and needful, for the part that he had in hand, and for the chief stay of our saveguard, that Christ should first deliver himself from death, and afterward assure us of safety by his uprising again.

Master. Thou hast touched, my son, the chief cause of Christ's rising again. Now would I fain hear thy mind of his going up into heaven. What answer, thinkest thou, is to be made to them, that say, It had been better for him to tarry here with us, presently [26] to rule and govern us? For, beside other divers causes, it is likely, that the love of the people toward their prince, specially being good and gracious, should grow the greater by his present company.

Scholar. All these things which he should do present, that is to say, if he were in company among us, he doth them absent. He ruleth, maintaineth, strengtheneth, defendeth, rebuketh, punisheth, correcteth, and performeth all such things as do become such a prince, or rather God himself. All those things (I say) performeth he, which belong either to our need or profit, honour or commodity. Beside this, Christ is not so altogether absent from the world, as many do suppose. For albeit the substance of his body be taken up from us, yet is his Godhead perpetually present with us, although not subject to the sight of our eyes. For things that

---

[23] Mark 15:31.
[24] Ps. 16:10.
[25] I Cor. 15:13 ff.
[26] In his presence.

be not bodily, can not be perceived by any bodily mean. Who ever saw his own soul? No man. Yet what is there more present? or what to each man nearer than his own soul? Spiritual things are not to be seen, but with the eye of the spirit. Therefore he that in earth will see the Godhead of Christ, let him open the eyes, not of his body, but of his mind, but of his faith; and he shall see him present, whom eye hath not seen; he shall see him present, and in the midst of them, wheresoever be two or three gathered together in his name; he shall see him present with us, even unto the end of the world. What said I? shall he see Christ present? Yea, he shall both see and feel him dwelling within himself, in such sort as he doth his own proper soul. For he dwelleth and abideth in the mind and heart of him which fasteneth all his trust in him.

Master. Very well: but our confession is that he is ascended up into heaven. Tell me therefore how that is to be understood.

Scholar. So use we commonly to say of him, that hath attained to any high degree or dignity, that he is ascended up, or advanced into some high room, some high place or state. Because he hath changed his former case, and is become of more honour than the rest. In such case is Christ gone up, as he before came down. He came down from highest honour to deepest dishonour, even the dishonour and vile state of a servant, and of the cross. And likewise afterward he went up, from the deepest dishonour, to the highest honour, even that same honour, which he had before. His going up into heaven, yea, above all heavens, to the very royal throne of God, must needs be evident by most just reason, that his glory and majesty might in comparison agreeably answer to the proportion of his baseness and reproachful estate. This doth Paul teach us in his writing to the Philippians: "he became obedient even unto death, yea, the very death of the cross. Wherefore God hath both advanced him to the highest state of honour, and also given him a name above all names; that at the name of Jesus every knee should bow, of all things in heaven, earth and hell." [27] But although he be already gone up into heaven, nevertheless by his nature of Godhead, and by his Spirit, he shall always be present in his Church, even to the end of the world. Yet this proveth not that he is present among us in his body. For his Godhead hath one property, his manhead another. His manhead was create, his Godhead uncreate. His manhead is in some one place of heaven; his Godhead is in such sort eachwhere, that it filleth both heaven and earth. But to make this point plainer, by a similitude

[27] Phil. 2:5 ff.

or comparing of like to like. There is nothing that doth trulier, like a shadow, express Christ, than the sun; for it is a fit image of the light and brightness of Christ. The sun doth alway keep the heaven; yet do we say that it is present also in the world: for without light there is nothing present, that is to say, nothing to be seen of any man; for the sun with his light fulfilleth all things. So Christ is lifted up above all heavens, that he may be present with all, and fully furnish all things, as S. Paul doth say.[28] But as touching the bodily presence of Christ here in earth (if it be lawful to place in comparison great things with small), Christ's body is present to our faith, as the sun, when it is seen, is present to the eye; the body whereof, although it do not bodily touch the eye, nor be presently with it together here in earth, yet is it present to the sight, notwithstanding so large a distance of space between. So Christ's body, which at his glorious going up was conveyed from us, which hath left the world, and is gone unto his Father, is a great way absent from our mouth, even then when we receive with our mouth the holy sacrament of his body and blood. Yet is our faith in heaven: and beholdeth that Sun of righteousness: and is presently together with him in heaven, in such sort as the sight is in heaven with the body of the sun, or in earth the sun with the sight. And as the sun is present to all things by his light: so is Christ also in his Godhead. Yet neither can from the body the light of the sun be sundered, nor from his immortal body the Godhead of Christ. We must therefore so say, that Christ's body is in some one place of heaven, and his Godhead every where; that we neither of his Godhead make a body, nor of his body a God.

Master. I see, my son, thou art not ignorant, after what sort Christ is rightly said to be from us in body, and with us in spirit. But this one thing would I know of thee: why Christ our Lord is thus conveyed away from the sight of our eyes; and what profit we take by his going up to heaven.

Scholar. The chief cause thereof was to pluck out of us that false opinion, which sometime deceived the apostles themselves, that Christ should in earth visibly reign, as other kings, and ruffling princes of the world. This error he minded to have utterly suppressed in us, and that we should think his kingdom to consist in higher things. Which thing he therefore thought fitter, because it was more for our commodity and profit, that some such kingdom should be set up, as the foundations thereof should rest upon our faith. Wherefore it was necessary that he should be conveyed away from us, past perceiving of all bodily sense; that by

[28] Eph. 4:10.

this mean our faith might be stirred up and exercised to consider his government and providence, whom no sight of bodily eyes can behold. And forasmuch as he is not king of some one country alone, but of heaven and earth, of quick and dead, it was most convenient that his kingdom should be otherwise governed, than our senses may attain unto. For else he should have been constrained, sometime to be carried up to heaven, sometime to be driven down to the earth, to remove sometime into one country, sometime into another; and like an earthly prince to be carried hither and thither, by divers change of chanceable affairs. For he could not be presently with all at once, unless his body were so turned into Godhead, that he might be in all or in many places together; as Eutyches, and certain like heretics held opinion.[29] If it so were that he might be eachwhere present with all, at one very instant time, then were he not man, but a ghost; neither should he have had a true body, but a fantastical: whereof should have sprung forthwith a thousand errors. All which he hath dispatched by carrying his body up whole to heaven. In the mean season he, remaining invisible, governeth his kingdom and commonweal, that is his church, with sovereign wisdom and power. It is for men to rule their commonweals by a certain civil policy of men; but for Christ and God, by a heavenly godlike order.

But all that I have hitherto said containeth but a small parcel of the profit that we take by the carrying up of Christ's body into heaven. For there are many more things that here might be rehearsed, whereof large store of fruit is to be gathered. But specially this may not be left unspoken: that the benefits are such, and so great, which come unto us by the death, rising again, and going up of Christ, as no tongue either of men or angels is able to express. And that you may know my mind herein, I will rehearse certain of the chief, whereunto, as it were two principal points, the rest may be applied. I say therefore, that both by these and other doings of Christ, two commodities do grow unto us: the one, that all the things that ever he hath done, for our profit and behoof he hath done them; so that they be as well our own, if we will cleave thereunto with stedfast and lively faith, as if we had done them ourselves. He was nailed to the cross: we were also nailed with him: and in him our sins punished. He died, and was buried: we likewise with our sins are dead, and buried; and that in such sort, that all remembrance of our sins is utterly taken out of mind. He is risen again: and we are also risen again with him; that is,

---

[29] A reference to Eutychianism and the Monophysite controversy of the fifth century.

are so made partakers of his rising again and life, that from henceforth death hath no more rule over us. For the same Spirit is in us that raised up Jesus from the dead. Finally, as he is gone up into heavenly glory: so are we lifted up with him. Albeit that these things do not now appear, yet then shall they all be brought to light, when Christ, the light of the world, shall shew himself in his glory, in whom all our bliss is laid up in store.

Moreover by his going up are granted us the gifts of the Holy Ghost, as Paul doth sufficiently witness (Ephe. iiii.).[30] The other commodity, which we take by the doings of Christ, is that Christ is set for an example unto us, to frame our lives thereafter. If Christ hath been dead, if he hath been buried for sin, he was so but once. If he be risen again, if he be gone up to heaven, he is but once risen, but once gone up. From henceforth he dieth no more, but liveth with God, and reigneth in everlasting continuance of glory. So if we be dead, if we be buried to sin, how shall we hereafter live in the same? If we be risen again with Christ, if by stedfast hope we live now in heaven with him, heavenly and godly things, not earthly and frail, we ought to set our care upon. And even as heretofore we have borne the image of the earthly man, so from henceforward let us bear the image of the heavenly. As the Lord Christ never ceased to do us good, by bestowing upon us his Holy Spirit, by garnishing his Church with so many notable gifts, and by perpetual praying to his Father for us, like reason ought to move us to aid our neighbour with all our endeavour, to maintain, as much as in us lieth, the bond of charity, and to honour Christ our Lord and Saviour, not with wicked traditions and cold devices of men, but with heavenly honour and spiritual in deed, most fit for us that give it, and him that shall receive it, even as he hath honoured and doth honour his Father. For he that honoureth him honoureth also the Father, of which he himself is a substantial witness.[31]

Master. The end of the world holy scripture calleth the fulfilling and performance of the kingdom and mystery of Christ, and the renewing of all things. For (saith the Apostle Peter in his second Epistle the third chapter), "We look for a new heaven, and a new earth, according to the promise of God: wherein dwelleth righteousness."[32] And it seemeth reason that corruption, unstedfast change, and sin, whereunto the whole world is subject, should at length have an end. Now by what way, and what fashion circumstances these things shall come to pass, I would fain hear thee tell.

Scholar. I will tell you as well as I can, according to the witness

[30] Eph. 4:7 ff.   [31] John 5:23.   [32] II Peter 3:13.

of the same apostle.³³ The heavens shall pass away like a storm, the elements shall melt away, the earth, and all the works therein, shall be consumed with fire; as though he should say, "As gold is wont to be fined, so shall the whole world be purified with fire, and be brought to his full perfection." The lesser world, which is man, following the same, shall likewise be delivered from corruption and change. And so for man this greater world (which for his sake was first created) shall at length be renewed, and be clad with another hue, much more pleasant and beautiful.

Master. What then remaineth?

Scholar. The last and general doom. For Christ shall come; at whose voice all the dead shall rise again, perfect and sound both in body and soul. The whole world shall behold him, sitting in the royal throne of his majesty; and after the examination of every man's conscience, the last sentence shall be pronounced. Then the children of God shall be in perfect possession of that kingdom of freedom from death and of everlasting life, which was prepared for them before the foundations of the world were laid. And they shall reign with Christ for ever. But the ungodly that believed not, shall be thrown from thence into everlasting fire, appointed for the devil and his angels.

Master. Thou hast said enough of the again rising of the dead. Now remaineth, that thou speak of the holy church: whereof I would very fain hear thy opinion.

Scholar. I will rehearse that in few words shortly which the holy scriptures set out at large and plentifully. Afore that the Lord God had made the heaven and earth, he determined to have for himself a most beautiful kingdom and holy commonwealth. The apostles and the ancient fathers that wrote in Greek, called it Ecclesia, in English, a congregation or assembly; into the which he hath admitted an infinite number of men, that should all be subject to one king as their sovereign and only one head. Him we call Christ, which is as much to say as "anointed." For the high bishops and kings among the Jews (who in figure betokened Christ, whom the Lord anointed with his holy Spirit), were wont by God's appointment at their consecration to have material oil poured on them. To the furnishing of this commonwealth belong all they, as many as do truly fear, honour and call upon God, wholly applying their mind to holy and godly living, and all those that putting all their hope and trust in him, do assuredly look for the bliss of everlasting life. But as many as are in this faith stedfast, were forechosen, predestinate, and appointed out to everlasting life,

---

³³ II Peter 3:10.

before the world was made. Witness hereof they have within in their hearts the Spirit of Christ, the author, earnest and unfailable pledge of their faith. Which faith only is able to perceive the mysteries of God, only bringeth peace unto the heart, only taketh hold on the righteousness that is in Christ Jesus.

Master. Doth then the Spirit alone and faith (sleep we never so soundly, or stand we never so reckless and slothful) so work all things for us, as without any help of our own to carry us idle up to heaven?

Scholar. I use, master, as you have taught me, to make a difference between the cause and the effects. The first, principal, and most perfect cause of our justifying and salvation, is the goodness and love of God, whereby he chose us for his, before he made the world. After that, God granteth us to be called by the preaching of the gospel of Jesus Christ, when the Spirit of the Lord is poured into us; by whose guiding and governance we be led to settle our trust in God, and hope for the performance of all his promises. With this choice is joined, as companion, the mortifying of the old man, that is of our affection and lust. From the same Spirit also cometh our sanctification, the love of God, and of our neighbour, justice: and uprightness of life; finally, to say all in sum, whatsoever is in us, or may be done of us, pure, honest, true and good, that altogether springeth out of this most pleasant root, from this most plentiful fountain, the goodness, love, choice and unchangeable purpose of God. He is the cause; the rest are the fruits and effects. Yet are also the goodness, choice and Spirit of God, and Christ himself, causes conjoined and coupled each with other, which may be reckoned among the principal causes of our salvation. As oft therefore as we use to say, that we are made righteous and saved by only faith, it is meant thereby that faith, or rather trust alone, doth lay hand upon, understand and perceive, our righteous-making to be given us of God freely; that is to say, by no deserts of our own, but by the free grace of the Almighty Father. Moreover faith doth engender in us the love of our neighbour, and such works as God is pleased withal. For if it be a lively and true faith, quickened by the Holy Ghost, she is the mother of all good saying and doing. By this short tale is it evident, whence, and by what means, we attain to be made righteous. For not by the worthiness of our deservings were we either heretofore chosen, or long ago saved, but by the only mercy of God and pure grace of Christ our Lord, whereby we were in him made to those good works, that God hath appointed for us to walk in. And although good works cannot deserve to make us righteous before God, yet do they so cleave unto faith, that neither can faith be found without them, nor good works be any where without faith.

Master. I like very well this short declaration of faith and works; for Paul plainly teacheth the same. But canst thou yet further depaint me out that congregation, which thou callest a kingdom or commonweal of Christians; and so set it out before mine eyes, that it may severally and plainly be known asunder from each other fellowship of men?

Scholar. I will prove how well I can do it. Your pleasure is, master, as I take it, that I point ye out some certain congregation, that may be seen.

Master. That it is indeed; and so it shall be good for ye to do.

Scholar. That congregation is nothing else but a certain multitude of men, which, wheresoever they be, profess the pure and upright learning of Christ, and that in such sort, as it is faithfully set forth in the holy testament, by the evangelists and apostles; which in all points are governed and ruled by the laws and statutes of their king and high Bishop Christ, in the bond of charity; which use his holy mysteries, that are commonly called sacraments, with such pureness and simplicity (as touching their nature and substance) as the apostles of Christ used and left behind in writing. The marks therefore of this Church are: first, pure preaching of the Gospel; then brotherly love, out of which, as members of all one body, springeth good will of each to other; thirdly, upright and uncorrupted use of the Lord's sacraments, according to the ordinance of the Gospel; last of all, brotherly correction, and excommunication, or banishing those out of the Church, that will not amend their lives. This mark the holy fathers termed discipline. This is that same Church, that is grounded upon the assured rock, Jesus Christ, and upon trust in him. This is that same Church which Paul calleth the pillar and upholding stay of truth. To this Church belong the keys wherewith heaven is locked and unlocked; for that is done by the ministration of the word, whereunto properly appertaineth the power to bind and loose, to hold for guilty, and forgive sins. So that whosoever believeth the Gospel preached in this Church, he shall be saved; but whosoever believeth not, he shall be damned.

Master. Now would I fain hear thy belief of the Holy Ghost.

Scholar. I confess him to be the third person of the holy Trinity; and sith he is equal with the Father and the Son, and of the very same nature, that he ought egally [34] to be worshipped with them both.

[34] Equally.

Master. Why is he called holy?

Scholar. Not only for his own holiness, but for that by him are made holy the chosen of God, and members of Christ. And therefore have the scriptures termed him the Spirit of sanctification or making holy.

Master. Wherein consisteth this sanctification?

Scholar. First, we be new gotten by his inward motion. And therefore said Christ, we must be new born of water, and of the Spirit.[35] Then by his inspiration are we adopted, and as it were by choice made the children of God. For which cause he is not causeless called the Spirit of adoption. By his light are we enlightened to understand God's mysteries. By his judgment are sins pardoned and retained. By his power is the flesh with her lusts kept down and tamed. By his pleasure are the manifold gifts dealt among the holy. Finally, by his means shall our mortal bodies be relieved. Therefore in the author of so great gifts we do not without a cause believe, honour, and call upon him.

Master. Well, thou hast now said sufficiently of the Holy Ghost. But this would I hear of thee: why it immediately followeth, that we believe the holy universal Church and the communion of saints.

Scholar. These two things I have alway thought to be most fitly coupled together, because the fellowships and incorporations of other men proceed and be governed by other means and policies, but the Church, which is an assembly of men called to everlasting salvation, is both gathered together and governed by the Holy Ghost, of whom we even now made mention. Which thing, sith it can not be perceived by bodily sense or light of nature, is by right and for good reason here reckoned among things that are known by belief. And therefore this calling together of the faithful is called universal, because it is bound to no one special place. For God throughout all coasts of the world hath them that worship him; which, though they be far scattered asunder by divers distance of countries and dominions, yet are they members most nearly joined of that same body, whereof Christ is the head, and have one spirit, faith, sacraments, prayers, forgiveness of sins, and heavenly bliss, common among them all, and be so knit with the bond of love, that they endeavour themselves in nothing more, than each to help other, and to build together in Christ.

Master. Seeing thou hast already spoken of the knowledge of God, and his members, I would also hear, what is the true service of God.

[35] John 3:5.

Scholar. First we must consider, that the right and true knowledge of God is the principal and only foundation of God's service. The same knowledge fear doth foster and maintain, which in scriptures is called the beginning of wisdom.[36] Faith and hope are the props and stays, whereupon lean all the rest that I have rehearsed. Furthermore charity, which we call love, is like an everlasting bond, by the strait knot whereof all other virtues be bound in one together, and their force increased. These be the inward parts of God's service, that is to say, which consist in the mind.

Master. What hast thou to say of the Sabbath, or the holy day, which even now thou madest mention of, among the laws of the first table?

Scholar. Sabbath is as much to say, as rest. It was appointed for only honour and service of God; and it is a figure of that rest and quietness, which they have that believe in Christ. For our trust in Christ doth set our minds at liberty from all slavish fear of the law, sin, death and hell, assuring us in the mean season, that by him we please God, and that he hath made us his children and heirs of his kingdom; whereby there groweth in our hearts peace and true quietness of mind, which is a certain foretaste of the most blessed quiet, which we shall have in his kingdom. As for those things that are used to to done on the Sabbath day, as ceremonies, and exercises in the service of God, they are tokens and witnesses of this assured trust. And meet it is, that faithful Christians, on such days as are appointed out for holy things, should lay aside unholy works, and give themselves earnestly to religion and serving of God.

Master. What be the parts of that outward serving God, which thou saidest even now did stand in certain bodily exercises, which are also tokens of the inward serving him?

Scholar. First, to teach and hear the learning of the gospel; then the pure and natural use of the ceremonies and sacraments; last of all, prayer made unto God by Christ, and in the name of Christ, which without fail obtaineth the Holy Ghost, the most assured author of all true serving God, and upright religion.

Master. Tell me what thou callest sacraments.

Scholar. They are certain customable reverent doings and ceremonies ordained by Christ; that by them he might put us in remembrance of his benefits, and we might declare our profession, that we be of the number of them, which are partakers of the same benefits, and which fasten all their affiance in him; that we

[36] E.g., Ps. 111:10.

are not ashamed of the name of Christ, or to be termed Christ's scholars.

Master. Tell me, my son, how these two sacraments be ministered: baptism; and that which Paul calleth the supper of the Lord.

Scholar. Him that believeth in Christ, professeth the Articles of the Christian religion, and mindeth to be baptized (I speak now of them that be grown to ripe years of discretion, sith for the young babes their parents' or the church's profession sufficeth), the minister dippeth in, or washeth with pure and clean water only, in the name of the Father, and of the Son, and of the Holy Ghost, and then commendeth him by prayer to God, into whose Church he is now openly as it were enrolled, that it may please God to grant him his grace, whereby he may answer in belief and life agreeably to his profession.

Master. What is the use of the Lord's supper?

Scholar. Even the very same, that was ordained by the Lord himself, Jesus Christ: which (as S. Paul saith), "the same night, that he was betrayed, took bread; and when he had given thanks, brake it, and said, This is my body, which is broken for you: Do this in the remembrance of me. In like manner, when supper was ended, he gave them the cup, saying: This cup is the new testament in my blood. Do this, as oft as ye shall drink thereof, in the remembrance of me." [37] This was the manner and order of the Lord's supper: which we ought to hold and keep; that the remembrance of so great a benefit, the passion and death of Christ, be alway kept in mind; that, after that the world is ended, he may come, and make us to sit with him at his own board.

Master. What doth baptism represent and set before our eyes?

Scholar. That we are by the Spirit of Christ new born, and cleansed from sin; that we be members and parts of his church, received into the communion of saints. For water signifieth the Spirit. Baptism is also a figure of our burial in Christ, and that we shall be raised up again with him in a new life, as I have before declared in Christ's resurrection.

Master. What declareth and betokeneth the supper unto us, which we solemnly use in the remembrance of the Lord?

Scholar. The Supper (as I have shewed a little before) is a certain thankful remembrance of the death of Christ, forasmuch as the bread representeth his body, betrayed to be crucified for us; the wine standeth in stead and place of his blood, plenteously shed for us. And even as by bread and wine our natural bodies are sus-

---

[37] I Cor. 11:23–25.

tained and nourished, so by the body, that is the flesh and blood of Christ, the soul is fed through faith, and quickened to the heavenly and godly life.

Master. How come these things to pass?

Scholar. These things come to pass by a certain secret mean, and lively working of the Spirit, when we believe that Christ hath, once for all, given up his body and blood for us, to make a sacrifice and most pleasant offering to his heavenly Father, and also when we confess and acknowledge him our only Saviour, high Bishop, Mediator, and Redeemer, to whom is due all honour and glory.

Master. All this thou dost well understand. For methinketh thy meaning is, that faith is the mouth of the soul, whereby we receive this very heavenly meat, full both of salvation and immortality, dealt among us, by the means of the Holy Ghost. Now, sith we have entreated of the sacraments, pass forward to the other parts of God's service.

Scholar. I will do your commandment. There remain two things, belonging to the perfection of God's service. First, our Lord Jesus Christ's will was, that there should be teachers and evangelists, that is to say, preachers of the gospel; to this intent, that his voice might continually be heard sound in his church. He that coveteth (as all ought to covet) to bear the name of a Christian, may have no doubt that he ought with most earnest affection and fervent desire endeavour himself to hear and soak into his mind the word of the Lord; not like the words of any man, but like (as it is indeed) the word of Almighty God. Secondarily, because all that is good and that ought of a Christian to be desired, cometh unto us from God, and is by him granted, therefore of him we ought to require all things, and by thanksgiving acknowledge them all received of him. Which thing he so well liketh, that he esteemeth it instead of a passing pleasant sacrifice; as it is most evident by the witness of the prophets and apostles.

Master. Hast thou any certain and appointed manner of praying?

Scholar. Yea forsooth: even the very same, that our Lord taught his disciples, and in them all other Christians. Who, being on a time required to teach them some sort of prayer, taught them this. "When ye pray," quod he, "say: Our Father which art in heaven, hallowed be thy name. Thy kingdom come. Thy will be done in earth as it is in heaven. Give us this day our daily bread, and forgive us our trespasses, as we forgive them that trespass against us.

And lead us not into temptation; But deliver us from evil. For thine is the kingdom, power and glory for ever. Amen." [38]

Master. How thinkest thou? is it lawful for us to use any other words of prayer?

Scholar. Although in this short abridgment are sufficiently contained all things that every Christian ought to pray for, yet hath not Christ in this prayer tied us up so short, as that it were not lawful for us to use other words and manner of prayer. But he hath set out in this prayer certain principal points, whereunto all our prayers should be referred. But let each man ask of God as his present need requireth. "Whatsoever ye ask the Father in my name," saith Christ, "he shall give it you." [39]

Master. Forasmuch as there is in all this prayer nothing doubtful or beside the purpose, I would hear thy mind of it.

Scholar. I do well perceive what the words do signify.

Master. Thinkest thou then that there is in it nothing dark, nothing hid, nothing hard to understand?

Scholar. Nothing at all. For neither was it Christ's pleasure, that there should be any thing in it dark or far from our capacity, specially since it belongeth egally to all, and is as necessary for the lewd,[40] as the learned.

Master. Therefore declare unto me, in few words, each part by itself.

Scholar. When I say, "Our Father which art in heaven," this do I think with myself: that it can not be but that he must hear me, and be pleased with my prayers. For I am his son (although unprofitable and disobedient), and he on the other side is my most bountiful Father, most ready to take pity and pardon me.

Master. Why dost thou say, he is in heaven? is he in some one certain and limited place in heaven? What meaneth that which he saith of himself, "I fill both heaven and earth"; [41] again, "The heaven is my seat and the earth my footstool?" [42]

Scholar. Hereof have I spoken somewhat before: whereunto I will join this that followeth. First of all, as oft as we do say, "which art in heaven," it is as much to say as heavenly and divine. For we ought to think much higher of our heavenly Father than of our earthly. He is also said to be in heaven for this cause: that in that high and heavenly place the notable and wonderful works of God do the more clearly and gloriously shew themselves. And he is now declared to be in everlasting and full felicity; whereas we abide

---

[38] Conflation of Luke 11:1 ff. and Matt. 6:9 ff.
[39] John 16:23.
[40] Unlearned.
[41] Jer. 23:24.
[42] Isa. 66:1.

yet banished in earth full wretchedly. Moreover as the heaven by unmeasurable wideness of compass containeth all places, the earth, and the sea, and no place is there, that may be hid from the large reach of heaven, sith it is at every instant of time to every thing present; so hereby may we understand, that God is likewise present to each thing in each place. He seeth, heareth and governeth all things; he being himself a spirit, and most far from all earthly and mortal state. Witness whereof Hieremy the prophet. "Am not I," saith the Lord, "a God near unto you? And am not I a God far off? Shall any man be able to shroud himself in such a corner, that I can not espy him?" [43] This is a pithy sentence, to drive fear into us, that we offend not that Lord of so large a dominion: whereby also we are persuaded assuredly to believe, that God will hear whensoever we shall stand in need. For he is at all times and in all places present. This foundation then laid, and so sweet and pleasant entrance prepared, there followeth the first part of the Lord's prayer, wherein we require, that not only we, but also all other whosoever, may in holiness honour, reverence, and worship his name.

Master. How is that to be done?

Scholar. I shall shew you: then we do that, when leaving all those that have the name of gods, be they in heaven or in earth, or worshipped in temples, in divers shapes and images, we acknowledge him alone our Father, pray to the true God, and Jesus Christ his only Son, whom he hath sent, and by pure unfeigned prayer call upon him alone, with uprightness of life and innocency.

Master. Thou hast said very well: proceed.

Scholar. In the second part we require that his kingdom come. For we see not yet all things in subjection to Christ; we see not the stone hewed off from the mountain without work of man, which all-to brosed [44] and brought to nought the image which Daniel descriveth, that the only rock Christ may obtain and possess the dominion of the whole world, granted him of his Father. Antichrist is not yet slain. For this cause do we long for, and pray that it may at length come to pass and be fulfilled, that Christ may reign with his saints, according to God's promises; that he may live and be Lord in the world, according to the decrees of the holy Gospel: not after the traditions and laws of men, nor pleasure of worldly tyrants.

Master. God grant his kingdom may come, and that speedily!

Scholar. Moreover, sith it is the children's duty to frame their life to their father's will, and not the father's to bow to the chil-

[43] Jer. 23:23–24.   [44] Bruised.

dren's pleasure; forasmuch as our will is commonly by tickling of affections, and stirring of lusts, drawn to do those things, that God is displeased with: it is reason, that we hang wholly upon the beck of our heavenly Father, and wholly submit ourselves to his heavenly government. Wherefore, for this cause, we mortal men do pray that we may in like case be obedient to his commandment, as are the sun and moon and other stars in heaven, which both by ordinary courses, and by lightening the earth with uncessant beams, execute the Lord's will continually; or that we, as the angels and other spirits divine, in all points obey him; which bestow all their travail diligently to accomplish his godly commandments.

Next after that he teacheth us to ask of our heavenly Father our bread; whereby he meaneth not meat only, but also all things else needful for maintenance, and preserving of life; that we may learn, that God alone is author of all things; which maketh the fruits of the earth both to grow and increase to plenty. Wherefore it is meet that we call upon him alone in prayer, which (as David saith) alone feedeth and maintaineth all things.[45]

Master. Some suppose this place to mean that bread that Christ maketh mention of in the sixth of John; that is, of the true knowledge and taste of Christ, that was born and died for us; wherewith the faithful soul is fed. The reason whereupon they gather this is the Greek word *epiousion,* whereby they understand supernatural, ghostly, heavenly and divine. This meaning I refuse not; for both these expositions may fitly agree with this place. But why calleth he it daily bread, which is also signified by this word *epiousion?*

Scholar. We ask daily bread, that might be always present and accompany us continually, to slake and satisfy our thirsty desire, and unsatiate stomach; lest otherwise we should be, as Christ sayeth, careful for tomorrow; because the morrow shall care for itself. For it shall come not without his own discommodity and care. Wherefore it is not reason that one day should increase the evil of another. It shall be sufficient for us daily to ask that our most bountiful Father is ready daily to give.

Now followeth the fifth request, wherein we beseech the Father to forgive us our trespasses and defaults, that we have committed. This request doubtless is very necessary, sith there is no man living free from sin. Here therefore must we cast away all trust of ourselves. Here must we pluck down our courage. Here must we pray our most merciful Father, for the love of Jesu Christ his most dear and obedient Son, to pardon, forgive, and utterly blot

[45] E.g., Ps. 145:15–16.

out of his book, our innumerable offences. Here ought we in the mean season to be mindful of the covenant we make with God: That it may please God so to forgive us our trespasses, as we ourselves forgive them that trespass against us. Therefore it is necessary, that we forgive and pardon all men all their offences, of what sort or condition soever they be. If we forgive men their faults, our heavenly Father shall forgive us ours.

Master. Were these things, my son, thus used, there should not, at this day, thus violently reign so many brawls, so many contentions, so many and so heinous disagreements, enmities and hatreds of one man to another. But now, whereas each man so standeth in his own conceit, that he will not lese an inch of his right, neither in honour or wealth, it chanceth oft that they lese both their wealth, their honour, and their life itself withal. Yea they put from themselves and turn away the favour of God, and everlasting glory. But thou, my son, must not be ignorant of Christ's commandment; nor of that which Paul teacheth, that thou suffer not thyself to be overcome of evil,[46] that is, suffer not thyself so to be seduced by any other man's offence, as to repay evil for evil, but rather overcome evil with good: I mean, by doing him good, that hath done thee evil; by using him friendly, that hath shewed himself thy most cruel foe. Now go forward to the sixth request.

Scholar. I will, with a good will, as you command me. Forasmuch as we be feeble, weak, subject to a thousand perils, a M. temptations, easy to be overcome, ready to yield to every light occasion, either to men fraught with malice, or to our own lust and appetite, or finally to the crafty malicious serpent, the devil; Therefore we beseech our Father, that he bring us into no such hard escape and peril, nor leave us in the very plunge of danger, but, if it come to that point, that he rather take us away from the present mischief, and engines of the devil, the author and principal cause of all evil, than suffer us to run headlong into destruction. Now have you, good master, in few words, all that you have taught me, unless peradventure somewhat be overslipped in the rehearsal.

Master. Because thine is the kingdom, power and glory for ever. Amen. Why was it Christ's pleasure to knit up our prayer with this clause in the end?

Scholar. Partly that we should declare our assured trust to obtain all things that we before have required. For there is nothing which, if it be asked with faith, he is not able or not willing to give, who ruleth and governeth all things, who is able to do all

[46] Rom. 12:21.

things, who is garnished with endless glory. These things when we rehearse of God our Father, there remaineth no cause to doubt, or suspect, that we shall receive denial. Partly by so saying, we teach ourselves how meet it is to make our suit to God; sith beside him none glistereth with so shining glory, none hath dominion so large, or force so great, to be able to stay him from giving that he hath appointed according to his pleasure, or to take away that he hath already given us. And there is no evil of ours so great, that may not be put away by his exceeding great power, glory and wisdom.

Master. I like well, my son, this thy short declaration, and I see nothing left out, that ought to have been spoken.[47] But yet this one thing will I add thereto. The chief and principal thing required in prayer, is that without all doubting we stedfastly believe that God our Father will grant what we do ask; so that it be[48] neither unprofitable for us to receive, nor unfit for him to give. For he that is not assured but doubtful, let him not think (as James saith) to get any thing at the hands of God.[49]

I see now, my dear son, how diligently and heedfully thou hast applied thy mind to those things that I have taught thee, how godly and upright a judgment thou hast of God's true service, and of the duties of neighbours one to another. This remaineth, that from henceforth thou so frame thy life, that this heavenly and godly knowledge decay not in thee, nor lie soulless and dead, as it were, in a tomb of the flesh. But rather see that thou wholly give thyself continually and earnestly to these godly studies. So shalt thou live, not only in this present life, but also in the life to come, which is much better and blesseder than this life present. For godliness (as Paul saith) hath a promise, not in this life only, but in the other.[50] It is convenient therefore, that we earnestly follow godliness, which plainly openeth the way to heaven, if we will seek to attain thereunto.

And the principal point of godliness is (as thou hast declared even now very well) to know God only; to covet him only as the chief felicity; to fear him as our Lord; to love and reverence him as our Father; with his Son our Saviour Jesus Christ. This is he that hath begotten and regenerate us. This is he which at the be-

---

[47] The English versions give the next sentences: "But yet . . . at the hands of God," to *Scholar,* with *Master* coming in again at "I see now . . ." We have followed the Latin, which gives the sense better.
[48] So long as it is.
[49] James 1:7.
[50] I Tim. 4:8.

ginning gave us life and soul, which maintaineth, which blesseth us with life of everlasting continuance. To this godliness is directly contrary godlessness. As for superstition and hypocrisy, they counterfeit indeed, and resemble it, whereas nevertheless they are most far different from all true godliness; and therefore we ought to avoid them as a pestilence, as the venom, and most contagious enemies of our soul and salvation.

The next point of godliness is to love each man, as our brother. For if God did at the beginning create us all, if he doth feed and govern us, finally, if he be the cause and author of our dwelling in this wide frame of the world, the name of brother must needs most fitly agree with us. And with so much straiter bond shall we be bound together, as we approach nearer to Christ, which is our brother, the first begotten and eldest; whom he that knoweth not, he that hath no hold of, is unrighteous indeed, and hath no place among the people of God. For Christ is the root and foundation of all right and justice, and he hath poured into our hearts certain natural lessons, as: "Do that," saith he, "to another, that thou wouldst have done unto thyself." [51] Beware therefore, thou do nothing to any man, that thou thyself wouldst not willingly suffer. Measure always another by thine own mind, and as thou feelest in thyself. If it grieve thee to suffer injury; if thou think it wrong that another man doth to thee; judge likewise the same in the person of thy neighbour that thou feelest in thyself: and thou shalt perceive, that thou dost no less wrongfully in hurting another, than other do in hurting thee. Here if we would stedfastly fasten our foot, hereunto if we would earnestly travail, we should attain to the very highest top of innocency. For the first degree thereof is to offend no man; the next to help, as much as in us lieth, all men; at least to will and wish well to all; the third (which is accounted the chief and perfectest) is to do good even to our enemies that wrong us.

Let us therefore know ourselves, pluck out the faults that are in us, and in their place plant virtues; like unto the husbandmen, that first use to shrubbe and root out the thorns, brambles and weeds, out of their ley-land and unlooked to; and then each where therein scatter and throw in to the womb of the earth good and fruitful seeds, to bring forth good fruit in their due season. Likewise let us do. For first let us labour to root out froward and corrupt lusts: and afterward plant holy and fit conditions for Christian hearts. Which, if they be watered, and fatted with the dew

[51] Matt. 7:12.

of God's word, and nourished with warmth of the Holy Ghost, they shall bring forth doubtless the most plentiful fruit of immortality and blessed life, which God hath by Christ prepared for his chosen, before the foundations of the world were laid. To whom be all honour and glory. Amen.

The end of the Cathechism.

John Hooper

A DECLARACION OF CHRISTE AND OF HIS OFFYCE

John Hooper: A Declaracion of Christe and of his offyce

INTRODUCTION

HOOPER BELONGED TO THE LEFT WING OF THE REFORMATION. AS such he represented in his particularly powerful way the new trend in the English scene, the increasing influence of Zurich. Even before he went abroad in 1539 to avoid trouble under the Six Articles, he had been a follower of Zwingli and Bullinger. Indeed, a letter of his to Bullinger seems to suggest that he embraced the Reformed faith as the result of reading their writings. Abroad, he ended up in the city of Zwingli and Bullinger after a time in Strasbourg, and became a complete man of Zurich, as advanced and militant as his masters. He returned to England in 1549 and occupied important posts as chaplain to the Protector Somerset and then to Northumberland and finally as Bishop of Gloucester. But it cannot be said that he fitted happily into English Church life. First his views on divorce provoked one controversy; then his doctrine of predestination touched off another; and at last, when he was nominated Bishop of Gloucester, he had scruples on the wearing of "vestments" at his consecration. Unmoved by the arguments of Thomas Cranmer, Nicholas Ridley, Martin Bucer, Peter Martyr, and others, Hooper needed a month in the Fleet Prison to convince him that the prescribed garments were not, after all, inconsistent with the New Testament. He was, indeed, a jagged, awkward, unapproachable man, but full of energy and zeal, and remarkably efficient in his diocese.

As a writer he had a wider range than most of the other English Reformers who, apart from their sermons, were immersed in the Eucharistic controversy or Biblical work or practical affairs. Hooper was also an exceedingly active bishop, at one time administering Worcester and Gloucester together and journeying backward and forward between the two. Even before this he was preaching, according to his wife, "four, or at least three times every day," and she begs Bullinger to write and tell him "to be more moderate in his labour."[1] Nevertheless, he found time also to write, if not voluminously, at least widely. He left what we might call a little dogmatics (*A briefe and clear confession of the Chrïstian faith*), an ethics (*A Declaration of the ten holy commaundementes*), a set of sermons on Jonah, a theological discussion of the incarnation, a reply to Gardiner on the Eucharist, and various expositions on parts of Romans and of the Psalter, besides some miscellaneous pieces.

Hooper wrote *A Declaracion of Christe and of his offyce*, according to his dedicatory epistle to Somerset, so "that every godly man may put to his helping hand to restore [Christ] again unto his kingdom." In other words, he wants to expound the heart of Christology as the means to reform theology. We may first summarize the book before assessing it:

Man has sinned, but God is merciful and provides Christ as the means of salvation. (Cap. I.) Jesus Christ is both God and man, the Son of God and the son of Mary, perpetual virgin. (Cap. II.) But it is chiefly of his office that we must now speak. This office is twofold. It is first that of priest. Christ is the priest primarily in his teaching and preaching. He has passed on this teaching office to the Church in commanding her to preach the gospel. (Cap. III.) Therefore the Church is bound to the word of Christ (i.e., the message of the New Testament) and must not adulterate it with human inventions. (Cap. IV.) Secondarily (Hooper speaks here and in the two following sections of Christ's second, third, and fourth offices, but it is clear that these are only subdivisions of his priestly office), Christ's priestly office lies in his making intercession, or in being the Mediator through whom his people may have access to the Father. It follows that there is no need of the saints or of images in approaching God. (Cap. V.) Thirdly, his priesthood consists in his offering his unique sacrifice for sin. (Cap. VI.) There are two necessary corollaries to this. The first is justification by faith. "To be justified by faith in Christ is as much to say as, we obtain remission of sin, and are accepted into the favour of God, by the merits of Christ. To be justified by works is as much to say as, to deserve remission of sin by works.... So that faith doth not only show us Christ that died, and now sitteth at the right hand of God; but also applieth the merits of this death unto us, and maketh Christ ours." (Cap.

---

[1] *Original Letters* (PS, I.108).

VII.) The second is the true doctrine of the Lord's Supper, which is not a sacrifice for sin, and in which no transubstantiation takes place. Yet Christ, who is absent corporally, "communicates by faith in spirit that most precious body, and the merits of the same." (Cap. VIII.) Fourthly, it is part of Christ's priestly office to sanctify his own people by the Word, the Spirit, and faith. (Cap. IX.) From this flows the new life of faith proving itself by works. (Cap. X.)

The second office of Christ is his Kingship. His Kingdom is spiritual and the only sword to be wielded in its defense is the Word. It is a persecuted Kingdom, which has God as its only defender, as he is also its only ruler. In this Kingdom the gospel is law, to which all God's people must submit. And the interpreter of the gospel is not men but Christ (that is, if I am not mistaken, the gospel is to be interpreted through the New Testament alone). Certainly it is a help and confirmation to our faith to find the fathers of the Church interpreting the gospel as we do, but our faith must be placed in the gospel and not in the interpreters. The gift of interpretation is the light of the Holy Spirit which God gives to the humble and penitent. (Cap. XI.) In three hasty, inconclusive and frankly gloomy chapters, Hooper then turns to the knowledge of man and his duty toward Christ.

The chief point in all this is his concept of Christ's offices. Here Hooper shows himself firmly within the tradition of the Reformed Church. The history of the "offices" of Christ in the Reformation before Calvin is not clear in detail. Both Luther and Melanchthon speak of Christ as the king and the priest. In Melanchthon the priestly office (in which he is more interested) consists in his preaching, his sacrificing of himself, his praying and blessing. For Bullinger also, it is a twofold office, and again his priesthood consists in teaching, making intercession, blessing, and sacrificing himself: but Bullinger adds Christ's sanctifying of his people with the Spirit. In his summary a page later, however, he omits blessing, perhaps because he sees it as a part of his sacrifice for sin.[2] Apparently only Osiander, among the Reformers, taught the *munus triplex* before Calvin, although it was not unknown in the early Church and in the Middle Ages. Calvin himself moved from a twofold office in the 1536 *Institutio* to the threefold office in the 1559 edition. It seems to be stated clearly first in the 1545 edition.

Hooper's thought is not original: he teaches the twofold office and divides it into teaching, making intercession, sacrifice, and sanctification. (Here, by the way, he was not relying on Bullinger's

[2] Sermon VII. Fourth Decade (PS, III.283 ff.).

sermon, which was not published until 1550.) But his treatment has its importance in the history of the doctrine both on account of his application of the doctrine to the life of the Church (so that it may be said that he bases this, not on the Bible *per se,* as the Elizabethan Puritans did, but on a Christology) and also in that his was the first English book on the subject, indeed, so far as I can find, the only English book on it, for the doctrine was little used in England. Hooper moved very quickly from the twofold office which he held in 1547 to the threefold which he propounds with complete clarity in *A briefe and clear confession of the Christian faith* in 1550. The Twentieth Article states: "I believe that the same Jesus Christ is verily Christ, that is to say, the Messias, anointed by the Holy Ghost, because he was the very King, the Prophet, and great Sacrificer." [3] And the Twenty-second: "I believe that Jesus Christ hath verily exercised these three offices, that is to say, of a prophet, of a king, of a sacrificer, not only in this world, being a mortal man as we are; but also that he exerciseth yet daily the same in heaven before the face of the Father." [4] We must suppose that in the meanwhile he had read Calvin's 1545 *Institutio.*

[3] PS, II.29.   [4] *Ibid.*

BIBLIOGRAPHY

A Declaracion of Christe and of his offyce was printed first at Zurich in 1547, the year in which Hooper went to live there and so, no doubt, while he was himself present to superintend the printing. This makes the more strange the chaotic state of the book. Christopher Rosdell revised it for the next generation and (in a piece of prose of which he was doubtless very proud and which shows us where he drew his inspiration from) tells us why he thinks the text was so corrupt: "As that famous river Hypanis, the prince of rivers amongst the Scythians, which in itself is most pure and sweet, by running through the bitter pool Exampeus or [ere] it come to the sea, is infected," etc., etc., etc., "so this godly and profitable tract, in itself most pure and pleasant, by passing through the press of an unskilful printer at Zurich in Germany, or it came to be published in the sea of this world, was so infected and corrupted, not with small and petty scapes, but with gross and palpable faults, not here and there, but in every leaf, in every page, and almost in every line, that it might truly be said, Either this is not Master Hooper's work, or else, *quam dissimilis sui prodit.*" (This dedication is well worth reading for amusement.) The title page says definitely that the printer was "a man of another Nation."

It has therefore been generally taken by the few who have since written on Hooper that the cause for the corruption of the text was that the compositor knew no English. This seems to have been so; but I believe it is only half the story. There are indications that 1547 was a translation from an earlier Latin work, and an unskillful translation at that. These indications are as follows:

1. It is a habit of Hooper's to quote Scripture in Latin, as can be seen in other of his writings. But elsewhere he will at once translate it with "that is to say, . . ." Many examples will be found in *A Declaration of the X holie commaundements*. But in the 1547 edition, the Latin is left untranslated. For the later edi-

tion, Rosdell had to translate it himself. As he says in the preface: "The allegations and testimonies alleged out of holy scripture, or fathers . . . (which in the first edition were all in Latin) might now, for the use and benefit of the simple reader, come forth in English." If the whole book was originally in Latin, these quotations would, of course, not be translated into English.

2. Often the gloss as well as the quotation is in Latin:
   a. "And mark this manner of speech: *Fide iustificamur; hoc est, fiducia misericordiae sumus iusti.*"—"*Fide iustificamur*" is the quotation from Romans, "*hoc est . . .*" Hooper's gloss, which should be in English.
   b. "*Nisi granum frumenti deiectum in terram mortuum fuerit, ipsum solum manet. Mortua prodest caro, non comesa.*"—The text is John 12:24. "*Mortua prodest . . .*" ("Only the flesh that died is profitable, not the flesh eaten") is the gloss—a quotation from a father?
   c. "I will interpretate this article of my creed thus: *Christus ascendit ad dextram Patris. Patris dextra est ubique: ergo Christus ascendit ad ubique.*"—Here he is putting words into the mouth of a Lutheran, or perhaps quoting a Lutheran writer. The first sentence is from the Creed. The rest forms a syllogism on it; strictly it should be in English, though it is happier in Latin.
   d. "*Similis est fratribus, perfectus Deus et perfectus homo.*" —Heb. 2:17. The gloss itself is perhaps an inflation by translator or printer of "*perfectus homo,*" which the sense demands.
   e. "*Ego aliquando vivebam sine lege, id est, fui securus, non sentiens iram Dei.*"—Rom. 7:9. "*id est . . .*" ("that is, I was secure and did not feel the wrath of God") is Hooper's gloss.

3. Explanatory or connecting words are sometimes in Latin:
   a. "*Ego hodie genui te. Et alibi, Tu es sacerdos.*"—" 'This day have I begotten thee.' And elsewhere, 'Thou art a priest.' "
   b. Athanasius "*adversus gentes sic scribit. Philosophi . . .*" —Athanasius "writes thus against the Gentiles: *Philosophi . . .*"
   c. "The prophets and apostles doth use many times this word '*annunciare*' *pro* '*laudare*' *et* '*gratias agere.*' "— "*Pro*" and "*et*" should be in English, though scholars quite often, in quoting Greek, would put a copulative (e.g., καὶ) into Greek, no doubt to preserve the flow. (It should

be noted, however, that *inquit* [he says] in the middle of a quotation is not evidence here, for Hooper customarily uses it in other writings.)

4. On four occasions a whole long clause appears in Latin, irrespective of any Biblical quotation, a little island of Latin surrounded by a sea of English.
   a. "Naum the prophet doth give God a wonderful name. . . . *Noter hu leobau* (i.e., a transliteration of Hebrew), *quasi iniuriarum memoriam retinens, et ulciscendi occasionem expectans*" ("as though remembering injuries, and waiting an opportunity for vengeance").
   b. "And because the oration of Christ wroten by St. John is obscure, and lacketh a declaration somewhat of the purpose that Christ would prove, *omittit, Hebraeorum more, alteram similitudinis partem*" ("he omits, in the Hebrew manner, the other part of the similitude").
   c. "So St. Paul *admirandis enallagis et prosopopoeis in Epi. Rom. vii disputat*" ("So St. Paul argues with admirable figures of speech in Rom. 7").
   d. Likewise with another argument, *a liberatione Christi petitium, et ab honesto. Dedit semetipsum pro nobis, etc.*" ("argument drawn from the deliverance Christ won for us, and from integrity or honour").

This final category seems to be conclusive. We may therefore posit an earlier Latin form of the book, carelessly translated. Whether it was ever printed is another matter. A search by the present editor and by a member of the staff of the Cambridge University Library has failed to discover such a book.

A Declaracion/ of Christe and of his/ offyce compylyd by Jo-/ han Hoper, Anno/ 1547./ Matt. 7./ Hic est filius meus dilectus, in/ quo mihi bene complacuit, ipsum/ audite.
Colophon: Pryntyd/ in Zvrych by Av-/gustyne Fries. Anno M./ D.XLVII.

Rosdell's revised edition of 1582:
A Godlie and Pro-/fitable treatise contei-/nying a declaration of/ Christ and his/ Office./ compiled 1547 by the reverend/ father, and faithfull Minister of/ Christe and constant martyre in/ the truth Maister Jhon Hoper:/ and newly corrected, and purged/ by the Godlie industrie of C.R./ from a multitude of grosse faul-/tes, where withall it was peste-/red, through the corruption of the/ print, and great unskilfulnesse/ of the

Printer, beying/ a man of an other/ Nation./ Matt. vii./ This is my beloved Sonne in whom/ I am well pleased, heare hym./ Imprinted at London for John/ Perrin, and are to be sold at his/ shop in Paules Churchyard,/ at the Signe of the/ Aungell.

I am indebted to my friend the Reverend J. H. Jacques for letting me use as the basis of this present version one that he prepared for a stillborn volume of selections from the Anglican Reformers which was being compiled by members of the Diocese of Lincoln five or six years ago. This I have now made into a reprint of the 1547 edition, apart from punctuation.

Works on Hooper:

T. Vetter, *Johannes Hooper, Bischof von Gloucester und Worcester, und seine Beziehungen zu Bullinger und Zürich.* (From: Turricensia. Beiträge zur zürcherische Geschichte. Zürich, 1891.)

F. D. Price, *Gloucester Diocese under Bishop Hooper* (Transactions of Bristol and Gloucestershire Archaeological Society, Vol. lx [1938], pp. 51–151).

M. M. Knappen, *Tudor Puritanism: A Chapter in the History of Idealism.* The University of Chicago Press, 1939.

J. Gairdner, "Bishop Hooper's visitation of Gloucester, 1551," In *English Historical Review,* 1904, pp. 98–121.

John Hooper: A Declaracion of Christe and of his offyce

THE TEXT

Caput I

For as much as almighty God of his infinite mercy and goodness prepared a means whereby Adam and his posterity might be restored again unto their original justice and perfection both of body and soul, and to live eternally unto the same end that they were created for, to bless and magnify for ever the immortal and living God; it is the office of every true Christian, before all other studies, travails, and pains that he shall sustain for the time of this brief and miserable life, to apply himself with all diligent force and labour to know perfectly this means ordained by God for our salvation; and the thing once known, diligently with heart, soul, and mind to follow the means, until such time as the effect and end be obtained wherefore [5] the means was appointed. The means was shewed unto Adam at his first and original transgression—the seed of a woman, which should break the head of the serpent, destroy the kingdom of the devil, and restore Adam and as many as knew and believed in this seed unto life everlasting. . . . All the solace and joy of Adam's posterity consisteth solely and only in this, Rom. v.: "Where sin abounded, grace abounded much more." [6] The benefits and merits of this seed aboundeth and is more available before the judgment of God, than sin, the flesh, the devil, and the world. This treasure and inestimable riches must be perfectly known of every person that will be saved. It is only in Christ, and in the knowledge of him, what he is, and what is his office.

[5] For which.   [6] Rom. 5:20.

Caput II Containeth What Christ Is

He is the Son of the living God and perpetual virgin Mary; both God and man, the true Messias, promised unto man from the beginning of his fall: whom St. John calleth the Word of eternal essence and divine majesty, saying, "In the beginning was the Word, and the Word was with God, and the Word was God." Joan.i.[7] Saint Paul, ad Coloss. capite i. calleth him "the image of God, &c."[8] unto the Hebrews, cap.i., "the brightness of God."[9] The creed of Nice calleth him "Light of light," the natural Son of God, in whom dwelleth the fountain of all divinity naturally, as Paul said, Col.ii., "In him dwelleth the fulness of the Godhead bodily";[10] meaning, that he is not the Son of God by adoption or acceptation into grace, as Abraham, David and other holy saints; but naturally the Son of God, equal with the Father in all things, as John saith, "And we saw the glory of him as the glory of the only-begotten of the Father." Cap.i. . . .[11]

This scripture doth not only teach us the knowledge of salvation, but doth comfort us against all the assaults, subtilties, and crafts of the devil, that God would of his inestimable love rather suffer his only Son to die for the world, than all the world should perish. Remaining always, as he was, very God immortal, ⟨he⟩ received the thing he was not, the mortal nature and true flesh of man, in the which he died, as Peter saith, I Peter iv.[12] Irenaeus, p. 185, hath these godly words: Christ was crucified and dead, the Word giving place that he might be crucified and die.[13] . . . The divine nature of Christ was not rent, nor torn, nor killed; but it obeyed the will of the Father. It gave place unto the displeasure and ire of God, that the body of Christ might die. Being all ways[14] equal with his Father, he could, if he had executed his divine power, ⟨have⟩ delivered this body from the tyranny of the Jews. . . . Seeing he was sent into the world to suffer this most cruel death and passion, he would do nothing that should be contrary unto his vocation, but with patience praying for his enemies, submitted himself unto the ignominy and contempt of the cross, suffering pains innumerable without grudge or murmur against the holy will of his Father: his Godhead hiding itself until the third day, when it restored the soul again unto the body and caused it to rise with great triumph and glory. . . . Repeating the

---

[7] John 1:1.
[8] Col. 1:15.
[9] Heb. 1:3.
[10] Col. 2:9.
[11] John 1:14.
[12] I Peter 4:1.
[13] *Contra haereses*, III.xix.3 (PG 7.941).
[14] In every way.

doctrine that before his death he preached unto the world, that he was both king and lord high bishop and priest both of heaven and earth. . . . He that before was most vile and contemptible in the sight of the world, now by right and just title acclaimeth [15] the dominion and empire of all the world. How mighty a prince he is, the creation of the world and the preservation thereof declareth. How merciful towards them that repent, we know by daily experience in ourselves, and by the example of other, Adam, David, Manasse, and Peter. How cruel and rigorous for sin, the punishment that we suffer and the calamities of this world declareth, specially the death of his most innocent body. How immortal his ire is against such as repent not, Saul, Pharao, Judas, with other, declare. . . .

Caput III

Now that the scripture hath taught us to know that Christ is both God and man, I will briefly entreat of his office: first, of his priesthood, then of his kingdom and reign over his church till the world's end, then, for ever, in solace with his elects, in perpetual mercy and favour; with such as contemn in this world his holy commandment and pleasure, in severe justice and immortal hatred and ire for ever. John iii.[16]

Saint Paul, in the epistle to the Hebrews, proveth him to be the priest called by God unto that function and office of the high bishop: "Christ took not to himself this honour to be made the high priest; but he that said unto him, Thou art my Son, this day begat I thee. And in another place, Thou art a priest for ever after the order of Melchisedec." Caput v.[17] By whose obedience unto the cross he gave everlasting health to as many as obeyed him and in all things executed the very true office of a bishop, to whom it appertained to teach the people; which was the chiefest part of the bishop's office, and most diligently and straitly commanded by God. . . .

This authority to preach the Father gave unto him in the hearing of the apostles, Matt. iii., xvii.,[18] and bound his church to receive his doctrine, saying, "This is my dear beloved Son, in whom I delight, hear him." . . . He preached not only himself, but sent his apostles and disciples to manifest unto the world, that the acceptable time of grace was come and the sacrifice for sin born into

---

[15] Claimeth.
[16] John 3:36.
[17] Heb. 5:5–6.
[18] Matt. 3:17; 17:5.

the world, Matt. x., John x.[19] And after his resurrection he gave them commandment to preach, and likewise what they should preach. . . .[20]

Always in their doctrine they taught the thing that Christ first taught and God's holy Spirit inspired them. Gal. i. ii. Cor. iii.[21] Holy apostles never took upon them to be Christ's vicar in the earth, nor to be his lieutenant; but said, "Let a man so esteem us, as the ministers of Christ, and stewards of the secrets of God. i. Cor. iv. . . .[22] They ministered not in the church, as though Christ were absent, although his most glorious body was departed corporally into the heavens above, but as Christ present, that always governeth his church with his Spirit of truth, as he promised, Matt. xxviii. Behold, I am with you unto the end of the world. . . .[23]

In the absence of his body, he hath commended the protection and governance of his church unto the Holy Ghost, the same God, and one God with the Father and his divine nature: whose divine puissance and power overmatcheth the force of the devil, so that hell itself cannot take one of Christ's flock out of God's protection. John x.[24] And this defence dureth not for a day, nor year, but shall demour [25] for ever, till this church be glorified at the resurrection of the flesh. John xv.[26]

It was no little pain that Christ suffered in washing away the sins of this church. Therefore he will not commit the defence thereof unto man. It is no less glory to defend and keep the thing won by force, than it is by force to obtain the victory. Adam, Abel, Abraham, Moses, nor Aaron could not win this church out of the devil's tyranny: no more can they defend it, delivered. For although by imputation of Christ's justice these men and all other faithfuls be delivered from the tyranny of the devil and condemnation of the law, yet had and hath the devil his very friends dwelling within the nature of man, corrupt as long as he liveth—the concupiscence and rebellion of man's nature, who [27] ceaseth nor day nor night to betray man again to the devil, except with the motion of true penitence this concupiscence be kept under in fear and faith; which two virtues be so infirm in man, that be he never

---

[19] Matt. 10:7; Luke, ch. 10 (?).
[20] Mark 16:15 ff.; Matt. 28:19 f.
[21] Gal. 1:6–9, 11–12; I Cor. 3:5 ff.
[22] I Cor. 4:1.
[23] Matt. 28:20.
[24] John 10:29.
[25] Abide, remain.
[26] John 15:1–11.
[27] *Who* refers to *concupiscence and rebellion*.

so perfect, yet falleth he from God sometime, as Abraham, Isaac, Jacob, Moses, and Aaron. Isa. xliii. Num. xix.[28] Therefore he keepeth the defence and governance of the church only and solely himself, in whom the devil hath not a jot of right. Though the apostles were instructed in all truth and left the same written unto his church, yet were they ministers, servants, testimonies, and preachers of this verity, and not Christ's vicars in earth and lieutenant to keep the keys of heaven, hell, and purgatory; but only appointed to approve the thing to be good that God's laws commanded, and that to be ill, that the word of God condemned.

Seeing that Christ doth govern his church always by his holy Spirit and bindeth all the ministers thereof unto the sole word of God, what abomination is this, that any bishop of Rome, Hierusalem, Antioche, or elsewhere, should acclaim to be Christ's vicar in the earth, and take upon him to make any laws in the church of God to bind the conscience of man, beside the word of God; and in placing of their superstition and idolatry, put the word of God out of his place. By what law, by whom, or where hath any this title given unto him, to be God's vicar and lieutenant upon the earth? . . .

This knowledge of Christ's supremity and continual presence in the church admitteth no lieutenant nor general vicar. Likewise it admitteth not the decrees and laws of men, brought into the church contrary unto the word and scripture of God, which is only sufficient to teach all verity and truth for the salvation of man. . . .

Caput IIII

Christ . . . taught his disciples the truth by the only law, written by Moses and the prophets, and not by unwritten verities.[29] And in all controversies and doubtful questions he answered his contraries [30] by the word of God. . . . Nothing can be desired necessary for man, but in this law it is prescribed. Of what degree, vocation, or calling soever he be, his duty is shewed unto him in the scripture. And in this it differeth from man's laws, because it is absolute, perfect, and never to be changed, nothing added unto it, nor taken from it. And the church of Christ, the more it was

---

[28] Isa. 43:27. Numbers, ch. 19, is cited presumably for the sake of its account of ritual uncleanness needing purification.
[29] I.e., oral tradition entrusted to the apostles and forming the basis of "tradidition" as an authority alongside Scripture. Cf. *A confutation of unwritten verities*, in Cranmer, PS, II.1 ff.
[30] Opponents.

and is burdened with man's laws, the farther it is from the true and sincere verity of God's word. The more man presumeth and taketh authority to interpretate the scripture after his own brain and subtle wit, and not as the verity of ⟨the⟩ text requireth, the more he dishonoureth the scripture and blasphemeth God, the author thereof.

It is the office of a good man to teach the church as Christ taught, to revoke [31] all errors, and such as err, unto the fold of Christ only by the word of Christ. For the water at the fountain's head is more wholesome and pure, than when it is carried abroad in rotten pipes or stinking ditches. I had rather follow the shadow of Christ, than the body of all general councils or doctors since the death of Christ. . . .

The church must therefore be bound to none other authority than unto the voice of the gospel and unto the ministry thereof. . . . And seeing the church is bound unto this infallible truth, the only word of God, it is a false and usurped authority that men attribute unto the clergy, and [32] bind the word of God and Christ's church to the succession of bishops or any college of cardinals, schools, ministers, or cathedral churches. . . .

Men may have the gift of God to understand and interpretate the scripture unto other, but never authority to interpretate it, otherwise than it interpretateth itself, which the godly mind of man by study, meditation, and conferring of one place thereof with the other, may find; howbeit some more, some less, as God giveth his grace. For the punishment of our sins God leaveth in all men a great imperfection; and such as were endued with excellent wit and learning saw not always the truth. As it is to be seen in Basilius, Ambrose, Epiphanius, Augustine, Bernard, and other, though they stayed themselves in the knowledge of Christ, and erred not in any principal article of the faith, yet they did inordinately and more than enough extol the doctrine and tradition of men, and after the death of the apostles every doctor's time was subject unto such ceremony and man's decrees that was neither profitable nor necessary. Therefore diligently exhorted Paul the church of Christ principally to consider and regard the foundation of all verity; meaning that doctors of the church had their imperfection and faults. "Another foundation can no man lay than that which is already laid, which is Jesus Christ." [33] In these few words

---

[31] *Revoke* is used in dual sense of refuting and calling back, and governs both *all errors* and also *such as err*.
[32] When they.
[33] I Cor. 3:11.

is stablished all our faith, and all false religion reprehended. . . .

Unto the rules and canons of the scripture must man trust, and reform his errors thereby; or else he shall not reform himself, but rather deform his conscience. . . . Therefore it shall be the office of every man that loveth God and his word to follow the scripture only, . . . and with all humility and humbleness submit himself to the judgment and censure of the judge of all judges, the word of God, that he may wisely and godly discern what is to be believed and accepted of any doctor's writings, and what is not to be accepted; what is to be pardoned, and what is not to be pardoned; and by the perils and dangers of other learn to be wise, that we commit not the same fault. . . .

He that took the pains to die and suffer his passion for the redemption of the world solely and only, solely and only hath taken the pains to teach the world how and which way they should keep this passion in mind, and left it unto the world in writing by the hands of his holy apostles; unto the which writing only he hath bound and obligated his church, and not to the writings of men.

In this passage I admonish the christian reader, that I speak not of the laws of magistrates, or princes, that daily ordain new laws for the preservation of their commonwealth, as they see the necessity of their realms or cities require; but of such laws as men hath ordained for the church of Christ, which should be now and for ever governed by the word of God. . . .

Concerning acts indifferent, which of themselves are neither good neither ill, as to refrain from eating of flesh the Friday, observing of the feasts kept holy in the remembrance of such holy martyrs as died for the faith of Christ, or in keeping holy Easter and Whitsunday, there is two respects most diligently to be observed; the one good and to be suffered, the other ill and to be eschewed. Such as abstain from flesh and think they do better service to God, and would likewise obtain remission of their sins by those works, do declare both themselves and their works to be ill. But such as abstain because the spirit may be more ardent, and the mind more given to study and prayer, doth well and as they be bound to do; and to come unto the temple to pray for themselves and the church of Christ, and to hear the word of God, doth well. For as God commandeth his word to be preached and heard, so he hath appointed a certain time, as the sabbath, when people should hear it. And not only this order to be observed in the church, but also in every family and household. Of what degree soever he be, he should cause his family and children to read some part of the Bible for their erudition, to know God. Likewise he should constrain them to pray unto God for the promotion of his holy word, and for the preservation of the governors of the commonwealth, so that no day should pass without prayer and augmentation of knowledge in the religion of Christ.

But our new evangelists hath another opinion; they dream of faith that justifieth, the which neither repentance precedeth, neither honesty of life followeth; which shall be to their double damnation, if they amend not. He that will conform his knowledge unto the word of God, let him likewise convert his life withal, as the word requireth, and as all the examples of Christ and his gospel teacheth; or else what will he do with the doctrine of Christ, which only teacheth, and sufficiently teacheth, all verity and virtuous life? Let him tarry still in the doctrine of man, and live as manly and as carnally as he list, and not profess to know God, neither his truth, rather than so to slander them both. This sufficeth to prove the only word of God to be sufficient to teach the truth; all other men's laws to be neither necessary, neither profitable. And certain we be that the church of the apostles did want these decrees that papistry of late days faithed [34] the church withall.

Caput V

The second office of Christ is to pray and to make intercession for his people. . . . This intercession of Christ only sufficeth. No man should seek any other mediator of intercession or expiation of sin, as Paul saith, declaring the sufficiency and ability of Christ's death and intercession, "Christ abideth for ever, having a perpetual priesthood: whereby he is able perfectly to save those which come to God through him; he liveth always to make intercession for them." . . .[35]

This doctrine of Christ's intercession must be always diligently preached unto the people; and likewise, that in all necessities, calamities, and trouble, the afflicted person to seek none other means to offer his prayers unto God but Christ only, according as the scripture teacheth, and as we have example of holy saints in the same. . . .

What intolerable ill, blasphemy of God, and ethnical [36] idolatry is this, to admit and teach the invocation of saints departed out of this world! It taketh from God his true honour; it maketh him a

---

[34] 1547: *faythyd*. If we accept this as representing Hooper's meaning, the sense will be: "has given to the church to believe."
[35] Heb. 7:24-25.
[36] Heathenish.

fool, that only hath ordained only Christ to be Mediator between man and him. It diminisheth the merits of Christ, taketh from the law of God her perfection and majesty, whereas [37] God hath opened his will and pleasure unto the world in all things. It condemneth the old church of the patriarchs and prophets, likewise the church of the apostles and martyrs, that never taught the invocation of saints. It accuseth the scripture of God to be false, which saith, "Thou . . . shalt neither add, neither diminish any thing": [38] it maketh Christ a liar that said, "The Spirit which I will send from the Father shall teach you all truth." [39] If the men that teach, "Saint Mary, pray for us," be more holy than all the patriarchs, prophets and apostles, let the conscience of the christian reader judge. . . .

But there is another ill as great as this, to be reprehended of all such as know how to pray aright—the being of images in the temple, which the world saith may be suffered in the churches, and say they be good to put the people of God in remembrance of such godly saints as died for Christ's sake. . . . This use of images is taken away in many places, but now they be applied to another use, scilicet to teach the people, and to be the laymen's books; as Damascene [40] and many other saith. O blasphemous and devilish doctrine, to appoint the most noble creature of God, man endued with wit and reason, resembling the image of the everlasting God, to be instructed and taught of a mute, dumb, blind, and dead idol! The brute beast that goeth by the way, and the ass that serveth for the mill, is not taught by the rod of the carter, but by the prudence of him that useth the rod; and should those painted blocks be the books of reasonable man? Full well can the devil transform himself into an angel of light, and [to] deceive the people under the pretence of true religion. . . .

What although many learned men hath approved images, should their wisdom maintain any contrary unto the word of God? No, a christian man must not care who speaketh, but what is spoken; the truth (is) to be accepted, whosoever speaketh it. Balaam was as wise, learned, and replenished with God's gift, as man could be; notwithstanding, his ass telling the truth must be believed better than he.[41] The law of God teacheth no use of images, but saith, "Thou shalt not make, thou shalt not worship." Exod. xx.[42] Believe it. Yet the art of graving and painting is the gift of God. To have the picture or image of any martyr or other, so it be not put

[37] Wherein.
[38] Deut. 12:32.
[39] John 16:13.
[40] *De Imaginibus, Oratio* I.17 (*PG* 94.1247).
[41] Num. 22:21 ff.
[42] Ex. 20:4-5.

in the temple of God, nor otherwise abused, it may be suffered. Christ by the picture of Caesar taught his audience obedience unto the civil prince, saying, "Whose image is this?" And they said, "Caesar's." "Then give unto Caesar that is Caesar's." [43]

But if man will learn to know God by his creatures, let him not say, "Good morrow, master," to an old moth-eaten post, but behold the heavens which declareth the mighty power of God. Psalm xix.[44] Consider the earth, how it bringeth forth the fruits thereof, the water with fishes, the air with the birds. Consider the disposition, order, and amity, that is between the members of man's body, the one always ready to help the other, to save the other. The hand the head, the head the foot, the stomach to disperse the meat and drink into the exterial parts of the body. Yea, let man consider the hawk and the hound, that obey in their vocation, and so every other creature of the earth; and with true heart and unfeigned penitence come to the knowledge of himself, and say, All the creatures that ever the living God made, obeyeth in their vocation, saving the devil, and I, most wretched man.

Those things were made to be testimonies unto us of God's mighty power, and to draw men unto virtue; not these idols, which the devil caused to be set in the temple to bring men from God. Thus did Christ teach the people his most blessed death and passion, and the fruit of his passion, by the grain of corn cast into the earth; and said, Except the corn fall into the earth and die, it abideth alone, but if it die it bringeth forth much fruit.[45] He hanged not the picture of his body upon the cross, to teach them his death, as our late learned men hath done.

The ploughman, be he never so unlearned, shall better be instructed of Christ's death and passion by the corn that he soweth in the field, and likewise of Christ's resurrection, than by all the dead posts that hang in the church, or ⟨are⟩ pulled out of the sepulchre with Christ rising again.

Caput VI

The third Office of Christ is concerning his priesthood, to offer sacrifice unto God, and by the same to purge the world from sin.

All the sacrifices of the old law were figures and types of this only sacrifice, which was appointed by God to die and to suffer the ire and displeasure of God for the sin of man, as though he himself were a sinner, and had merited this displeasure. . . .

The signs of his ire and displeasure unto man is this, that he would not accept man again into his favour for no penance, no

---

[43] Matt. 22:19-21.   [44] Ps. 19:1.   [45] John 12:24.

A DECLARACION OF CHRISTE AND HIS OFFYCE

sorrow, no trouble, no adversity, no weeping, no wailing, no, nor for the death of any person, until his own Son, most dear beloved, by death appeased his displeasure, and became surety to satisfy the justice of God and the right that the devil had unto all mankind. This if ⟨a⟩ man remembered as deeply and as earnestly as the matter requireth, it should make his heart full sorry, and bring him unto an honest and virtuous trade [46] of life; to consider this example of God's justice and equity in the appeasing of his own just conceived ire, and likewise that he would do no wrong unto his mortal enemy, the devil. Except the Son of God had been an equal and just redemption, a price correspondent to contrepece [47] and satisfy the culpe [48] and guilt of man's sin, God would not have taken one soul from the right and justice of the devil.

Now of this infallible truth, that Christ hath sacrificed only for sin, and his death accompted only sufficient for the salvation of man, the church of Christ is aright instructed of two most necessary articles: first, of justification, and then of the right use of the sacrament of his holy body.

Caput VII

Saint Paul, when he saith that we be justified by faith, Rom. iii., iv., v., he meaneth that we have remission of sin, reconciliation, and acceptation into the favour of God. So doth this word "justify" signify (Deut. xxv.) *hisdich*,[49] whereas God commandeth the judge to justify, quit, and absolve the innocent and to condemn and punish the person culpable.

Paul declareth, that for the death and merits of Christ we be saved, and not by our own virtues. So that faith doth not only shew us Christ that died, and now sitteth at the right hand of God, but also applieth the merits of this death unto us and maketh Christ ours: faith laying nothing to gage [50] unto the justice of God but the death of Christ, and thereupon claimeth mercy and God's promise, the remission of sin, and desireth God to justify and deliver the soul from the accusation of the law and right of the devil, which he is bound to do for his promise sake. Ezek. xxxiii., Matt. xvii.[51] . . .

And although it be necessary and requisite that in the justifica-

---

[46] Way.
[47] Counterweigh.
[48] Blame.
[49] Deut. 25:1. *Hisdich:* הִצְדִּיק.
[50] Pledge, pawn.
[51] Ezek. 33:14 ff., 19 f. The Matthew reference is an error and the allusion is too general to assign any particular passage to it.

tion of a sinner contrition [to] be present, and that necessarily charity and virtuous life must follow, yet doth the scripture attribute the only remission of sin unto the mercy of God, which is given only for the merits of Christ, and received solely by faith. Paul doth not exclude those virtues to be present, but he excludeth the merits of those virtues, and deriveth the cause of our acceptation into [52] the grace of God only for Christ.

And mark this manner of speech: We are justified by faith; that is, through the confidence [53] of his mercy we are just. This word faith doth comprehend as well a persuasion and confidence that the promise of God appertaineth unto him for Christ's sake, as the knowledge of God. For faith, though it desire the company of contrition and sorrow for sin, yet contendeth it not in judgment upon the merits of no works, but only for the merits of Christ's death. In case it did, it availeth nothing. For if a man desire to be delivered from the law, the law must be satisfied which saith, Thou shalt love the Lord thy God with all thy mind, with all thy heart, and with all thy soul. Deut. vi.[54] Now there neither is, nor never was, any man born of the stock of Adam in original sin, that feared God as much as the law requireth, nor never had such constant faith as is required, nor such ardent love as it requireth: seeing those virtues that the law required be infirm and debile, for their merits we can obtain nothing of God. We must therefore only trust to the merits of Christ, which satisfied the extreme jot and uttermost point of the law for us. And this his justice and perfection he imputeth and communicateth with us by faith.

Such as say, that only faith justifieth not, because other virtues be present, they cannot tell what they say. Every man that will have his conscience appeased, must mark those two things: How remission of sin is obtained, and wherefore it is obtained. Faith is the mean whereby it is obtained, and the cause wherefore it is received is the merits of Christ. Although faith be the means whereby it is received, yet hath neither faith, nor charity, nor contrition, nor the word of God, nor all those knit together, sufficient merits wherefore we should obtain this remission of sin: but the only cause wherefore sin is forgiven, is the death of Christ.

Now mark the words of Paul: "Freely," saith he, "we are justified by his grace." [55] Let the man burst his heart with contrition, believe that God is good a thousand times, burn in charity; yet shall not all these satisfy the law, nor deliver man from the ire of God, until such time as faith letteth fall all hope and confidence

---

[52] He traces it back to.
[53] Trust; no doubt "confidence" is a translation of *fiducia*.
[54] Deut. 6:5.
[55] Rom. 3:24.

in the merits of such virtues as be in man, and say, "Lord, behold thy unfruitful servant; only for the merits of Christ's blood give me remission of sins; for I know no man can be justified otherwise before thee, as David saith: No man living shall be justified in thy sight. Psal. cxliii.[56] Again, Blessed is the man unto whom the Lord imputeth no sin. Psal. xxxii." . . .[57]

"As Moses lift up the serpent in the wilderness, so must the Son of man be lift up." [58] Moses was commanded to lift up this serpent in the wilderness for this cause, that whosoever was stung or venomed with the poison of the serpents, if he looked upon the serpent of brass, might be healed. . . . Now to the words of Christ: "So must Christ be lift up, that as many as believe in him shall have everlasting life." Here is Nicodemus taught the way unto everlasting life; and because he was a doctor of Moses' law, Christ by the law made open the matter unto him, and brought him from the shadow unto the true body, and from the letter unto the understanding of the letter, saying: "As those that by faith beheld the serpent were healed of the stings of the serpent, so such as behold me in faith hanging upon the cross, shall be healed from their sickness and sin, that the devil by the serpent infected mankind withal." . . .

This must be diligently marked. For as the fathers of the old church used the serpent, so must those of our church use the precious body of Christ. They looked upon him only with the eyes of faith, they kissed him not, they cast no water upon him, and so washed their eyes therewithal; they touched him not with their hands, they ate him not, nor corporally, nor really, nor substantially: yet by their belief they obtained health. So Christ himself teacheth us the use of his precious body: to believe and look upon the merits of his passion suffered upon the cross, and so to use his precious body against the sting of original and actual sin: not to eat his body transformed into the form of bread,[59] or in the bread, with the bread, under the bread, behind the bread, or before the bread,[60] corporally or bodily, substantially or really, invisibly, or any such ways, as many men, to the great injuries of Christ's body, doth teach. But as the children of Israel only by faith ate the body spiritually not yet born, so by faith doth the Christians eat him now, being ascended into heaven, and none otherwise, as Christ saith unto Nicodemus: "That every one which believeth in him should not perish." . . .[61]

---

[56] Ps. 143:2.
[57] Ps. 32:1.
[58] John 3:14.
[59] Transubstantiation.
[60] Consubstantiation.
[61] John 3:16.

This example of Nicodemus declareth that neither the works that go before justification, neither those that follow justification, deserve remission of sin. Though sole faith exclude not other virtues to be present at the conversion of every sinner, yet doth sole faith and only, exclude the merits of other virtues and obtaineth solely remission of sin for Christ's sake, herself alone: as Paul saith, Ephes. ii.: "Through grace ye are saved, by faith, and that not of yourselves; it is the gift of God; not of works, lest any should boast themselves." [62] Where as plainly he excludeth the dignity of works, and affirmeth us to be reconciled by faith. So doth John, chap. i. attribute those two singular gifts unto Christ, grace and verity, saying: "The law was given by Moses, but grace and truth came by Jesus Christ." [63] Here grace signifieth free remission of sin for the merits of Christ: verity is the true knowledge of God, and the gifts of the Holy Ghost that followeth the remission of sin. Therefore such as say they be not justified only by faith in the mercy of God through Christ, extenuate sin and God's ire against sin too much, and likewise spoil Christ of his honour, who is the only sacrifice that taketh away the sin of the world.

They that will justify themselves any other ways than by faith, doth doubt always whether their sins be forgiven or not; and by reason of this doubt they can never pray unto God aright. For he that doubteth whether God be his friend or not, prayeth not, but as [64] an ethnick saith his *Pater noster*, without faith and godly motion of the heart. He that is persuaded by the gospel, though his own unworthiness fear [65] him from God, yet beholdeth he the Son of God, and believeth that both he and his prayers be accepted in Christ; and thus accepted into grace, will follow the life of a justified man, as Paul commandeth (Rom. viii. Coloss. iii.), [66] and as all the scripture giveth example. For it is no profit to say sole faith justifieth, except godliness of life follow, as Paul saith: "If ye live according to the flesh, ye shall die." [67] He that hath obtained the remission of sin must diligently pray for the preservation of God's favour, as David giveth example unto the whole church, saying: "Create a clean heart, and renew a right spirit within me. Cast me not away from thy face, and take not thy holy Spirit from me. Restore unto me the joy of thy saving health, and stablish me with thy free spirit. Psalm. l." . . . [68]

These virtues must man practise and use, after he is justified, as

[62] Eph. 2:8.
[63] John 1:17.
[64] Like.
[65] Frighten.
[66] Rom. 8:12 ff.; Col. 3:1 ff.
[67] Rom. 8:13.
[68] Ps. 51:10–12.

well as to obtain remission of his sin, or else he is not justified at all: he is but a speaker of justification, and hath no justice within him. As he maketh Christ only his Saviour, so must he follow such as were of Christ's family, the patriarchs, prophets, and the apostles, in the life prescribed by Christ, as they did; or else they shall be no disciples of the prophets, that were the doers as well as the speakers of virtue. . . .

Caput VIII

Of this infallible verity, "Only the death of Christ to be the sacrifice for the expiation of sin," may be necessarily taught the right and true use of the Lord's supper, which men call the mass.

First, it is manifest, that it is not a sacrifice for sin, as men teach, contrary unto the word of God, that saith, "Christ by one sacrifice made perfect all things," Heb. vii. viii. ix. x.; [69] and as John saith, "The blood of Jesus Christ doth cleanse us from all sin:" [70] and there remaineth no more after it, as Paul saith, "Where remission of sins is, there is no more sacrifice for sin"; [71] and, to take away all doubt that remission of sin cannot be obtained for the merits of the mass, Paul saith plainly that without blood-shedding no sacrifice can merit remission of sin.[72]

Although Christ now sit at the right hand of God, and pray for his church, and likewise doth offer the prayers and complaint of us that believe, yet it is only for the merits of his death that we obtain the mercy of God's promise. . . .

As concerning the use of this Sacrament and all other the rites and ceremonies that be godly, they should be so kept and used in the church, as they were delivered unto us of the high bishop Christ, the author of all Sacraments. For this is true, that he most godly, most religiously, and most perfectly instituted and celebrated the supper, and none otherways than the evangelist doth record. The best manner and most godly way to celebrate this supper is to preach the death of Christ unto the church, and the redemption of man, as Christ did at his supper, and there to have common prayers, as Christ prayed with his disciples; then to repeat the last words of the supper, and with the same to break the bread and distribute the wine to the whole church; then, giving thanks to God, depart in peace. These ceremonies that God instituted not, but repugneth God's institution, be not necessary, but rather in any case to be left, because they abrogate the institution of Christ.

[69] Heb. 7:27; 9:12, 28; 10:10, 12, 14.
[70] I John 1:7.
[71] Heb. 10:18.
[72] Heb. 9:22.

It seemeth sufficient unto me, if the church do as Christ hath commanded it to do. . . .

This is therefore an ungodly disputation that the papists contend about the change and alteration of the bread; and also a false and pernicious doctrine, that teacheth the corporal presence of Christ, both God and man, in the bread. For although Christ said of the bread, "This is my body," it is well known that he purposed to institute a sacrament; therefore he spake of a sacrament sacramentally. To speak sacramentally is to give the name of the thing to the sign; so yet notwithstanding, that the nature and substance of the sign remaineth, and is not turned into the thing that it signifieth. Further, the verity of the scripture, and the verity of a christian faith, will not suffer to judge and believe Christ's body, invisible or visible, to be upon the earth. Acts. i., Luke ult., Mark ult., Acts iii.[73]

If we likewise consider the other places of the scripture, John vi. xvi. xvii.,[74] we shall find that Christ would not, nor meant not, to institute any corporal presence of his body, but a memory of the body slain, resuscitated, ascended into ⟨the⟩ heavens, and from thence to come unto judgment. True it is, that the body is eaten, and the blood drunken, but not corporally. In faith and spirit it is eaten, and by that sacrament the promise of God sealed and confirmed in us, the corporal body remaining in heaven. . . .

So in the sacrament the christian heart that is instructed in the law of God and knoweth the right use of the sacraments by the Holy Ghost, and a firm faith that he hath in the merits of Christ's body and soul, which is ascended corporally into heaven, may in spirit receive[th] the effect, marrow, sweetness, and commodity of Christ's precious body, though it never descend corporally. Thus doth faith and the scripture compel the church to believe. . . .

Further, Christ's body hath not lost his corporal qualities; but wheresoever he be corporally, there is he with all qualities of a body, and not without qualities, as these dreamers imagine. I will not judge my Saviour, that died for the sin of the world, to have a body in heaven, sensible with all qualities of true man, and in the sacrament, without all qualities and quantities of a true body; but abhor and detest with the scripture this opinion as an heresy, so little differing from Marcion, that I can scarce put diversity. . . .

To say that Christ's very natural body is in the earth, and yet invisible, it is to destroy the body, and not to honour the body.

---

[73] Hooper here cites the accounts of the Ascension. The final reference is to Acts 3:21.
[74] John 6:35 f.; 16:5 ff.; 17:20 ff. (?).

Aristotle, Lib. v., Metaphysicorum, cap.xxii., defineth what invisible is: That is invisible, (quoth he), which hath no colour at all.[75] Take this from Christ's body, that it is truly in the sacrament corporally, and yet invisible, is to say, Christ hath lost all the colour, shape, and form of his humanity. But what shall Aristotle do in this our faith? The scripture teacheth what we should believe: "He hath ascended into heaven, he sitteth on the right hand of God the Father Almighty, from thence he shall come to judge the quick and the dead," Act. i. Mark. ultimo. Luk. ultimo, and hath left us a sacrament of his blessed body, the which we are bound to use religiously and many times, to exercise and stablish our faith; and he, being absent corporally, doth communicate by faith in spirit that most precious body, and the merits of the same: and would to God people would use it with more reverence and more awe, as the scripture teacheth, with true amendment of life, and firm faith. . . .

Caput IX

The fourth office of Christ is to consecrate and sanctify these that believe in him. He is not only holy himself, but maketh holy others also; as he saith, John xvii., "For their sake sanctify I myself, that they also may be sanctified through the truth." [76]

This sanctification is none other but a true knowledge of God in Christ by the gospel, that teacheth us how unclean we are by the sin of Adam, and how that we are cleansed by Christ; for whose sake the Father of heaven doth not only remit the sins wrought willingly against the word of God, but also the imperfection and natural concupiscence which remaineth in every man, as long as the nature of man is mortal. How the Father doth sanctify his people, the prayer of Christ sheweth, John xvii. Sanctify them by thy truth, "sanctify them by thy word"; [77] purge their heart, teach them, hallow them, make them apt for thy kingdom. Wherewith? With thy word, which is everlasting verity.

The means to sanctify is the word of God, the Holy Ghost, and faith that receiveth the word of our redemption. So doth Peter say, Acto. xv.: "Our hearts are purged by faith." [78] Here is the cause expressed, whereby we accept our santification; "by faith," saith Saint Peter. Saint Paul, i. Cor. vi., sheweth for whose sake, and wherefore, we are sanctified: "You are washed, you are sanctified, you are justified by the name of Jesus Christ, and the Spirit of our

[75] *Metaph.* Bk. Δ, 22.
[76] John 17:19.
[77] John 17:17.
[78] Acts 15:9.

God, for the merits of Jesus Christ, by the operation of the Holy Ghost."[79] This is to be always marked, that when Christ had prayed his Father to sanctify his church by his word and by his holy Spirit, and desired him to preserve them from ill for his mercy's sake, he added the price, the merits, and just deserving of God's graces, and said, "I sanctify myself for them, because they may be sanctified by the truth."[80] He sanctified himself for the church, when he died for the detestable uncleanness and filthiness thereof, more stinking and filthy than ever was the abhorred and leprous body of Lazarus. As though he had said, "Forasmuch as I offer and submit myself unto the bitter and cruel pain of the cross for the church, thou must, most holy Father, sanctify them, and accept them as sanctified, nourish them, love them, and defend them, for the price and satisfaction of my death."

What a consolation is this for every troubled conscience to understand. Although it be unworthy of remission of sin for the greatness thereof, yet for the prayer of Christ he shall not be a cast-away, so that he believe: as Christ said, he prayed not only for his apostles, but also for as many as should believe his word till the world's end....[81]

Caput X

Of this verity and truth, that the gospel teacheth us only to be sanctified in the blood of Christ, is confuted the blasphemous pride of the Bishop of Rome.

This office of Christ doth abrogate all other things that man's constitutions attribute any holiness unto, as bewitched water,[82] candles, boughs, or any such ethnick superstition: for only Christ sanctifieth, and all holiness we must attribute unto him, as John said, "Behold the Lamb of God, that taketh away the sins of the world." John i.[83]

Although baptism be a sacrament to be received and honourably used of all men, yet it sanctifieth no man. And such as attribute the remission of sin unto the external sign, doth offend....

This new life cometh not, until such time as Christ be known and received. Now, to put on Christ is to live a new life. Such as be baptized must remember, that penance[84] and faith preceded this external sign, and in Christ the purgation was inwardly obtained, before the external sign was given. So that there is two kinds of baptism, and both necessary: the one interior, which is

---

[79] I Cor. 6:11.
[80] John 17:19.
[81] John 17:20.
[82] Holy water.
[83] John 1:29.
[84] Repentance.

the cleansing of the heart, the drawing of the Father, the operation of the Holy Ghost: and this baptism is in man, when he believeth and trusteth that Christ is the only author of his salvation. . . . Then is the exterior sign added, not to purge the heart, but to confirm, manifest, and open unto the world that this child is God's. . . .

Likewise no man should condemn nor neglect this exterior sign, for the commandment's sake: though it have no power to purge from sin, yet it confirmeth the purgation of sin, and the act of itself pleaseth God, for because the receivers thereof obey the will of his commandment. Like as the king's majesty, that now is, immediately after the death of his father, was the true and legitimate king of England, right heir unto the crown, and received his coronation, not to make himself thereby king, but to manifest that the kingdom appertained unto him before. He taketh the crown to confirm his right and title. Had all England said nay, and by force, contrary unto God's laws and man's laws, with an exterior ceremony and pomp, crowned any other man, he should have been an adulterous and wrong king, with all his solemnities and coronation. Though this ceremony confirm and manifest a king in his kingdom, yet it maketh not a king, but the laws of God and of the land, that giveth by succession the right of the kingdom to the old king's first heir male in England and other realms. And the babe in the cradle hath as good right and claim, and is as true a king in his cradle uncrowned, as his father was, though he reigned a crowned king forty years. And this right of the babe should be defended and manifested, not only by the ceremony of coronation, but with all obedience and true subjection.

So is it in the church of Christ: man is made the brother of Christ, and heir of eternal life by God's only mercy received by faith, before he receive any ceremony to confirm and manifest openly his right and title. He saith, he believeth in the Father, the Son, and the Holy Ghost, and believeth (he saith) the remission of sin; doth not only deny the devil, the world, and sin, but saith he will forsake him for ever, and serve his master, the Lord of virtue, King of heaven and earth.[85] Thus assured of God, and cleansed from sin in Christ, he hath the livery of God given unto him, baptism, the which no Christian should neglect; and yet not attribute his sanctification unto the external sign. As the king's majesty may not attribute his right unto the crown, but unto God and unto his father, who hath not only given him grace to be born into the world, but also to govern as a king in the world; whose right and

[85] A paraphrase of Baptism promises in BCP.

title the crown confirmeth, and sheweth the same unto all the world. Whereas this right by God and natural succession precedeth not the coronation, the ceremony availeth nothing. A traitor may receive the crown, and yet a true king nothing the rather. So an hypocrite and an infidel may receive the external sign of baptism, and yet no christian man nothing the rather; as Simon Magus [86] and other.

Sacraments must be used holily, and yet not to have the office of Christ added unto them. Solely it is his office to sanctify and purge from sin. I take nothing from the sacraments, but honour them and extol them in all things, as they be worthy. Howbeit, not too much. I call a sacrament a ceremony instituted in the law of God to this end, that it should be a testimony of God's promise unto all such as believe, and signs of God's good will and favour towards us. . . .

Such as be sanctified by Christ must live an honest and holy life, or else his sanctification availeth not. As God forsook the childer of Israel for sin, so will he do us. . . . Therefore, one of these two we must needs do, that say we be justified and sanctified in Christ: either from the bottom of our hearts amend, or else be eternally lost with all our ghostly knowledge. For the axe is put to the root of the tree. So far is the malice of man proceeded, that the ire of God can be no longer deferred. A great time hath the gospel been known of many men, yet the life of the gospel as new to seek, as though it were but now begun.

Therefore see we how God beginneth again to permit the darkness of error to overwhelm the world. Such blindness ever followeth the contempt of God's word and the unthankful receiving thereof. Therefore, as we be sanctified by Christ, so let us bear him and sanctify him in our breasts, or else we perish, Rom. vi.[87] For faith intendeth and always maketh haste unto this port, as Paul saith, Tit. ii.: "That we may live holily, justly, and godly." [88]

Caput XI

As the scripture teacheth Christ to be the very true Priest and Bishop of the church, which prayeth for the church, satisfieth the ire of God for the sin of the church, and only sanctifieth the church: so doth it prove Christ to be the King, Emperor, and Protector of the church, and that by the office and property of a king, that defendeth his subjects, not only by his godly laws, but also by force and civil resistance, as the enemies of his commonwealth

---

[86] Acts 8:9 ff.   [87] Rom. 6:1-11, 23.   [88] Titus 2:12.

shall minister occasion. . . . Although now the commonwealth of the church hath no certain place appointed where it shall remain, as it was appointed in the old law, yet certain we be, that this kingdom of Christ remaineth upon the earth, and shall do, till the earth be burned. Matt. xvi. xxviii. i. Cor. xv.[89] Howbeit, as Christ won and obtained this kingdom in the latter days without shield or spear, so doth he preserve it with his holy Spirit and not with carnal weapons. . . .

This kingdom is spiritual. Christ sitting at the right hand of God the Father prayeth for us, giveth us remission of sin, and the Holy Ghost, to fight and overcome the world, hath left here in the church his gospel, the only weapon to fight withal for the time of this mortal life. John. xvii. . . .[90]

This kingdom shall be ever persecuted till the world's end. . . . Thus the church shall remain, but always in affliction. I know such as favoureth not the truth, will interpretate my words, that I condemn all princes and kings, as enemies of the gospel, because they peaceably enjoy their kingdoms. So I wish them always to do, with hearty prayer to the glory ⟨of⟩ God. But of this one thing I will assure every prince of the world: the more sincere he is in the cause of God, the more shall be his cross. . . .

God preserveth above human reason his ministers, as he did Jacob from the hands of Esau, David from Saul, Daniel from the lions, and Paul in the ship, where as no human hope of salvation was at all, but only the protection of God. Those examples declare, that he doth defend his people against all the world by his mighty power.

Likewise he governeth his church with his only laws, and would his subjects to know him, to honour him, and to obey him, as he hath commanded in his law. Paul expresseth this law, Rom. i.: "The gospel is the power of God unto salvation to every one that believeth." [91] Mark xvi.: "Preach you the gospel to every creature." [92] The only law whereunto this congregation is bound, is the gospel, as Christ saith, John xiv.: "The Holy Spirit shall teach you all things, and bring all things to your remembrance which I have said unto you." [93] Here Christ bindeth the apostles and all the church unto the things that he had taught them.

This commonwealth of the true church is known by these two marks: the pure preaching of the gospel, and the right use of the sacraments. Thus proveth Paul, Eph. ii., that the church is bound

[89] Matt. 16:18; 28:18 ff.; I Cor. 15:25.
[90] John 17:14.
[91] Rom. 1:16.
[92] Mark 16:15.
[93] John 14:26.

unto the word of God: "You are builded upon the foundation of the apostles and prophets."[94] Likewise, Esa. lix.: "My spirit which is in thee, and my words which I have put in thy mouth, shall not depart from thy mouth, nor from the mouth of thy seed for ever."[95]

Of the right use of sacraments it is taught, i. Cor. xi. Mark. ult. Luk. ult. and Matt. ult.[96] Such as teacheth people to know the church by these signs, the traditions of men, and the succession of bishops, teach wrong. Those two false opinions hath given unto the succession of bishops power to interpretate the scripture, and power to make such laws in the church as it pleased them. There is no man hath power to interpretate the scripture. God, for the preservation of his church, doth give unto certain persons the gift and knowledge to open the scripture; but that gift is no power bound to any order, succession of bishops, or title of dignity. . . .

Such as will be the members of this church, must be a disciple of the gospel, and learn in fear and humbleness of spirit the articles of our religion, as they be taught there, and not stand unto the judgment of any man, whatsoever he be, though he say truth. For his truth is nothing, except the authority of God's word contain the said truth.

It is a great confirmation of our faith, when we see such as were godly persons before us interpretate the scripture, and use the sacraments as we do. As when the heresy of Samosatenus troubled the christian brothers, that said, this word, *Verbum,* in John, In the beginning was the word, did not signify any person nor substance divine; they were confirmed by the testimony of Ireneus, that heard Polycarpus, John the Evangelist's disciple, interpretate *Verbum* in the gospel, for the Son of God, second Person in Trinity.[97] Though we be bound to hear the church, to say, the true and faithful preachers of God's word, as was in this case Polycarpus and Ireneus. Notwithstanding our faith is not grounded upon the authority of the church, but in and upon the voice of the gospel, we pray and invoke the Son of God, second Person in Trinity. . . .[98]

The adversaries of the truth defend many a false error under the name of the holy church: therefore these treasons and secret

---

[94] Eph. 2:20.
[95] Isa. 59:21.
[96] I Cor. 11:23 ff.; Mark 16:16 ff. and par.
[97] Hooper's gloss on Eusebius, *Hist. eccles.* V.xxviii (*PG* 20.511 ff.).
[98] The argument in these two sentences is: "Although we be bound . . . that is to say, the true . . . Irenaeus, yet our faith . . . gospel, and therefore we pray . . ."

conspiracies must be taken heed of; and when the church is named, diligently to consider, when the articles they would defend were accepted of the church, by whom, and who was the author of them. Leave not, till the matter be brought unto the first, original, and most perfect church of the apostles. If thou find by their writings, that their church used the thing that the preacher would prove, then accept it; or else, not. Be not amazed, though they speak of never ⟨so⟩ many years, nor name never so many doctors. Christ and his apostles be grandfathers in age to the doctors and masters in learning. Repose thyself only ⟨upon⟩ the church that they have taught thee by the scripture. . . .

Remember, christian reader, that the gift of interpretation of the scripture is the light of the Holy Ghost given unto the humble and penitent person that seeketh it only to honour God; and not unto those persons that acclaim it by title or place, because he is a bishop, or followed by succession Peter or Paul. Remember, therefore, to examine all kind of doctrine by the word of God; for such as preach it aright, hath their infirmities and ignorancy. They may depart from the truth, or else build some superstition and false doctrine upon the gospel of Christ. Superstition is to be avoided, false doctrine to be abhorred, whosoever be the author thereof, prince, magistrate, or bishop; as the apostles made answer, Acto. v., "We must rather obey God than men." . . .[99]

Caput XII

Man fallen from his first dignity and original perfection is now the creature that fighteth with the law of God, full of darkness, ignorancy, and of the contempt of God, without obedience, fear and love of God, oppressed and subject unto all calamities and wilful concupiscences both of body and soul.

It is very difficile and hard for man to know himself. The only way thereunto is to examine and open himself before God by the light of the scripture. And he that will behold himself well in that mirror and glass, shall find such a deformity and disgraced [1] physiognomy, that he will abhor his own proportion so horribly disfigured. . . . Only the law declareth how great an ill sin is; and the man that beholdeth the will of God in the law, shall find himself, and all his life, guilty of eternal death. Read the seventh chapter to the Romans with judgment, and then know what man is, how miserably spoiled of virtue and oppressed with sin. So Paul learned to know himself, and knew not what sin was till the

---

[99] Acts 5:29. [1] Beauty taken away.

law had made him afraid, and shewed him that he was with all his holiness, being a Pharisee, damned. "Sin took an occasion by the commandment, and deceived me, and thereby slew me." Rom. vii.[2] And in the same chapter he sheweth plainly what he saw in the glass and contemplation of the law, that sin was manifested thereby, and the greatness thereof known: "Sin, that it might appear sin, wrought death in me by that which is good; that sin might be out of measure sinful by the commandment."[3] Mark the travice[4] and play between the law of God and the conscience of Paul, and see how he giveth thanks unto his master the law, and proclaimeth it to be a spiritual and holy thing, as a light or torch to shew man his filthy and stinking nature; saying, "The law is spiritual; but I am carnal, sold under sin,"[5] a bondman of sin and traitor of God.

Here thou seest, good reader, what a miserable wretch man is, and how man may know his misery by the law. Howbeit, though we read it many times, we be neither the wiser, neither the better. We be not taught a deal by this mistress the law: she cannot make us good scholars. We dally and play so with the world; we live in such security and ease, that, say she what she list, we turn the deaf ear and will not hear.

Therefore, to make man to know himself, God sendeth another mistress to school man, scilicet, adversity. . . . Now though these temporal pains be more than man can support, they be but sport and dalliance in respect of the pains eternal. Howbeit, man may learn by them how much God is displeased with sin, and know himself to be, as he is, a vile piece of earth, with all his pride and pomp, and a rebellion unto his Maker, as no creature else is, saving the devil and he.

This inward and secret ill, rebellion of the heart, blindness of the intendment,[6] and frowardness of will, is daily augmented by the malice of the devil and our own negligence, that regardeth not what the law teacheth ⟨that⟩ God requireth of man. Because the gospel teacheth, ⟨that⟩ we are only saved by the mercy of God for the merits of Christ, our gospellers hath set all at liberty, and careth not at all of such life as should and ought to follow every

---

[2] Rom. 7:11.
[3] Rom. 7:13.
[4] O.E.D. quotes this sentence as an example of "traverse" used in the fencing sense of moving from side to side. Hooper's meaning will therefore be that the law and Paul's conscience are the fencers, with the law attacking and Paul giving ground.
[5] Rom. 7:14.
[6] *Entendement,* understanding.

justified man and disciple of Christ. It is no marvel; for there is no discipline and punishment for sin: and wheresoever the gospel be preached, and this correction not used, as well against the highest as the lowest, there shall be never a godly church. As a king's army, though their hearts be never so good, cannot resist the force of his enemies without weapon and artillery necessary for men of war; no more can the king's majesty, the magistrates, and preachers, preserve the church against the devil and sin without the excommunication of such as openly offend the divine majesty of God and his word. . . .

This political and civil use of the law teacheth man to know his faults; and this discipline of the law exterior and civil is necessary for man for divers causes: first, to declare our obedience unto God; then, to avoid the punishment that always God, or else the magistrate, revengeth the transgression; thirdly, because of a public peace in every commonwealth, that the one should not do injuries to the other, neither in body nor in goods. There is yet another cause, why this discipline of the law is necessary, which few men regard. Paul saith, that it is a schoolmistress, *pedagogia,* unto Christ, because such as leaveth not to sin, and to do the thing contrary unto the express word of God, to those Christ is not profitable. . . . [7]

As for the second use of the law, which is to declare what sin is, I shewed before that it manifesteth the greatness and vileness thereof, as Paul writeth, it damneth sin, and delivereth not from sin: "By the law cometh the knowledge of sin. The law causeth wrath: by the law sin is made exceeding guilty." [8] Rom. vii. "The sting of death is sin; and the strength of sin is the law." i. Cor. xv.[9] In men that be addict unto the pleasure of this world, the law hath not this use, say the preacher what he list. Let the word of God threaten death eternal for sin, it availeth not. He thinketh that God is asleep, and will at last be pleased with a fig for sin. We shall find the contrary to our great pain, as other hath before our time, that would not believe the word, till they felt the vengeance and punishment of God. . . .

This use and office of the law none feeleth neither perceiveth so well as such as be God's friends, Adam, Abraham, Jacob, David, Ezechias, &c. David said that the fear of God's displeasure and ire was no less pain unto him, than though the fierce lion had rent and dismembered his body in pieces: "As a lion hath he broken my bones in sunder," Psal. xxii.[10] So saith Paul: "O wretched man

[7] Gal. 3:24.
[8] Rom. 7:7, 9–11, 13.
[9] I Cor. 15:56.
[10] Not Ps. 22, but Isa. 38:13.

that I am! who shall deliver me from the body of this death?"[11] He that before said: "I lived sometimes without law, that is to say, I was secure, not feeling the wrath of God"; [12] now converted from a Pharisee to be an apostle, and brought to a knowledge of himself, he confesseth his imbecility [13] and faults, and saith: "I know that in me, that is to say, in my flesh, there dwelleth no good thing." [14] Yet Paul confesseth that the law maketh us not afraid to be damned because we cannot satisfy it, but that we should come to Christ, with these comfortable words: "He hath shut all under sin, that he might have mercy on all." [15] A great consolation for every troubled conscience . . .

Caput XIII

The law is also necessary for the justified man to teach him with what works he should exercise his faith withal and obedience unto God. We may not choose works of our own wisdom to serve him withal; but ⟨he⟩ would us to be governed by his word, as David saith: "Thy word is a lantern unto my feet." [16] Also, "In vain do they worship me by the precepts of men." [17] The wisdom of man, not governed by the word of God, doth soon err. It is carried for the most part with affections, and chooseth the works that be contrary to the law of God. Therefore this is true, that the ordinance of God still remaineth in the justified man immutable, that he must obey the law, and serve in his vocation according to the scripture; that the exterior facts may bear testimony of the inward reconciliation. . . . The science [18] of the scripture is practive,[19] and not speculative; it requireth a doer and not a speaker only. . . .

[11] Rom. 7:24.
[12] Rom. 7:9.
[13] Weakness.
[14] Rom. 7:18.
[15] Rom. 11:32.
[16] Ps. 119:105.
[17] Isa. 29:13 as quoted Mark 7:7.
[18] Knowledge.
[19] That which must be put into practice.

Richard Taverner

POSTILS ON EPISTLES AND GOSPELS

Richard Taverner: Postils on Epistles and Gospels

INTRODUCTION

THE REFORMATION WAS A REDISCOVERY OF THE GOSPEL, THE joyful news that Jesus Christ is the Savior and Lord of the world. And because it was this, it entailed also the recovery of the responsibility of every believer to bear witness to him and to pass on the good news to those who did not yet know it. "Evangelical" has become, alas! a party title. These sixteenth-century evangelical believers were called rather gospelers, and this because they not only believed the gospel but bore witness to it. They were a vocal group.

Their witness, however, did not confine itself to private conversations, though of these there were plenty, as the pages of Foxe bear record. Those who were qualified (and not infrequently, those who were not) preached in public. On the Continent the amount of preaching that went on is almost unbelievable to the modern man, accustomed to the meager fare of two twenty-minute sermons a week. The major Reformers, whose sermons were taken down by skillful and zealous secretaries, left behind them thousands of sermons. But not every country minister and parson was a major Reformer; nor, indeed, did every parish or congregation have a Protestant pastor to care for it. Many congregations in France, for example, would read one of Calvin's printed sermons at their secret meetings. Such a solution was clearly only makeshift, however, and the leaders of all the Reformation Churches were deeply exercised with the problem. To have regular gospel preaching in every parish church, there would be needed a pastor who was both an Evangelical and who had been trained to preach. And in England the only places where youths could be trained "as Apprentices to learne the trade of preach-inge" (as George Fox put it a century later) were Oxford and Cambridge. And here at once we are in the realm of education. We need grammar schools to prepare boys for the university; we need university places; we need more lecturers. All this means more money. Why was not the money that was taken from the monasteries applied to this purpose? This is a constant cry of the Reformers. But it was many years before much fruit was seen.

In the meanwhile, what was being done to evangelize England? [1] ("Evangelize" is not too strong a word. The governments might be making use of preaching as anti-Papal or pro-government propaganda, but the preachers themselves had, in general, the intention of passing on the good news that Jesus Christ had died and risen again for the salvation of the world.) There were energetic preachers—*dum spiro, praedico!* Hooper with his three or four sermons a day (but surely not every day?), Latimer busy all King Edward's days, Bilney "a preacher to the prisoners and comfortless; a great doer in Cambridge and a great preacher in Suffolk and Norfolk." [2] Others were less mindful of the hungry sheep. Everywhere in the two volumes of the *Original Letters* in the Parker Society we come upon complaints on the scarcity of preaching. Richard Hilles wrote rhetorically to Bullinger in 1541, "A man may travel from the east of England to the west, and from the north to the south, without being able to discover a single preacher, who out of a pure heart and faith unfeigned is seeking the glory of our God." [3] Hilles is too despondent, of course, over the disaster that the Six Articles brought, but Peter Martyr in more measured tones tells Rudolph Gualter nine years later, even after the winter of the Reformers' discontent had yielded to the sunshine of Edward's reign, "There is no lack of preachers in London, but throughout the whole kingdom [or it might be better translated, "the kingdom as a whole"] they are very rare." [4] And Martin Bucer wrote sadly to Calvin in the same year, "Even our friends are so sparing of their sermons, that during the whole of Lent (which nevertheless they still seem to wish to observe, with the exception of one or two Sundays) they have not once preached to the people, not even on the day of commemoration of Christ's death or of his resurrection." [5]

The need was seen, however, though the measures taken to meet

---

[1] I believe that Traverner's *Postils* (and the Homilies, too) should be approached by way of preaching (common or garden sermons) rather than, as Cardwell, by way of official formularies, via Hilsey's *Manual*.
[2] Foxe, 6.620.
[3] *Original Letters*, PS, I.204.
[4] *Ibid.*, II.485.
[5] *Ibid.*, II.546–7.

it were strangely tentative. The Royal Injunctions of 1536 had commanded preaching only by inference, though they were specific enough on the subjects. For the next quarter, and thereafter at least twice a quarter, the clergy are to preach every Sunday against "the Bishop of Rome's usurped power"; they are to expound the Ten Articles of 1536; they are also "in the same their sermons and other collations" to admonish parents, masters, and tutors to teach their children and servants the Pater Noster, the Creed, and the Ten Commandments in English, and what is more, to recite a clause in every sermon so that their congregations may gradually learn the whole by heart.[6] The Injunctions of 1538 ordered that clergy should recite a clause of either the Pater Noster or the Creed every Sunday until it had been learned by rote and that they were to expound the same, and when they had finished these, they were to go on to the Ten Commandments; they were also to preach at least once a quarter, when they should declare "the very Gospel of Christ" and exhort their hearers to works of charity, mercy, and faith. It was all very well to command Sir John to expound the Lord's Prayer, the Creed, and the Ten Commandments on Sundays, but Sir John, working on his land during the week like his parishioners, might be handier at plowing than at the noble art of exposition. It is no good commanding Samuel Johnson's dog to walk on his hind legs unless you have trained him to do it. As an interim measure, the clergy had to be supplied with sermons to read. The forerunner of the Homilies was Taverner's *Postils* of 1540.

Butterworth is mistaken in saying that Taverner dedicated his work to the king.[7] He seems to have misread the title of the Preface as saying, "Rycharde Taverner, clerke of the Signet, to our soveraigne Lorde the Kynge wyssheth all grace . . ." whereas in fact it reads, "Rycharde Taverner, clerke of the Signet to our soveraigne Lorde the Kynge, wyssheth to the Christen reader all grace from God above and increase of knowledge in his worde." In this Preface, Taverner gives us a hint as to the origin and formation of his book:

"Forasmuch as, good Christian reader, at this present time, according to our Lord's word, the harvest is great and plenteous, but the labourers are few (I mean as thus, that the people be very desirous and greedy to receive God's Word, if they had plenty of sober, modest and sincere teachers; whereas now for scarcity of such in some places they

---

[6] *Visitation Articles and Injunctions of the Period of the Reformation,* ed. by W. H. Frere and W. M. Kennedy (London, 1910), Vol. II, pp. 1–11.
[7] Butterworth, *English Primers,* p. 215.

be destitute and scattered abroad even as sheep lacking faithful shepherds), I was instantly required, to the intent the Lord of the harvest might by this mean thrust forth his labourers into the harvest, to peruse and recognize this brief postil [8] which was delivered me of certain godly persons for that purpose and intent. Which thing to my little power and as the shortness of time would serve, I have done. And such sermons or homilies as seemed to want, I have supplied partly with mine own industry, and partly with the help of other sober men which be better learned than I myself." [9]

Perhaps we may interpret this obscure narration as follows: Taverner is asked by someone to look over and revise the collection handed over to him by certain persons.[10] This he did and where any epistles or Gospels lacked their sermon, he either wrote one himself or got someone else to do it for him. But who "instantly required" him to undertake the work? A certain air of authority surrounds the expression, and we can understand his using it of his master, Thomas Cromwell, or of the archbishop. For the rest, we may suppose that various theologians were asked (or perhaps required!) to write sermons on given passages and pass on the results to Taverner as the editor. Some, as happens in every collaboration, were slow to deliver their work, and in the end Taverner had to do his part in a hurry.

The suggestion of authority is maintained in the rest of the preface. After the promise that if "you priests and curates shall use this singular help and benefit," then "other fruitful works may be hereafter at the commandment of the king's majesty or of his most honourable council set forth and published unto you," [11] he mutters the threat that if they do not use it, then not only will there be no future benefits, but even what they have already (the *Postils?* their cures?) will be taken from them and they will be cast into utter darkness. He proceeds even more definitely:

"But there is good hope that ye will otherwise demean yourselves; namely now, sith ye be so benignly invited, injoined, and continually called upon to execute your office in this behalf by our high shepherd under Christ and supreme head, our most dread sovereign lord, the king's majesty, whom I doubt not but ye will gladly obey, I mean to feed more often your flock committed to your charge, not with rash, erroneous, heretical or fabulous sermons, but with sober, discreet,

---

[8] I.e., book of postils.
[9] Cardwell's edition, p. xix.
[10] Jacobs believes (*Study in Comparative Symbolics*, pp. 179 f.) that because Taverner translated Sarcerius' *Common-places*, the *Postils* are a translation of his *Postilla in Evangelia Dominicalia* and *Postilla in Evangelia Festivalia* (1538). I also have not seen this rare book, and therefore suspend judgment.
[11] Cardwell's edition, p. xix.

catholic, and godly instructions such as be here described unto you, or better, if better ye can desire." [12]

This can be read as suggesting that the *Postils* were issued with the royal authority, or it may merely be a reference to the Royal Injunctions, in which parish clergy are commanded to preach at least once a quarter, with the *Postils* put forward as an offering to help the clergy in this heavy task. One thing, however, is quite certain; the clergy were not commanded to use these homilies. Perhaps we may take Taverner's preface as a sailing as close to the wind as he dared in suggesting authority without claiming it.

The *Postils* ran through at least five editions in 1540 and seem also to have been printed again in the next five years, probably in 1542 and 1545 (at least, there are editions in the British Museum to which these dates have been assigned). It would therefore appear that the *Postils* continued to be used until the First Book of Homilies superseded them in 1547. It is surprising that they were able to hold their own in spite of an inauspicious beginning, when two facts militated against them. The lesser was that if, as is probable, Thomas Cromwell was responsible for the scheme, his sudden disappearance from the scene in 1540 told against his works also. The greater was that they were produced under the shadow of the anti-Reforming Six Articles of 1539. The official reform of the Church was halted in effect until Edward came to the throne. Cardwell supposes that Taverner and the other writers altered the *Postils* to conform with the Articles. "Whenever a hazardous tenet arose for discussion, it was either quietly surrendered, or treated in such a manner as to leave the special point of difficulty unmolested." [13] I do not know of any authority for this statement, although it would seem probable. But in fact, how closely do the *Postils* reflect the theology of the Six Articles? It will be remembered that these asserted (1) transubstantiation, (2) Communion in one kind, (3) celibacy of priests, (4) observation of vows of chastity, (5) the value of private masses, (6) auricular confession. The last is neither here nor there; both Calvin and Bucer thought that auricular confession should be retained until a better discipline could be introduced. For the rest, do the *Postils* teach these doctrines and urge these practices? Certainly these tenets can all be found, even though there are texts which we should expect to find them under and do not. But they are taught from such a generally Reformed position that most of their sting is drawn or becomes almost imperceptible unless one is looking for it. Not for nothing

[12] *Ibid.*, p. xx. [13] *Ibid.*, p. ix.

was Richard Taverner a lawyer. Transubstantiation is the best test here. Taverner has kept on the windy side of the law. In *An exhortation before the communion or receyvynge of the blessed sacrament of the aulter* [14] and again in the "Postil on the Gospel for Corpus Christi" [15] (John 6:55, 58) transubstantiation is technically asserted, as is also Communion in one kind (though, if we are to be hypercritical, so is Communion in both kinds [end of p. 185 to beginning of p. 186]), but it comes in so mildly and so very rarely and is surrounded by such an emphasis on the participation in Christ by faith that no congregation of nontheologians would have noticed it.

Cardwell is right in saying that the Six Articles made the *Postils* milder and less definite than they would have been. Hence, when the prohibitions were lifted and the First Book of Homilies could speak clearly and strongly, there was no need of Taverner. Yet the Church of England lost something when it dropped Taverner and the postil form. The Homilies are brief doctrinal and practical tracts. Taverner's *Postils* were expositions of the Biblical text, and fitted the good Reformed tradition that the Word must ordinarily not only be read but also explained. D. B. Knox has a penetrating assessment of the *Postils* and any reader of them will recognize his summary as true. "The most noteworthy feature of the sermons is the pre-eminence of Christ. This is set out on almost every page. Another conspicuous feature is the emphasis that falls on the work of the Holy Spirit. . . . The sermons are based on the doctrine of justification by faith only." [16]

[14] *Ibid.*, pp. 181 ff. [16] *The Doctrine of Faith*, pp. 212–214.
[15] *Ibid.*, pp. 339 ff.

BIBLIOGRAPHY

The bibliographical history is obscure and very complicated. I fear that I can say little here that will shed light on it. I have seen three separate copies and each differed from the other in details. Cardwell worked with four copies but gives the text of only one. He says that Dr. Cotton [17] mentions five, all of 1540. The reader may consult Cardwell, pp. xi–xiv, to find his solution of the problem.

It will be simplest if I relate the Bibliography to our present text, which is that given by Cardwell ("C" in the textual notes): *Postils on the Epistles and Gospels compiled and published by Richard Taverner in the year 1540, and now edited by Edward Cardwell, D.D.* Oxford. M.DCCC.XLI.

The two title pages given by Cardwell are:
The Epi-/stles and Gospelles with a brief/ Postyl vpon the same from Aduent/ tyll Lowe sondaye whiche is the/ (Wynter parte) drawen/ forth by diuerse learned/ men for the singuler/ commoditie of al/ good christen/ persons/ and namely of Prestes/ and Curates new-/ly recognized./ Cum priuilegio ad impri-/mendum solum.

Colophon: Imprinted in London by Richarde Bankes,/ and are to be solde in Fletestrete next to/ the sygne of the whyte Harte./ Cum priuilegio ad impri-/mendum solum.

The Epi-/stles and Gospelles with a brief Po-/stil vpon the same from after Easter/ TYLL Aduent, which is the Somer/ parte, set-forth for the singuler commoditie of all good chri-/sten men and namely/ of Prestes and/ Curates./ Roma. i./ Euangelium est virtus Dei in/ salutem omni credenti./ The Gospell is the power of God/ to the saluacion of every fayth-/full Christen man./ Cum priuilegio ad impri-/mendum solum.

Colophon: Imprinted at London by Richarde Bankes,/ and

---

[17] H. Cotton, *Editions of the Bible and Parts Thereof in English from the year MDV. to MDCCCL.* (Oxford, 1852), p. 18.

solde in Fletestrete at the sygne of/ the whyte Harte by Anthony/ Clerke./ Cum privilegio ad impri-/mendum solum.

I have collated this text with two others and give the variant readings from them both. The first I refer to as "A"; its Class mark in Cambridge University Library is SSS.56.24:

The Epi-/stles and Gospelles wyth a brief/ Postil upon the same from Aduent/ tyll Lowe sondaye whiche is the/ (Wynter parte) drawen/ forth by diuerse learned/ men for the singuler/ commoditie of all/ good christen/ persons and namely of Prestes and/ Curates newly re-/cognized./ Cum priuilegio ad impri-/mendum solum.

Colophon: Imprynted at London by Rycharde Bankes,/ and are to be solde in Powles churche yarde/ by Thomas Petyt./ Cum priuiligio ad impri-/mendum solum.

The Epi-/stles and Gospelles with a brief Po-/stil upon the same from after Easter/ tyll Aduent, which is the Somer/ parte, set forth for the singuler/ commoditie of all good chri-/sten men and namely/ of Prestes and/ Curates./ Roma. i. Euangelium est virtus dei in/ salutem omni credenti/ The Gospell is the power of God/ to the saluacion of euery fayth-/full Christen man./ Cum priuilegio ad impri-/mendum solum.

Colophon: Imprinted at London by Richarde Bankes/ and solde in Fletestrete at the sygne of/ the whyte Harte by Anthony/ Clerke./ Cum priuilegio ad impri-/mendum solum.

The second I refer to as "B"; the Class mark in Cambridge University Library is Syn. 7.54.30:

The Epi-/stles and Gospelles with a brief/ Postyl upon the same from Aduent/ tyll Lowe sonday whiche is the/ wynter parte drawen forth by/ diuerse learned men for/ the singuler commo-/ditie of al good/ christen per-/sons and/ namely of Prestes and/ Curates newly re-/cognized./ Cum priuilegio ad impri-/mendum solum.

Colophon: Imprinted in London by Richarde Bankes,/ and are to be solde in Fletestrete at/ the sygne of the whyte Harte./ Cum priuilegio Regali ad impri-/mendum solum.

The Epi-/stles and Gospelles with a brief Po-/stil upon the same from after Easter/ tyll Aduent, which is the Somer/ parte, set forth for the singuler/ commoditie of all good chri-/sten men and namely of/ Prestes and/ Curates./ Roma. i. Euangelium est virtus dei in/ salutem omni credenti/ The Gospell is the power of god to/ the saluacion of euery faythfull/ Christen man./ Cum priuilegio ad impri-/mendum solum.

Colophon: Imprinted in Fletestrete next to the white/ harte by Rycharde Bankes./ Cum priuilegio ad imprimendum solum.

These volumes contain yet more title pages:
A. After "the wednesday in Witson weke" comes the colophon: Imprinted at London by/ Rychard Bankes/ Cum priuilegio/ ad imprimen-/dum solum. Then follows the title page: *The Epi-/ stles and Gospels with a brief Po-/styll upon the same from Trini- tie/ sonday tyll Aduent, drawen forthe/ by diuers learned men for the sin-/guler commoditie of al good chri/stians and namely of Pre-/stes and Curates./ Christus Matt. iiij./ Poenitentiam agite, appropin-/quauit enim regnum/ coelorum./* Cum priuilegio ad impri-/mendum solum./ The colophon is the same as that given above for Part 2 of A.
B. A secondary title page (not given in A) is printed after "The table" (i.e., of contents) of the second part: *Postilles or/ Homilies vpon the Epist/les and Gospels from Ester/ untyll Trinitie son- daye, wyth certayne other/ frutefull and godly Sermons drawen/ forth by dyuerse lerned men for the syn-/gular edificacion and commoditie/ of al good Christen/ parsons and in especi-/all of prestes and/ Cvrates./* Cum priuilegio ad impri-/mendum solum./ Anno .M.D.XL.
After "the .iiij. daye of Pentecost" (fol. lxx^b) is the colophon to this section: Imprinted at London by Richarde Ban-/kes, and are to be solde in Fletestrete/ at the sygne of the whyte Harte./ Cum priuilegio ad imprimen-/dum solum. Then comes the fol- lowing title page: *The Epi-/stles and Gospelles with a brief Postyll/ upon the same from Trinitie sonday tyll/ Aduent, drawen forth by dyuerse lear-/ned men for the singuler commo-/ditie of al good christians/ and namely of prestes/ and Curates./ Christus Matt. iiij./ Poenitentiam agite, appropinquauit/ enim regnum coelorum./* Cum priuilegio ad impri-/mendum solum./ Anno .M.D.XL. The colophon to this is the same as for Part 2 of B given above.
After Part 2 (fol. clxxxvi^b) is the colophon: Imprinted at Lon- don by Richarde Bankes,/ and solde in Fletestrete at the sygne of/ the whyte Harte by Anthony/ Clerke./ Cum priuilegio ad impri-/ mendum solum. There follows the final title page: *On saynt An- drewes day./ The Gos-/pels with brief sermons upon them/ for al the holy dayes in ỹ yere.*

[I have since seen, in Westminster Abbey Library, yet another example of 1540, as well as a copy of 1542, published by Rychard Bankes.]

Richard Taverner: Postils on Epistles and Gospels

THE TEXT

The Epistle on the First Sunday in Advent [18]
The xiii. Chapter to the Romans

The Argument upon this Epistle.[19]
Paul prepareth and exhorteth men's hearts to a Christian life.

Brethren, we know the season, how it is time that we should now awake out of sleep. For now is our salvation nearer than when we believed. The night is passed, the day is come nigh. Let us therefore cast away the deeds of darkness and put on the armour of light. Let us walk honestly as it were in the day light; not in eating and drinking, neither in chambering and wantonness, neither in strife and envying: but put ye on the Lord Jesus Christ.[19a]

My brethren and sisters in Jesu Christ, Saint Paul the apostle of God in this present epistle doth teach and admonish us how we ought to know the time wherein we now be. For it is assuredly the time of grace, the time (I say) in which it hath pleased almighty God the Father, which is the fountain and well of all mercy, mercifully and tenderly to visit us by his most dearly beloved Son our Lord Christ Jesu, which undoubtedly is the only Health, Redeemer and Saviour of the whole world. By reason whereof, most dear brethren, we ought diligently to know, that now at last is the time to awake out of this our drowsy and deep sleep, that is to wit, to leave and utterly to renounce and forsake all vanity, idleness, sloth, dreams of our own fancy, and briefly to conclude, all kinds and sorts of sin, which doubtless is the sleep of death, yea, and that of everlasting death.

[18] A, B, fol. i^a; C, Part 1, p. 1.   [19a] Vs. 11–14.
[19] A, omit: upon this Epistle.

Why then, most dear brethren, should we not now arise out of this horrible and foul sleep, sith the apostle declareth and signifieth unto us that our health and salvation is nearer than it was what time we saw nothing but shadows and promises, that is to wit, in the time of the law? And as the apostle writeth to the Ephesians, "Ye that sometime were afar off, be made now near by the blood of Christ." [20] Forasmuch as the darkness of the old law is now past and the light of the new law (which is the light of our Saviour Jesu Christ) is come upon us. The night of sin and the shadow of death wherein the Gentiles did sit (as witnesseth the prophet Esaye [21]) is passed and the day of grace is at hand. For lo! Christ hath brought us grace, pardon, and full remission of all our sins. Lo! all is pardoned unto us in Jesu Christ only, if [22] we have a constant and unfeigned faith in him that it is he to whom God the Father hath given all and for whom and by whom he will give all and forgive all and so make us the children of faith and of light in him, which is the only very clear day and very light of faith and consequently of everlasting life. He is our day, he is our light, our grace, our faith, our health, our life, and altogether ours; without him we are nothing at all. Yea, of ourselves we be but night, but darkness, but infidelity, sin, perdition and death. And what death? Certes, death without end.

Let us then with Christian and faithful hearts do the thing which the apostle (that is to say, the ambassador and messenger of God) doth monish and exhort us to do. Let us leave, I say, all works and deeds of darkness, that is to wit, ignorance and blindness of godly works, and take we upon us the armours of light, which be the graces of our Lord Jesu Christ; that is to say, all faith, all trust, all fear, all reverence, and all love in him which hath so much loved us that he, being God, would become man and suffer death for us and give himself a sacrifice and ransom for us, to the intent that in that sacrifice God should forgive all sins unto all them that ever were from the beginning of the world and that be at this present season and that shall be unto the end of it, so that they have this knowledge, this faith, this fear and trust in him. And of this ought we not to doubt; for it is not so true that we be and speak the one to the other, as this is true; nor that the sky and the earth is, as this is true.

Then go to, dear brethren; let us walk gladly in spirit,[23] armed

---

[20] Eph. 2:13.
[21] Isa. 9:2.
[22] Or: Christ, only if. In this case, only if = provided that.
[23] I.e., in the Spirit, corresponding with "in flesh" (= in the flesh) below.

with faith and trust, in all honesty and cleanness as in daylight in this time of grace, the time, I say, of the coming and visitation of the Son of God, our Lord Jesu Christ. Flee we all surfeiting, revelling, and drunkenness, all foul lusts and filthiness, all strifes and envies, and let us clothe ourselves with Christ, be we shining and glistering with his faith. Let us raise up ourselves to him by faith, by true hope and trust all inflamed in his love and armed with all his graces. And albeit we must live in flesh, that is to wit, by eating and drinking, yet let us so live in flesh, let us so eat and drink, that excess and lust be away, according to the example of Christ. To whom be given all praise, glory, and thanks, world without end. Amen.

THE GOSPEL ON ASCENSION DAY [24]
THE XVI. CHAPTER OF MARK

The Argument.
Of the commission that Christ gave to his apostles to preach his Gospel throughout the whole world. And how Christ stied [25] up to heaven.

After this [26] *Jesus appeared again unto the eleven as they sat at meat, and cast in their teeth their unbelief and hardness of heart, because they believed not them which had seen him* [27] *risen again.* [28] *And he said unto them: Go ye into all the world, and preach the Gospel to every creature.* [29] *He that believeth and is baptized shall be saved. He that believeth not shall be damned. And these tokens shall follow them that believe. In my name they shall cast out devils, they shall speak with new tongues, they shall drive away serpents. And if they drink any deadly thing, it shall not hurt them. They shall lay their hands on the sick, and they shall recover. And* [30] *when the Lord had* [31] *spoken unto them, he was received into heaven, and is set* [32] *on the right hand of God. They therefore* [33] *went forth and preached everywhere, the Lord working with them and confirming the word with miracles following.* [34]

[24] A, B, Part 2, fol. xxxviii^b; C, p. 288.
[25] B, ascended (= stied).
[26] A, omit: After this.
[27] B, that he was.
[28] B, add: from the dead.
[29] B, all creatures.
[30] B, So then.
[31] A, B, hath.
[32] B, omit: set.
[33] B, And they.
[34] Verses 12–19. A, title: The sermon upon this Gospel. B omits.

The Christian man's life in this Gospel, good people, is set before our eyes.[35] For faith and charity are here propounded unto us as in all the rest of the Gospels. Wherefore, sith the Gospel bringeth ever these [36] two with it, we ought also continually to practise [37] them and entreat of them. For he sayeth, "Whoso believeth and be baptized shall be saved." [38]

First of all, therefore,[39] Christ upbraideth in this Gospel his apostles of their faint believe and hardness of heart, and [40] blameth them, declaring what they wanted, and yet nevertheless,[41] he rejecteth them not, neither is moved rigorously and hastily against them, but he gently blameth them none other wise than if one of us would say to an other, "Art thou not ashamed to do the thing thou goest about?" speaking after this sort to bring him to know himself and to make him ashamed, that he may leave of his evil enterprise or work; and yet we forsake [42] him not, nor hate him, nor [43] pluck our love from him. Neither was it a light matter why the Lord rebuked his disciples, for surely infidelity or lack of believe is of all sins that can be named the greatest. Wherefore he upbraideth them of unfaithfulness, as Saint Jerome saith, that faithfulness might succeed.[44] He upbraideth the hardness of their stony heart, that a fleshy heart replenished with charity might follow in the place.[45]

All these things were done to our comfort and instruction,[46] that we should not be discouraged, though we be found [47] anything faulty in our faith, as if we doubt, stumble, or fall, but rather that we should quickly rise again, stablish [48] our faith and run to God, taking trust and affiance at him, and constantly also retaining it, namely sith he dealeth not with us [49] according to rigour, but can wink at our falls and infirmities. And he that reputeth God [50] to

[35] A, C, eyen.
[36] A, those.
[37] B, preach.
[38] B, add: Which things we shall now in order peruse and consider.
[39] B, omit: therefore.
[40] B, add: consequently.
[41] B, omit: nevertheless.
[42] B, reject.
[43] B, nor yet.
[44] In what Migne calls an *opus supposititium, Commentarius in Ev. sec. Marc. XVI*, (*PL* 30.642).
[45] For: He upbraideth . . . place, B reads: And he expresseth unto them the manner of their misbelieve when he sayeth, that their hearts were hardened, and yet notwithstanding he handleth them gently and mildly.
[46] B, consolation.
[47] B, omit: found.
[48] B, establish.
[49] B, with us not.
[50] B, him.

be such, shall also find him such one; I say, if we [51] can take him for a merciful God, he will suffer himself to be found such one, and will so declare himself towards us.[52] Contrary wise, he that hath [53] an evil conscience and an unfaithful heart doth not so. He beareth no such affiance towards God, but fleeth [54] from him, counting [55] him a sore and rigorous judge; and therefore he [56] also findeth him such one. The same we must also do with our neighbours. If we see any swerve from the faith, we may not maintain him [57] in his malice, but we ought to reprove and lay his fault [58] before his eyes; but yet not after such sort that we should hate him or be against him or turn our friendship and love from him. For thus saith Saint Paul: "Brethren, although a man be found in any fault, you that be ghostly [59] redress such a person with the spirit of meekness." [60]

But the most holy father, or god rather, the Bishop of Rome, which will be called Pope, his bishops, his priests, his monks, his canons, his friars, and his nuns, cannot abide, when that they be found in any notable crime, to be reproved. For whatsoever evil do chance, they pretend and allege for them that it come not through their fault, but through the fault of their subjects. Their subjects and such as be under their obedience shall be cruelly and roughly handled. Certainly, all manner [61] injury and wickedness ought to be punished, but love [62] and verity must [63] be kept towards every man. Neither ought we to suffer our mouth to be stopped. For none of us shall so live, as long as we be in this flesh, that we can be found on every part blameless and without sin.[64] But I am faulty in this thing, and another in that.

Namely, sith it is right plain and evident [65] to all men, that even the apostles themselves lacked that which was chief and the highest point of all, whereas notwithstanding they were the corner-stones

---

[51] B, he.
[52] B, him.
[53] B, omit: he that hath.
[54] B, flyeth.
[55] B, reputing.
[56] B, omit: he.
[57] For: we may . . . him, B reads: he is not to be beloved.
[58] B, add: and shrinking.
[59] B, spiritual.
[60] Gal. 6:1.
[61] For: Certainly, all manner, B reads: *Summa summarum,* any.
[62] For: to be . . . love, A reads: to be so punished that charity.
[63] A, omit: must.
[64] B, omit: and without sin.
[65] For: plain and evident, B reads: manifest.

and the rocks of foundation, yea, and the best and the most excellent part of Christendom. No man yet thinketh that the apostles were utterly and altogether unfaithful or [66] infidels. For they believed the things that were written in the law and in the prophets, albeit they had not yet the full perfection of faith. Faith was in them, and it was not in them. Faith therefore is a thing which always groweth bigger and bigger, according to the parable of the mustard seed which our Saviour Christ declareth in the xiii. chapter of Matthew.[67] So the apostles were not utterly void [68] of faith, for they had a part of it. For verily [69] it is with faith as it is with a man that is sick, and beginneth by little and little to creep up and wax strong. The [70] Lord then expresseth [71] to his apostles wherein they believed not, and what they wanted, that is to wit,[72] that they perfectly believed [73] not his resurrection. For albeit they believed all the rest, yet in this behalf they remained [74] infidels. For haply they believed also this, that God would be merciful unto them, but yet this was not enough. For it was needful [75] also that they should believe Christ's resurrection. Wherefore he upbraideth them of their lack of faith,[76] because, notwithstanding [77] they had seen altogether,[78] yet they believed it not, and that they yet wanted this article of resurrection.

What is it then to believe the resurrection of Christ, which beareth so great a stroke, and is of such strength,[79] that the disciples were called infidels and misbelieving persons for the default of it? Verily,[80] to believe the resurrection of Christ is nothing else than to believe we have a spokesman and peacemaker [81] before God—which is Christ, which maketh us at one with God the Father and justifieth us in his sight. For whatsoever is in man of his own nature and birth, without regeneration, is but sin and death, whereby he heapeth upon himself God's vengeance. Again, God is

[66] B, omit: unfaithful or.
[67] Matt. 13:31 f. B, omit: which our . . . Matthew.
[68] B, add: and destitute.
[69] B, omit: verily.
[70] A, our.
[71] B, add: and declareth.
[72] For: that . . . wit, B reads: which doubtless was.
[73] A, believeth.
[74] A, remaineth.
[75] B, necessary.
[76] For: lack of faith, B reads: infidelity.
[77] For: because notwithstanding, B reads: saying that, albeit.
[78] I.e., all things.
[79] B, importance.
[80] B, Certes.
[81] For: spokesman and peacemaker, B reads: reconciler.

the everlasting [82] justice and clearness, which of his nature hateth sin. Hereof it cometh that between God and man, being in such case,[83] is perpetual enmity, neither can they be friends or agree together. Christ therefore, by taking our flesh upon him [84] did both translate our sins upon himself, and drowned the wrath of the Father in himself, to make us at one with [85] his Father. Without this faith we be the children of vengeance; we can do no good work that may please [86] God, neither will God hear our prayers. For thus sayeth the prophet: [87] "They cried and there was no helper, to the Lord, and he answered them not." [88] Yea, the most excellent work whereby we thought to obtain grace, help and comfort of God, was imputed unto us for sin, as the self-same [89] prophet [90] saith: *"Oratio eius in peccatum fiat:* Be his prayer counted for sin." [91] For surely we cannot with all our powers of our own nature pacify God. We needed therefore Christ to be a suitor [92] for us to the Father, and to make us at one with him, and finally, to obtain whatsoever is needful [93] for us.

By the same Christ it behoveth us to ask of God whatsoever [94] we need, as Christ himself instructeth us, saying: "Whatsoever ye ask the Father in my name [95] shall be done unto you." [96] Whatsoever we demand of God, surely we must [97] by this Christ (which hath satisfied for our sins) obtain and get it. For Christ is he which protecteth [98] us; he is the defence and buckler under whom we be shadowed,[99] even as the chickens be nourished and hid under the wings of the hen. By him only our prayer is allowed before God. By him only we be heard and get the favour and grace of the Father.

This is then,[1] to believe upon Christ's resurrection, if, as it is

[82] B, eternal.
[83] B, omit: being . . . case.
[84] For: by taking . . . him, B reads: being incarnate.
[85] For: make . . . with, B reads: reconcile us to.
[86] B, be acceptable to.
[87] For: sayeth the prophet, B reads: in the xviii. Psalm it is written.
[88] Ps. 18:41.
[89] B, omit.
[90] B, add: in the cix. psalm.
[91] Ps. 109:7.
[92] For: a suitor, B reads: mediator.
[93] B, necessary.
[94] B, add: thing.
[95] B, add: it.
[96] John 16:23.
[97] B, transpose "we must" to before "obtain."
[98] B, layeth a garrison about.
[99] B, hidden.
[1] B, now.

rehearsed,[2] we believe that Christ hath borne upon him as well our sins as the sins of the whole world, and hath drowned in himself the one and the other and also the displeasure [3] of the Father, by whom [4] we be reconciled to God and made righteous before him.

But here I cannot sufficiently lament the fewness of [5] Christian men and women that [6] have this steadfast [7] faith that by Christ they be released of [8] their sins and [9] made righteous. Few, I say, have such opinion [10] in the resurrection of Christ that they think [11] their sins be taken away [12] by Christ. But what do they? They [13] go about to be justified by works of their own imagination.[14] This man entereth into the cloister, and is made a monk or friar, she a nun, some one thing, some another; [15] and yet they say they believe in the resurrection of Christ, where their works do show clean contrary. Wherefore this article have the holy fathers preached and taught [16] specially before other. For thus [17] Paul in [18] his first epistle to the Corinthians sayeth: "If Christ hath not risen from death to life, then vain is our preaching, vain also is your faith." [19] And a little after: "If Christ hath [20] not risen, vain is your faith, ye be yet in your sins." [21] Ye will ask how this doth follow of S.[22] Paul's words.[23] Thus, truly: If Christ rose not from death to life, it followeth that sin and death did swallow him up and killed him. After that we could not rid ourselves out of our sins, Jesus Christ took them upon him, to tread under his feet death

---

[2] B, recited.
[3] B, ire.
[4] B, whereby.
[5] For: But . . . of, B reads: Now ye see yourselves how few.
[6] B, there be which; A, which.
[7] B, omit: steadfast.
[8] For: that . . . of, B reads: whereby all men be delivered from.
[9] B, add: he.
[10] For: Few . . . opinion, B reads: For they believe not in.
[11] B, omit: they think.
[12] B, add: also.
[13] B, omit: what . . . they.
[14] For: by . . . imagination, B reads: their own works.
[15] B, add: that they may be delivered from their sins.
[16] B, inculked.
[17] B, add: saint.
[18] B, add: the xv. chapter of.
[19] I Cor. 15:14.
[20] B, have.
[21] I Cor. 15:17.
[22] A, saint.
[23] For: Ye . . . words, B reads: What manner consequence is this? how do this follow?

and hell, and to be made Lord over them. But [24] if he rose not again, then surely he overcame not sin, but was overcome of sin. And thereupon it followeth,[25] if he rose not again, he redeemed us not, and so we be yet in our sins.

Furthermore, in the Epistle [26] to the Romans he saith: [27] "if thou confessest with thy mouth Jesus to be the Lord, and believest in thy heart that God hath raised him from death, thou shalt be saved." [28] Hereunto agreeth all Scripture both Old and New. But it is not yet sufficient barely [29] to believe the resurrection of Christ. For [30] wicked persons believe this, yea, the devil [31] doubteth not but that God suffered and rose again. We therefore [32] must also believe the effect [33] of the resurrection and must know [34] what fruit and profit we have taken thereby; that is to say, pardon of our guilt and, as it were, a gale delivery [35] of all our sins, that Christ passed through death and by it overcame sin and death, yea, and whatsoever could hurt us he trod under his foot, and is ordained and set [36] at the right hand of the Father in heaven, the mighty Lord over sin, death, hell, the devil,[37] and whatsoever hurteth us; and that all these things be done for our sake, which thing the wicked persons believe not.

Ye see, then, my friends, how much is contained [38] in this article of resurrection, so that ye [39] may better want all the rest than this one article. For what were it to believe all other [40] articles, as that God was born of the virgin Mary, that he died and was buried, if we do [41] not also believe that he rose again? And this God meaneth in the prophecy of [42] Habakkuk, where he sayeth: "I shall work a work in you which men shall not [43] believe when it shall

---

[24] B, Now.
[25] B, omit: thereupon it followeth.
[26] B, tenth.
[27] B, add: thus.
[28] Rom. 10:9.
[29] B, omit: barely.
[30] B, add: all.
[31] B, Satan.
[32] B, But we.
[33] B, sum.
[34] For: must know, B reads: also.
[35] Remittance of payment.
[36] For: ordained and set, B reads: constitute and made.
[37] B, omit.
[38] B, laid.
[39] A, we.
[40] B, the.
[41] B, thou doest.
[42] B, omit: the prophecy of.
[43] For: men . . . not, B reads: no man shall.

be told." [44] And this is the cause why Paul in all his epistles handleth no work or miracle of Christ so busily,[45] as he doth the resurrection of Christ. Yea, he letteth pass all the works and miracles of Christ, and chiefly teacheth us the fruit of this; [46] so that none of the apostles hath so painted Christ unto us as Paul, of whom [47] not without cause Christ said to Ananias: "This is my chosen vessel,[48] to bear my name before the heathen people, and kings, and the children of Israel." [49]

It followeth in the text: *Go ye into the whole world* (saith Christ to his disciples) [50] *and preach the Gospel to every creature.* But I pray you,[51] what shall they preach? Verily,[52] none other thing but that Christ is risen from death, and that he hath vanquished and taken away sin and all misery; he that believeth this, is saved. For the Gospel (which betokeneth [53] a glad tidings) is nothing else but a preaching or showing of Christ's rising again.[54] He that believeth this,[55] is safe; he that doth not, is lost. And here consider me the nature of faith. Faith constraineth none to the Gospel, but leaveth every man to his own liberty and choice. He that believeth, may freely believe; he that cometh, let him come; he that will not, choose him. And here again ye shall mark that the Romish Bishop erreth and doth naught,[56] in that he goeth about by violence to draw heathen [57] men to the Christian faith. For besides the preaching of the Gospel, Christ gave nothing in commission unto his disciples. So they preached it, according to their commission, and left it in men's free liberty to come to it or not. They said not: "Either believe it, or I will kill thee." So ye see that infidels, as Turks, Saracens and Jews, ought not violently to be drawn to our faith, but lovingly rather provoked [58] and allured.

But here is a doubt, how this text ought to be understand—"Go into all the world"—sith the apostles never passed

[44] Hab. 1:5.
[45] B, diligently.
[46] B, it.
[47] For: of whom, B reads: wherefore.
[48] For: chosen vessel, B reads: vessel of election.
[49] Acts 9:15.
[50] B, omit: saith . . . disciples.
[51] B, omit: But . . . you.
[52] B, omit: Verily.
[53] For: betokeneth, B reads: in the Greek soundeth.
[54] B, resurrection.
[55] For: believeth this, B reads: giveth faith unto it.
[56] Wrong.
[57] B, omit: heathen.
[58] B, invited.

throughout all the world. For none of the apostles came so far as to us. Furthermore, there be many islands found out now in our time which be inhabited with people to whom God's Word was never preached; whereas yet the Scripture witnesseth that [59] their sound went forth into all the world.[60] I say therefore, that [61] their preaching went [62] into all lands, although it be not yet come into the whole world. And this coming out is begun, albeit it be not yet [63] ended; but nevertheless [64] it spreadeth continually more and more, and shall do till the last day. And it is with this commission or ambassade [65] of preaching, as it is with a stone that [66] is cast into the water. For, like as a stone that is cast into the sea [67] maketh waves about it, and one wave driveth forth another till they come to the shore, and albeit there be in the middes a great calm, yet the waves cease not, but go continually forth, even [68] so it is with the preaching of the Gospel. It began by the apostles; and it still goeth forth; and by still preaching [69] it spreadeth further and further. It suffereth in the world persecution and chasing away; yet it is always opened more and more to such as heard not of it before, though in the mid journey it be driven down and be made stark heresy. Or it may be likened to an ambassage that one sendeth out. As, if our sovereign lord the King of England should send his ambassadors into France or Spain, we say that an ambassady is gone forth from our king thither, albeit the ambassadors be not in deed as yet come thither. For, like as Christ died for all, so he rose again for all, and therefore he would have his Gospel preached to all.[70]

Whosoever, then,[71] *that believeth and is baptized, shall be saved.* Here ye shall mark [72] that God doth hang an outward sign to his Word, which sign maketh his Word to be the stronger unto us, so that it assureth [73] our hearts and maketh us not to doubt thereof.

[59] For: witnesseth that, B reads: confirmeth, saying: *In omnem terram exivit sonus eorum,* that is.
[60] Not Ps. 8 as margin, but Ps. 19:4.
[61] B, omit: therefore, that.
[62] B, add: out.
[63] B, add: finished and.
[64] B, omit.
[65] B, ambassadie.
[66] B, when it.
[67] For: like . . . sea, B reads: it.
[68] B, forth. Even.
[69] For: still preaching, B reads: preachers.
[70] Margin refers to Erasmus' *Paraphrasis.* This is "For I died for all, I rose again for all" (*Opera omnia* VII.271). B, omit: For, . . . to all.
[71] For: whosoever, then, B reads: It followeth in the text.
[72] B, note.
[73] B, confirmeth.

Thus God did set the rainbow for a sign to Noah, to assure him he would no more destroy the world with floods. So that this rainbow is, as it were, a seal or surety both to Noah and to all us, none otherwise than a seal is put to writings to make them sure. And like as princes and noblemen be known by their colours, badges and arms, even so dealeth God with us, and hast established his words as with a seal, that we should nothing doubt. He gave to Abraham circumcision for a sign of Christ's coming, that should bless the world. Likewise hath he done here, by putting to this promise of salvation an outward sign—I mean baptism. For baptism is, as it were, a watchword to put God in remembrance of his promise. Which, if it can be had, ought of necessity [74] to be taken (as Saint Austin saith) [75] and not to be omitted.[76] But, if it cannot be had, or if it be denied a man, yet he shall not be damned, so that[77] he believeth the Gospel.[78] And therefore the Lord saith, "He that believeth not shall be damned." He saith not, "He that is not baptised." For baptism without faith (either of the party self, or of them that bring him to baptism, if it be a child that is baptised) [79] is nothing [80] worth, but it is like to a paper that hath a seal hanging to it, and hath no writing in it.[81] Wherefore they that have the visible signs [82] without the invisible [83] faith, they have seals without writings.

Furthermore, we [84] see here that [85] the office of such as will be called Christ's apostles is [86] to go into the world and preach Christ's Gospel. And so here we may judge whether the Bishop of Rome with his gallant prelates, which ride like princes upon their moils [87] and never preach one word, but rather stop the mouths of true preachers, ought to be called the successors of the apostles and persons apostolic [88] or no.

And [89] *these tokens,* saith Christ,[90] *shall follow them that believe.*

[74] B, in any wise.
[75] *De peccatorum meritis et remissione* III.8 (*PL* 44.190).
[76] B, despised.
[77] Provided that.
[78] B, add: For where the Gospel is, there is baptism and all that pertaineth to Christianity.
[79] B, omit: either . . . baptised.
[80] A, little.
[81] A, therein.
[82] For: the visible signs, B reads: signs (which we call sacraments).
[83] B, omit: the invisible.
[84] B, ye.
[85] For: that, B reads: good people, what is.
[86] For: is, B reads: that is to wit.
[87] Mules.
[88] For: the successors . . . apostolic, B reads: apostolic persons.
[89] B, It followeth in the text, And.
[90] B, omit: saith Christ.

In my name they shall cast out devils, they shall speak with new tongues, they shall take [91] *away serpents. And if they drink any deadly thing, it shall not hurt them. They shall lay their hands on the sick, and they shall recover.* But ye will ask, "How [92] shall we verify this text, that he that believeth shall have power to work all these? [93] For our [94] Lord saith that these tokens shall follow the believers; and yet it is certain [95] that not all the apostles wrought them. For it is recorded of none to have drunken poison, but of John the Evangelist.[96] Yea,[97] if this saying of Christ must needs stand, few shall be saved, for very few of the saints have done all these." Some [98] therefore, to avoid this inconvenience, do expound these signs mystically, saying that they do speak with new tongues which whereas before they taught devilish doctrines, now [99] confess Christ and so [1] be new men. By taking away of serpents, they understand the destroying of pestiferous doctrines, heresies and sects. By drinking of poison without hurt they understand that the reading or hearing of false doctrines shall not hurt them. By healing and curing of sick persons they understand the healing of the soul. Albeit this interpretation is honest and a matter of truth that such as believe shall work these feats, yet it is no doubt but that

---

[91] B, drive.
[92] For: But . . . How, B reads: My friends, how.
[93] B, add: signs.
[94] B, the.
[95] For: and . . . certain, B reads: Moreover, it is certainly known unto us.
[96] Hastings' *Dictionary of the Bible* (1899), II.682, note *, ascribes this legend to Isidore of Seville. Our Postil may have received it from Nicholas of Lyra or Faber Stapulensis.
[97] B, furthermore.
[98] A common allegorical interpretation of this passage. Thus Aquinas, in the so-called *Catena aurea (Diui Thomae Aqui–/natis enarrationes . . . In quatuor Euangelia . . . Venundantur Parisiis in edibus Ambrosii girault. M.D.xxxi.* The copy I looked it up in was Cranmer's, by the way). But the Postil is probably referring to the *Glossa ordinaria* in the *Biblia* of Nicholas of Lyra, which is worth quoting: "*They shall cast out demons.* Today the Church does this spiritually, when for the sake of exorcism she lays hands on believers and drives out evil spirits. *They shall speak.* This happens when believers leave the profane language (*secularia verba*) and speak holy mysteries and magnify the praises and power of God so far as they may. *They shall take up serpents.* That is, they shall disperse the wise. . . . It is to be understood intellectually. *If they drink* . . . When they hear noxious ideas they will not be led astray to put them into practice. . . . *They shall lay hands on the sick.* . . . When they strengthen their neighbours to do good deeds by their own example of good works, they lay hands on the sick and they will recover. These miracles are the greater inasmuch as they are spiritual; for by this souls are raised and not just bodies."
[99] B, add: they.
[1] B, add: they.

whensoever the profit of the Gospel, as Erasmus saith,[2] requireth an outward miracle, he shall do any of the foresaid miracles even outwardly [3] and they shall follow him, as Christ himself sayeth in another place: "Verily, verily, I say unto you, he that believeth in me, the works that I do, he shall do, yea, and he shall do greater than they be." [4] For the Christian man hath the same power which our Saviour [5] Christ hath; [6] Christ is a community; he is set in the same goods with Christ. Furthermore, our Saviour [7] Christ gave them power against wicked spirits, to cast them out, and to heal all manner of sicknesses, as it is read in the tenth of Matthew.[8] Also the prophet David,[9] in the xix. Psalm sayeth: [10] "Thou shalt walk upon lions and dragons." [11] Wherefore, where a Christian man is, the power to work these signs and miracles is not taken away, as by many examples it hath been proved.

But no man ought to do them, unless [12] the case require it. For the apostles themselves wrought not these miracles but only to the testification of God's Word, that so by miracles the Gospel might be confirmed, as the text saith: "They went and preached everywhere, the Lord working with them and strengthening [13] the word with miracles following." But now after [14] the Gospel is spread abroad and open [15] to the whole world, miracles be not [16] necessary as they were in the apostles' time. For, as Saint Gregory [17] full well saith, in the beginning of the Church, these signs were necessary. For to the intent that the faith of the believers might increase, it was to be nourished with miracles even like as we also, when we plant young trees, do pour so long water into them till we see them take hold in the earth; but when they be once thoroughly rooted, we cease from watering them any more.[18]

[2] *Opera omnia* VII.272.
[3] For: no doubt . . . outwardly, B reads: not the right sense and meaning of this text. This then is the meaning: Where a Christian man hath faith, he shall have power to work these signs.
[4] John 14:12.
[5] For: which . . . Saviour, B reads: with.
[6] B, omit: hath.
[7] B, omit: our Saviour.
[8] Matt. 10:1.
[9] B, omit: the prophet David.
[10] B, ye read.
[11] Not Ps. 19 as margin, but Ps. 91:13.
[12] B, add: it be necessary and.
[13] B, confirming.
[14] A, add: that.
[15] B, opened.
[16] A, add: so.
[17] *Moralium* XXVII.xviii (*PL* 76.420).
[18] B, omit: For, as . . . any more.

Now [19] *when the* [20] *Lord had spoken these things* [21] *unto them, he was received into heaven;* that is,[22] he went up to begin his spiritual and heavenly kingdom and drew with him our hopes [23] that thither, whither we saw him ascend, we should also follow. And he sitteth on the right hand of God; that is to say,[24] he is God, equal and of like power with the Father. And, as the prophet sayeth: "He ascended up on high, and hath led captivity a prisoner." [25] So that now we be no longer in thraldom, for Christ hath carried it away with him and made us the children of his Father, to live eternally with him in heaven. To whom be glory for ever and ever. Amen.

The Gospel on the III. Sunday After Trinity [26]
The xv. Chapter of Luke

The Argument.
The Parable of the Hundred Sheep and of the Groat.

The publicans and sinners resorted unto Jesus [27] *to hear him. And the Pharisees and scribes murmured, saying, He receiveth sinners and eateth with them. But he put forth this parable unto them, saying, What man of you, having an hundred sheep, if he lose one of them, leaveth not* [28] *ninety and nine in the wilderness, and go after that which is lost until he find it? And when he hath found it, he layeth it on his shoulders with joy. And as soon as he cometh home, he calleth together his lovers and neighbours, saying unto them, Rejoice with me, for I have found my sheep which was lost. I say unto you, that likewise joy shall be in heaven over one sinner that repenteth, more than over ninety and nine just persons which need no repentance. Either what woman having ten groats, if she lose one, doth not she light a candle and sweep the house and seek diligently till she find it? And when she hath found it, she calleth her lovers and her neighbours together, saying, Rejoice with me, for I have found the groat which I had lost. Likewise I*

---

[19] B, It followeth, Now.
[20] A, our.
[21] B, omit: these things.
[22] B, add: to say.
[23] B, add: into heaven.
[24] For: that is to say, B reads: This is a manner or figure of speaking and it signifieth.
[25] Ps. 68:18; Eph. 4:8.
[26] A, B, Part 2, fol. lxxxviii^b. C, p. 371.
[27] B, Then resorted unto him all the p. and s. for.
[28] B, doth not leave.

say unto you, there shall [29] *be joy in the presence of the angels of God over one sinner that repenteth.*[29a]

In this Gospel, dear brethren, is set before our eyen the notable example of the loving kindness and mercy of Christ towards us wretched sinners and lost sheep, unto whom only this Gospel is proponed for a singular comfort. For the Pharisees and scribes which be blinded with their own proper justice, be not only no partakers of this most comfortable Gospel but moreover they utterly understand it not. Yea, when they see that Christ bestoweth his Gospel upon sinners they grudge [30] thereat and envy that they should have such favour and grace at his hands. The publicans, then, that is to say, customers, tribute gatherers, or bailiffs, which amongst the Jews and namely, amongst the religious Pharisees, were counted unholy persons, and the other notorious and open sinners resorted to Christ to hear him. They had heard much of him and what wonders and miracles he had showed amongst the people and namely they had heard of his comfortable doctrine. Wherefore they come now, knowing themselves sinners and therefore not quiet in their conscience, to seek rest to their souls and to hear Christ, whom forthwith he lovingly receiveth and like a tender and a good physician goeth about to lay his medecine and salve to their diseases. All his patient hearers and humble suitors he healeth, not only in body, but also in soul. But the most holy and religious Pharisees and famous doctors of the law and scribes are nothing content herewith. They murmur, they grudge, they snouf [31] at him. And what say they? "Lo! this fellow which is reported to be the Son of God and which maketh himself so perfect and holy a person receiveth sinful persons into his company and eateth and drinketh with them."

But he put forth this parable unto them, etc. Good people, ye shall understand that our Master Christ, because he would not give a just cause of offence to the Pharisees and scribes, studieth to heal them with two feat [32] parables, by which he teacheth that not without cause he receiveth sinners and eateth with them. Yea, he declareth that his office requireth to preach glad tidings to the poor, not to break a bruised reed nor to quench the smoking flax, as Esay had prophesied of him. Moreover, that his office and feat [33] was to feed his flock like a shepherd, to gather together the lambs with his arm, to relieve them in his bosom, also such as be lost to seek up, such as go astray to bring again, such as be wounded to

[29] B, shall there.
[29a] Vs. 1–10.
[30] Grumble.
[31] Sniff; turn up their noses.
[32] Apt.
[33] Property.

bind up, such as be weak to make strong, and so forth. All these offices of Christ be everywhere recorded in Scripture and he doth express them here in the parables ensuing, to the intent he would show that he doth not amiss in that he receives sinners and taketh meat with them. Indeed, Christ might have made answer to the Pharisees and scribes without parables, even with open texts out of the prophets concerning his offices. But this he doth not, that hearing they should not hear, and seeing they should not see, but at last should perish by the just judgement of God. And in these parables lieth hid the right dreadful judgement of God against these proud religious and holy Pharisees that will evermore justify themselves, which shall be rejected and shaken off with their justices, whereas the penitent and lowly sinners shall be received.

What man of you, saith Christ, *which if he hath* [34] *an hundred sheep, and fortune to lose one of them, will not forthwith leave the four score and nineteen in wilderness and go after that which is lost until he find it? And when he hath found it, for joy he layeth it on his shoulders, and he cometh not so soon home but he calleth together his friends and his neighbours and desireth them to rejoice with him for the finding again of his lost sheep.* So, sayeth Christ, *joy shall be in heaven over one sinner that repenteth more than over four score and xix persons which need no repentance.* My friends, what meaneth this parable? Who is this shepherd or sheepmaster? Surely it is our Master Christ, he feedeth his sheep, he teacheth all men in the wildsome and desert world. Of these sheep, one strayeth abroad and is lost; the other, in their own conceits and judgement, err not but be still in the right way and therefore they need not to be sought and to be redeemed. And truly, good people, the number is very small of them that shall be saved, for the rest of the people think themselves just and righteous persons by the merits of their own works. The sheep that goeth astray signifieth them which know themselves sinners. These doth Christ seek up. Yea, he came for these persons' [35] sakes, that he might redeem them. Hear then, ye see the final cause and use of Christ. "The Son of Man came to seek and save that was lost." [36] He came into this world to save sinners. So then, there be ii. sorts of just or righteous persons in the world. He that knowledgeth his sins and unworthiness and believeth on him that justifieth the wicked is just by faith and he is the true just and good person. The other is he that will be justified and made good by the works of the

---

[34] B, have.
[35] B, men's.
[36] Luke 19:10. Margin, Isa. 42, a general reference to ch. 42:7–9.

law. This justice is called the Pharisaical justice. Of this justice Christ speaketh thus: "Unless your righteousness pass the righteousness of the scribes and Pharisees, ye shall not enter into the kingdom of God." [37] And in the xvi. chapter of Luke, he sayeth: "Ye be they which justify yourselves before men, but God knoweth your hearts." [38]

The second parable, of the women which had lost a groat and after much seeking found it again, meaneth the same thing that the other parable doth. Indeed, the woman is a weak vessel. So Christ applieth [39] himself to the weak and unperfect persons. The woman lighteth a candle, sweepeth her house, seeketh diligently her coin that she hath lost. She never ceaseth till she hath found it again. Even so careful and desirous is our Saviour Christ to call sinners to repentance.

Now, if ye will know the cause of our salvation,[40] ye shall understand that it is not our own work nor our own merit and deserving but because Christ our Shepherd seeketh us. Yea, we should utterly perish straying in the wilderness if Christ our herdman sought us not up. But how doth he seek us? Truly, by his Word, which being preached unto us reproveth us of our wandering and straying abroad. Which known, we be brought again by Christ our pastor and shepherd to the flock, that is to wit, we be made the true members of the true Church. And after we be once reduced and brought home again to the flock, we be not set in a field alone by ourselves where we alone shall feed, but together with that rest of the flock and under our shepherd we seek all one and the same food and do the same that the rest of the sheep do.

Finally, forasmuch as Christ sayeth that the angels in heaven do joy upon such as repent, we be here taught that repentance is a work very acceptable and pleasing to God. Wherefore, my friends, let us not be likened to these religious, proud, and presumptuous Pharisees and scribes, which murmured and grudged at the tender heart and kindness of our Saviour Christ, and which justified themselves, despising all other in comparison of them, because of their own traditions and observances, and therefore thought they had no need of Christ. But let us humbly and thankfully, at the preaching of Christ's holy Word (which it hath pleased him now in these last days to disclose and open again unto us), repent ourselves [41] of our wandering out of the right way. And then, doubtless, the angels in heaven shall have more joy over us than over all those which were counted most holy and perfect persons in the sight of

---

[37] Matt. 5:20.
[38] Luke 16:15.
[39] Accommodates.
[40] B, repentance.
[41] B, to repent us.

the world. Which angels also at our departure out of this vale of misery shall carry up our souls into heaven, where we shall have the most full fruition of all joy with Christ our Lord. To whom, with the Father and Holy Ghost, be all glory. Amen.

The Epistle on the iiii. Sunday After Trinity [42]
The viii. Chapter to the Romans

The Argument.
In this epistle we be comforted to bear adversity well in worth, seeing it is the way to everlasting glory.

Brethren, I suppose that the afflictions of this life are not worthy of the glory which shall be showed upon us. For the fervent desire of the creature abideth, looking when the sons of God shall appear, because the creature is subdued to vanity, against the will thereof, but for his will which hath subdued the same in hope. For the same creature shall be delivered from the bondage of corruption into the glorious liberty of the sons of God. For we know that every creature groaneth with us also, and travaileth in pain, even unto this time. Not only it, but we also which have the first fruits of the spirit, mourn in ourselves also and wait for the adoption of the children of God even the deliverance of our body.[42a]

The Sermon upon this Epistle.[43]

The holy apostle Saint Paul, well-beloved brethren and sisters, considering the state of true Christian men which live godly in this world to be full of adversities and troubles which be offered unto them both by the world, the flesh, and the devil, and knowing the weak power of frail men to be far unable to stand steadfastly in them unless they be armed and fenced with the armour of God's Word, exhorteth us therefore in this epistle by divers reasons to patience and sufferance, and comforteth us with the great joy and glory that shall be declared unto us in the world to come. He affirmeth unto us that whatsoever we can suffer in this world is but short and transitory, but the joy that we shall receive is durable and everlasting. How great soever the pain be of our adversity that we suffer here, I think it nothing, sayeth Saint Paul, to the glory that shall appear unto us, which is so great and infinite that it cannot be comprehended of any man's understanding. It far passeth the eye of man to see through it, or the ear to hear the greatness thereof, or the heart of man to understand the glory that

---

[42] A, B, Part 2, fol. xci[b]. C, p. 380.   [42a] Vs. 18–23.   [43] B, omit title.

God hath prepared for them that love him,[44] which are content after the example of his well-beloved Son Christ to suffer and to bear their cross with good heart and will.

Let us therefore behold not so much the grief and despite of persecution and displeasures of this world, as the brightness and excellency of the glory that we shall be in, which, although we see it not with our corporal eye, yet with the eye of our faith in the mirror of God's Word we see it much more clearly, and shall more surely enjoy it than we see and enjoy those things which be under our corporal sight. If the greatness of adversity feareth us, let us call to mind that when we suffer innocently we suffer with Christ and Christ with us. If we be of the body by true faith, then may we be sure that the Head beareth part with us and helpeth us in our adversity. In his power and assistance we shall overcome. Of our self we be too weak, but in his power, sayeth Saint Paul, in whom is my comfort, I can do all things.[45] Let no men think it impossible to bear patiently the loss of name, of goods, of wife and children, to bear the great assaults of the devil's temptations. For to overcome the strong and unruly affections of our corrupt nature, and thereupon by [46] cowardness to give over and suffer ourselves to be led under their captivity, nay, there is nothing too hard to be performed of a Christian man in whom the Spirit of God is abiding. "Take good heart," sayeth our Saviour and Captain, Christ, "I have overcome the world and all these for you." [47] It is not impossible for you to resist and to have the victory; for faith subdueth all things and hath the victory of all things that be against you, for all things be possible to faith. This is the comfort that a Christian man may have, if he [48] consider that it is not his adversity alone which he suffereth but Christ his Head and Captain suffereth with him. As he said to Saul when he persecuted the Christian men, "Saul, Saul, why doest thou persecute me?" [49] It ought to be no strange thing to us to suffer; for Saint Paul sayeth that we be ordained for this use and purpose. In chastisement doth God nurture his children whom he loveth. If our life be in chastisement and adversity, and we live in patience, we may have good hope that as we be made like to Christ in trouble and affliction, so shall we be like to him in glory. The way to pleasure is by adversity, to wealth by infirmity, to glory by rebuke and shame, to riches everlasting by transitory poverty. After none other sort walked our Saviour Christ in this world. It were unmeet the disciple to be above the master. It were not meet the soldier to be more delicately handled

[44] Isa. 64:4; I Cor. 2:9. [46] B, in. [48] For: if he, B reads: to.
[45] Phil. 4:13. [47] John 16:33. [49] Acts 9:4.

than his captain. Who can require of God to be spared from his cross, where God spared not his own dear and well-beloved Son, Christ? He suffered all reproofs and afflictions, and suffered to the death of the cross and yet deserved it not. Why then, should not we that be sinners content ourselves to suffer, whether God ordaineth adversity to fall upon us for our sins, to the intent to purge us of them, or whether he would have us suffer for the trial of our faith, that so, by our patience we might glorify his name and edify our neighbour by our example? Let us bless ourselves in the name of the Father, of the Son, and the Holy Ghost, and offer ourselves to bear whatsoever he thinketh meet for our soul. Let us pray that we may have faith to stand and not be overcome of the temptation of adversity. It is no small comfort to us that we suffer not alone. Such an unity and consent is there between the members of Christ's mystical body, that what one member suffereth, all the residue feel the grief of the same and bear their part of the burthen. And if this seemeth not enough, all the creatures of God seem to feel our adversity and to suffer with us, and desire and tarry for, in hope, their deliverance. They seem to understand, as they be abused in the world, that so also be the elect. They see themselves created of God to the use and necessity of man, whom they serve with right good will, and they see themselves otherwhiles sore abused in excess and riot, and therefore they be grieved therewith. And yet, though it be against their wills, they are still subject for his sake that ordained them and are content for his pleasure to be subject to mutability and bear patiently the vanity of men in their abuse, in hope yet once [50] of deliverance. They desire not to be above the dignity of God's dear and chosen servants, whom they see unworthily dealt withal in the world, but bear their bondage and captivity well in worth, taking such part as God's most worthy creatures do, for they know that they shall once be delivered, not only from their pain and travail in changing and renewing themselves from time to time for man's use and commodity, in perpetual generation and corruption, but shall also be delivered from the abuse which the ungodly hold and occupy them unjustly in. A liberty and deliverance they look for in hope, which they know certainly shall then chance to them when they shall see the children of God delivered from their labours and travails and set in their glory and [51] joyful rest. This is the deliverance which all creatures sorrow and wail daily for, and are in as fervent desire to see this deliverance as the woman which is in travail of her child longeth for the deliverance thereof.

[50] One day.   [51] B, of.

In a parable, good friends, thus Saint Paul speaketh unto you, to comfort you, that for some solace of your pain and adversity, ye have all the creatures of God suffer with you. Count it not for any vain invention feigned of Saint Paul, for he said that he knew it to be thus indeed, that all creatures do suffer part with God's elect in their troubles. Which thing might we learn and know also if we will consider with better advisement the thing which he speaketh. For consider me what doth it signify to us when we see the weary ox wail and pant under his yoke, the horse groan under his burthen, and the poor lamb bleat when he is drawn and driven to his slaughter, when all beasts travail with pain and dolour to increase in their kind, when all creatures are subject to such continual alteration, formed and reformed from one fashion to another, what signifieth it unto us but that they be partakers of such pains as God's servants be put to? They suffer and resist not, for so they see such portion to fall to the elect of God. And therefore in hope of deliverance they abide whatsoever the use and necessity of man requireth of them, or yet whatsoever abuse and tyranny man's malice put them to. And thus in their painful travail, they continue till the day come when God's children shall be delivered of all their misery, which they long for, both for the elects' sake and their own also.

This desire and carefulness is not in unreasonable creatures only, neither do they alone suffer such vexation and abuse in the world to be wrongfully dealt with; but we ourselves, sayeth Saint Paul, which have the first-fruits of God's Spirit, endowed with singular prerogatives above other of God's household, being the heads and teachers of the people and made of God the vessels to receive and keep the most worthy and excellent treasure of his Gospel, we ourself are in danger and subject to manifold adversities in the world, insomuch that we are as men daily in danger and judged to death, and are reputed as sheep evermore ready to the slaughter. We see so many unworthy things done in the world, that we desire to be out of the world and to be with Christ. Such cumbrance and grievance we feel in this corruptible body that we sigh and daily long to be delivered. We desire much to have this tabernacle of our bodies to be changed and altered, that we may be endowed with our heavenly house from above.

Now, my friends, these things well considered, let us take upon us the armour of God to fight against our invisible enemies. Let us patiently abide all griefs and displeasures of this life, that we may reign with Christ another day. It is no small joy that we be called to. It is far passing all the passions that we can suffer here. And let us, as I said, call to mind that we suffer not alone. Christ our Head suffereth with us, by whose assistance we shall be able to stand. And such communion and fellowship is there between the members of Christ's body that what the one suffereth all other suffer with it. Yea, all the creatures of God are partakers with us, and, in hope to be delivered, they suffer patiently. No creature should desire to be exempt from trouble in this world, seeing Christ, God's natural Son, was not exempt, seeing God's holy prophets and apostles were not exempt. Let us then, commit ourselves into the hands of God and arm ourselves with patience, so that we may glorify God's holy name by our well doing, that another day we may be taken for his well-beloved children. To whom be all glory for ever and ever. Amen.

Thomas Cranmer

CERTAIN SERMONS, OR HOMILIES

Thomas Cranmer: Certain Sermons, or Homilies

INTRODUCTION

WE HAVE ALREADY SPOKEN OF THE PREACHING OF THE ENGLISH Reformation in the Introduction to Taverner's *Postils* and can take the story up from that point.

Taverner was no doubt used to some extent during the rest of King Henry's reign, though as early as 1542 plans were set in motion to supplant or supplement him with a book of homilies. But when Edward VI succeeded to the throne at the end of January, 1547, the first positive work of the Reformers was the compiling of a fresh set of sermons for the parish clergy to read. *Certain Sermons, or Homilies,* popularly called the First Book of Homilies, was printed in July, 1547. It is worth noting that the very first reforming move, when the Reformers enjoyed more freedom, was the supplying of this need.

Clearly, for the work to come out so soon after the new king's accession, most of the homilies must have been prepared and ready some time before Henry's death. Although uncertainty surrounds the book's making, the evidence supports such a conclusion. A correspondence was carried on between Gardiner, the Bishop of Winchester, and Cranmer. Unfortunately, Cranmer's letters are lost and we have to infer their contents from Gardiner's second letter to him and two to the Protector Somerset. From Gardiner's letter to Cranmer it appears that the archbishop had asked him to supply a homily for the book. It can hardly be supposed that Cranmer's letter which he received on June 10 contained this request, for the set must surely have been complete and ready for the printers by then. Nor do Gardiner's words necessarily suggest this: "Your grace . . . mindeth nothing now but only homilies, wherein your grace would I should write."¹ To Somerset he reports that "I have received this day letters from my lord of Canterbury, touching certain homilies, which the bishops, in the convocation holden A.D. 1542, agreed to make for stay of such errors as were then by ignorant preachers sparkled among the people."² Yet Gardiner's next letter to Somerset (undated) says that he has received other letters from Cranmer "requiring the said homilies."³ Unless we are to convict Cranmer of double dealing with Gardiner, we must suppose that he wrote in June to remind Gardiner that he needed his contribution immediately. It would be consistent that he had been deputed to supply one of the homilies. At any rate, Gardiner will have nothing to do with the scheme. To Cranmer he sketches out a homily on faith and works which he would contribute if he were not aware that it would contradict another homily (meaning the one on salvation). And what do we want homilies for anyway? The people got on all right without homilies in the past and they will go to heaven now without any homilies.

Gardiner's mention of the 1542 Convocation suggests that what was happening now had its roots in Cranmer's abortive attempt to compile and publish a book of sermons at that time. It may even be that some of those known to have been written in consequence of that Convocation and presented to another held in the following year were kept in hand by Cranmer against a more propitious season. It would also be strange if he had not made plans to be put into effect when that season should come, especially when Henry's death was seen to be not far distant. Thus he was able, not only to bring out the book of homilies within six months, but also to "instigate"⁴ the Royal Visitation, details of which were settled in April and began to be realized in May. In this nationwide visitation "for the better reformation of religion," as Strype puts it, the Book of Homilies was distributed to the bishops and, through the archdeacons, to the parishes.

Not every homily can be assigned to an author. As an official compilation they were, of course, published anonymously. Cranmer's authorship of that on salvation is in little doubt, thanks to

¹ *Memorials of . . . Thomas Cranmer*, by John Strype (Oxford, 1848), II.464.
² Foxe, 6.41.
³ *Ibid.*
⁴ R. W. Dixon speaks of the Visitation as Somerset's scheme (*History of the Church of England*, II.428). But Strype sees Cranmer behind it: "By these and other pious instigations of the archbishop . . . he began to think of the church. . . . For about April there was a royal visitation resolved upon" (*Cranmer*, II.10).

CERTAIN SERMONS, OR HOMILIES 257

further letters from Gardiner to Somerset. Writing from prison in October, 1547, he tells the Lord Protector that Cranmer had sent for him the previous Friday and, along with two bishops and Cox and Aire, had held a conference with him about the Homily on Salvation: "My lord of Canterbury was in hand with his Homily of Salvation." [5] In his next letter (undated) he says: "As for the Book of Homilies, in that point where my lord of Canterbury would have taught how faith excluded charity in the office of justifying . . ." [6] And again in the same letter: "My lord hath, in the homily of Salvation, taken such a matter in hand, and so handled it as, if I were his extreme enemy, I would have wished him to have taken that piece in hand." [7] And again: "My lord of Canterbury told me, his intent is only to set out the freedom of God's mercy." [8] And in the last of these letters: "As for my lord of Canterbury's Homily of Salvation, [it] hath as many faults, as I have been weeks in prison, which be seven." [9]

The evidence for the authorship of the other two is less satisfactory. The only evidence adduced by Jenkyns, the Parker Society, and Griffiths is a statement in 1576 by Bishop Wootten, the nephew of Alexander Nowell. If we say that the style, the presentation, and the doctrine in these two are similar to what we find in the Homily of Salvation, that is as far as we can go.

It is sometimes said that the Homily of the Salvation of Mankind propounds a mediating doctrine of justification and is something less wholehearted than Continental statements. Thus Dr. T. M. Parker suggests that the book "expounded a moderate version of justification by faith only." [10] We will not press the embarrassing question as to how any doctrine of justification by faith *only* can be moderate when the alternative is justification by something else as well as faith. But it is surprising that Dr. Parker should write this three years after Professor Rupp had dealt so faithfully with another little book on this doctrine.[11]

In fact, a summary of this homily shows that it is a quite typical statement of the Reformation belief. After an introductory paragraph in which it is denied that our own activities are accepted by God as righteousness, and in which justification is defined as the forgiveness of sins, the homily begins with the redeeming work of Christ. He fulfilled the law for man, and by his sacrifice on the cross "made amends" for sin, to appease God's anger. Be-

[5] Foxe, 6.45.
[6] Foxe, 6.47.
[7] Foxe, 6.49.
[8] Foxe, 6.50.
[9] Foxe, 6.55.
[10] *The English Reformation to 1558*, p. 124.
[11] *The English Protestant Tradition*, pp. 171 ff.

cause of his sacrifice, baptized children who die are cleansed from sin and those who live on and fall into sin are cleansed when they repent—i.e., when they return to their baptismal position. (It is noteworthy that justification is here dealt with practically and experientially, within the framework of the hearer's life. He has been baptized; his baptism was the sacrament of justification; his daily repentance and renewed faith is a realization of his once for all baptism and justification.)

The homily turns to resolve the apparent difficulty that justification is free and yet that a ransom must be paid. The answer lies primarily in the love and justice of God, the one freely pardoning, the other demanding punishment for sin. Both demands are met in Jesus Christ and his redeeming work. It was by the love of God that Jesus Christ was given; it was the justice of God that was satisfied by his sacrifice. For there are three parts to be considered in justification. The first is God's mercy and grace; the second Christ's satisfaction of God's justice; and the third our faith in his merits.

The formula "by faith alone" is not intended to exclude repentance, hope, love, and so forth, as qualities of the Christian man. It is, however, intended to exclude them from "the office of justifying," that is, from being meritorious causes of justification. Nor does "by faith alone" absolve the Christian man from obedience to the commandments and will of God; it does, however, deny that these works of obedience deserve God's favor, for they themselves are imperfect.

Part II takes up the point again at once. "Faith alone" does not mean that repentance, hope and love should not be present in the Christian man, nor does "freely" mean that the believer can be idle. Such qualifying terms are meant to take away "the merits of works." But justification by faith alone is a very dangerous doctrine, easily liable to misunderstanding and perversion; and misunderstood or perverted it may lead to ruin in this world and the next. It is therefore necessary to explain it most carefully.

In justification we must distinguish between God's office to man and man's office to God. It belongs to God, and to him alone, to justify. All that man can do in the matter is to accept the state of affairs that God pronounces to be so. But it is not this acceptance (i.e., faith) that justifies us.[12] Even faith has to be renounced as a

---

[12] Note that Cranmer here anticipates and refuses the view (as expressed by Dr. T. M. Parker) that justification is "brought about as a result of a psychological act by which a man accepted Christ consciously as his personal Saviour" (*The English Reformation to 1558*, p. 118).

meritorious cause, for it also is imperfect. The efficacy of faith lies rather in the object of faith than in faith itself, which "putteth us from itself . . . and appointeth us unto Christ." [13] Faith is represented as speaking to us: "It is not I that take away your sins, but it is Christ only; and to him only I send you for that purpose, renouncing therein all your good virtues, words, thoughts, and works, and only putting your trust in Christ." [14]

After reiterating this, Part III continues with man's office to God. We must not waste our lives by careless living or by opposition to God. This would, indeed, be a sign that we had no faith or a false faith. For there is an attitude which may be called faith, inasmuch as it is an assent to the truth of historical events. But it is only partial and lacks the distinctive life-giving quality of whole faith. True faith is not only belief in the truth of doctrine and assent to the reliability of historical records, but also trust and confidence in God's promises and in Christ's redeeming work. Such a faith, which is given by God, is quickening and powerful to produce love to God and the neighbor. The doctrine that justification is freely given to us by God and is "by faith alone" does not produce hardness and carelessness but moves us to give up our lives to God, to serve him and seek his glory.

[13] P. 268. [14] P. 268.

BIBLIOGRAPHY

The bibliographical history of the First Book of Homilies would, because of its complications, take too long to describe here, but may be read in Griffiths, pp. xlix–lxii. He enumerates six editions printed by Grafton in 1547 and three by Whitchurch in the same year. Grafton's first he regards as the *editio princeps:*

Certain/ Sermons, or Homi/lies, appoynted by the/ Kynges Maiestie, to be/ declared and redde, by all/ Persones, Uicars, or/ Curates, every Son/day in their Chur/ches, where thei/ have Cure./ Anno. 1547.

Colophon: Imprynted at London,/ the laste daye of Iulii, in the fyrste yere/ of the reigne of our souereigne lord/ Kynge Edward the .VI: By/ Rychard Grafton Printer/ to his moste royall/ Maiestie./ In the yere of our Lord./ M.D.XLVII./ Cum priuilegio ad impri/ mendum solum.

The basis of the present text is that of Griffiths. His text is 1559, "the earliest known Elizabethan text." But as we are printing these homilies in relation to Cranmer, who died in 1555, the revisions of 1559 are obviously too late for our purpose. The latest edition in Cranmer's lifetime was 1552; but this "seems to follow the quarto of 1551" (p. lviii), which in turn follows the 1549 Grafton. It is to this text, therefore, that we are pressed back. Our text will for this reason be seen to differ in detail from the Parker Society edition of Cranmer, Jenkyns' *Remains* and also that of Griffiths himself.

Other editions of the Homilies are:

The Two Books of Homilies, edited by John Griffiths. Oxford, 1859.

Certain Sermons . . . , edited by G. E. Corrie. Cambridge, 1850.

The literature devoted to the Homilies is not extensive. There were two interesting books at the end of the nineteenth century. The first thinks to find the source of the Homily of Salvation in

Cajetan's commentary on Romans: R. C. Jenkins, *Pre-Tridentine Doctrine*. London, 1891. The second looks to Melanchthon as the source: W. Fitzgerald, *Lectures on Ecclesiastical History*. 2 vols. London, 1885 (II. 214 f.).

Works of Cranmer:
The Remains of Thomas Cranmer, D.D., Archbishop of Canterbury. Collected and arranged by the Rev. Henry Jenkyns, M.A. 4 vols. Oxford, 1833.
Writings and Disputations of Thomas Cranmer . . . Relative to the Sacrament of the Lord's Supper. Edited for the Parker Society by the Rev. John Edmund Cox, M.A. Cambridge, 1844.
Miscellaneous Writings and Letters of Thomas Cranmer . . . Edited for the Parker Society by the Rev. John Edmund Cox, M.A. Cambridge, 1846.

Biography:
The latest biography, J. G. Ridley, *Thomas Cranmer* (Oxford, 1962), has not won universal acceptance, and in some respects A. F. Pollard, *Thomas Cranmer and the English Reformation* (New York and London, 1904) is to be preferred. Both books are deficient in theological understanding and should be supplemented by the valuable but too brief *Thomas Cranmer, Theologian*, by G. W. Bromiley (London, 1956).

Thomas Cranmer: *Certain Sermons, or Homilies*

AN HOMILY OF THE SALVATION OF MANKIND BY ONLY CHRIST OUR SAVIOUR FROM SIN AND DEATH EVERLASTING

THE TEXT

Because all men be sinners and offenders against God, and breakers of his law and commandments, therefore can no man by his own acts, works, and deeds, seem they never so good, be justified and made righteous before God; but every man of necessity is constrained to seek for another righteousness or justification, to be received at God's own hands, that is to say, the remission, pardon, and forgiveness of his sins and trespasses in such things as he hath offended. And this justification or righteousness, which we so receive by God's mercy and Christ's merits, embraced by faith, is taken, accepted, and allowed of God for our perfect and full justification.

For the more full understanding hereof, it is our parts and duty ever to remember the great mercy of God; how that, all the world being wrapped in sin by breaking of the law, God sent his only Son our Saviour Christ into this world to fulfil the law for us; and by shedding of his most precious blood, to make a sacrifice and satisfaction, or (as it may be called) amends, to his Father for our sins, to assuage his wrath and indignation conceived against us for the same. Insomuch that infants, being baptized and dying in their infancy, are by this sacrifice washed from their sins, brought to God's favour, and made his children and inheritors of his Kingdom of Heaven. And they which actually do sin after their baptism, when they convert and turn again to God unfeignedly, they are likewise washed by this sacrifice from their sins in such sort that there remaineth not any spot of sin that shall be imputed to their damnation. This is that justification or righteousness which St. Paul speaketh of when he saith, "No man is justified by the works of the law, but freely by faith in Jesus

Christ." [15] And again he saith, "We believe in Jesu Christ, that we be justified freely by the faith of Christ, and not by the works of the law; because that no man shall be justified by the works of the law." [16]

And although this justification be free unto us, yet it cometh not so freely unto us that there is no ransom paid therefore at all.

Objection. But here may man's reason be astonied, reasoning after this fashion. If a ransom be paid for our redemption, then is it not given us freely: for a prisoner that payeth his ransom is not let go freely; for, if he go freely, then he goeth without ransom; for what is it else to go freely than to be set at liberty without payment of ransom?

An answer. This reason is satisfied by the great wisdom of God in this mystery of our redemption; who hath so tempered his justice and mercy together, that he would neither by his justice condemn us unto the perpetual captivity of the devil and his prison of hell, remediless for ever without mercy; nor by his mercy deliver us clearly without justice or payment of a just ransom, but with his endless mercy he joined his most upright and equal justice. His great mercy he shewed unto us in delivering us from our former captivity, without requiring of any ransom to be paid or amends to be made upon our parts; which thing by us had been impossible to be done. And, whereas it lay not in us that to do, he provided a ransom for us, that was, the most precious body and blood of his most dear and best beloved Son Jesu Christ; who, besides his ransom, fulfilled the law for us perfectly. And so the justice of God and his mercy did embrace together, and fulfilled the mystery of our redemption. And of this justice and mercy of God knit together speaketh St. Paul in the third chapter to the Romans: "All have offended and have need [17] of the glory of God, justified freely by his grace by redemption which is in Jesu Christ; whom God hath set forth to us for a reconciler and peacemaker through faith in his blood, to shew his righteousness." [18] And in the tenth chapter, "Christ is the end of the Law unto righteousness to every man that believeth." [19] And in the eighth chapter, "That which was impossible by the Law, inasmuch as it was weak by the flesh, God sending his own Son in the similitude of sinful flesh by sin damned sin in the flesh, that the righteousness of the Law might be fulfilled in us, which walk not after the flesh, but after the Spirit." [20]

In these foresaid places the apostle toucheth specially three

[15] Gal. 3:11 (?).
[16] Gal. 2:16.
[17] Vulg.: *egent*.
[18] Rom. 3:23 f.
[19] Rom. 10:4.
[20] Rom. 8:3 f.

things, which must concur and go together in our justification: upon God's part, his great mercy and grace; upon Christ's part, justice, that is, the satisfaction of God's justice, or price of our redemption by the offering of his body and shedding of his blood with fulfilling of the law perfectly and throughly; and upon our part, true and lively faith in the merits of Jesu Christ; which yet is not ours but by God's working in us. So that in our justification is not only God's mercy and grace, but also his justice, which the apostle calleth "the justice of God"; [21] and it consisteth in paying our ransom and fulfilling of the law. And so the grace of God doth not exclude the justice of God in our justification, but only excludeth the justice of man, that is to say, the justice of our works, as to be merits of deserving our justification. And therefore St. Paul declareth here nothing upon the behalf of man concerning his justification, but only a true and lively faith; which nevertheless is "the gift of God," and not man's only work without God. And yet that faith doth not exclude repentance, hope, love, dread, and the fear of God, to be joined with faith in every man that is justified; but it excludeth them from the office of justifying. So that although they be all present together in him that is justified, yet they justify not all together. Nor that faith also doth not exclude the justice of our good works, necessarily to be done afterward of duty towards God (for we are most bounden to serve God in doing good deeds commanded by him in his Holy Scripture all the days of our life;), but it excludeth them, so that we may not do them to this intent, to be made good by doing of them. For all the good works that we can do be unperfect, and therefore not able to deserve our justification: but our justification doth come freely, by the mere mercy of God, and of so great and free mercy that, whereas all the world was not able of their selves to pay any part towards their ransom, it pleased our heavenly Father, of his infinite mercy, without any our desert or deserving, to prepare for us the most precious jewels of Christ's body and blood, whereby our ransom might be fully paid, the law fulfilled, and his justice fully satisfied. So that Christ is now the righteousness of all them that truly do believe in him. He for them paid their ransom by his death. He for them fulfilled the law in his life. So that now in him and by him every true Christian man may be called a fulfiller of the law; forasmuch as that which their infirmity lacketh, Christ's justice hath supplied.

[21] Vulg., *iustitia Dei:* righteousness of God.

The Second Part of the Sermon of Salvation

Ye have heard of whom all men ought to seek their justification and righteousness, and how also this righteousness cometh unto men by Christ's death and merits. Ye heard also how that three things are required to the obtaining of our righteousness; that is, God's mercy, Christ's justice, and a true and a lively faith, out of the which faith springeth good works. Also before was declared at large that no man can be justified by his own good works, because that no man fulfilleth the law according to the full request of the law. And St. Paul in his epistle to the Galatians proveth the same, saying thus, "If there had been any law given which could have justified, verily righteousness should have been by the law." [22] And again he saith, "If righteousness be by the law, then Christ died in vain." [23] And again he saith, "You that are justified by the law are fallen away from grace." [24] And furthermore he writeth to the Ephesians on this wise, "By grace are ye saved through faith; and that not of yourselves for it is the gift of God; and not of works, lest any man should glory." [25] And, to be short, the sum of all Paul's disputation is this: that, if justice come of works, then it cometh not of grace; and if it come of grace, then it cometh not of works. And to this end tendeth all the Prophets, as St. Peter saith in the tenth of the Acts, "Of Christ all the Prophets," saith St. Peter, "do witness, that through his name all they that believe in him shall receive the remission of sins." [26]

And after this wise to be justified, only by this true and lively faith in Christ, speaketh all the old and ancient authors, both Greeks and Latins. Of whom I will specially rehearse three, Hilary, Basil, and Ambrose. St. Hilary saith these words plainly in the ninth Canon upon Matthew: "Faith only justifieth." [27] And St. Basil, a Greek author, writeth thus: "This is a perfect and a whole rejoicing in God, when a man avaunteth [28] not himself for his own righteousness, but knowledgeth himself to lack true justice and righteousness, and to be justified by the only faith in Christ. And Paul," saith he, "doth glory in the contempt of his own righteous-

---

[22] Gal. 3:21.
[23] Gal. 2:21.
[24] Gal. 5:4.
[25] Eph. 2:9.
[26] Acts 10:43.
[27] *Comm. in Matth.*, cap. VIII (not IX) (*PL* 9.961).
[28] *Avaunteth* (1547 G1) is to be preferred to the reading of 1547 G2, etc., *advanceth,* since the first edition reads *doth not boast himself.*

ness, and that he looketh for his righteousness of God by faith." [29] These be the very words of St. Basil. And St. Ambrose, a Latin author, saith these words: "This is the ordinance of God, that he which believeth in Christ should be saved without works, by faith only, freely receiving remission of his sins." [30] Consider diligently these words: "Without works," "by faith only," "freely we receive remission of our sins." What can be spoken more plainly than to say that freely, without works, by faith only, we obtain remission of our sins?

These and other like sentences, that we be justified by faith only, freely, and without works, we do read ofttimes in the most best and ancient writers. As, beside Hilary, Basil, and St. Ambrose before rehearsed, we read the same in Origen, St. Chrysostom, St. Cyprian, St. Augustine, Prosper, Œcumenius, Photius, Bernardus, Anselm, and many other authors, Greek and Latin.[31] Nevertheless, this sentence, that we be justified by faith only, is not so meant of them, that the said justifying faith is alone in man, without true repentance, hope, charity, dread, and the fear of God, at any time or season. Nor when they say that we be justified freely, they mean not that we should or might afterward be idle, and that nothing should be required on our parts afterward; neither they mean not so to be justified without our good works, that we should do no good works at all, like as shall be more expressed at large hereafter. But this proposition, that we be justified by faith only, freely, and without works, is spoken for to take away clearly all merit of our works, as being insufficient to deserve our justification at God's hands; and thereby most plainly to express the weakness of man and the goodness of God, the great infirmity of ourselves and the might and power of God, the imperfectness of our own works and the most abundant grace of our Saviour Christ; and thereby wholly for to ascribe the merit and deserving of our justification unto Christ only and his most precious bloodshedding.

This faith the Holy Scripture teacheth: this is the strong rock and foundation of Christian religion: this doctrine all old and ancient authors of Christ's Church do approve: this doctrine advanceth and setteth forth the true glory of Christ, and suppresseth the vainglory of man: this whosoever denieth is not to be reputed for a Christian man,[32] nor for a setter forth of Christ's glory, but

---

[29] *Homilia de humilitate* (PG 31.529–530).
[30] Ambrosiaster, *Comm. in Ep. B. Pauli ad Corinthios Primam* (PL 17.185).
[31] Cranmer is here drawing on his manuscript notes of quotations, printed in PS, II.203 ff., as *Notes on Justification*.
[32] Until 1547 G6: *a true Christian man*.

for an adversary to [33] Christ and his gospel, and for a setter forth of men's vainglory.

And although this doctrine be never so true, as it is most true indeed, that we be justified freely without all merit of our own good works (as St. Paul doth express it), and freely by this lively and perfect faith in Christ only (as the ancient authors use to speak it), yet this true doctrine must be also truly understand, and most plainly declared; lest carnal men should take unjustly occasion thereby to live carnally after the appetite and will of the world, the flesh, and the devil. And because no man should err by mistaking of this doctrine,[34] I shall plainly and shortly so declare the right understanding of the same, that no man shall justly think that he may thereby take any occasion of carnal liberty to follow the desires of the flesh, or that thereby any kind of sin shall be committed, or any ungodly living the more used.

First, you shall understand that in our justification by Christ it is not all one thing, the office of God unto man, and the office of man unto God. Justification is not the office of man, but of God. For man cannot justify himself by his own works, neither in part, nor in the whole; for that were the greatest arrogancy and presumption of man that Antichrist could erect against God, to affirm that a man might by his own works take away and purge his own sins, and so justify himself. But justification is the office of God only, and is not a thing which we render unto him, but which we receive of him; not which we give to him, but which we take of him, by his free mercy, and by the only merits of his most dearly beloved Son, our only Redeemer, Saviour, and Justifier, Jesus Christ. So that the true understanding of this doctrine, We be justified freely by faith without works, or that we be justified by faith in Christ only, is not that this our own act, to believe in Christ, or this our faith in Christ, which is within us, doth justify us and merit our justification unto us; for that were to count ourselves to be justified by some act or virtue that is within ourselves. But the true understanding and meaning thereof is, that, although we hear God's word and believe it, although we have faith, hope, charity, repentance, dread, and fear of God within us, and do never so many good works thereunto, yet we must renounce the merit of all our said virtues of faith, hope, charity, and all our other virtues and good deeds, which we either have done, shall do, or can do, as things that be far too weak and insufficient and unperfect to deserve remission of our sins and our justification; and therefore we must trust only in God's mercy, and in that sacrifice

---

[33] Until 1547 G6: *of.*   [34] 1547 G1: *this true doctrine.*

which our High Priest and Saviour Christ Jesus, the Son of God, once offered for us upon the cross, to obtain thereby God's grace, and remission, as well of our original sin, in baptism, as of all actual sin committed by us after our baptism, if we truly repent, and convert unfeignedly to him again. So that, as St. John Baptist, although he were never so virtuous and godly a man, yet in this matter of forgiving of sin he did put the people from him, and appointed them unto Christ, saying thus unto them, "Behold, yonder is the Lamb of God, which taketh away the sins of the world": [35] even so, as great and as godly a virtue as the lively faith is, yet it putteth us from itself, and remitteth or appointeth us unto Christ, for to have only by him remission of our sins or justification. So that our faith in Christ, as it were, saith unto us thus: It is not I that take away your sins, but it is Christ only; and to him only I send you for that purpose, renouncing therein all your good virtues, words, thoughts, and works, and only putting your trust in Christ.

The Third Part of the Sermon of Salvation

It hath been manifestly declared unto you, that no man can fulfil the law of God, and therefore by the law all men are condemned: whereupon it followed necessarily that some other thing should be required for our salvation than the law; and that is a true and a lively faith in Christ, bringing forth good works and a life according to God's commandments. And also you heard the ancient authors' minds of this proposition, Faith in Christ only justifieth man, so plainly declared, that you see that the very true sense of this proposition, We be justified by faith in Christ only, according to the meaning of the old ancient authors, is this: We put our faith in Christ, that we be justified by him only, that we be justified by God's free mercy and the merits of our Saviour Christ only, and by no virtue or good work of our own that is in us, or that we can be able to have or to do, for to deserve the same, Christ himself only being the cause meritorious therof.

Here you perceive many words to be used, to avoid contention in words with them that delight to brawl about words, and also to shew the true meaning, to avoid evil taking and misunderstanding: and yet peradventure all will not serve with them that be contentious; but contenders will ever forge matter of contention, even when they have none occasion thereto. Notwithstanding, such be the less to be passed upon,[36] so that the rest may profit,

---

[35] John 1:29.   [36] To be heeded.

which will be more desirous to know the truth, than, when it is plain enough, to contend about it, and with contentions and captious cavillations to obscure and darken it. Truth it is that our own works do not justify us, to speak properly of our justification; that is to say, our works do not merit or deserve remission of our sins, and make us, of unjust, just before God; but God of his mere mercy, through the only merits and deservings of his Son Jesus Christ, doth justify us. Nevertheless, because faith doth directly send us to Christ for remission of our sins, and that by faith given us of God we embrace the promise of God's mercy and of the remission of our sins, which thing none other of our virtues or works properly doeth, therefore Scripture useth to say, that faith without works doth justify. And forasmuch that it is all one sentence in effect to say, Faith without works, and Only faith, doth justify us, therefore the old ancient fathers of the Church from time to time have uttered our justification with this speech, Only faith justifieth us; meaning none other thing than St. Paul meant, when he said, Faith without works justifieth us. And, because all this is brought to pass through the only merits and deservings of our Saviour Christ, and not through our merits, or through the merit of any virture that we have within us, or of any work that cometh from us, therefore, in that respect of merit and deserving, we renounce as it were altogether again faith, works, and all other virtues. For our own imperfection is so great, through the corruption of original sin, that all is imperfect that is within us, faith, charity, hope, dread, thoughts, words, and works, and therefore not apt to merit and deserve any part of our justification for us. And this form of speaking we use, in the humbling of ourselves to God, and to give all the glory to our Saviour Christ, which is best worthy to have it.

Here you have heard the office of God in our justification, and how we receive it of him freely, by his mercy, without our deserts, through true and lively faith. Now you shall hear the office and duty of a Christian man unto God, what we ought on our part to render unto God again for his great mercy and goodness. Our office is not to pass the time of this present life unfruitfully and idly after that we are baptized or justified, not caring how few good works we do to the glory of God and profit of our neighbours: much less it is our office, after that we be once made Christ's members, to live contrary to the same, making ourselves members of the devil, walking after his enticements and after the suggestions of the world and the flesh; whereby we know that we do serve the world and the devil, and not God. For that faith which bringeth forth, without repentance, either evil works, or no good works, is not a right, pure, and lively faith, but a dead, devilish, counterfeit, and feigned faith, as St. Paul and St. James call it.[37] For even the devils know and believe that Christ was born of a virgin, that he fasted forty days and forty nights without meat and drink, that he wrought all kind of miracles, declaring himself very God. They believe also that Christ for our sakes suffered most painful death, to redeem us from eternal death, and that he rose again from death the third day: they believe that he ascended into heaven, and that he sitteth on the right hand of the Father, and at the last end of this world shall come again and judge both the quick and the dead. These articles of our faith the devils believe; and so they believe all things that be written in the New and Old Testament to be true: and yet for all this faith they be but devils, remaining still in their damnable estate, lacking the very true Christian faith. For the right and true Christian faith is, not only to believe that Holy Scripture and all the foresaid articles of our faith are true, but also to have a sure trust and confidence in God's merciful promises to be saved from everlasting damnation by Christ; whereof doth follow a loving heart to obey his commandments. And this true Christian faith neither any devil hath, nor yet any man which, in the outward profession of his mouth and in his outward receiving of the Sacraments, in coming to the church and in all other outward appearances, seemeth to be a Christian man, and yet in his living and deeds sheweth the contrary. For how can a man have this true faith, this sure trust and confidence in God, that by the merits of Christ his sins be remitted, and he reconciled to the favour of God, and to be partaker of the Kingdom of Heaven by Christ, when he liveth ungodly and denieth Christ in his deeds? Surely no such ungodly man can have this faith and trust in God. For, as they know Christ to be the only Saviour of the world, so they know also that wicked men shall not possess the Kingdom of God. They know that God "hateth unrighteousness"; that he will "destroy all those that speak untruly"; [38] that those that have done good works," which cannot be done without a lively faith in Christ, "shall come forth into the resurrection of life, and those that have done evil shall come unto the resurrection of judgment." [39] And very well they know also, that "to them that be contentious, and to them that will not be obedient unto the truth, but will obey unrighteousness, shall come indignation, wrath, and affliction, &c." [40]

[37] Titus 1:16; James 2:14 ff.
[38] Ps. 5:6.
[39] John 5:29.
[40] Rom. 2:8.

Therefore, to conclude, considering the infinite benefits of God shewed and exhibited unto us mercifully without our deserts; who hath not only created us of nothing, and from a piece of vile clay, of his infinite goodness, hath exalted us, as touching our soul, unto his own similitude and likeness; but also, whereas we were condemned to hell and death eternal, hath given his own natural Son (being God eternal, immortal, and equal unto himself in power and glory) to be incarnated, and to take our mortal nature upon him with the infirmities of the same, and in the same nature to suffer most shameful and painful death for our offenses, to the intent to justify us and to restore us to life everlasting; so making us also his dear beloved children, brethren unto his only Son our Saviour Christ, and inheritors for ever with him of his eternal Kingdom of Heaven: these great and merciful benefits of God, if they be well considered, do neither minister unto us occasion to be idle and to live without doing any good works, neither yet stirreth us by any means to do evil things; but contrariwise, if we be not desperate persons, and our hearts harder than stones, they move us to render ourselves unto God wholly with all our will, hearts, might, and power; to serve him in all good deeds, obeying his commandments during our lives; to seek in all things his glory and honour, not our sensual pleasures and vainglory; evermore dreading willingly to offend such a merciful God and loving Redeemer in word, thought, or deed. And the said benefits of God, deeply considered, do move us for his sake also to be ever ready to give ourselves to our neighbours, and, as much as lieth in us, to study with all our endeavour to do good to every man. These be the fruits of the true faith: to do good, as much as lieth in us, to every man; and, above all things and in all things, to advance the glory of God, of whom only we have our sanctification, justification, salvation, and redemption. To whom be ever glory, praise, and honour world without end. Amen.

A SHORT DECLARATION OF THE TRUE, LIVELY, AND CHRISTIAN FAITH

THE TEXT

The first entry unto God, good Christian people, is through faith; whereby, as it is declared in the last Sermon, we be justified before God. And, lest any man should be deceived for lack of right understanding thereof, it is diligently to be noted that faith is taken in the Scripture two manner of ways. There is one faith which in Scripture is called a dead faith, which bringeth forth no good works, but is idle, barren, and unfruitful. And this faith by the holy apostle St. James is compared to the faith of devils, which believe God to be true and just, and tremble for fear, yet they do nothing well, but all evil.[41] And such a manner of faith have the wicked and naughty Christian people; "which confess God," as St. Paul saith, "in their mouth, but deny him in their deeds, being abominable and without the right faith and in all good works reprovable."[42] And this faith is a persuasion and belief in man's heart, whereby he knoweth that there is a God, and assenteth unto all truth of God's most holy Word contained in Holy Scripture. So that it consisteth only in believing of the Word of God, that it is true. And this is not properly called faith: but as he that readeth Caesar's *Commentaries*, believing the same to be true, hath thereby a knowledge of Caesar's life and noble acts, because he believeth the history of Caesar, yet it is not properly said that he believeth in Caesar, of whom he looketh for no help nor benefit; even so he that believeth that all that is spoken of God in the Bible is true, and yet liveth so ungodly that he cannot look to enjoy the promises and benefits of God, although it may be said that such a man hath a faith and belief to the words of God, yet it is not properly said that he believeth in God, or hath such a

[41] James 2:19. [42] Titus 1:16.

faith and trust in God whereby he may surely look for grace, mercy, and eternal life at God's hand, but rather for indignation and punishment according to the merits of his wicked life. For, as it is written in a book intituled to be of Didymus Alexandrinus, "Forasmuch as faith without works is dead, it is not now faith; as a dead man is not a man." [43] This dead faith therefore is not that sure and substantial faith which saveth sinners.

Another faith there is in Scripture, which is not, as the foresaid faith, idle, unfruitful, and dead, but "worketh by charity," as St. Paul declareth (Gal. 5) : [44] which as the other vain faith is called a dead faith, so may this be called a quick or lively faith. And this is not only the common belief of the articles of our faith,[45] but it is also a sure trust and confidence of the mercy of God through our Lord Jesus Christ, and a steadfast hope of all good things to be received at God's hand; and that, although we through infirmity or temptation of our ghostly [46] enemy do fall from him by sin, yet if we return again unto him by true repentance, that he will forgive and forget our offences for his Son's sake our Saviour Jesus Christ, and will make us inheritors with him of his everlasting Kingdom; and that in the mean time, until that Kingdom come, he will be our protector and defender in all perils and dangers, whatsoever do chance: and that, though sometime he doth send us sharp adversity, yet that evermore he will be a loving Father unto us, correcting us for our sin, but not withdrawing his mercy finally from us, if we trust in him, and commit ourselves wholly unto him, hang only upon him, and call upon him, ready to obey and serve him. This is the true, lively, and unfeigned Christian faith, and is not in the mouth and outward profession only, but it liveth, and stirreth inwardly in the heart. And this faith is not without hope and trust in God, nor without the love of God and of our neighbours, nor without the fear of God, nor without the desire to hear God's word, and to follow the same in eschewing evil and doing gladly all good works. This faith, as St. Paul describeth it, is the sure ground and foundation of the benefits which we ought to look for and trust to receive of God, a certificate and sure expectation of them, although they yet sensibly appear not unto us.[47] And after he saith: "He that cometh to God must believe both that he is, and that he is a merciful rewarder of welldoers." [48] And nothing commendeth

[43] *Enarratio in Ep. B. Iacobi,* cap. II, v. 26 (PG 39.1752).
[44] Gal. 5:6.
[45] I.e., to believe in a general way in the articles of the Creed.
[46] Spiritual.
[47] Heb. 11:1.
[48] Heb. 11:6.

good men unto God so much as this assured faith and trust in him.

Of this faith three things are specially to be noted: first, that this faith doth not lie dead in the heart, but is lively and fruitful in bringing forth good works; second, that without it can no good works be done that shall be acceptable and pleasant to God; third, what manner of good works they be that this faith doth bring forth.

For the first. As the light cannot be hid, but will shew forth itself at one place or other; so a true faith cannot be kept secret, but, when occasion is offered, it will break out and shew itself by good works. And as the living body of a man ever exerciseth such things as belongeth to a natural and living body for nourishment and preservation of the same, as it hath need, opportunity, and occasion; even so the soul that hath a lively faith in it will be doing alway some good work, which shall declare that it is living, and will not be unoccupied.

Therefore, when men hear in the Scriptures so high commendations of faith, that it maketh us to please God, to live with God, and to be the children of God; if then they phantasy that they be set at liberty from doing all good works, and may live as they list, they trifle with God, and deceive themselves. And it is a manifest token that they be far from having the true and lively faith, and also far from knowledge what true faith meaneth. For the very sure and lively Christian faith is not only to believe all things of God which are contained in Holy Scripture, but also is an earnest trust and confidence in God, that he doth regard us, and hath cure [49] of us, as the father of the child whom he doth love, and that he will be merciful unto us for his only Son's sake; and that we have our Saviour Christ our perpetual advocate and priest; in whose only merits, oblation and suffering, we do trust that our offences be continually washed and purged, whensoever we, repenting truly, do return to him with our whole heart, steadfastly determining with ourselves, through his grace, to obey and serve him in keeping his commandments, and never to turn back again to sin. Such is the true faith that the Scripture doth so much commend: the which, when it seeth and considereth what God hath done for us, is also moved, through continual assistance of the Spirit of God, to serve and please him, to keep his favour, to fear his displeasure, to continue his obedient children, shewing thankfulness again by observing his commandments, and that freely, for true love chiefly, and not for dread of punishment or love of temporal reward, considering how clearly without our deservings, we have received his mercy and pardon freely.

[49] Care.

This true faith will shew forth itself, and cannot long be idle. For, as it is written, "The just man doth live by his faith," [50] he neither sleepeth nor is idle, when he should wake and be well occupied. And God by his prophet Jeremy saith, that "he is a happy and blessed man which hath faith and confidence in God: for he is like a tree set by the water side, that spreadeth his roots abroad toward the moisture, and feareth not heat when it cometh; his leaf will be green, and will not cease to bring forth his fruit." [51] Even so faithful men, putting away all fear of adversity, will shew forth the fruit of their good works, as occasion is offered to do them.

The Second Part of the Sermon of Faith

Ye have heard in the first part of this Sermon that there be two kinds of faith, a dead and an unfruitful faith, and a faith lively that worketh by charity: the first to be unprofitable, the second necessary for the obtaining of our salvation; the which faith hath charity always joined unto it, and is fruitful, bringing forth all good works. Now as concerning the same matter you shall hear what followeth.

The Wise Man saith, "He that believeth in God will hearken unto his commandments." For, if we do not shew ourselves faithful in our conversation,[52] the faith which we pretend to have is but a feigned faith; because the true Christian faith is manifestly shewed by good living, and not by words only, as St. Augustine saith, "Good living cannot be separated from true faith, which worketh by love." [53] And St. Chrysostom saith, "Faith of itself is full of good works: as soon as a man doth believe, he shall be garnished with them." [54]

How plentiful this faith is of good works, and how it maketh the work of one man more acceptable to God than of another, St. Paul teacheth at large in the eleventh chapter to the Hebrews, saying that faith made the oblation of Abel better than the oblation of Cain. This made Noe to build the ark. This made Abraham to forsake his country and all his friends, and to go unto a far country, there to dwell among strangers. So did also Isaac and Jacob, depending only of the help and trust that they had in God. And when they came to the country which God promised them, they would build no cities, towns, nor houses; but lived like strangers in tents,

---

[50] Hab. 2:4; Rom. 1:7, etc.
[51] Jer. 17:7 f.
[52] Way of life.
[53] *De fide et operibus*, cap. xvi (*PL* 40.215).
[54] Pseudo-Chrysostom, *De fide et lege naturae* (*PG* 48.1081).

that might every day be removed. Their trust was so much in God, that they set but little by any worldly thing, for that God had prepared for them better dwelling-places in heaven, of his own foundation and building. This faith made Abraham ready at God's commandment to offer his own son and heir Isaac, whom he loved so well, and by whom he was promised to have innumerable issue, among the which one should be born, in whom all nations should be blessed; trusting so much in God, that though he were slain, yet that God was able by his omnipotent power to raise him from death, and perform his promise. He mistrusted not the promise of God, although unto his reason every thing seemed contrary. He believed verily that God would not forsake him in dearth and famine that was in the country. And, in all other dangers that he was brought unto, he trusted ever that God would be his God and his protector, whatsoever he saw to the contrary. This faith wrought so in the heart of Moses, that he refused to be taken for king Pharaoh his daughter's son, and to have great inheritance in Egypt; thinking it better with the people of God to have affliction and sorrow, than with naughty men in sin to live pleasantly for a time. By faith he cared not for the threatening of king Pharaoh: for his trust was so in God, that he passed not of the felicity of this world, but looked for the reward to come in heaven; setting his heart upon the invisible God, as if he had seen him ever present before his eyes. By faith the Children of Israel passed through the Red Sea. By faith the walls of Jericho fell down without stroke; and many other wonderful miracles have been wrought. In all good men that heretofore have been, faith hath brought forth their good works, and obtained the promises of God. Faith hath stopped the lions' mouths; faith hath quenched the force of fire; faith hath escaped the sword's edges; faith hath given weak men strength, victory in battle; overthrown the armies of infidels; raised the dead to life. Faith hath made good men to take adversity in good part: some have been mocked and whipped, bound and cast in prison; some have lost all their goods, and lived in great poverty; some have wandered in mountains, hills, and wilderness; some have been racked, some slain, some stoned, some sawn, some rent in pieces, some headed, some brent [55] without mercy, and would not be delivered, because they looked to rise again to a better state.

All these fathers, martyrs, and other holy men, whom St. Paul spake of, had their faith surely fixed in God, when all the world was against them. They did not only know God to be the Lord,

[55] Burnt.

Maker, and governor of all men in the world; but also they had a special confidence and trust that he was and would be their God, their comforter, aider, helper, maintainer, and defender. This is the Christian faith; which these holy men had, and we also ought to have. And, although they were not named Christian men, yet was it a Christian faith that they had; for they looked for all benefits of God the Father through the merits of his Son Jesu Christ, as we now do. This difference is between them and us; for they looked when Christ should come, and we be in the time when he is come. Therefore saith St. Augustine, "The time is altered, but not the faith. For we have both one faith in one Christ." [56] The same Holy Ghost also that we have, had they, saith St. Paul.[57] For, as the Holy Ghost doth teach us to trust in God, and to call upon him as our Father, so did he teach them to say, as it is written, "Thou, Lord, art our Father and Redeemer, and thy name is without beginning and everlasting." [58] God gave them then grace to be his children, as he doth us now. But now, by the coming of our Saviour Christ, we have received more abundantly the Spirit of God in our hearts, whereby we may conceive a greater faith and a surer trust than many of them had. But in effect they and we be all one: we have the same faith that they had in God, and they the same that we have. And St. Paul so much extolleth their faith, because we should no less, but rather more, give ourselves wholly unto Christ, both in profession and living, now when Christ is come, than the old fathers did before his coming. And by all the declaration of St. Paul it is evident that the true, lively, and Christian faith is no dead, vain, or unfruitful thing, but a thing of perfect virtue, of wonderful operation and strength, bringing forth all good motions and good works.

All Holy Scripture agreeably beareth witness that a true lively faith in Christ doth bring forth good works: and therefore every man must examine himself diligently, to know whether he have the same true lively faith in his heart unfeignedly or not; which he shall know by the fruits thereof. Many that professed the faith of Christ were in this error, that they thought they knew God and believed in him, when in their life they declared the contrary. Which error St. John in his first epistle confuting writeth in this wise, "Hereby we are certified that we know God, if we observe his commandments. He that saith he knoweth God, and observeth not his commandments, is a liar, and the truth is not in him." [59]

[56] *In Ioan. Ev.,* Tract. XLV (*PL* 35.1722).
[57] II Cor. 4:13 (?).
[58] Isa. 63:16.
[59] I John 2:3–4.

And again he saith, "Whosoever sinneth doth not see God, nor know him. Let no man deceive you, well beloved children." [60] And moreover he saith: "Hereby we know that we be of the truth, and so we shall persuade our hearts before him. For, if our own hearts reprove us, God is above our hearts, and knoweth all things. Well beloved, if our hearts reprove us not, then have we confidence in God, and shall have of him whatsoever we ask, because we keep his commandments, and do those things that please him." [61] And yet further he saith, "Every man that believeth that Jesus is Christ is born of God;" [62] and, "We know that whosoever is born of God, doth not sin; but the generation of God purgeth him, and the devil doth not touch him." [63] And finally he concludeth, and shewing the cause why he wrote this epistle saith, "For this cause have I thus written unto you, that you may know that you have everlasting life which do believe in the Son of God." [64] And in his third epistle he confirmeth the whole matter of faith and works in few words, saying: "He that doth well is of God, and he that doth evil knoweth not God." [65] And as St. John saith that the lively knowledge and faith of God bringeth forth good works, so saith he likewise of hope and charity that they cannot stand with evil living. Of hope he writeth thus: "We know that when God shall appear, we shall be like unto him, for we shall see him even as he is. And whosoever hath this hope in him doth purify himself, like as God is pure." [66] And of charity he saith these words: "He that doth keep God's word" or commandment "in him is truly the perfect love of God." [67] And again he saith: "This is the love of God, that we should keep his commandments." [68]

And St. John wrote not this as a subtile proposition devised of his own phantasy, but as a most certain and necessary truth, taught unto him by Christ himself, the eternal and infallible Verity; who in many places doth most clearly affirm that faith, hope, and charity cannot consist without good and godly works. Of faith he saith: "He that believeth in the Son hath everlasting life; but he that believeth not in the Son shall not see that life, but the wrath of God remaineth upon him." [69] And the same he confirmeth with a double oath, saying: "Forsooth and forsooth, I say unto you, he that believeth in me hath everlasting life." [70] Now, forasmuch as he that believeth in Christ hath everlasting life, it must needs consequently follow, that he that hath this faith must have also good

[60] I John 3:6–7.
[61] I John 3:19–22.
[62] I John 5:1.
[63] I John 5:18.
[64] I John 5:13.
[65] III John 11.
[66] I John 3:2 f.
[67] I John 2:5.
[68] I John 5:3.
[69] John 3:36.
[70] John 6:47.

works, and be studious to observe God's commandments obediently. For to them that have evil works, and lead their life in disobedience and transgression of God's commandments, without repentance, pertaineth not everlasting life, but everlasting death, as Christ himself saith: "They that do well shall go into life eternal; but they that do evil shall go into the eternal fire." [71] And again he saith: "I am the first letter and the last, the beginning and the ending. To him that is athirst I will give of the well of the water of life freely. He that hath the victory shall have all things, and I will be his God, and he shall be my son: but they that be fearful, mistrusting God and lacking faith, they that be cursed people, and murderers, and fornicators, and sorcerers, and idolaters, and all liars, shall have their portion in the lake that burneth with fire and brimstone, which is the second death." [72] And as Christ undoubtedly affirmeth that true faith bringeth forth good works, so doth he say likewise of charity: "Whosoever hath my commandments and keepth them, that is he that loveth me." [73] And after he saith: "He that loveth me will keep my word," and, "He that loveth me not keepth not my words." [74]

And as the love of God is tried by good works, so is the fear of God also; as the Wise Man saith: "The dread of God putteth away sin." [75] And also he saith: "He that feareth God will do good works." [76]

The Third Part of the Sermon of Faith

You have heard in the second part of this Sermon, that no man should think that he hath that lively faith which Scripture commandeth, when he liveth not obediently to God's laws; for all good works spring out of that faith. And also it hath been declared unto you by examples, that faith maketh men constant, quiet, and patient in all afflictions. Now as concerning the same matter, you shall hear what followeth.

A man may soon deceive himself, and think in his own phantasy that he by faith knoweth God, loveth him, feareth him, and belongeth to him, when in very deed he doeth nothing less. For the trial of all these things is a very godly and Christian life. He that feeleth his heart set to seek God's honour, and studieth to know the will and commandments of God, and to conform himself thereunto, and leadeth not his life after the desire of his own flesh, to serve the devil by sin, but setteth his mind to serve God for God's

[71] Matt. 25:46.
[72] Rev. 21:6-8.
[73] John 14:21.
[74] John 14:23 f.
[75] Ecclus. 1:21.
[76] Ecclus. 15:1.

own sake, and for his sake also to love all his neighbours, whether they be friends or adversaries, doing good to every man, as opportunity serveth, and willingly hurting no man; such a man may well rejoice in God, perceiving by the trade of his life that he unfeignedly hath the right knowledge of God, a lively faith, a constant hope, a true and unfeigned love and fear of God. But he that casteth away the yoke of God's commandments from his neck, and giveth himself to live without true repentance, after his own sensual mind and pleasure, not regarding to know God's word, and much less to live according thereunto; such a man clearly deceiveth himself, and seeth not his own heart, if he thinketh that he either knoweth God, loveth him, feareth him, or trusteth in him.

Some peradventure phantasy in themselves that they belong to God, although they live in sin; and so they come to the church, and shew themselves as God's dear children. But St. John saith plainly: "If we say that we have any company with God, and walk in darkness, we do lie." [77] Other do vainly think that they know and love God, although they pass not of his commandments. But St. John saith clearly: "He that saith, I know God, and keepeth not his commandments, he is a liar." [78] Some falsely persuade themselves that they love God, when they hate their neighbours. But St. John saith manifestly: "If any man say, I love God, and yet hateth his brother, he is a liar." [79] "He that saith that he is in the light, and hateth his brother, he is still in darkness. He that loveth his brother dwelleth in the light: but he that hateth his brother is in darkness, and walketh in darkness, and knoweth not whither he goeth, for darkness hath blinded his eyes." [80] And moreover he saith: "Hereby we manifestly know the children of God from the children of the devil: he that doeth not righteously is not the child of God, nor he that hateth his brother." [81]

Deceive not yourselves therefore, thinking that you have faith in God, or that you love God, or do trust in him, or do fear him, when you live in sin; for then your ungodly and sinful life declareth the contrary, whatsoever ye say or think. It pertaineth to a Christian man to have this true Christian faith, and to try himself whether he hath it or no, and to know what belongeth to it, and how it doth work in him. It is not the world that we can trust to: the world, and all that is therein, is but vanity. It is God that must be our defence and protection against all temptation of wickedness and sin, errors, superstition, idolatry, and all evil. If all the world were on our side, and God against us, what could the world

[77] I John 1:6.
[78] I John 2:4.
[79] I John 4:20.
[80] I John 2:9–11.
[81] I John 3:10.

avail us? Therefore let us set our whole faith and trust in God, and neither the world, the devil, nor all the power of them, shall prevail against us.

Let us therefore, good Christian people, try and examine our faith, what it is: let us not flatter ourselves, but look upon our works, and so judge of our faith, what it is. Christ himself speaketh of this matter, and saith: "The tree is known by the fruit." [82] Therefore let us do good works, and thereby declare our faith to be the lively Christian faith. Let us, by such virtues as ought to spring out of faith, shew our election to be sure and stable; as St. Peter teacheth: "Endeavour yourselves to make your calling and election certain by good works." [83] And also he saith: "Minister or declare in your faith virtue, in virtue knowledge, in knowledge temperance, in temperance patience; again, in patience godliness, in godliness brotherly charity, in brotherly charity love." [84] So shall we shew indeed that we have the very lively Christian faith, and may so both certify our conscience the better that we be in the right faith, and also by these means confirm other men. If these fruits do not follow, we do but mock with God, deceive ourselves, and also other men. Well may we bear the name of Christian men, but we do lack the true faith that doth belong thereunto. For true faith doth ever bring forth good works; as St. James saith: "Shew me thy faith by thy deeds." [85] Thy deeds and works must be an open testimonial of thy faith; otherwise thy faith, being without good works, is but the devils' faith, the faith of the wicked, a phantasy of faith, and not a true Christian faith. And like as the devils and evil people be nothing the better for their counterfeit faith, but it is unto them the more cause of damnation, so they that be christened, and have received knowledge of God and of Christ's merits, and yet of a set purpose do live idly, without good works, thinking the name of a naked faith to be either sufficient for them, or else setting their minds upon vain pleasures of this world do live in sin without repentance, not uttering the fruits that do belong to such an high profession; upon such presumptuous persons and wilful sinners must needs remain the great vengeance of God, and eternal punishment in hell, prepared for the devil and wicked livers.

Therefore, as you profess the name of Christ, good Christian people, let no such phantasy and imagination of faith at any time beguile you; but be sure of your faith; try it by your living; look upon the fruits that cometh of it; mark the increase of love and

[82] Matt. 7:20.
[83] II Peter 1:10.
[84] II Peter 1:5-7.
[85] James 2:18.

charity by it towards God and your neighbour; and so shall you perceive it to be a true lively faith. If you feel and perceive such a faith in you, rejoice in it, and be diligent to maintain it and keep it still in you: let it be a daily increasing and more and more be [86] well working: and so shall ye be sure that you shall please God by this faith; and at the length, as other faithful men have done before, so shall you, when his will is, come to him, and receive "the end and final reward of your faith," as St. Peter nameth it, "the salvation of your souls." [87] The which God grant us, that hath promised the same unto his faithful. To whom be all honour and glory world without end. Amen.

[86] Only 1547W reads *be*. All others have *by*. If this latter is accepted, it will make the syntax very involved, if not impossible.
[87] I Peter 1:9.

AN HOMILY OR SERMON OF GOOD WORKS ANNEXED UNTO FAITH

THE TEXT

In the last sermon was declared unto you what the lively and true faith of a Christian man is, that it causeth not a man to be idle, but to be occupied in bringing forth good works, as occasion serveth. Now, by God's grace, shall be declared the second thing that before was noted of faith, that without it can no good work be done, acceptable and pleasant unto God. For "as a branch cannot bear fruit of itself," saith our Saviour Christ, "except it abide in the vine, so cannot you except you abide in me. I am the vine, and you be the branches. He that abideth in me, and I in him, he bringeth forth much fruit: for without me you can do nothing." [88] And St. Paul proveth that Enoch had faith, because "he pleased God"; for "without faith," saith he, "it is not possible to please God." [89] And again to the Romans he saith: "Whatsoever work is done without faith, it is sin." [90]

Faith giveth life to the soul; and they be as much dead to God that lack faith, as they be to the world whose bodies lack souls. Without faith all that is done of us is but dead before God, although the work seem never so gay and glorious before man. Even as a picture graven or painted is but a dead representation of the thing itself, and is without life or any manner of moving; so be the works of all unfaithful persons before God. They do appear to be lively works, and indeed they be but dead, not availing to the eternal life. They be but shadows and shews of lively and good things, and not good and lively things indeed. For true faith doth give life to the works; and out of such faith come good works, that be very good works indeed; and without it no work is good before God.

[88] John 15:4–5.   [89] Heb. 11:6.   [90] Rom. 14:23.

As saith St. Augustine: "We must set no good works before faith, nor think that before faith a man may do any good work. For such works, although they seem unto men to be praiseworthy, yet indeed they be but vain," and not allowed before God. "They be as the course of a horse that runneth out of the way, which taketh great labour, but to no purpose. Let no man therefore," saith he, "reckon upon his good works before his faith: where as faith was not, good works were not. The intent," saith he, "maketh the good works; but faith must guide and order the intent of man." [91] And Christ saith: "If thine eye be naught, thy whole body is full of darkness." [92] "The eye doth signify the intent," saith St. Augustine, "wherewith a man doeth a thing. So that he which doeth not his good works with a godly intent and a true faith that worketh by love, the whole body beside (that is to say, all the whole number of his works) is dark, and there is no light in it." [93] For good deeds be not measured by the facts themselves, and so dissevered from vices, but by the ends and intents for the which they be done. If a heathen man clothe the naked, feed the hungry, and do such other like works; yet, because he doeth them not in faith for the honour and love of God, they be but dead, vain, and fruitless works to him. Faith is it that doth commend the work to God: "for," as St. Augustine saith, "whether thou wilt or no, that work that cometh not of faith is naught." [94] Where the faith of Christ is not the foundation, there is no good work, what building soever we make. There is one work, in the which be all good works, that is, "faith which worketh by charity." If thou have it, thou hast the ground of all good works; for the virtues of strength, wisdom, temperance, and justice be all referred unto this same faith. Without this faith we have not them, but only the names and shadows of them; as St. Augustine saith: "All the life of them that lack the true faith is sin; and nothing is good without him that is the Author of goodness: where he is not, there is but feigned virtue, although it be in the best works." [95] And St. Augustine, declaring this verse of the psalm, "The turtle hath found a nest where she may keep her young birds," [96] saith that Jews, heretics, and pagans do good works; they clothe the naked, feed the poor, and do other works of mercy; but, because they be

[91] *Enarr. in Ps. XXXI*, ii.4 (PL 36.259).
[92] Matt. 6:23.
[93] *De Sermone Domini in Monte*, Lib. II, cap. xiii (PL 34.1289).
[94] *Contra Iulianum Pelagianum*, Lib. IV (PL 44.754).
[95] This is Prosperus Aquitanus, *Liber sententiarum ex operibus S. Augustini delibatum* §cvi (PL 51.441).
[96] Ps. 84:3.

not done in the true faith, therefore the birds be lost. But, if they remain in faith, then faith is the nest and safeguard of their birds; that is to say, safeguard of their good works, that the reward of them be not utterly lost.[97]

And this matter, which St. Augustine at large in many books disputeth, St. Ambrose concludeth in few words, saying: "He that by nature would withstand vice, either by natural will or reason, he doth in vain garnish the time of this life, and attaineth not the very true virtues: for without the worshipping of the true God that which seemeth to be virtue is vice." [98]

And yet most plainly to this purpose writeth St. John Chrysostom in this wise: "You shall find many which have not the true faith and be not of the flock of Christ, and yet, as it appeareth, they flourish in good works of mercy; you shall find them full of pity, compassion, and given to justice; and yet, for all that, they have no fruit of their works, because the chief work lacketh. For, when the Jews asked of Christ what they should do to work good works, he answered: 'This is the work of God, to believe in him whom he sent': [99] so that he called faith the work of God. And as soon as a man hath faith, anon he shall flourish in good works: for faith of itself is full of good works, and nothing is good without faith." [1] And for a similitude he saith that "they which glister and shine in good works without faith in God be like dead men, which have goodly and precious tombs, and yet it availeth them nothing. Faith may not be naked without good works, for then it is no true faith: and, when it is adjoined to works, yet it is above the works. For, as men, that be very men indeed, first have life, and after be nourished; so must our faith in Christ go before, and after be nourished with good works. And life may be without nourishment, but nourishment cannot be without life." [2] "A man must needs be nourished by good works, but first he must have faith. He that doeth good deeds, yet without faith he hath no life. I can shew a man that by faith without works lived and came to heaven: but without faith never man had life. The thief that was hanged when Christ suffered did believe only, and the most merciful God did justify him. And, because no man shall object that he lacked time to do good works, for else he would have done them, truth it is, and I will not contend therein: but this I will surely affirm, that faith only saved him. If he had lived, and not

---

[97] *Enarr. in Ps. LXXXIII* (i.e., Ps. 84:3) (*PL* 37.1060 f.).
[98] Ambrosiaster, *De vocatione Gentium*, Lib. I, cap. iii (*PL* 17.1078).
[99] John 6:29.
[1] Pseudo-Chrysostom, *De fide et lege naturae* (*PG* 48.1081).
[2] *Ibid.*

regarded faith and the works thereof, he should have lost his salvation again. But this is the effect that I say, that faith by itself saved him, but works by themselves never justified any man." [8]
Here ye have heard the mind of St. Chrysostom; whereby you may perceive, that neither faith is without works, having opportunity thereto, nor works can avail to eternal life without faith.

[8] *Ibid.* (PG 48.1081–2).

Nicholas Ridley

A TREATISE AGAYNST THE
ERROUR OF TRANSUBSTANTIATION,
AND EXTRACTS FROM
HIS EXAMINATIONS

Nicholas Ridley: A Treatise Agaynst the Errour of Transubstantiation, and Extracts from His Examinations

INTRODUCTION

THERE IS A CONSIDERABLE LITERATURE ON THE EUCHARISTIC doctrine of Cranmer and Ridley, but the differences of opinion are so many and so great that any student who relied on secondary works would be quite bewildered, and wonder how the scholars, with the same documents before them, could arrive at such divergent conclusions. For this there are, I believe, three main reasons. The first lies, quite frankly, in the ecclesiastical vested interests at stake. Cranmer's doctrine is not a purely historical matter but one affecting the character of the Church of England today. We might therefore expect that if a really balanced account is to be given, it should come from a foreign scholar. In England poor Cranmer has become a wax nose. Secondly, the English controversy has been too much isolated from the Continental. Given due weight to its local peculiarities, the Eucharistic debate in England ought to be treated in a wider context. It was one battle front, with its own peculiar problems, but it was part of a much wider war. And thirdly, this doctrine has been most unrealistically isolated from the main body of doctrine. How is it possible to arrive at conclusions about the Eucharistic doctrine of Cranmer or Ridley without knowing also about their doctrine of the Trinity, their Christology, or their concept of revelation? Until we know far more about these matters, we cannot arrive at a satisfactory and conclusive account of this particular doctrine. I, at any rate, will confess my ignorance here; but I will make one negative contribution to the debate—I will not darken counsels by attempting a critique of Ridley's doctrine of the Lord's Supper without such knowledge. It will be quite enough to set ourselves the humble task of expounding his thought in *A Treatise agaynst the errour of Transubstantiation*. We shall then be left with something quite tangible; and if we go wrong, here is the text, and the misinterpretation can be corrected by recourse to Ridley himself.

A Treatise agaynst . . . Transubstantiation was written, the title page tells us, while Ridley was a prisoner in Oxford "a little before" his death; in other words, sometime between April, 1554, and October, 1555. It therefore belongs to the same period as the Disputations, which took place during April, 1555. The first impression of the Disputations on the reader's mind is one of incoherence and bittyness. The argument does not pursue an ordered course but switches at the will of the interrogator. A point will suddenly occur to one of the questioners and we are off on a new track. Yet the coherence appears at last, and that on both sides. The accusers and the accused not only have a considerable area of agreement in their fundamental presuppositions on the Eucharist, but they both pursue their own doctrines consistently throughout the discussions—so much so that it is rather hard to see why they bothered to argue the matter at all, unless for the sake of publicity. That the accusers should maintain a consistent doctrine is not surprising, but it must be said that Ridley did very well to maintain his, confronted with so many opponents and in such a dangerous situation. The position that he took up in the Disputations was both a confirming and a supplementing of what he had taught in *Treatise agaynst the errour of Transubstantiation*.

He begins this book with a prayer for understanding of the truth in general and in particular for light on the Eucharistic controversy and for ability to teach the unlearned. His prayer leads into a preliminary statement of the way he intends to treat the matter, that is, by an exposition of the relevant Biblical texts. He therefore begins by quoting Matt. 26:26-30 and Mark 14:22-25, indicating the differences between them, and Luke 22:19-20 and I Cor. 11:23-25, with similar distinctions. These passages are recitals of the sacramental action, the Sacrament being defined as the "perpetual remembrance, until his coming again, of himself," i.e., "of his body given for us and of his blood shed for the remission of sins" (PS, p. 8). In this context, "remembrance" refers, not to the mental act of remembering by the believer, but to the initial act of Christ. It is Christ who makes the remembrance, and by God's power "it far passeth all kinds of remembrances that any other man is able to make, either of himself, or of any other thing" (*ibid.*). It has this transcendent importance because of its effect, in that the recipient "receiveth therewith either death or life" (*ibid.*). This is not to say that believers, who are already alive in God's sight, can receive death, or unbelievers, who are dead before God, life. Those alive receive life; those dead are condemned.

So far everyone in England will agree with him, whether they be Protestants, Pharisees, Papists, or gospelers. They all likewise abhor the notion that the Sacrament can do neither good nor ill, or that the sacramental elements are no different from common food. Therefore, let the opponents of the Reformers stop slandering them of saying that the Sacrament is merely a piece of bread, or that it is a bare sign, like the ivy bush outside a tavern. All this is completely irrelevant to the controversy.

And what is the controversy? It concerns five main points: "(1) Whether there be any transubstantiation of the bread, or no? (2) Any corporal and carnal presence of Christ's substance, or no? (3) Whether adoration, only due unto God, is to be done unto the sacrament, or no? (4) And whether Christ's body be there offered indeed unto the heavenly Father by the priest, or no? (5) Or whether the evil man receiveth the natural body of Christ, or no?" (p. 298). But the last three points depend on the first two. If these can be disproved, then all the others fail with them. Yet, if we attack the real presence of the natural substance of Christ's body and blood in the Sacrament, it is plain that we are in fact attacking transubstantiation, upon which it depends. Hence *A Treatise agaynst the errour of Transubstantiation*, the original English title, better expresses the contents than does the later *A treatise of the Lordes Supper* (1574), translated from half the Latin title *De Coena Dominica assertio*. The attack is directed against transubstantiation.

We must found our arguments on Scripture, in this instance on the two sets of parallel passages already mentioned, Matt., ch. 26, with Mark, ch. 14, and Luke, ch. 22, with I Cor., ch. 11. All these say that Jesus called the bread his body. The point at issue is how these words are to be interpreted. Now, if I do not misinterpret him, Ridley's ensuing argument runs thus (apart from one or two digressions): You say that these words must be interpreted literally. If so, the whole passage in each writer must also be interpreted literally. Let us see where this will lead us. We say that the bread, "retaining still its own very [true] natural substance" is the body of Christ "by grace and in a sacramental signification" (p. 301). It has been said, however, that a strict exegesis of the passages will do justice to the fact that, between the words "took bread" and the naming it his body, comes Christ's blessing of it. Since it was by the blessing that the bread was converted into his body, Christ was calling that his body which was indeed, since the blessing, his body. Nor did he break bread, but only its "form." This line of argument was invented by Innocentius III, worked out more fully by Duns Scotus, and revived in our own days by Stephen Gardiner. But interpreting the passages literally we find that St. Paul speaks of "the bread which we break," and five times in the passage he calls it bread after consecration. Again, Scripture calls the sacramental bread the mystical body. But the mystical body means also the congregation or Church. Therefore, if we are to be literal in our identifications, we must say that the sacramental bread is transubstantiated in the congregation.

Apply the same literal interpretation to the wine and even stranger conclusions follow. We may note first that Christ says, in Matthew and Mark, "I will not drink henceforth of *this* fruit of the vine tree. . . ." He is here calling the contents of the cup natural wine. Moreover, if the bread is transubstantiated by the blessing, then the wine is unchanged, since none of the four record that Christ blessed the wine. Again, we may assume (and this will be granted) that St. Paul sometimes used the I Cor., ch. 11, passage when he was himself celebrating the Lord's Supper. If so, was not the recitation of Christ's words, "This cup is the new covenant in my blood," as effectual as that of his words, "This is my body"? Certainly this must be so. But if the word *is* "mightily signifies" the change of the substance of bread into the substance of Christ's body, it must perform the same office in regard to the cup. A strict literalness will then land us into saying that the metal cup has been converted into the substance of the new covenant. If you say that this is absurd, I entirely agree. It is as absurd as saying that the substance of the bread is converted into the substance of Christ's body. If you say that "cup" means "wine" and is merely a figurative expression, I agree again; but now we have deserted the literal interpretation of the passages and admitted a figurative. We on our side say that "is" must also be interpreted figuratively.

How are we to decide what is literal and what figurative in the Bible? Augustine's rule in *De doctrina christiana* is as good as any. If Scripture commands ungodliness or forbids "charity," it must be taken as speaking figuratively. The example he gives is John 6:52 ff., where Jesus commands his followers to eat his flesh and drink his blood. Cannibalism is ungodly; therefore, Jesus was speaking figuratively. This rule and its example both support us. In effect, Christ is commanding in the Last Supper precisely the same thing that he did in John, ch. 6. If it is figurative in the one instance, it is figurative in the other.

Gardiner has also revived Duns Scotus' theory on the word "this." Does "this" refer to the bread that Christ took, or not? No, says Duns, its object is left undetermined when it is spoken. Its nature will become plain in its predicate (i.e., "my body"). But I reply that this will not hold true of the passages in question, where "this" in Matthew and Mark becomes "this cup" (i.e., "this wine") in Luke and Paul. In other words, speaking grammatically "this" is not a demonstrative pronoun but a demonstrative adjective in the second instance and therefore in the first instance too. The same is true of "This is my body," where "this" is the demonstrative adjective before "bread," which is to be supplied.

The rest of the work is taken up with a demonstration of support from three Greek and three Latin fathers.

It remains now to examine some of the concepts Ridley used to express his doctrine of the Eucharist. For this we will go to the Disputations as well as to *A Treatise agaynst the errour of transubstantiation*.

1. *Communication.* Smith has accused Ridley of teaching that the Sacraments are figures of Christ's body and blood. *"Ridley:* I never said that Christ gave only a figure of his body; for indeed he gave himself in a real communication, that is, he gave his flesh after a communication of his flesh." Weston at once repeated the charge (he seems to have been looking up a passage in Augustine and perhaps did not hear Ridley's reply). *"Ridley:* I say not so: I say, he gave his own body verily; but he gave it by a real, effectual, and spiritual communication."[1] Since elsewhere he uses "communication" to translate *koinōnia* in I Cor. 10:16, we may infer that it bears the same meaning and reference here. Thus Ridley is saying that in the Eucharist we receive really and effectually Christ's true body, and that we receive him by "spiritual communion." But we may not take him here as advocating some sort of sacramental mysticism. "Communion" means "union with," "being made one with." "Spiritual" means, as we shall see more fully later, "by the Holy Spirit." In the Eucharist, therefore, the believer is united to Christ, made one with Christ and Christ with him. Ridley views this sometimes in relation to the incarnation and sometimes to the cross and resurrection. On the one hand, the believer is united with the crucified and risen Christ and therefore receives forgiveness and life, and on the other, he is united with the "flesh" of Jesus which, because it is itself "united in the

[1] PS, p. 234.

divine nature in Christ, the second person of the Trinity . . . hath not only life in itself, but is also able to give . . . life unto so many as be . . . partakers thereof." [2]

2. *By grace.* In one of the most remarkable passages in the Disputations, first Curtop and then Weston are pressing Ridley to give a direct and unequivocal answer to what is in the chalice after consecration. To both he gives the same answer. He tells Curtop that "it is his true blood which is in the chalice . . . but by way of a sacrament." [3] Curtop retorts, "The sacrament of the blood is not the blood." Ridley insists, "The sacrament of the blood is the blood." [4] Weston then chimes in, to whom Ridley replies, "The blood of Christ is in the chalice indeed; but not in the real presence, but by grace, and in a sacrament." *Weston:* "That is very well. Then we have blood in the chalice." *Ridley:* "It is true; but by grace, and in a sacrament." [5] With this agree his words: We "deny the presence of Christ's body in the natural substance of his human and assumed nature, and grant the presence of the same by grace." [6] He defines grace in two ways. First, it is equivalent to an act of giving: "By grace, I say, that is, by the gift of this life . . . the same body of Christ is here present with us." [7] This needs a further definition, however, if it is to cast any light on the passage from the Disputations: "The society or conjunction with Christ through the Holy Ghost is grace; and by the sacrament we are made the members of the mystical body of Christ, for that by the sacrament the part of the body is grafted in the head." [8] We are back at the concept of *koinōnia:* grace is spiritual communication with Christ. Then what does Ridley mean by saying that the blood is in the chalice "by grace"? If grace means "gift," the statement is a platitude. If grace means "communion with Christ," it is difficult to see that it has any meaning at all. Only if we put the emphasis on "spiritual" does anything meaningful emerge. This is supported by his statement in the Examination before the Commissioners: "I confess . . . Christ's natural body to be in the sacrament indeed by spirit and grace." [9]

3. *Spiritual.* This is the heart of Ridley's doctrine of the Eucharist. We may expound it from a dispute between Watson and Ridley. Watson asks him whether Christ's words in John, ch. 6 ("He that eateth my flesh," etc.), refer to the eating of his "natural flesh" or of the sacramental bread. Ridley, of course, cannot

[2] PS, p. 13.
[3] PS, p. 237.
[4] PS, p. 238.
[5] PS, p. 238.
[6] PS, p. 13.
[7] PS, p. 13.
[8] PS, p. 239.
[9] PS, p. 274.

answer such a question directly, and in fact, the way that Watson in his next question ignores his reply, shows that he regarded it as completely irrelevant or meaningless. *"Ridley:* I understand that place of the very flesh of Christ to be eaten, but spiritually. And further I say that the sacrament also pertaineth unto the spiritual manducation; for without the spirit to eat the sacrament is to eat it unprofitably. For whoso eateth not spiritually, he eateth his own condemnation." [10] "Spiritually" is here not be understood subjectively, as if it referred to a certain religious quality on the part of the recipient, but objectively of the activity of the Holy Spirit. As a sound Trinitarian, Ridley believed that the works of God toward his creatures are the activity of the whole Godhead— of the Father, the Son, and the Holy Spirit. Moreover, he believed that the work which Christ wrought for his people is effected in them by the creative activity of the Spirit. The Spirit works generally through creaturely media—the preaching of the gospel and the Sacraments. He converts them, not into the actual voice of God or into the substantial body and blood of Christ, but into the effectual media of God's voice and of the incarnate Christ.

We should note how careful Ridley usually is not to call the Sacraments figurative. He will apply the term to the Scriptural accounts; his opponents frequently accuse him of applying it to the Sacraments; but he himself has quite another set of words. Although he will use the common concepts of remembrance and representation and effectuality, he comes back always to communion, grace, and Spirit. A complete study of Ridley would have to begin with a thorough lexicographical study—something that here we have had the space to do only very sketchily, though perhaps sufficiently to show the need for it.

[10] PS, p. 238.

BIBLIOGRAPHY

Certen godly, learned, and/ comfortable conferences, betwene the/two Reuerende Fathers, and holye Martyrs of/ Christe, D. Nicolas Rydley late Bysshoppe/ of London, and M. Hughe Latymer/ Sometyme Bysshoppe of Wor-/cester, during the tyme of/ theyr empryson-/mentes./ Wherunto is added./ A Treatise agaynst the errour of Transubstan-/tiation, made by the sayd Reuerende Father D./ Nicolas Rydley./ M.D.LVI./ Ryghte deare in the sighte of the Lor-/de is the death of his sainctes./ Psalm 116.
(No colophon.)

The same year appeared a Latin edition in Geneva:
D. Nicolai/ Ridleii Episcopi Lon-/dinensis De Coena/ Dominica assertio,/ Contra/ Sceleratam Illam Trans-/substantiationis haerisim, quam e carcere author/ scripserat: vnde etiam paulo post, id est XVI./ Octobr. die .M.D.LV. igni comburendus ex-/trahebatur./ Psal. LXXIX./ Fuderunt sanguinem tuorum, Domine, velut aquam per/ vniuersam Hierosolymam, nec quisquam inuentus/ est, qui occisos sepeliret./ Genevae./ Apud Ioannem Crispinum./ M.D.LVI.
(No colophon.)

Further editions were printed in 1574 (John Awdeley, London) and 1586 (for Abraham Veale, London).
Parker Society:
The Works of Nicholas Ridley, D.D. sometime Lord Bishop of London, Martyr, 1555. Edited for the Parker Society, by the Rev. Henry Christmas, M.A., F.S.A. Cambridge, 1841.
Biography:
J. G. Ridley, *Nicholas Ridley: A Biography.* London, 1957.

Cranmer's *A defence of the True and Catholike doctrine of the sacrament of the body and bloud of our sauiour Christ* (1550) was given in the first volume of his works in the Parker Society, edited by J. E. Cox (Cambridge, 1844), and in the Jenkyns edition (Oxford, 1833). The latter has been reprinted in *The Work of Thomas Cranmer*, edited by G. E. Duffield (Sutton Courtenay Press, 1964).

The chief opponent against whom Ridley directs his attack is Gardiner, with three books:

A Detec/tion of the/ Deuils Sophistrie, wher-/with he robbeth the un-/learned people, of the/ true byleef, in the/ most blessed Sa-/crament of the aulter/ . . . 1546.

An explication/ and assertion of the true Ca-/tholique fayth, touchyng the moost blessed/ Sacrament of the aulter with confuta-/cion of a booke written agaynst the/ same. Made by Steuen Byshop/ of Wynchester, and exhibi-/ted by his owne hande/ for his defence/ to the Kynges maiesties Commis-/sioners at Lambeth./ Anno 1551.

Confvtatio cavillationvm, qvibvs sacrosanctvm Evcharistiae Sacramentum, ab impiis Capernaitis, impeti solet, Authore Marco Antonio Constantio, Theologo Louaniensi. Parisiis. 1552.

There are several modern books on the subject. They will be found in the bibliography in Father Clark's book:

Francis Clark, *Eucharistic Sacrifice and the Reformation*. London, 1960.

The latest book seems to the present writer the most satisfying:

Peter Brooks, *Thomas Cranmer's Doctrine of the Eucharist*. London, 1965.

Nicholas Ridley: *A Treatise Agaynst the Errour of Transubstantiation, and Extracts from His Examinations*

THE TEXT

It is neither to be denied nor dissembled, that in the matter of this sacrament there be divers points, wherein men counted to be learned cannot agree. As whether there be any transubstantiation of the bread or no? Any corporal and carnal presence of Christ's substance or no? Whether adoration only due unto God, is to be done to the sacrament or no? And whether Christ's body be there offered in deed unto the heavenly Father by the priest or no? Or whether the evil man receive the natural body of Christ or no?

Yet nevertheless, as in a man diseased in divers parts, commonly the original cause of such divers diseases which are spread abroad in the body do come from one chief member, as from the stomach, or from the head; even so, all those five aforesaid points do chiefly hang upon this one question, which is, What is the matter of the sacrament, whether is it the natural substance of bread, or the natural substance of Christ's own body?

The truth of this question, truly tried out and agreed upon, no doubt shall cease the controversy in all the rest. For if it be Christ's own natural body, born of the Virgin, then assuredly (seeing that all learned men in England, so far as I know, both new and old, grant there to be but one substance), then, I say, they must needs grant transubstantiation, that is, a change of the substance of bread into the substance of Christ's body: then also they must grant the carnal and corporal presence of Christ's body: then must the sacrament be adored with the honour due unto Christ himself, for the unity of the two natures in one person: then, if the priest do offer the sacrament, he doth offer indeed Christ himself; and finally, the murderer, the adulterer, or wicked man, receiving the sacrament, must needs then receive also the natural substance of Christ's own blessed body, both flesh and blood.

Now, on the other side, if, after the truth shall be truly tried out, it be found that the substance of bread is the material substance of the sacrament; although, for the change of the use, office, and dignity of the bread, the bread indeed sacramentally is changed into the body of Christ, as the water in Baptism is sacramentally changed into the fountain of regeneration, and yet the material substance thereof remaineth all one as was before; if (I say) the true solution of that former question, whereupon all these controversies do hang, be that the natural substance of bread is the material substance in the holy sacrament of Christ's blessed body; then must it follow of that former proposition, (confessed of all that be named to be learned, so far as I do know, in England) which is, that there is but one material substance in the sacrament of the body, and one only likewise in the sacrament of the blood; that there is no such thing indeed and in truth as they call transubstantiation, for the substance of bread remaineth still in the sacrament of the body; then also the natural substance of Christ's human nature which he took of the Virgin Mary, is in heaven, where it reigneth now in glory, and not here inclosed under the form of bread; then that godly honour which is due unto God the Creator and may not be done to the creature without idolatry and sacrilege, is not to be done to the holy sacrament; then also the wicked (I mean the impenitent murderer, adulterer, or such-like) do not receive the natural substance of the blessed body and blood of Christ; finally, then doth follow that Christ's blessed body and blood, which was once only offered and shed upon the cross, being available for the sins of all the world, is offered up no more in the natural substance thereof, neither by the priest, nor any other thing.

But here, before we go any further to search in this matter and to wade, as it were, to search and try out, as we may, the truth thereof in the Scripture, it shall do well by the way to know, whether they that thus make answer and solution unto the former principal question, do take away simply and absolutely the presence of Christ's body and blood from the sacrament ordained by Christ, and duly ministered according to his holy ordinance and institution of the same. Undoubtedly, they do deny that utterly, either so to say, or to mean the same. And thereof if any man do or will doubt, the books which are written already in this matter of them that thus do answer will make the matter plain.

Now then you will say, what kind of presence do they grant, and what do they deny? Briefly, they deny the presence of Christ's body in the natural substance of his human and assumpt nature, and grant the presence of the same by grace. That is, they affirm and say that the substance of the natural body and blood of Christ is only remaining in heaven, and so shall be unto the latter day, when he shall come again in glory, accompanied with the angels of heaven, to judge both the quick and the dead. And the same natural substance of the very body and blood of Christ, because it is united to the divine nature in Christ, the second Person of the Trinity, therefore it hath not only life in itself, but is also able and doth give life unto so many as be, or shall be, partakers thereof; that is, that to all that do believe on his name, (which are not born of blood, as St. John saith, or of the will of the flesh, or of the will of man, but are born of God [11]) though the selfsame substance abide still in heaven, and they, for the time of their pilgrimage, dwell here upon the earth, by grace (I say), that is, by the life mentioned in John and the properties of the same meet for our pilgrimage here upon earth, the same body of Christ is here present with us. Even as, for example, we say the sun, which in substance never removeth his place out of the heavens, is yet present here by his beams, light, and natural influence, where it shineth upon the earth. For God's Word and his sacraments be as it were the beams of Christ, which is *Sol justitiae,* the Sun of righteousness.[12] . . .

And the places of Scripture whereupon this my faith is grounded, be these, both concerning the sacrament of the body, and also of the blood.

First let us repeat the beginning of the institution of the Lord's Supper, wherein all the three Evangelists and St. Paul almost in words do agree; [13] saying, that Jesus took bread, gave thanks, brake, and gave it to the disciples, saying, "Take, eat, this is my body." Here it appeareth plainly, that Christ calleth very bread his body. For that which he took was very bread (in this all men do agree); and that which he took, after he had given thanks, he brake; and that which he took and brake, he gave it to his disciples; and that which he took, brake, and gave to his disciples, he said himself of it: "This is my body." So it appeareth plainly that Christ called very bread his body. But very bread cannot be his body in very substance thereof. Therefore it must needs have another meaning, which meaning appeareth plainly, what it is, by the next sentence that followeth immediately, both in Luke and in Paul.

[11] John 1:13.
[12] Mal. 4:2.
[13] Mark 14:22 ff. and par.; I Cor. 11:23 ff.

And that is this: "Do this in remembrance of me." Whereupon it seemeth unto me to be evident, that Christ did take bread, and called it his body, for that he would institute thereby a perpetual remembrance of his body, specially of that singular benefit of our redemption, which he would then procure and purchase unto us by his body upon the cross. But bread, retaining still his own very natural substance, may be thus by grace, and in a sacramental signification, his body: whereas else, the very bread, which he took, brake, and gave them, could not be in any wise his natural body, for that were confusion of substances. And therefore the very words of Christ, joined with the next sentence following, both enforceth us to confess the very bread to remain still, and also openeth unto us, how that bread may be, and is thus by his divine power, his body which was given for us.

But here I remember I have read in some writers of the contrary opinion; which do deny, that that which Christ did take, he brake. For, say they, after his taking, he blessed it, as Mark doth speak; and by his blessing he changed the natural substance of the bread into the natural substance of his body: and so, although he took the bread and blessed it, yet because in blessing he changed the substance of it, he brake not the bread, which then was not there, but only the form thereof.

Unto this objection I have two plain answers, both grounded upon God's Word. The one I will here rehearse; the other answer I will defer until I speak of the sacrament of the blood. Mine answer here is taken out of the plain words of St. Paul, which doth manifestly confound this fantastical invention, first invented, I ween, of Pope Innocentius, and after confirmed by the subtle sophister Duns, and lately renewed now in our days with an eloquent style and much fineness of wit.[14] But what can crafty invention, subtilty in sophisms, eloquence or fineness of wit, prevail against the infallible Word of God? What need have we to strive and contend what thing we break? For Paul saith, speaking undoubtedly of the Lord's Table: "The bread," saith he, "which we break, is it not the partaking or fellowship of the Lord's body?" Whereupon it followeth, that after the thanksgiving it is bread which we break. And how often in the Acts of the Apostles is the Lord's Supper signified by breaking of bread? "They did persevere," saith St. Luke, "in the Apostles' doctrine, communion,

---

[14] A marginal note in 1555 reads: "It is mente of a book firste sette forth under the name of M. Antonius Constantius. And afterward of Ste. Gard, Bishop of Winch." This is *Confutatio cavillationum, quibus sacrosanctum Eucharistiae Sacramentum, ab impiis Capernaitis, impeti solet, Authore Marco Antonio Constantio, Theologo Lovaniensi.* Parisiis. 1552.

and breaking of bread." [15] And again, "They brake bread in every house." [16] And again, in another place, "When they were come together to break bread." [17] St. Paul, which setteth forth most fully in his writing both the doctrine and the right use of the Lord's Supper, and the sacramental eating and drinking of Christ's body and blood, calleth it five times, Bread, bread, bread, bread, bread.[18]

The sacramental bread is the mystical body, and so is called in Scripture, i. Cor. x.,[19] as it is called the natural body of Christ. But Christ's mystical body is the congregation of Christians. Now no man was ever so fond, as to say that that sacramental bread is transubstantiated and changed into the substance of the congregation. Wherefore no man should likewise think or say that the bread is transubstantiated, and changed into the natural substance of Christ's human nature.

But my mind is not here to write what may be gathered out of Scriptures for this purpose, but only to write here briefly those which seem to me to be the most plain places. Therefore, contented to have spoken thus much of the sacramental bread, now I will speak a little of the Lord's cup.

And this shall be my third argument, grounded upon Christ's own words. The natural substance of the sacramental wine remaineth still, and is the material substance of the sacrament of the blood of Christ: therefore it is likewise so in the sacramental bread.

I know, that he that is of a contrary opinion, will deny the former part of my argument. But I will prove it thus, by the plain words of Christ himself, both in Matthew and in Mark. Christ's words be thus, after the words said upon the cup: "I say unto you," saith Christ, "I will not drink henceforth of this fruit of the vine tree, until I shall drink that new in my Father's Kingdom." [20] Here note, how Christ calleth plainly his cup the fruit of the vine tree. But the fruit of the vine tree is very natural wine. Wherefore the natural substance of the wine doth remain still in the sacrament of Christ's blood.

And here, in speaking of the Lord's cup, it cometh unto my remembrance the vanity of Innocentius his fantastical invention, which by Paul's words I did confute before,[21] and here did promise somewhat more to speak; and that is this: If the transubstantia-

---

[15] Acts 2:42.
[16] Acts 2:46.
[17] Acts 20:7.
[18] In I Cor., chs. 10 and 11.
[19] I Cor. 10:16.
[20] Mark 14:25 and par.
[21] See p. 301.

tion be made by this word "blessed" in Mark, said upon the bread, as Innocentius that Pope did say; then surely, seeing that word is not said of Christ, neither in any of the Evangelists, nor in Paul, upon the cup, there is no transubstantiation of the wine at all. For where the cause doth fail, there cannot follow the effect. But the sacramental bread, and the sacramental wine, do both remain in their natural substance alike; and if the one be not changed, as of the sacramental wine it appeareth evidently, then there is no such transubstantiation in neither of them both.

All that put and affirm this change of the substance of bread and wine into the substance of Christ's body and blood (called transubstantiation), do also say and affirm this change to be made by a certain form of prescript words and none other. But what they be that make the change either of the one or of the other, undoubtedly even they that do write most finely in these our days,[22] almost confess plainly that they cannot tell. For although they grant to certain of the old doctors, as Chrysostom and Ambrose,[23] that these words, "This is my body," are the words of consecration of the sacrament of the body: "yet," say they, "these words may well be so called, because they do assure us of the consecration thereof, whether it be done before these words be spoken, or no." But, as for this their doubt concerning the sacrament of the body, I let it pass.

Let us now consider the words which pertain unto the cup. This is first evident, that as Matthew much agreeth with Mark, and likewise Luke with Paul doth much agree, herein in form of words; so, in the same, the form of words in Matthew and Mark is diverse from that which is in Luke and Paul. The old authors do most rehearse the form of words in Matthew and Mark, because, I ween, they seemed to them most clear. But here I would know, whether it is credible or no, that Luke and Paul, when they celebrated the Lord's Supper with their congregations, that they did not use the same form of words at the Lord's Table which they wrote, Luke in his Gospel, and Paul in his epistle. Of Luke, because he was a physician, whether some will grant that he might be a priest or no, and was able to receive the order of priesthood, which (they say) is given by virtue of these words said by the Bishop, "Take thou authority to sacrifice for the quick and the

---

[22] Gardiner, in Cranmer, PS, I.59.
[23] Chrysostom, *In sermone de Eucharistia in Encaenis* (*PG* 49:345-6) and *De proditione Judae.*, Hom. i (*PG* 49.380; as quoted Gardiner, in Cranmer, PS, I.182).
Ambrose, *De Sacramentis*, Lib. V, cap. iv (*PL* 16.452 as quoted Gardiner, in Cranmer, PS, I.178 f.).

dead," I cannot tell. But, if they should be so strait upon Luke, either for his craft, or else for lack of such power given him by virtue of the aforesaid words: then I ween both Peter and Paul are in danger to be deposed of their priesthood; for the craft either of fishing, which was Peter's, or of making tents, which was Paul's, were more vile than the science of physic. And, as for those sacramental words of the order of priesthood, to have authority to sacrifice both for the quick and the dead, I ween Peter and Paul (if they were both alive) were not able to prove that ever Christ gave them such authority, or ever said any such words unto them. But I will let Luke go: and because Paul speaketh plainly for himself, I will rehearse his words. "That," saith Paul, "which I received of the Lord, I gave unto you: for the Lord Jesus, &c." And so he setteth forth the whole institution and right use of the Lord's Supper. Now, seeing that Paul here saith, that which he received of the Lord, he had given them; and that which he had received and given them before by word of mouth, now he rehearseth and writeth the same in his epistle: is it credible that Paul would never use this form of words upon the Lord's cup, which (as he saith) he received of the Lord, that he had given them before, and now rehearseth in his epistle? I trust no man is so far from all reason but he will grant me that this is not likely so to be.

Now then, if you grant me that Paul did use the form of words which he writeth, let us then rehearse and consider Paul's words, which he saith Christ spake thus upon the cup: "This cup is the new testament in my blood; this do as often as ye shall drink it in the remembrance of me."

Here I would know whether that Christ's words spoken upon the cup were not as mighty in work, and as effectual in signification, to all intents, constructions, and purposes (as our Parliament men do speak), as they were, spoken upon the bread? If this be granted, which thing, I think, no man can deny, then further I reason thus: But the word "is" in the words spoken upon the Lord's bread, doth mightily signify (say they) the change of the substance of that which goeth before it, into the substance of that which followeth after; that is, of the substance of bread into the substance of Christ's body, when Christ saith, "This is my body." Now then, if Christ's words, which be spoken upon the cup, which Paul here rehearseth, be of the same might and power both in working and signifying, then must this word "is," when Christ saith, "This cup is the new testament, &c." turn the substance of the cup into the substance of the new testament. And if thou wilt say that this word "is" neither maketh nor signifieth any such change of the cup, although it be said of Christ that this cup is the new testament, yet Christ meant no such change as that. Marry, sir, even so say I, when Christ said of the bread which he took, and after thanks given, brake, and gave them, saying, "Take, eat, this is my body," he meant no more any such change of the substance of bread into the substance of his natural body, than he meant of the change and transubstantiation of the cup into the substance of the new testament.

And, if thou wilt say, that the word "cup" here in Christ's words doth not signify the cup itself, but the wine, or thing contained in the cup, by a figure called *metonymy*,[24] for that Christ's words meant, and so must needs be taken; thou sayest very well. But I pray thee by the way, here note two things: first, that this word "is" hath no such strength or signification in the Lord's words, to make or to signify any transubstantiation: secondly, that in the Lord's words, whereby he instituted the sacrament of his blood, he useth a figurative speech. How vain then is it, that some so earnestly do say, as it were an infallible rule, that in doctrine and in the institution of the sacraments Christ useth no figures, but all his words are to be strained to their proper significations; when as here, whatsoever thou sayest was in the cup, yet neither that nor the cup itself was (taking every word in his proper signification) the new testament: but in understanding that which was in the cup, by the cup, that is a figurative speech. Yea and also thou canst not verify, or truly say of that (whether thou sayest it was wine or Christ's blood) to be the new testament, without a figure also. Thus, in one sentence spoken of Christ in the institution of the sacrament of his blood, the figure must help us twice. So untrue is it that some do write, that Christ useth no figure in the doctrine of faith, nor in the institution of his sacraments.

But some say: if we shall thus admit figures in doctrine, then shall all the articles of our faith, by figures and allegories, shortly be transformed and unloosed. I say, it is like fault, and even the same, to deny the figure where the place so requireth to be understood, as vainly to make it a figurative speech, which is to be understanded in his proper signification.

The rules, whereby the speech is known when it is a figurative, and when it is none, St. Austin, in his book called *De doctrina christiana*, giveth divers learned lessons, very necessary to be known of the student in God's Word. Of the which one I will rehearse, which is this: "If," saith he, "the Scripture doth seem to command a thing which is wicked or ungodly, or to forbid a

[24] The substitution of an attribute of a thing for its proper name.

thing that charity doth require, then know thou (saith he) that the speech is figurative." [25] And for example he bringeth the saying of Christ in the sixth chapter of St. John: "Except ye eat the flesh of the Son of Man, and drink his blood, ye cannot have life in you." [26] It seemeth to command a wicked or an ungodly thing. Wherefore it is a figurative speech, commanding to have communion and fellowship with Christ's passion, and devoutly and wholesomely to lay up in memory that his flesh was crucified and wounded for us.

And here I cannot but marvel at some men,[27] surely of much excellent fineness of wit, and of great eloquence, that are not ashamed to write and say that this aforesaid saying of Christ is (after St. Austin) a figurative speech indeed, but not unto the learned, but unto the unlearned. Here let any man that indifferently understandeth the Latin tongue, read the place in St. Augustine; and if he perceive not clearly St. Augustine's words and mind to be contrary, let me abide thereof the rebuke.

This lesson of St. Augustine I have therefore the rather set forth; because, as it teacheth us to understand that place in John figuratively, even so surely the same lesson with the example of St. Augustine's exposition thereof teacheth us, not only by the same to understand Christ's words in the institution of the sacrament both of his body and of his blood figuratively, but also the very true meaning and understanding of the same. For if to command to eat the flesh of the Son of Man and to drink his blood, seemeth to command an inconvenience [28] and an ungodliness; and is even so indeed, if it be understanded as the words do stand in their proper signification, and therefore must be understanded figuratively and spiritually, as St. Augustine doth godly and learnedly interpretate them; then surely Christ, commanding in his Last Supper to eat his body and to drink his blood, seemeth to command, in sound of words, as great and even the same inconvenience and ungodliness, as did his words in the sixth chapter of St. John; and therefore must even by the same reason be likewise understanded and expounded figuratively and spiritually, as St. Augustine did the other. Whereunto that exposition of St. Augustine may seem to be the more meet, for that Christ in his Supper, to the commandment of eating and drinking of his body and

---

[25] *De doct. christ.* III.16 (*PL* 34.74 f.).
[26] John 6:53.
[27] Gardiner, in Cranmer, PS, I.116. His distinction, however, is not between learned and unlearned, but between believers and unbelievers.
[28] Something unfitting, an impropriety.

blood, addeth: "Do this in the remembrance of me." Which words, surely, were the key that opened and revealed this spiritual and godly exposition unto St. Augustine.

But I have tarried longer in setting forth the form of Christ's words upon the Lord's cup, written by Paul and Luke, than I intended to do. And yet, in speaking of the form of Christ's words spoken upon his cup, it cometh now unto my remembrance the form of words used in the Latin Mass upon the Lord's cup. Whereof I do not a little marvel, what should be the cause, seeing the Latin Mass agreeth with the Evangelists and Paul in the form of words said upon the bread, why in the words upon the Lord's cup it differeth from them all; yea, and addeth unto the words of Christ, spoken upon the cup, these words, *Mysterium fidei*, that is, "the mystery of faith"; [29] which are not read to be attributed unto the sacrament of Christ's blood, neither in the Evangelists, nor in Paul, nor (so far as I do know) in any other place of Holy Scripture. Yea, and if it may have some good exposition, yet, why it should not be as well added unto the words of Christ upon his bread, as upon his cup, surely I do not see that mystery.[30]

And, because I see in the use of the Latin Mass the sacrament of the blood abused, when it is denied to the lay men, clean contrary to God's most certain Word; for why, I beseech thee, should the sacrament of Christ's blood be denied unto the lay Christian, more than to the priest? Did not Christ shed his blood as well for the lay godly man as for the godly priest? If thou wilt say: "Yes, that he did so. But yet the sacrament of the blood is not to be received without the offering up and sacrificing thereof unto God the Father, both for the quick and for the dead; and no man may make oblation of Christ's blood unto God but a priest, and therefore the priest alone (and that but in his Mass only) may receive the sacrament of the blood." And call you this, masters, *mysterium fidei?* Alas! alas! I fear me this is before God *mysterium iniquitatis.* . . .[31]

To speak of this oblation, how much it is injurious unto Christ's passion, how it cannot but with high blasphemy, and heinous arrogance, and intolerable pride, be claimed of any man, other than of Christ himself, how much and how plainly it repugneth unto the manifest words, the true sense and meaning, of Holy Scrip-

[29] *Hic est enim calix sanguinis mei, novi et aeterni testamenti: mysterium fidei* . . . (from Innocentius, *De sac. alt. myst.* [PL 217.770]).
[30] Intended ironically. The Latin version reads: I confess that I do not know the reason for such mystery.
[31] II Thess. 2:7.

ture in many places, especially in the epistle to the Hebrews, the matter is so long, and other have written in it at large,[32] that my mind is now not to entreat thereof any further. For only in this my scribbling I intended to search out and set forth by the Scriptures (according to God's gracious gift of my poor knowledge) whether the true sense and meaning of Christ's words in the institution of his Holy Supper do require any transubstantiation (as they call it), or that the very substance of bread and wine do remain still in the Lord's Supper, and be the material substance of the holy sacrament of Christ our Saviour's blessed body and blood.

Yet there remaineth one vain quiddity of Duns in this matter, the which, because some that write [33] now do seem to like it so well, that they have stripped him out of Duns' dusty and dark terms, and pricked him and painted him in fresh colours of an eloquent style, may therefore deceive the more, except the error be warily eschewed.

Duns saith [34] in these words of Christ, "This is my body": "This pronoun demonstrative, meaning the word 'this,' if ye will know what it doth shew or demonstrate, whether the bread that Christ took or no," he answereth, "no; but only one thing in substance it pointeth, whereof the nature and name it doth not tell, but leaveth that to be determined and told by that which followeth the word, 'is,' that is, by *predicatum*, as the logician doth speak": and therefore he calleth this pronoun demonstrative "this," *individuum vagum*, that is, a wandering proper name, whereby we may point out and shew any one thing in substance, what thing soever it be.

That this imagination is vain and untruly applied unto those words of Christ, "This is my body," it may appear plainly by the words of Luke and Paul said upon the cup, conferred with the form of words spoken upon the cup in Matthew and Mark. For as upon the bread it is said of all, "This is my body"; so of Matthew and Mark is said of the cup, "This is my blood." Then, if in the words, "This is my body," the word "this" be, as Duns calleth it, "a wandering name," to appoint and shew forth any one thing, whereof the name and nature it doth not tell; so must it be likewise in these words of Matthew and Mark upon the Lord's cup, "This is my blood." But in the words of Matthew and Mark, it signifieth and pointeth out the same that it doth in the Lord's words upon the cup in Luke and Paul, where it is said,

[32] E.g., Cranmer, *Defensio verae et catholicae doctrinae*, Lib. V (PS, I.344 ff.).
[33] Gardiner, in Cranmer, PS, I.106.
[34] *Quaestiones in Lib. IV Sententiarum*, Lib. IV, Dist. VIII, Quaest. II.

"This cup is the new testament in my blood, &c." Therefore, in Matthew and Mark the pronoun demonstrative "this" doth not wander to point only one thing in substance, not shewing what it is, but telleth plainly what it is, no less in Matthew and Mark to the eye, than is done in Luke and Paul, by putting to this word "cup" both unto the eye and unto the ear.

For, taking the cup, and demonstrating or shewing it unto his disciples by this pronoun demonstrative "this," and saying unto them, "Drink ye all of this," it was then all one to say, "This is my blood," as to say, "This cup is my blood," meaning by the cup, as the nature of the speech doth require, the thing contained in the cup. So likewise, without all doubt, when Christ had taken bread, given thanks, and broken it, and giving it to his disciples, said, "Take"; and so demonstrating and shewing that bread which he had in his hands, to say then, "This is my body," and to have said, "This bread is my body." As it were all one, if a man, lacking a knife, and going to his oysters, would say to another, whom he saw to have two knives, "Sir, I pray you lend me the one of your knives"; were it not now all one to answer him: "Sir, hold, I will lend you this to eat your meat, but not to open oysters withal": and, "Hold, I will lend you this knife to eat your meat, but not to open oysters"?

This similitude serveth but for this purpose, to declare the nature of speech withal; whereas the thing that is demonstrated and shewed is evidently perceived and openly known to the eye. But, O good Lord, what a wonderful thing is it to see, how some men do labour to teach what is demonstrated and shewed by the pronoun demonstrative "this" in Christ's words, when he saith: "This is my body"; "this is my blood"; how they labour (I say) to teach what that "this" was then in deed, when Christ spake in the beginning of the sentence the word "this," before he had pronounced the rest of the words that followed in the same sentence; so that their doctrine may agree with their transubstantiation: which indeed is the very foundation wherein all their erroneous doctrine doth stand. And here the transubstantiators do not agree amongst themselves, no more than they do in the words which wrought the transubstantiation, when Christ did first institute his sacrament. Wherein Innocentius, a Bishop of Rome of the latter days, and Duns (as was noted before), do attribute the work unto the word *benedixit*, "he blessed." [35] But the rest for the most part to *hoc est corpus meum*, "this is my body." Duns, therefore, with his sect, because he putteth the change before, must needs say, that "this,"

[35] See p. 301.

when Christ spake it in the beginning of the sentence, was indeed Christ's body. For in the change the substance of bread did depart, and the change was now [36] done in *"benedixit,"* saith he, that went before. And therefore after him and his, that "this" was then indeed Christ's body, though the word did not import so much, but only one thing in substance, which substance, after Duns, the bread being gone, must needs be the substance of Christ's body.

But they that put their transubstantiation to be wrought by these words of Christ, "This is my body," and do say that, when the whole sentence was finished, then this change was perfected, and not before: they cannot say, but that Christ's "this" in the beginning of the sentence, before the other words were fully pronounced, was bread indeed. For as yet the change was not done, and so long the bread must needs remain; and so long as the substance of the bread doth remain, so long, with the universal consent of all transubstantiators, the natural substance of Christ's body cannot come; and therefore must their "this" of necessity demonstrate and shew the substance which was as yet in the pronouncing of the first word "this" by Christ, but bread. But how can they make and verify Christ's words to be true, demonstrating the substance, which, in the demonstration, is but bread, and say thereof, "This is my body," that is, as they say, the natural substance of Christ's body; except they would say, that the verb "is" signifieth, "is made," or "is changed into"? And so then, if the same verb "is" be of the same effect in Christ's words spoken upon the cup, and rehearsed by Luke and Paul, the cup, or the wine in the cup, must be made or turned into the new testament, as was declared before. . . .

Thus much have I spoken, in searching out a solution for this principal question, which was, What is the material substance of the holy sacrament in the Lord's Supper?

[We continue with passages extracted from the Disputation at Oxford in April, 1555, between Ridley and a number of opponents, chiefly Dr. Richard Smith.[37]]

The First Proposition

In the sacrament of the altar, by the virtue of God's word spoken of the priest, the natural body of Christ, born of the Virgin Mary,

---

[36] "Now" in sense of Latin *iam,* "already."
[37] From Foxe, *Actes and Monuments,* 1563, pp. 958 ff.

and his natural blood, is really present under the forms of bread and wine.

The Answer of N. R.

In matters pertaining unto God, we may not speak according to the sense of man nor of the world: therefore this first proposition or conclusion is framed after another manner of phrase or kind of speech than the Scripture useth. Again, it is very obscure and dark, by means of sundry words of doubtful signification. And being taken in the sense which the schoolmen teach, and at this time the Church of Rome doth defend, it is false and erroneous and plain contrary to the doctrine which is according to godliness.

The Explication

How far the diversity and newness of the phrase in all this first proposition is from the phrase of the holy Scripture (and that in every part almost), it is so plain and evident to any that is but meanly exercised in holy writ, that I need not now (especially in this company of learned men) to spend any time therein, except the same shall be required of me hereafter.

There is also a doubtful sense in these words *by the virtue of God's Word*. For it is doubtful what word of God this is; whether it be that which is read in the Evangelists, or in Paul, or any other. And if it be that that is in the Evangelists, or in Paul, yet it is in doubt which it is. If it be in none of them, then how may it be known to be God's word, and of such virtue that it should be able to work so great a matter.

Again, there is a doubt in these words *of the priest*, whether no man may be called a priest, but he which hath authority to make propitiatory sacrifice for the quick and the dead: and how it may be proved that this authority was committed of God to any man but to Christ alone.

It is likewise doubted after what order the sacrificing priest shall be, whether after the order of Aaron or else after the order of Melchizedek. For as far as I know, the holy Scripture doth allow no more. . . .

Moreover, there is ambiguity in this word *really*, whether it be to be taken as the logicians [38] term it *transcendenter*, that is most generally; (and so it may signify any manner of thing which belongeth to the body of Christ by any means: after which sort we also grant Christ's body to be really in the sacrament of the Lord's

---
[38] I.e., the Schoolmen, following Aristotle.

supper . . .) or whether it be taken to signify the very same thing, having body, life and soul, which was assumed and taken of the word of God into the unity of person. In which sense, since the body of Christ is really in heaven, because of the true manner of his body, it may not be said to be here in the earth.

There is yet a further doubtfulness in these words *under the forms of bread and wine,* whether *the forms* be there taken to signify the only accidental and outward shows of bread and wine, or therewithal the substantial natures thereof, which are to be seen by their qualities and perceived by ⟨the⟩ [39] exterior senses.

Now the error and falseness of the proposition, after the sense of the Roman Church, and schoolmen, may hereby appear in that they affirm the bread to be transubstantiated and changed into the flesh assumed of the word of God, and that (as they say) by the virtue of the word, which they have devised by a certain number of words and ⟨which⟩ [40] cannot be found in none of the evangelists, nor in Paul. And so they gather that Christ's body is really contained in the sacrament of the altar. Which position is grounded upon the foundation of transubstantiation; which foundation is monstrous, against reason and destroyeth the analogy or proportion [41] of the sacraments; and therefore this proposition also, which is builded upon this rotten foundation is false, erroneous and to be counted as a detestable heresy of the sacramentaries. . . .

This carnal presence is contrary to the word of God, as appeareth John 16:7: "I tell you the truth; it is profitable to you that I go away; for if I go not away the Comforter shall not come unto you." Acts 3:21: "Whom the heavens must receive until the time of restoring of all things which God hath spoken." Matt. 9:15: "The children of the bridegroom cannot mourn so long as the bridegroom is with them: but now is the time of mourning." John 16:22: "But I will see you again and your hearts shall rejoice." John 14:3: "I will come again and take you to myself." Matt. 24:23, 28: "If they shall say unto you, Behold, here is Christ, or there is Christ, believe them not: for wheresoever the dead carcass is, thither the eagles will resort."

It varieth from the articles of faith: "He ascended into heaven and sitteth on the right hand of God the Father, from whence"

---

[39] Not *their* as 1563.
[40] *Which* not in 1563.
[41] I.e., the Sacraments are not to be regarded as either identical with Christ or completely separate from him but as related to him in such a way that they, although different in themselves, are nevertheless used by him as the means of his redeeming revelation of himself.

(and not from any other place, saith St. Augustine) "he shall come to judge both the quick and the dead." [42]

It destroyeth and taketh away the institution of the Lord's supper, which was commanded only to be used and continued until the Lord himself should come. If therefore he be now really present in the body of his flesh then must the supper cease, for a remembrance is not of a thing present but of a thing past and absent. And there is a difference between remembrance and presence, and as one of the fathers saith: "A figure is in vain where the thing figured is present." [43]

It maketh precious things common to profane and ungodly persons, and constraineth men to confess many absurdities. For it affirmeth that whoremongers and murderers, yea, and as some of them hold opinion, that the wicked and faithless, mice, rats also and dogs may receive the very real and corporal body of the Lord, wherein the fulness of the Spirit of light and grace dwelleth; contrary to the manifest words of Christ in six places and sentences of the sixth chapter of Saint John.

It confirmeth also and maintaineth that beastly kind of cruelty of the *Anthropophagi*,[44] that is the devouring of man's flesh: for it is a more cruel thing to devour a quick man than to slay him. . . .

But now, my brethren, think not because I disallow that presence which this first proposition maintaineth . . . that I therefore go about to take away the true presence of Christ's body in his supper, rightly and duly ministered, which is grounded upon the word of God and made more plain by the commentaries of the faithful fathers. They that think so of me, the Lord knoweth how far they are deceived. And to make the same evident unto you, I will in few words declare, what true presence of Christ's body in the sacrament of the Lord's supper I hold and affirm with the word of God and the ancient fathers.

I say and confess with the evangelist Luke and with the apostle Paul, that the bread on the which thanks are given is the body of Christ in the remembrance of him and of his death, to be set forth perpetually of the faithful until his coming.

I say and confess the bread which we break to be the communion and partaking of Christ's body, with the ancient and the faithful fathers.

[42] *Ep. ad Dardanum* (PL 33.835).
[43] Lactantius, *Divinae Institutiones*, Lib. I, cap. ii (PL 6.259).
[44] Cannibals.

I say and believe that there is not only a signification of Christ's body set forth by the sacrament, but also that therewith is given to the godly and faithful the grace of Christ's body, that is, the food of life and immortality. And this I hold with Cyprian.

I say also with St. Augustine, that we eat life and we drink life; with Emissene that we feel the Lord to be present in grace; with Athanasius that we receive celestial food, which cometh from above; the property of natural communication, with Hilary; the nature of flesh and benediction which giveth life, in bread and wine, with Cyril; and with the same Cyril, the virtue of the very flesh of Christ, life and grace of his body, the property of the only begotten, that is to say, life, as he himself in plain words expoundeth it.

I confess also with Basil, that we receive the mystical advent and coming of Christ, grace and the virtue of his very nature; the sacrament of his very flesh, with Ambrose; the body by grace, with Epiphanius; spiritual flesh, but not that which was crucified, with Jerome; grace flowing into a sacrifice, and the grace of the Spirit, with Chrysostom; grace and invisible verity, grace and society of the members of Christ's body, with Augustine. Finally, with Bertram (which was the last of all these) I confess that Christ's body is in the sacrament in this respect: namely, as he writeth, because there is in it the Spirit of Christ, that is, the power of the word of God, which not only feedeth the soul, but also cleanseth it. Out of these I suppose it may clearly appear unto all men how far we are from that opinion whereof some go about falsely to slander us to the world, saying we teach that the godly and faithful should receive nothing else at the Lord's table but a figure of the body of Christ. . . .

The Third Proposition

In the mass is the lively sacrifice of the church, propitiable and available for the sins as well of the quick as of the dead. . . .

The Explication of Dr. Ridley

Concerning the Romish mass which is used at this day or the lively sacrifice thereof, propitiatory and available for the sins of the quick and the dead, the holy Scripture hath not so much as one syllable.

There is ambiguity also in the name of the mass, what it signifieth and whether at this day there be any such indeed as the ancient fathers used, seeing that now there be neither catechists nor *poenitentes* to be sent away.[45]

Again, touching these words *the lively sacrifice of the church,* there is a doubt whether they are to be understood figuratively and sacramentally for the sacrament of the lively sacrifice (after which sort we deny it not to be in the Lord's supper) or properly and without any figure; after the which manner there was but one only sacrifice and that once offered, namely upon the altar of the cross. . . .

There is also a doubt in the word *propitiable,* whether it signify here that which taketh away sin or that which may be made available for the taking away of sin; that is to say, whether it is to be taken in the active or in the passive signification.

Now the falseness of the proposition, after the meaning of the schoolmen and the Roman Church and impiety in that sense which the words seem to import is this, that they, leaning to the foundation ⟨of⟩[46] their fond transubstantiation, would make the quick and lively body of Christ's flesh, united and knit to the divinity, to lurk under the accidents and outward shows of bread and wine; which is very false, as I have said afore. And they, building upon this foundation, do hold that the same body is offered unto God by the priest in his daily massings to put away the sins of the quick and the dead. Whereas by the Apostle to the Hebrews it is evident that there is but one oblation and one true and lively sacrifice of the church offered upon the altar of the cross, which was, is and shall be for ever the propitiation for the sins of the whole world, and where there is remission of the same there is (saith the Apostle) no more offering for sin.[47]

Syllogisms in Confirmation

1. Where there is no meet priest to offer a sacrifice propitiable, there can no such sacrifice be offered.

But there is no meet priest for that office, but Christ alone.

Ergo, such a sacrifice cannot be offered of the priests in their daily masses.

2. The office of offering is a great honour.

But no man ought to take unto himself this honour, but he

---

[45] A reference to the supposed derivation of the word "mass," that in the early church the catechumens and penitents were sent out (*missi*) before the celebration of the mass.
[46] Read *of* for *and* 1563.
[47] Heb. 10:18.

that is called thereto of God; and no man is called thereto but only Christ our Saviour.

Ergo, it followeth that no man but Christ alone can offer the same. That alone it is evident, for there are but two only orders of priesthood allowed in the word of God, namely the order of Aaron and the order of Melchizedek. But now the order of Aaron is come to an end, by reason that it was unprofitable and weak, and of the order of Melchizedek there is but one priest alone, even Christ the Lord, which hath a priesthood that cannot pass to any other.

3. That thing is in vain and to no effect, where no necessity is wherefore it is done.

But there is no such necessity to offer up any more sacrifice propitiatory for the quick and the dead, for Christ our Saviour did that fully and perfectly once for all.

Ergo, to do the same in the mass it is in vain.

4. After that eternal redemption is found and obtained, there needeth no more daily offering for the same.

But Christ coming an high bishop, etc., found and obtained for us eternal redemption.

Ergo, there needeth now no more daily oblation for the sins of the quick and the dead.

5. Without shedding of blood there is no remission of sins.

But in the mass there is no shedding of blood.

Ergo, in the mass there is no remission of sins: and so it followeth also that there is no propitiatory sacrifice.

6. In the mass the passion of Christ is not in verity, but in a mystery representing the same, yea, even there where the Lord's supper is duly ministered.

But where Christ suffereth not, there is he not offered in verity: for the Apostle saith, "Not that he might offer up himself oftentimes, for then must he have suffered oftentimes sith the beginning of the world." [48] Now where Christ is not offered, there is no propitiatory sacrifice.

Ergo, in the mass there is no propitiatory sacrifice. . . .

7. Where there is any sacrifice that can make the comers thereunto perfect, there ought men to cease from offering any more expiatory and propitiatory sacrifices.

But in the New Testament there is one only sacrifice now already long since offered which is able to make the comers thereto perfect for ever.

Ergo, in the new testament they ought to cease from offering any more propitiatory sacrifice. . . .

[48] Heb. 9:26.

[He quotes then Heb. 10:10, 12, 14 and 1:3; Col. 1:21-22; and I John 2:1-2, and continues:]

I know that all these places of the Scripture are eluded and avoided by two manner of subtle shifts. The one is by the distinction of the bloody and unbloody sacrifice, as though our unbloody sacrifice of the church were any other than the sacrifice of praise and thanksgiving, than a commemoration, a showing-forth and a sacramental representation of that one only bloody sacrifice offered up once for all. The other is by depraving and wresting the sayings of the ancient faithful fathers unto such a strange kind of sense as the fathers themselves indeed never meant. For what the meaning of the fathers was, it is evident by that which St. Augustine writeth in his epistle to Boniface [49] and in the eighty-third chapter of his ninth book against Faustus the Manichee,[50] besides many other places; likewise by Eusebius, Emissene, Cyprian, Chrysostom, Fulgentius, Bertram and others, which do wholly concord and agree together in this unity in the Lord, that the redemption, once made in verity for the salvation of man, continueth in full effect for ever, and worketh without ceasing unto the end of the world; that the sacrifice once offered cannot be consumed; that the Lord's death and passion is as effectual, the virtue of that blood once shed as fresh at this day for the washing away of sins as it was even the same day it flowed out of the blessed side of our Saviour; and finally that the whole substance of our sacrifice which is frequented of the church in the Lord's supper, consisteth in prayers, praise and giving of thanks and in remembering and showing forth of that sacrifice once offered upon the altar of the cross, that the same might continually be had in reverence by mystery, which once only and no more was offered for the price of our redemption. . . .

[The debate then began, as follows:]

Smith: . . . Me seemed you did in your supposition abuse the testimonies of Scripture concerning the ascension of Christ, to take away his presence in the sacrament, as though this were a strong argument to enforce your matter withal:
  Christ did ascend unto heaven.
  Ergo, he is not in the sacrament.
Now therefore I will go about to disprove this reason of yours.
  Christ's ascension is no let to his real presence in the sacrament.
  Ergo, you are deceived, whereas you do ground yourself upon those places.

[49] *Ep. clxxxv*, cap. 1 (*PL* 33.815).
[50] *Contra Faustum* xix.16 (not ix.83) (*PL* 42.356 f.).

Ridley: You import as though I had made a strong argument by Christ's going up into heaven. But howsoever mine argument is made, you collect it not rightly. For it doth not only stay upon his ascension, but both upon his ascension and his abiding there also.

Smith: Christ's going up into heaven and his abiding there hinder not his real presence in the sacrament.
Ergo, you are deceived.

Ridley: Of Christ's real presence there may be a double understanding. If you take the real presence of Christ according to the real and corporal substance which he took of the Virgin, that presence being in heaven cannot be on the earth also. But if you mean a real presence *secundum rem aliquam quae ad corpus Christi pertinent*—according to something that doth appertain to Christ's body—certes the ascension and abiding in heaven are no let at all to that presence. Wherefore Christ's body after that sort is here present to us in the Lord's supper; by grace, I say, as Epiphanius speaketh it.

Weston: I will cut off from henceforth all equivocation and doubt. For whensoever we speak of Christ's body, we mean that which he took of the Virgin.

Ridley: Christ's ascension and abiding in heaven cannot stand with this presence.

Smith: Christ appeared corporally and really on the earth, for all his ascension and continual abode in heaven until the day of doom.
Ergo, his ascension and abiding in heaven is no let to his real presence in the sacrament.

Ridley: Master doctor, this argument is nothing worth. I do not so straitly tie Christ up in heaven, that he may not come into the earth at his pleasure. For when he will, he may come down from heaven and be on the earth, as it liketh himself. Howbeit I do affirm that it is not possible for him to be both in heaven and earth at one time.

Smith: Mark, I pray you my masters, diligently, that be here, what he answereth. First he saith that the sitting of Christ at the right hand of his Father is a let to the real presence of his body in the sacrament, and then afterward he flieth from it again.

Ridley: I would not have you think that I do imagine or dream upon any such manner of sitting as these men here sit in the school.

Smith: Ergo, it is lawful for Christ then to be here present on the earth when he will himself.

Ridley: Yea, when he will, it is lawful indeed.

Smith: Ergo, his ascending into heaven doth not restrain his real presence in the sacrament.

Ridley: I do not gainsay but that it is lawful for him to appear on the earth when he will. But prove you that he will.

Smith: Then your answer dependeth upon the will of Christ, I perceive. Wherefore I will join again with you in this short argument:

Christ, albeit he doth alway abide in heaven after his ascension, was seen really and corporally of them.

Ergo, notwithstanding his ascension and continual sitting at the right hand of the Father, he may be really and corporally in the sacrament.

Ridley: If the notaries should so record your argument as you have framed it, you peradventure would be ashamed thereof hereafter.

Smith: Christ after his ascension was seen really and corporally upon the earth.

Ergo, notwithstanding his ascension and abiding with his Father, he may be corporally in the sacrament.

Ridley: I grant the antecedent, but I deny the consequence. . . .

Smith: Christ after his ascension was seen really and corporally on earth, albeit he do abide in heaven continually.

Ergo, notwithstanding his ascension and continual abiding at the right hand of the Father, he may be really and corporally on the earth.

Ridley: Let us first agree about the continual sitting at the right hand of the Father.

Smith: Doth he so sit at the right hand of his Father, that he doth never forsake the same?

Ridley: Nay, I do not bind Christ in heaven so straitly. I see you go about to craft with your equivocations. Such equivocations are to be distinguished. If you mean by his sitting in heaven, to reign with his Father, he may be both in heaven and also in earth. But if ye understand his sitting to be after a corporal manner of sitting, so he is always permanent in heaven. For Christ to be corporally here on earth, when corporally he is resident in heaven, is clean contrary to the holy Scriptures; as Augustine saith: "The body of Christ is in heaven, but his truth is dispersed in every place." [51] Now, if continually he abide in heaven after the manner of his corporal presence, then his perpetual abiding there stoppeth or letteth that the same corporal presence of him cannot be in the sacrament.

[51] *In Ioan. Ev.*, Tract. XXX.1. (*PL* 35.1632).

[This argument is pursued at length between the disputants, with considerable recourse to the fathers and debate as to their actual intentions. In the course of it occurs the following passage between the contestants and the remarkable statement by Ridley:]

Curtop: Reverend sir, I will prove and declare that the body of Christ is truly and really in the eucharist. And whereas the holy fathers both of the west and east church have written both many things and no less manifest of the same matter, yet I will bring forth only Chrysostom. The place is in cap. x. Corinth. i. Hom. xxiv.: [52]

That which is in the cup is the same that flowed from the side of Christ.
But his true and pure blood did flow from the side of Christ.
Ergo, his true and pure blood is in the cup.

Ridley: It is his true blood which is in the chalice, I grant, and the same which sprang from the side of Christ. But how? It is blood indeed, but not after the same manner after which manner it sprang from his side. For here is the blood, but by the way of sacrament. Again I say, like as the bread of the sacrament and of thanksgiving is called the body of Christ given for us, so the cup of the Lord is called the blood which sprang from the side of Christ. But that sacramental bread is called the body, because it is the sacrament of his body. Likewise the cup is called the blood also, which flowed out of Christ's side, because it is the sacrament of that blood which flowed out of his side, instituted of the Lord himself for our singular commodity, namely, for our spiritual nourishment; like as baptism is ordained in water to our spiritual regeneration.

Curtop: The sacrament of the blood is not the blood.
Ridley: The sacrament of the blood is the blood; and that is attributed to the sacrament which is spoken of the thing of the sacrament.

Here Weston repeateth Curtop's argument in English.

Weston: That which is in the chalice is the same which streamed out of Christ's side.
But there came out very blood.
Ergo, there is very blood in the chalice.

Ridley: The blood of Christ is in the chalice indeed, but not in real presence, but by grace and in a sacrament.
Weston: Why, then we are glad we have blood in the chalice.
Ridley: It is true. But by grace and in a sacrament.

---

[52] *In Ep. I ad Corinthios,* Hom. XXIV (*PG* 61.199-200).

Hugh Latimer

A SERMON ON THE
LORD'S PRAYER

Hugh Latimer: A Sermon on the Lord's Prayer

INTRODUCTION

LATIMER SPENT THE AUTUMN AND WINTER MONTHS (PERHAPS until the end of February) of 1552–1553 in Lincolnshire. For much, possibly all, of this time he was the guest of the Dowager Duchess of Suffolk at Grimsthorpe Castle, between Bourne and Grantham, in Lincolnshire. According to the original editor of his sermons, he preached in Grimsthorpe Castle the seven sermons on the Lord's Prayer, and those on Christmas Day, St. Stephen's Day, St. John the Evangelist's Day, and Twelfth Day (i.e., Epiphany). The ten sermons preached during October, November, and December are assigned to Lincolnshire, but not specifically to Grimsthorpe. Those on the five Sundays after the Epiphany, Septuagesima, and Sexagesima seem to follow on from the Christmas sermons at Grimsthorpe.

For congregation he had the duchess herself,[1] her household, and, as he put it, "other that be willing to hear,"[2] presumably villagers from Edenham and farther afield, and a neighboring landowner or two. The duchess was one of those strong-willed women that sixteenth-century England seemed to breed so easily. Her mother had come to England with Katharine of Aragon, to whom she was related. She herself was married young to her guardian, the already three times married Charles Brandon, Duke of Suffolk. She was left a widow after nine years, in 1545, and then lost both her sons in one day in 1551. It was about the time of Latimer's visit to Grimsthorpe that she married her second husband, Richard Bertie. Thomas Fuller described her as "a lady of a sharp wit and sure hand to thrust it home and make it pierce when she pleased." She was, indeed, insufferably insolent to

[1] PS, I.319.   [2] PS, I.326.

Stephen Gardiner and paid dearly for it when he was back in power under Mary. She and her husband had to flee the country and for several years lived in some danger and in real poverty on the Continent.

As for Latimer himself, he was now an old man "above three score and seven years of age," and certainly feeling it. Not long after resigning his bishopric in July, 1539, "he was almost slain, but sore bruised with the fall of a tree." [3] In the fourth sermon on the Lord's Prayer he says, "I intend not to tarry long, for I am not very well at ease this morning; therefore I will make it short." [4] (This does not prevent him, however, from preaching for about an hour.) Cambridge, his days as a fellow of Clare, the preaching in St. Edward's Church and the Austin Friars, are now far behind him. So too the troublesome and frustrating years as Bishop of Worcester. It is thirteen years since he danced for joy at resigning. Since the accession of Edward VI to the throne, the sun has shone on him. He has lived chiefly with Thomas Cranmer and has been busy as a preacher, usually preaching twice a Sunday (according to Foxe [5]), though only a few of his sermons are extant.

He seems to have preached extemporarily, and we are therefore dependent upon others for taking his sermons down at the time of preaching. Whether this was by short or long hand is not said. But both his scribes confess their own shortcomings. Thus Thomas Some in his dedicatory preface to the seven sermons preached in Lent, 1549, before the king, says: "I have gathered, writ, and brought to light, the famous Friday sermons of Master Hugh Latimer. . . . And let no man be grieved though it be not so exactly done as he did speak it; for in very deed I am not able so to do, to write word for word as he did speak: that passeth my capacity, though I had twenty men's wits, and no fewer hands to write withal." [6] The other scribe was Augustine Bernher. He is usually referred to as Latimer's servant, but we shall be far wide of the mark if we think of him as a valet. He was a not unlearned man in his own right, and in one respect surpassed his master, in that he knew some Hebrew, and probably more Greek too. After the restoration of the Reformed Church in England, he became vicar of Southam in Warwickshire. It is to be presumed that he took down the sermons at Grimsthorpe, for although he says in the Dedication only, "I thought it good . . . to put forth these sermons here following in print" [7] and "I have set forth these sermons," [8] a colophon declares "Exceptae per me, Augustinum

[3] Foxe, 7.463.
[4] PS, I.370.
[5] Foxe, 7.463.
[6] PS, I.82.
[7] PS, I.319.
[8] PS, I.324.

Bernerum, Helvetium"[9] and since no selection or collection is involved, *exceptae* means, in this context, "gathered as they were spoken." The sermon on October 28, 1552, is ascribed by the printer John Day to "Augustine Bernher hys servaunt," in 1571. The remaining Lincolnshire sermons mention Bernher in the title: "Collected and gathered by Augustine Bernherre an Helvetian: and albeit not so fully and perfectly gathered as they were uttered; yet nevertheles truly."[10]

This brings up the question of the authenticity of the sermons. Thomas Some distinctly admits that his transcriptions were neither complete nor accurate. Bernher admits only that his were not complete but claims accuracy for them as far as they go. If we accept his plea, we can, at any rate, say that we have the *ipsissima verba* of Latimer in the Sermons of 1552–1553. More than this cannot be said at the moment; it would need a very careful examination of Latimer's style and thought to settle their authenticity. We need not be too quick despairers, however. If Some and Bernher were responsible for these sermons to any great degree, they were men of genius and deserve a major place in English literature.

Latimer is perhaps the strangest figure among all the English Reformers. If we take his sermons at their face value, he emerges as one of the old brigade, a good old-fashioned, no-nonsense Englishman. A countryman, and born in a farmhouse; knowledgeable about cattle and horses, about the crooked ways of country markets, about the lives of common people, always with a wise country saw on his lips. A veritable Mr. Hardcastle in hating novelties and loving the past. Does he tell the story about St. Antony and the cobbler? Then he cannot avoid telling us that cobblers really were cobblers in the good old days: "I warrant you, he did not so many false stitches as cobblers do nowadays."[11] Everything that he touches becomes Old English. Even his exposition of the Bible transforms it from its Eastern setting to the towns and countryside of England. Like the painters of his day, he sees the people of the Bible as his contemporaries. Mary was a poor woman and wore shabby clothes; she could not afford a farthingale, and wouldn't have wasted her money on one in any case: "for she used no such superfluities as our fine damsels do nowadays."[12] Jairus is churchwarden of one of the city churches, and Capernaum "was such a town as Bristol or Coventry is."[13] It is all so artless and homely that we wonder what this latter-day friar is

[9] PS, I.446.
[10] PS, I.455.
[11] PS, I.393.
[12] PS, II.108.
[13] PS, I.533.

doing among the gospelers. It does not surprise us that he held on to the doctrine of transubstantiation until the late fifteen forties.

But is he quite so artless? C. S. Lewis doubted whether many of his best touches were not calculated. He was right to doubt. But his complete picture of Latimer as no "humanist" but a clever high-pressure evangelist is, I believe, quite wrong.[14] Foxe gives us a hint that we should not neglect: "Not to speak of here his indefatigable travail and diligence in his own private studies, who, notwithstanding both his years and other pains in preaching, every morning ordinarily, winter and summer about two of the clock in the morning was at his book most diligently."[15] If we follow up this clue and start to look for learning in Latimer, the artless old countryman steeped in the only version of the Bible that he knew, the Vulgate, becomes considerably less convincing. How many of his anecdotes and his proverbs come not from Leicestershire but from ancient Greece and Rome, perhaps by way of Erasmus' *Adagia*? He said at his trial that he knew no Greek.[16] But this does not prevent his telling his congregation that he had examined the Greek of some particular text or occasionally mentioning a Greek word. Moreover, later in the same trial, on being told to speak in Latin, he said, "I cannot speak Latin so long and so largely."[17] This is hard to accept, and we can sympathize with one of his examiners retorting to his "I understand you not" with "I know your learning well enough, and how subtle ye be."[18] And when we come to the Latin version of the Bible that he is continually quoting, we find that this is not the Vulgate at all, but comes from divers sources. If we examine the thirty Latin quotations in the present sermon, we find that not one of them agrees precisely with the Vulgate. It is true that they do not agree precisely with any other version that I have examined, but they have closer affinities with some than with others. The first five will serve as a sample:

I Tim. 2:1. Latimer: *pro regibus et qui in sublimitate*
Vulgate: *pro regibus et omnibus qui in sublimitate sunt*
Pellicanus: *pro regibus et omnibus qui in sublimitate constituti sunt*

---

[14] *English Literature in the Sixteenth Century* (Oxford, 1954), pp. 192–194.
[15] Foxe, 7.463.
[16] PS, II.263.
[17] PS, II.268.
[18] PS, II.269.

A SERMON ON THE LORD'S PRAYER 327

I Tim. 2:2.	Latimer:	*ut placidam et quietam vitam agamus*
	Vulgate:	*ut quietam et tranquillam vitam agamus*
	Erasmus, 1535:	*ut placidam ac quietam vitam degamus*
Luke 16:15.	Latimer:	*Quod excelsum est hominibus, abominabile est coram deo*
	Vulgate:	*quod hominibus altum est, abominatio est ante Deum*
	Erasmus, 1535:	*quod hominibus excelsum est, abominandum est coram deo*
Heb. 13:4.	Latimer:	*et adulteros et fornicatores iudicabit dominus*
	Vulgate:	*fornicatores enim et adulteros iudicabit deus*
	Erasmus, 1535:	*Scortatores autem et adulteros iudicabit deus*
I Cor. 7:32.	Latimer:	*volo vos absque solicitudine esse*
	Vulgate:	*volo autem vos sine solicitudine esse*
	Erasmus, 1535:	*velim vos absque solicitudine esse*

It is safe to say that Latimer, although he must have known his Vulgate intimately, prefers the modern renderings, that he makes use of Erasmus' version and the commentaries of Pellicanus [19] and of Münster or Vatablus. As this is only in five examples we might expect a fairly wide range of reading to be revealed by an examination of all his Bible quotations.

Yet it would be foolish to suggest that Latimer was a great scholar or that he was in the forefront of sixteenth-century Biblical studies. Far from it. He warbled his native wood-notes wild, undoubtedly; but he knew how to use them to the best effect and he mingled them with considerable bookishness. We should not forget that if he spent his first fifteen years in rural Leicestershire, the next twenty-five were passed in Cambridge.

C. S. Lewis seems to me to be equally astray on Latimer's theology. "Latimer assents, indeed, to the doctrine of justification by faith, but he is no theologian; some of his apparent tergiversations may perhaps result from the bewilderment (even the impatience) of a 'plain man' entangled in matters above his capacity.

---

[19] The edition of Pelicanus in the Cambridge University Library bears the autograph "H. latymere" at the head of the title page.

Whatever he may say (when he remembers) about faith, he is really so interested in works that not only a Papist but a Pelagian or even a good pagan could read nine-tenths of his sermons without a qualm!" [20] This is only a surface judgment. Certainly a good many of Latimer's pages are given up to anecdotes and some to political chidings and forebodings. If we are looking for theological dissertations in him, we shall be disappointed. But he must be judged according to his purpose and method. Compared with Luther's preaching or Calvin's, or with the Homilies, his sermons might be called nondoctrinal. But this is not to say that they are not based on a very definite and strongly held theology. The present sermon is a good example. There are hardly any technical theological terms, and no doctrinal arguments. His feet are firmly on the ground, his language simple and direct, his thought concrete. He is concerned about such things as peace being better than war, family life better than monasteries, about servants and masters, distribution of wealth, cheating in business, and so on. But none of these is treated secularly; always it is the activity of God in the world, the relationship of God to man, of man to God, that is the issue. He views it all *sub specie aeternitatis*. When the need and the text demands, he will show his doctrine. If I were to put forward some quotations to prove the point, it would be suspected that I had discovered half a dozen grains of corn in a heap of chaff. Read therefore the Sermon of the Plough, or the Seventh before King Edward, or the Sermon on St. Stephen's Day at Grimsthorpe. These alone are sufficient to convince us that Latimer had a very sound grasp of Reformation theology. It may be a measure of his success as a preacher that he has managed to deceive the scholars. We might take as the motive force of his preaching one of his most splendid sayings: "Again, *Deus vult omnes homines salvos fieri,* God will have all men to be saved. He excepts not the Englishmen here, nor yet expressly nameth them; and yet I am as sure that this realm of England, by this gathering, is allowed to hear God's word, as though Christ had said a thousand times, 'Go preach to Englishmen: I will that Englishmen be saved.'" [21] Latimer harnesses his powers as a surpassing orator and a moderate scholar and theologian to obeying this command.

[20] C. S. Lewis, *op. cit.,* p. 192.   [21] PS, I.234.

BIBLIOGRAPHY

The sermons on the Lord's Prayer were first printed in 1562. Unfortunately the first title page of both the copies in Cambridge University Library is missing. The second part contains the sermons preached before Edward VI in 1549 and those at Stamford. The whole was printed by John Daye in 1562.

The colophon to the sermons on the Lord's Prayer runs:
Here endeth the sermons upon the Lordes/ praier made by the right reuerend father in god, Mai/ster Doctour Latymer, before the righte vertuous/ and honorable Lady Katherine Duchesse of/ Suffolke, at Grymstorpe, the yere of/ our Lord. 1552./ Exceptae per me Augustinum Bernerum Heluetium.
This provides the text for the present sermon.

Parker Society:
Sermons by Hugh Latimer, sometime Bishop of Worcester, Martyr, 1555. Edited for the Parker Society by the Rev. George Elwes Corrie, B.D. Cambridge, 1844.
Sermons and Remains of Hugh Latimer . . . Edited . . . by the Rev. George Elwes Corrie, B.D. Cambridge, 1845.
The Sermons on the Lord's Prayer come in the former volume, pp. 311 ff.

Secondary Works:
R. Demaus, *Hugh Latimer: A Biography.* London, 1923.
H. S. Darby, *Hugh Latimer.* London, 1953.
A. G. Chester, *Hugh Latimer, Apostle to the English.* University of Pennsylvania Press, 1954.
C. M. Gray, *Hugh Latimer and the Sixteenth Century: An Essay in Interpretation.* Harvard University Press, 1950.
G. R. Owst, *Literature and Pulpit in Medieval England: A Neglected Chapter in the History of English Letters and of the English People* (Oxford, 1961), pp. 98 ff.

J. W. Blench, *Preaching in England in the Late Fifteenth and Sixteenth Centuries: A Study of English Sermons 1450–c.1600.* Oxford, 1964.

Bernhard Schulze, *Latimers Beredsamkeit in der Entwickelung der kirchlichen Prosa seit den Mystikern.* Münster, 1924.

Hugh Latimer: A Sermon on the Lord's Prayer

THE TEXT

Panem nostrum quotidianum da nobis hodie. Give us this day our daily bread. Every word is to be considered, for they have their importance. This word *bread* signifieth all manner of sustenance for the preservation of this life: all things whereby man should live are contained in this word Bread.

You must remember what I said by that petition, "Hallowed be thy name."[22] There we pray unto God that he will give us grace to live so, that we may with all our conversations and doings hallow and sanctify him, according as his word telleth us. Now forasmuch as the preaching of God's Word is most necessary to bring us into this hallowing, we pray in the same petition for the office of preaching. For the sanctifying of the name of God cannot be, except the office of preaching be maintained, and his Word be preached and known; therefore in the same petition, when I say, *Sanctificetur,* "Hallowed be thy name," I pray that his Word may be spread abroad and known, through which cometh sanctifying.

So likewise in this petition, *Give us this day our daily bread,* we pray for all those things which be necessary and requisite to the sustenance of our souls and bodies. Now the first and principal thing that we have need of in this life is the magistrates: without a magistrate we should never live well and quietly. Then it is necessary and most needful to pray unto God for them, that the people may have rest, and apply their business, every man in his calling; the husbandman in tilling and ploughing, the artificer in his business. For you must ever consider, that where war is, there be all discommodities; no man can do his duty according

[22] See *Sermons,* pp. 344 ff.

unto his calling, as it appeareth now in Germany, the Emperor and the French king being at controversy.[23] I warrant you, there is little rest or quietness. Therefore in this petition we pray unto God for our magistrates, that they may rule and govern this realm well and godly, and keep us from invasions of aliants [24] and strangers, and to execute justice, and punish malefactors: and this is so requisite, that we cannot live without it. Therefore when we say, "Give us this day our daily bread," we pray for the king, his counsellors, and all his officers. But not every man that saith these words understandeth so much. For it is obscurely included, so that none perceive it but those which earnestly and diligently consider the same. But St. Paul he expresseth it with more words plainly, saying, "I exhort you to make supplications and prayers for all men, but specially *pro regibus et qui in sublimitate constituti sunt,* for the kings and for those which be aloft." Whereto? *Ut placidam et quietam vitam agamus,* "That we may live godly and quietly, in all honesty and godliness." [25] And when I pray for them, I pray for myself. For I pray for them that they may rule so, that I and all men may live quietly and at rest. And to this end we desire a quiet life, that we may the better serve God, hear his Word, and live after it.

For in the rebels' time,[26] I pray you, what godliness was shewed amongst them? They went so far (as it was told) that they defiled other men's wives. What godliness was this? In what estate, think you, were those faithful subjects which at the same time were amongst them? They had sorrow enough, I warrant you. So it appeareth, that where war is, there is right godliness banished and gone. Therefore to pray for a quiet life, that is as much as to pray for a godly life, that we may serve God in our calling, and get our livings uprightly. So it appeareth that praying for magistrates is as much as to pray for ourselves.

They that be children, and live under the rule of their parents, or have tutors, they pray in this petition for their parents and tutors; for they be necessary for their bringing up. And God will accept their prayer as well as theirs which be of age. For God hath no respect of persons; he is as ready to hear the youngest as the oldest. Therefore let them be brought up in godliness, let them know God. Let parents and tutors do their duties to bring

---

[23] In 1552 the culmination of the long struggle between the Habsburg and the Valois dynasties (now represented by the Emperor Charles V and Henry II of France) was under way.
[24] Aliens.
[25] I Tim. 2:1–2.
[26] Presumably a reference to the uprisings in Cornwall and Norfolk in opposition to the 1549 Book of Common Prayer.

them up so, that as soon as their age serveth, they may taste and savour God. Let them fear God in the beginning, and so they shall do also when they be old. Because I speak here of orphans, I shall exhort you to be pitiful unto them; for it is a thing that pleaseth God, as St. James witnesseth, saying, *Religio pura*, &c., "Pure religion." [27]

It is a common speech amongst the people and much used, that they say, "All religious houses [28] are pulled down": which is a very peevish saying, and not true, for they are not pulled down. That man and that woman that live together godly and quietly, doing the works of their vocation, and fear God, hear his Word and keep it; that same is a religious house, that is, that house that pleaseth God. For religion, pure religion (I say), standeth not in wearing of a monk's cowl, but in righteousness, justice, and well-doing, and, as St. James saith,[29] in visiting the orphans, and widows, that lack their husbands, orphans that lack their parents; to help them when they be poor, to speak for them when they be oppressed: herein standeth true religion, God's religion, I say. The other which was used was an unreligious life, yea rather, an hypocrisy. There is a text in Scripture, I never read it but I remember these religious houses: *Estque recta homini via, cujus tamen postremum iter est ad mortem;* "There is a way, which way seemed to men to be good, whose end is eternal perdition." [30] When the end is naught, all is naught. So were these monks' houses, these religious houses. There were many people, specially widows, which would give over housekeeping, and go to such houses, when they might have done much good in maintaining of servants, and relieving of poor people; but they went their ways. What a madness was that? Again, how much cause we have to thank God, that we know what is true religion; that God hath revealed unto us the deceitfulness of those monks, which had a goodly shew before the world of great holiness, but they were naught within. Therefore Scripture saith, *Quod excelsum est hominibus, abominabile est coram Deo;* "That which is highly esteemed before men is abominable before God." [31] Therefore that man and woman that live in the fear of God are much better than their houses were.

I read once a story of a holy man, some say it was St. Anthony,[32]

---

[27] James 1:27.
[28] Monasteries.
[29] James 1:27.
[30] Prov. 14:12.
[31] Luke 16:15.
[32] *Vitae Patrum*, Lib. III.130 (*PL* 73.785) and repeated Lib. VII, cap. xv.2 (*PL* 73.1038).

which had been a long season in the wilderness, eating nor drinking no thing but bread and water: at the length he thought himself so holy, that there should be nobody like unto him. Therefore he desired of God to know who should be his fellow in heaven. God made him answer, and commanded him to go to Alexandria; there he should find a cobbler which should be his fellow in heaven. Now he went thither and sought him out, and fell in acquaintance with him, and tarried with him three or four days to see his conversation. In the morning his wife and he prayed together; then they went to their business, he in his shop, and she about her housewifery. At dinner time they had bread and cheese, wherewith they were well content, and took it thankfully. Their children were well taught to fear God, and to say their Pater noster, and the Creed, and the Ten Commandments; [33] and so he spent his time in doing his duty truly. I warrant you, he did not so many false stitches as cobblers do nowadays. St. Anthony perceiving that, came to knowledge of himself, and laid away all pride and presumption. By this ensample you may learn that honest conversation and godly living is much regarded before God; insomuch that this poor cobbler, doing his duty diligently, was made St. Anthony's fellow. So it appeareth that we be not destituted of religious houses: those which apply their business uprightly and hear God's Word, they shall be St. Anthony's fellows, that is to say, they shall be numbered amongst the children of God.

Further, in this petition the man and wife pray one for the other. For one is a help unto the other, and so necessary the one to the other. Therefore they pray one for the other, that God will spare them their lives, to live together quietly and godly, according to his ordinance and institution; and this is good and needful. As for such as be not married, you shall know that I do not so much praise marriage, that I should think that single life is naught; as I have heard some which will scant allow single life. They think in their hearts that all those which be not married be naught: therefore they have a common saying amongst them, "What!" say they, "they be made of such metal as we be made of," thinking them to be naught in their living; which suspicions are damnable afore God. For we know not what gifts God hath given unto them; therefore we cannot with good conscience condemn them or judge them. Truth it is, "marriage is good and honourable amongst all men," as St. Paul witnesseth; *Et adulteros et fornicatores iudicabit Dominus,* "And the Lord shall and will

---

[33] I.e., they learned their Catechism from the Prayer Book, like good Anglicans, or perhaps were brought up on one of the Primers.

judge," that is, condemn, "adulterers and whoremongers"; [34] but not those which live in single life. When thou livest in lechery, or art a whore or whoremonger, then thou shalt be damned: but when thou livest godly and honestly in single life, it is well and allowable afore God; yea, and better than marriage. For St. Paul saith, *Volo vos absque solicitudine esse,* "I will have you to be without carefulness," that is, unmarried; and sheweth the commodities, saying, "They that be unmarried set their minds upon God, how to please him, and to live after his commandments. But as for the other, the man is careful how to please his wife; and again, the woman how to please her husband." [35] And this is St. Paul's saying of the one as well as of the other. Therefore I will wish you not to condemn single life, but take one with the other; like as St. Paul teacheth us; not so extol the one, that we should condemn the other. For St. Paul praiseth as well single life as marriage; yea, and more too. For those that be single have more liberties to pray and to serve God than the other: for they that be married have much trouble and afflictions in their bodies. This I speak, because I hear that some there be which condemn single life. I would have them to know that matrimony is good, godly, and allowable unto all men: yet for all that, the single life ought not to be despised or condemned, seeing that Scripture alloweth it; yea, and he affirmeth that it is better than matrimony, if it be clean without sin and offence.

Further, we pray here in this petition for good servants, that God will send unto us good, faithful, and trusty servants; for they are necessary for this bodily life, that our business may be done: and those which live in single life have more need of good trusty servants than those which are married. Those which are married can better oversee their servants. For when the man is from home, at the least the wife overseeth them, and keepeth them in good order. For I tell you, servants must be overseen and looked to: if they be not overseen, what be they? It is a great gift of God to have a good servant. For the most part of servants are but eye-servants; when their master is gone, they leave off from their labour, and play the sluggards: but such servants do contrary unto God's commandment, and shall be damned in hell for their slothfulness, except they repent. Therefore, I say, those that be unmarried have more need of good servants than those which be married; for one of them at the least may always oversee the family. For, as I told you before, the most part of servants be eye-servants; they be nothing when they be not overseen. There was

[34] Heb. 13:4.   [35] I Cor. 7:32 f.

once a fellow asked a philosopher a question,[36] saying, *Quomodo saginatur equus?* "How is an horse made fat?" The philosopher made answer, saying, *Oculo domini,* "With his master's eye," not meaning that the horse should be fed with his master's eye, but that the master should oversee the horse, and take heed to the horse-keeper, that the horse might be well fed. For when a man rideth by the way and cometh to his inn and giveth unto the hostler his horse to walk and so he himself sitteth at the table and maketh good cheer and forgetteth his horse, the hostler cometh and saith, "Sir, how much bread [37] shall I give unto your horse?" He saith, "Give him two-penny worth." [38] I warrant you, this horse shall never be fat. Therefore a man should not say to the hostler, "Go, give him"; but he should see himself that the horse have it. In like manner, those that have servants must not only command them what they shall do, but they must see that it be done: they must be present, or else it shall never be done. One other man asked that same philosopher this question,[39] saying, "What dung is it that maketh a man's land most fruitful in bringing forth much corn?" "Marry," said he, "*vestigia domini,* the owner's footsteps." Not meaning that the master should come and walk up and down and tread the ground; but he would have him to come and oversee the servants' tilling of the ground, commanding them to do it diligently, and so to look himself upon their work: this shall be the best dung, saith the philosopher. Therefore never trust servants, except you may be assured of their diligence. For I tell you truly, I can come nowhere but I hear masters complaining of their servants. I think verily, they fear not God, they consider not their duties. Well, I will burthen them with this one text of Scripture, and then go forward in my matters. The prophet Jeremy saith, *Maledictus qui facit opus Domini negligenter.* Another translation hath *fraudulenter,* but it is one in effect: "Cursed be he," saith the prophet Jeremy, "that doth the work of the Lord negligently or fraudulently," [40] take which you will.

It is no light matter that God pronounceth them to be cursed. But what is "cursed"? What is it? Cursed is as much to say as, it

---

[36] This and the following proverb on the master's footsteps are common to many countries and are still sometimes heard in England. In antiquity they occur not infrequently (e.g., in Pliny and Plutarch). Latimer perhaps adapts them from Aristotle, *Oeconomica* I.vi.3.
[37] Food in general.
[38] 1562: ii d.
[39] See n. 36.
[40] Jer. 48:10. Vulg.: *fraudulenter.* LXX, Vatablus, Münster: *negligenter.*

shall not go well with them; they shall have no luck; my face shall be against them. Is not this a great thing? Truly, consider it as you list, but it is no light matter to be cursed of God, which ruleth heaven and earth. And though the prophet speaketh these words of warriors going to war, yet it may be spoken of all servants, yea, of all estates, but specially of servants. For St. Paul saith, *Domino Christo servitis:* "You servants," saith he, "you serve the Lord Christ, it is his work." [41] Then, when it is the Lord's work, take heed how you do it; for cursed is he that doth it negligently. But where is such a servant as Jacob was to Laban? How painful was he! How careful for his master's profit! Insomuch that when somewhat perished, he restored it again of his own.[42] And where is such a servant as Eleazer was to Abraham his master? What a journey had he! How careful he was, and when he came to his journey's end, he would neither eat nor drink afore he had done his master's message; [43] so that all his mind was given only to serve his master, and to do according to his commandments: insomuch that he would neither eat nor drink till he had done according to his master's will. Much like to our Saviour's saying, *Cibus meus est ut faciam voluntatem ejus qui misit me;* "This is my meat, to do the will of him that sent me." [44] I pray you servants, mark this Eleazer well; consider all the circumstances of his diligent and faithful service, and follow it: else if you follow it not, you read it to your own condemnation. Likewise consider the true service which Joseph (that godly young man) did unto his master Potiphar, lieutenant of the Tower; [45] how faithfully he served without any guile or fraud: [46] therefore God promoted him so, that he was made afterwards the ruler over all Egypt.

Likewise consider how faithful Daniel was in serving King Darius.[47] Alack, that you servants be stubborn-hearted, and will not consider this! You will not remember that your service is the work of the Lord; you will not consider that the curse of God hangeth upon your heads for your slothfulness and negligence. Take heed, therefore, and look to your duties.

Now further, whosoever prayeth this prayer with a good faithful heart, as he ought to do, he prayeth for all ploughmen and hus-

[41] Col. 3:24.
[42] Gen. 31:39.
[43] Gen. 24:33.
[44] John 4:34.
[45] I.e., of the Tower of London. A pleasant example of Latimer's transmutation of the Bible world into his own society.
[46] Gen. 39:1–6.
[47] Dan. 6:4.

bandmen, that God will prosper and increase their labour. For except he give the increase, all their labour and travail is lost. Therefore it is needful to pray for them, that God may send his benediction by their labour; for without corn and such manner of sustenance we cannot live. And in that prayer we include all artificers; for through their labours God giveth us many commodities which we could not lack. We pray also for wholesome air. Item, we pray for seasonable weather. When we have too much rain, we pray for fair weather: again, when we lack rain, we pray that God will send rain. And in that prayer we pray for our cattle, that God will preserve them to our use from all diseases: for without cattle we cannot live; we cannot till the ground, nor have meat: therefore we include them in our prayer too. . . .

And here we be admonished of our estate and condition, what we be, namely, beggars. For we ask bread: of whom? Marry, of God. What are we then? Marry, beggars: the greatest lords and ladies in England are but beggars afore God. Seeing then that we all are but beggars, why should we then disdain and despise poor men? Let us therefore consider that we be but beggars; let us pull down our stomachs.[48] For if we consider the matter well, we are like as they be afore God: for St. Paul saith, *Quid habes quod non accepisti?* "What hast thou that thou hast not received of God?"[49] Thou art but a beggar, whatsoever thou art: and though there be some very rich and have great abundance, of whom have they it? Of God. What saith he, that rich man? He saith, "Our Father, which art in heaven, give us this day our daily bread." Then he is a beggar afore God as well as the poorest man. Further, how continueth the rich man in his riches? Who made him rich? Marry, God. For it is written, *Benedictio Dei facit divitem,* "The blessings of God maketh rich."[50] Except God bless, it standeth to no effect: for it is written, *Comedent et non saturabuntur;* "They shall eat, but yet never be satisfied."[51] Eat as much as you will, except God feed you, you shall never be full. So likewise, as rich as a man is, yet he cannot augment his riches, nor keep that he hath, except God be with him, except he bless him. Therefore let us not be proud, for we be beggars the best of us.

Note here that our Saviour biddeth us to say, *Us*. This *Us* lappeth in all other men with my prayer; for every one of us prayeth for another. When I say, "Give us this day our daily bread," I pray not for myself only (if I ask as he biddeth me) but I pray for all others. Wherefore say I not, "Our Father, give me

[48] Pride.
[49] I Cor. 4:7.
[50] Prov. 10:22.
[51] Isa. 9:20.

this day my daily bread"? For because God is not my God alone, he is a common God. And here we be admonished to be friendly, loving and charitable one to another: for what God giveth, I cannot say, "This is my own"; but I must say, "This is ours." For the rich man cannot say, "This is mine alone, God hath given it unto me for my own use." Nor yet hath the poor man any title unto it, to take it away from him. No, the poor man may not do so; for when he doth so, he is a thief afore God and man. But yet the poor man hath title to the rich man's goods, so that the rich man ought to let the poor man have part of his riches to help and to comfort him withal. Therefore when God sendeth unto me much, it is not mine, but *Ours;* it is not given unto me alone, but I must help my poor neighbours withal.

But here I must ask you rich men a question. How chanceth it you have your riches? "We have them of God," you will say. But by what means have you them? "By prayer," you will say. "We pray for them unto God, and he giveth us the same." Very well. But I pray you tell me, what do other men which are not rich? Pray they not as well as you do? "Yes," you must say; for you cannot deny it. Then it appeareth that you have your riches not through your own prayers only, but other men help you to pray for them: for they say as well, "Our Father, give us this day our daily bread," as you do; and peradventure they be better than you be, and God heareth their prayer sooner than yours. And so it appeareth most manifestly, that you obtain your riches of God, not only through your own prayer, but through other men's too: other men help you to get them at God's hand. Then it followeth, that seeing you get not your riches alone through your own prayer, but through the poor man's prayer, it is meet that the poor man should have part of them; and you ought to relieve his necessity and poverty. But what meaneth God by this inequality, that he giveth to some an hundred pound, unto this man five thousand pound, unto this man in a manner nothing at all? What meaneth he by this inequality? Here he meaneth, that the rich ought to distribute his riches abroad amongst the poor: for the rich man is but God's officer, God's treasurer: he ought to distribute them according unto his Lord God's commandment. If every man were rich, then no man would do any thing: therefore God maketh some rich and some poor. Again, that the rich may have where to exercise his charity, God made some rich and some poor: the poor he sendeth unto the rich to desire of him in God's name help and aid. Therefore, you rich men, when there cometh a poor man unto you, desiring your help, think none otherwise but God hath sent him unto you; and remember that thy riches be not thy own, but thou art but a steward over them. If thou wilt not do it, then cometh in St. John, which saith: "He that hath the substance of this world, and seeth his brother lack, and helpeth him not, how remaineth the love of God in him?" [52] He speaketh not of them that have it not, but of them that have it: that same man loveth not God, if he help not his neighbour, having wherewith to do it. This is a sore and hard word. There be many which say with their mouth, they love God: and if a man should ask here this multitude, whether they love God or no, they would say, "Yes, God forbid else!" But if you consider their unmercifulness unto the poor, you shall see, as St. John said, "The love of God is not within them." Therefore, you rich men, ever consider of whom you have your riches: be it a thousand pound, yet you fetch it out of this petition. For this petition, "Give us this day our daily bread," is God's storehouse, God's treasure-house: here lieth all his provision, and here you fetch it. But ever have in remembrance that this is a common prayer: a poor man prayeth as well as thou, and peradventure God sendeth this riches unto thee for another man's prayers' sake, which prayeth for thee, whose prayer is more effectual than thine own. And therefore you ought to be thankful unto other men, which pray for you unto God, and help you to obtain your riches. Again, this petition is a remedy against this wicked carefulness of men, when they seek how to live, and how to get their livings, in such wise, like as if there were no God at all. And then there be some which will not labour as God hath appointed unto them; but rather give them to falsehood; to sell false ware, and deceive their neighbours; or to steal other men's sheep or conies. Those fellows are far wide; let them come to God's treasure-house, that is to say, let them come to God and call upon him with a good faith, saying, "Our Father, give us this day our daily bread." Truly God will hear them. For this is the only remedy that we have here in earth, to come to his treasure-house, and fetch there such things as we lack.

Consider this word *daily*. God promiseth us to feed us daily. If ye believe this, why use you then falsehood and deceit? Therefore, good people, leave your falsehood; get you rather to this treasure-house; then you may be sure of a living: for God hath determined that all that come unto him, desiring his help, they shall be holpen; God will not forget them. But our unbelief is so great, we will not come unto him: we will rather go about to get our living with falsehood, than desire the same of him.

[52] I John 3:17.

A SERMON ON THE LORD'S PRAYER

O what falsehood is used in England, yea, in the whole world! It were no marvel if the fire from heaven fell upon us, like as it did upon the Sodomites, only for our falsehoods' sake. I will tell you of some which are practised in my country where I dwell.[53] But I will not tell it you to teach you to do the same, but rather to abhor it. For those which use such deceitfulness shall be damned world without end, except they repent. I have known some that had a barren cow: they would fain have had a great deal of money for her; therefore they go and take a calf of another cow, and put it to this barren cow, and so come to the market, pretending that this cow hath brought that calf; and so they sell their barren cow six or eight shillings dearer than they should have done else. The man which bought the cow cometh home: peradventure he hath a many of children, and hath no more cattle but this cow, and thinketh he shall have some milk for his children; but when all things cometh to pass, this is a barren cow, and so this poor man is deceived. The other fellow, which sold the cow, thinketh himself a jolly fellow and a wise merchant; and he is called one that can make shift for himself. But I tell thee, whosoever thou art, do so if thou lust, thou shalt do it of this price: thou shalt go to the devil, and there be hanged on the fiery gallows world without end: and thou art as very a thief as when thou takest a man's purse from him going by the way, and thou sinnest as well against this commandment, *Non facies furtum,* "Thou shalt do no theft."[54] But these fellows commonly, which use such deceitfulness and guiles, can speak so finely, that a man would think butter should scant melt in their mouths.

I tell you one other falsehood. I know that some husbandmen go to the market with a quarter of corn. Now they would fain sell dear the worst as well as the best. Therefore they use this policy: they go and put a strike [55] of fine malt or corn in the bottom of the sack, then they put two strike of the worst they had; then a good strike aloft in the sack's mouth, and so they come to the market. Now there cometh a buyer, asking, "Sir, is this good malt?" "I warrant you," saith he, "there is no better in this town." And so he selleth all his malt or corn for the best, when there be but two strikes of the best in his sack. The man that buyeth it thinketh he hath good malt. He cometh home. When he putteth the malt out of the sack, the strike which was in the bottom

---

[53] Presumably a reference to his native county, Leicestershire, although he had lived elsewhere since he was a boy.
[54] Ex. 20:15.
[55] Strike was a measurement varying, in different districts, from a half bushel to four bushels.

covereth the ill malt which was in the midst. And so the good man shall never perceive the fraud, till he cometh to the occupying of the corn. The other man that sold it taketh this for a policy: [56] but it is theft afore God, and he is bound to make restitution of so much as those two strikes which were naught were sold too dear; so much he ought to restore, or else he shall never come to heaven, if God be true in his word.

I could tell you of one other falsehood, how they make wool to weigh much: but I will not tell it you. If you learn to do those falsehoods whereof I have told you now, then take the sauce with it, namely, that you shall never see the bliss of heaven, but be damned world without end with the devil and all his angels. Now go to; when it please you, use falsehood. But I pray you, wherefore will you deceive your neighbour, whom you ought to love as well as your own self? Consider the matter, good people, what a dangerous thing it is to fall into the hands of the ever-living God. Leave falsehood; abhor it: be true and faithful in your calling. *Quaerite regnum Dei, et iustitiam eius, et cetera omnia adiicientur vobis:* "Seek the Kingdom of God and the righteousness thereof, then all things necessary for you shall come unto you unlooked for." [57]

Therefore in this petition, note first God's goodness, how gentle he is towards us; insomuch that he would have us to come unto him and take of him all things. Then again, note what we be, namely, beggars, for we beg of him; which admonisheth us to leave stoutness and proudness, and to be humble. Note what is *Our;* namely, that one prayeth for another, and that this storehouse is common unto all men. Note again, what we be when we be false; namely, the children of the devil and enemies unto God. . . .

But you must not take my sayings after such sort, as though you should do nothing but sit and pray; and yet you should have your dinner and supper made ready for you. No, not so; but you must labour, you must do the work of your vocation. *Quaerite regnum Dei,* "Seek the Kingdom of Heaven": you must set those two things together, works and prayer. He that is true in his vocation, doth according as God willeth him to do, and then prayeth unto God, that man or woman may be assured of their living; as sure (I say) as God is God. As for the wicked, indeed God of his exceeding mercy and liberality findeth them; and sometimes they fare better than the good man doth: but for all that the wicked man hath ever an ill conscience; he doth wrong unto God; he is an usurper, he hath no right unto it. The good and godly man he

[56] Clever trick.   [57] Matt. 6:33.

hath right unto it; for he cometh by it lawfully, by his prayer and travail. But these covetous men, think ye, say they this prayer with a faithful heart, "Our Father, which art in heaven; Give us this day our daily bread"? Think ye they say it from the bottom of their hearts? No, no; they do but mock God, they laugh him to scorn when they say these words. For they have their bread, their silver and gold in their coffers, in their chests, in their bags or budgets; [58] therefore they have no savour of God, else they would shew themselves liberal unto their poor neighbours, they would open their chests and bags, and lay out and help their brethren in Christ. They be as yet but scorners; they say this prayer like as the Turk might say it.

Consider this word, *Give*. Certainly, we must labour, yet we must not so magnify our labour as though we gat our living by it. For labour as long as thou wilt, thou shalt have no profit by it, except the Lord increase thy labour. Therefore we must thank him for it; he doth it; he giveth it. To whom? *Laboranti et poscenti*, "Unto him that laboureth and prayeth." That man that is so disposed shall not lack, as he saith, *Dabit Spiritum Sanctum poscentibus illum;* "He will give the Holy Ghost unto them that desire the same." [59] Then, we must ask; for he giveth not to sluggards. Indeed, they have his benefits; they live wealthily: but, as I told you afore, they have it with an ill conscience, not lawfully. Therefore Christ saith, *Solem suum oriri sinit super iustos et iniustos;* "He suffers his sun to rise upon the just and unjust." [60] Item, *Nemo scit an odio vel amore sit dignus;* "We cannot tell outwardly by these worldly things, which be in the favour of God, and which be not"; [61] for they be common unto good and bad. But the wicked have it not with a good conscience; the upright, good man hath his living through his labour and faithful prayer. Beware that you trust not in your labour, as though ye got your living by it: for, as St. Paul saith, *Qui plantat nihil est, neque qui rigat, sed qui dat incrementum Deus;* "Neither he that planteth is aught, nor he that watereth, but God that giveth the increase." [62] Except God give the increase, all our labour is lost. They that be the children of this world (as covetous persons, extortioners, oppressors, caterpillars,[63] usurers), think you they come to God's storehouse? No, no, they do not; they have not the understanding

---

[58] Wallets.
[59] Luke 11:13.
[60] Matt. 5:45.
[61] Eccl. 9:1.
[62] I Cor. 3:7.
[63] "A rapacious person; an extortioner; one who preys on society." (O.E.D.)

of it; they cannot tell what it meaneth. For they look not to get
their livings at God's storehouse, but rather they think to get it
with deceit and falsehood, with oppression, and wrong doings.
For they think that all things be lawful unto them; therefore they
think that though they take other men's goods through subtilty
and crafts, it is no sin. But I tell you, those things which we buy,
or get with our labour, or are given us by inheritance, or otherways, those things be ours by the law; which maketh *meum* and
tuum, "mine" and "thine." Now all things gotten otherwise are
not ours; as those things which be gotten by crafty conveyances,
by guile and fraud, by robbery and stealing, by extortion and
oppression, by hand-making,[64] or howsoever you come by it beside the right way, it is not yours; insomuch that you may not
give it for God's sake, for God hateth it.

But you will say, "What shall we do with the good gotten by
unlawful means?" Marry, I tell thee: make restitution; which is
the only way that pleaseth God. O Lord, what bribery, falsehood,
deceiving, false getting of goods is in England! And yet for all
that, we hear nothing of restitution; which is a miserable thing.
I tell you, none of them which have taken their neighbour's good
from him by any manner of falsehood, none of them, I say, shall
be saved, except they make restitution, either in affect or effect; in
effect, when they be able; in affect, when they be not able in no
wise. Ezekiel saith, *Si impius egerit pœnitentiam, et rapinam
reddiderit;* "When the ungodly doth repent, and restoreth the
good gotten wrongfully and unlawfully." [65] For unlawful good
ought to be restored again: without restitution look not for salvation. Also, this is a true sentence used of St. Augustine, *Non remit-
tetur peccatum, nisi restituatur ablatum;* "Robbery, falsehood, or
otherwise ill-gotten goods, cannot be forgiven of God, except it be
restored again." [66] Zacheus, that good publican, that common officer, he gave a good ensample unto all bribers and extortioners.[67]
I would they all would follow his ensample. He exercised not open
robbery; he killed no man by the way; but with crafts and subtilties he deceived the poor. When the poor men came to him, he
bade them to come again another day, and so delayed the time,
till at the length he wearied poor men, and so gat somewhat of
them. Such fellows are now in our time very good cheap; [68] but

[64] Undue profit.
[65] Ezek. 18:21. *Et rapinam reddiderit* seems to be Latimer's gloss on the latter part of the verse.
[66] *Ep.* CLIII. xx (*PL* 33.662).
[67] Luke 19:1–10.
[68] Plentiful.

they will not learn the second lesson. They have read the first lesson, how Zachee was a bribe-taker; but they will not read the second: they say A, but they will not say B. What is the second lesson? *Si quem defraudavi, reddam quadruplum;* "If I have deceived any man, I will restore it fourfold." [69] But we may argue that they be not such fellows as Zacheus was, for we hear nothing of restitution; they lack right repentance.

It is a wonderful thing to see that Christian people will live in such an estate, wherein they know themselves to be damned: for when they go to bed, they go in the name of the devil. *In summa,* whatsoever they do, they do it in his name, because they be out of the favour of God. God loveth them not; therefore (I say) it is to be lamented that we hear nothing of restitution. St. Paul saith, *Qui furabatur non amplius furetur;* "He that stale, let him steal no more." [70] Which words teach us, that he which hath stolen or deceived, and keepeth it, he is a strong [71] thief so long till he restore again the thing taken; and shall look for no remission of his sins at God's hand, till he hath restored again such goods. There be some which say, "Repentance or contrition will serve; it is enough when I am sorry for it." Those fellows cannot tell what repentance meaneth. Look upon Zacheus. He did repent, but restitution by and by followed. So let us do too: let us live uprightly and godly; and when we have done amiss, or deceived any body, let us make restitution. And after, beware of such sins, of such deceitfulness; but rather let us call upon God, and resort to his storehouse, and labour faithfully and truly for our livings. Whosoever is so disposed, him God will favour, and he shall lack nothing. As for the other impenitent sluggards, they be devourers and usurpers of God's gifts, and therefore shall be punished world without end in everlasting fire. . . .

You have heard now, how men had things in common in the first Church: [72] but St. Paul he teacheth us how things ought to be in common amongst us, saying, *Sitis necessitatibus sanctorum communicantes;* "Help the necessity of those which be poor." [73] Our good is not so ours that we may do with it what us listeth; but we ought to distribute it unto them which have need. No man (as I told you before) ought to take away my good from me; but I ought to distribute that that I may spare, and help the poor withal.

[69] Luke 19:8.
[70] Eph. 4:28.
[71] "Strong" usually = "gross" or "flagrant"; but here it seems to mean "obdurate."
[72] Acts 2:44.
[73] Rom. 12:13.

Communicantes necessitatibus, saith St. Paul; "Distribute them unto the poor," let them lack nothing; but help them with such things as you may spare. For so it is written, *Cui plus datum est, plus requiretur ab illo;* "He that hath much, must make account for much; and if he have not spent it well, he must make the heavier account." [74] But I speak not this to let poor folks from labour; for we must labour and do the works of our vocation, every one in his calling: for so it is written, *Labores manuum tuarum manducabis et bene tibi erit,* "Thou shalt eat thy handlabour, and it shall go well with thee." [75] That is to say, every man shall work for his living, and shall not be a sluggard, as a great many be: every man shall labour and pray; then God will send him his living. St. Paul saith, *Qui non laborat, non comedat;* "He that laboureth not, let him not eat." [76] Therefore those lubbers which will not labour, and might labour, it is a good thing to punish them according unto the king's most godly statutes. For God himself saith, *In sudore vultus tui vesceris pane tuo;* "In the sweat of thy face thou shalt eat thy bread." [77] Then cometh in St. Paul, which saith, *Magis autem laboret ut det indigentibus;* "Let him labour the sorer, that he may have wherewith to help the poor." [78] And Christ himself saith, *Melius est dare quam accipere;* "It is better to give than to take." [79] So Christ and all his apostles, yea, the whole Scripture, admonisheth us ever of our neighbour, to take heed of him, to be pitiful unto him: but God knoweth there be a great many which care little for their neighbours. They do like as Cain did, when God asked him, "Cain, where is thy brother Abel?" "What," saith he, "am I my brother's keeper?" [80] So these rich franklings,[81] these covetous fellows, they scrape all things to themselves, they think they should care for nobody else but for themselves: God commandeth the poor man to labour the sorer, to the end that he may be able to help his poor neighbour: how much more ought the rich to be liberal unto them?

But you will say, "Here is a marvellous doctrine, which commandeth nothing but 'Give, Give': if I shall follow this doctrine,

---

[74] Luke 12:48.
[75] Ps. 128:2.
[76] II Thess. 3:10.
[77] Gen. 3:19.
[78] Eph. 4:28.
[79] Acts 20:35.
[80] Gen. 4:9.
[81] Franklins: he probably intends "landowners," and refers to one of the foremost sixteenth-century problems, the enclosure of land for sheep-farming.

I shall give so much, that at the length I shall have nothing left for myself." These be words of infidelity; he that speaketh such words is a faithless man. And I pray you, tell me, have ye heard of any man that came to poverty, because he gave unto the poor? Have you heard tell of such a one? No, I am sure you have not. And I dare lay my head to pledge for it, that no man living hath come, or shall hereafter come to poverty, because he hath been liberal in helping the poor. For God is a true God, and no liar: he promiseth us in his Word, that we shall have the more by giving to the needy. Therefore the way to get is to scatter that that you have. Give, and you shall gain. If you ask me, "How shall I get riches?" I make thee this answer: "Scatter that that thou hast; for giving is gaining." But you must take heed, and scatter it according unto God's will and pleasure; that is, to relieve the poor withal, to scatter it amongst the flock of Christ. Whosoever giveth so shall surely gain: for Christ saith, *Date, et dabitur vobis;* "Give, and it shall be given unto you." *Dabitur,* "it shall be given unto you." [82] This is a sweet word, we can well away with that; but how shall we come by it? *Date,* "Give". . . .

For no rich man can say before God, "This is my own." No, he is but an officer over it, an almoner, God's treasurer. Our Saviour saith, *Omnis qui reliquerit agrum, &c., centuplum accipiet;* "Whosoever shall leave his field, shall receive it again an hundred fold." [83] As, if I should be examined now of the Papists, if they should ask me, "Believe you in the Mass?" I say, "No; according unto God's word, and my conscience, it is naught, it is but deceitfulness, it is the devil's doctrine." Now I must go to prison, I leave all things behind me, wife and children, good and land, and all my friends: I leave them for Christ's sake, in his quarrel.[84] What saith our Saviour unto it? *Centuplum accipiet;* I shall have an hundred times so much. Now though this be spoken in such wise, yet it may be understanden of alms-giving too. For that man or woman that can find in their hearts for God's sake to leave ten shillings or ten pounds, they shall have an hundred fold again in this life, and in the world to come life everlasting. If this will not move our hearts, then they are more than stony and flinty; then our damnation is just and well deserved. For to give alms, it is like as when a man cometh unto me, and desireth an empty purse of me: I lend him the purse, he cometh by and by and

---

[82] Luke 6:38.
[83] Matt. 19:29.
[84] This was to become the lot of a good many Protestants within the next five years. Is Latimer being prophetic, or should we regard the sentence as an editorial insertion after the event?

bringeth it full of money, and giveth it me; so that I have now my purse again, and the money too. So it is to give alms: we lend an empty purse, and take a full purse for it. Therefore let us persuade ourselves in our hearts, that to give for God's sake is no loss unto us, but great gain. And truly the poor man doth more for the rich man in taking things of him, than the rich doth for the poor in giving them. For the rich giveth but only worldly goods, but the poor giveth him by the promise of God all felicity.

Quotidianum, Daily. Here we learn to cast away all carefulness, and to come to this storehouse of God, where we shall have all things competent [85] both for our souls and bodies. Further, in this petition we desire that God will feed not only our bodies but also our souls; and so we pray for the office of preaching. For like as the body must be fed daily with meat, so the soul requireth her meat, which is the Word of God. Therefore we pray here for all the clergy, that they may do their duties, and feed us with the Word of God according to their calling.

Now I have troubled you long, therefore I will make an end. I desire you remember to resort to this storehouse: whatsoever ye have need of, come hither; here are all things necessary for your soul and body, only desire them. But you have heard how you must be apparelled; you must labour and do your duties, and then come, and you shall find all things necessary for you. And specially now at this time let us resort unto God; for it is a great drought, as we think, and we had need of rain. Let us therefore resort unto our loving Father, which promiseth, that when we call upon him with a faithful heart, he will hear us. Let us therefore desire him to rule the matter so, that we may have our bodily sustenance. We have the ensample of Elias, whose prayer God heard.[86] Therefore let us pray this prayer, which our Saviour and Redeemer Jesus Christ himself taught us, saying, "Our Father, which art in heaven," &c. *Amen.*

[85] Fit, necessary.   [86] I Kings 18:41 ff.

INDEXES

NAMES

Ælfric, 79
Aeneas Sylvius, 79n
Aire, 257
Albigensians, 81
Alferus, Duke, 80
Alfrida, Queen, 80
Ambrose, 19, 24, 26 ff., 50, 53, 198, 265 f., 285, 303, 314
Ambrosiaster, 266n, 285n
Anselm, 266
Antoninus, 75
Antony, St., 325, 333 f.
"Antwerp" Bible, 92
Apollinarius, 151, 155
Apollonius, 40
Apologia Ecclesiae Anglicanae, xx, 3 ff.
Apologists, 4, 9
Aquinas. *See* Thomas Aquinas
Arians, 53
Aristotle, 209, 311, 336
Arnoldus Carnotensis, 29n
Ascham, 150
Athanasius, 53n, 190, 314
Augsburg, Confession of, xvii
Augusta, Bishop of. *See* Udalrichus (Pseudo-)
Augustine of Canterbury (or Austen), 79
Augustine of Hippo (also Austin), 18, 21, 22, 26 ff., 36, 40, 50, 147, 198, 241, 266, 275, 277, 284 f., 292 f., 305 ff., 313 f., 317, 319, 344
Authorized Version, 95 f.
Auxentius, 53

Bacon, John, 83
Bacon, Lady, 7
Bale, 67 f., 77, 89, 90
Basil, 26, 198, 265 f., 314
Becon, xxi, 147

Bede, 65, 79
Berengarius, 81
Bernard of Clairvaux, 41n, 198, 266
Bernher, 324 f.
Bertie, Richard, 323
Bertram, Berthramus. *See* Ratramnus
Bevan, xviii
Bilney, 222
Bonner, xvi
Book of Common Prayer, xv, xvii, xx f., 31n, 332, 334
Booty, John E., 6 ff.
Boucher, 63
Brandon, Charles. *See* Suffolk, Duke of
Brentius, 89
British saints, 65, 78
Bruschius, 82
Bucer, xx, 89, 185, 222, 225
Bullinger, 89, 150, 185 ff., 222
Burleigh, Lord. *See* Cecil, William
Butterworth, 223

Caesar, Julius, 202, 272
Cajetan, 261
Calixtus, 27
Calvin, 17n, 89, 92, 187 f., 221 f., 225, 328
Cardwell, 222, 224 ff.
Cassiodorus, 40n
Cecil, William, 4, 8 ff., 150
Chadwick, xvi f.
Charlemagne, 53
Charles V, Emperor, 332
Cheke, 150 f.
Chichele (Chichesly), 84
Christopher, J. P., 147
Chrysostom, 24 ff., 29, 38, 39, 50, 266, 275, 285, 303, 314, 317, 320
Chrysostom (Pseudo-), 38n, 275n, 285n
Cicero, 73
Colet, xx, 89, 92, 147

349

Colinaeus, 92
Conrad, 76
Cornish rebellion, 332n
Cotton, 227
Councils
  Ancyra, 52
  Aquila, 53
  Carthage III, 22 f., 41, 52 f.
  Chalcedon, 51, 53
  Constantinople, 51
  Elvira, 39
  Ephesus, 51
  Frankfurt, 53
  Gangra, 40 f., 52
  Hippo, 41n
  Neo-Caesarea, 52
  Nicaea, 22, 29, 51 ff.
  Nicaea II, 53
  Rome, Synod of, 40
  Trent, 3, 16 f., 42, 48, 54
  Trident. See Trent
  Vercelli, Synod of, 81n
Cox, 8, 150, 257
Crabbe, P., 25n
Cranmer, xvi, xxi, 148 ff., 185, 197, 224, 225 ff., 289, 308, 324
Creighton, Mandell, 84n
Crispin, 61
Cromwell, Thomas, 224 f.
Curtop, 294, 320
Cyprian, 22, 29, 39, 266, 314, 317
Cyril of Alexandria, 26, 29, 314

Day, John, 325
Didymus of Alexandria, 273
Dionysius, 26
Dixon, R. W., 10, 256n
Donatists, 18, 53
Duns Scotus, 6, 293, 301, 308, 309
Dunstan, 80

Eastern Church, 45, 51, 53
Edgar, King, 80
Edward, Saxon prince, 80
Edward VI, 3, 150, 328
Egidius, 35
Elizabeth I, xvi f., 3, 10, 61, 63 f.
Emissene. See Eusebius
Emperors of Rome
  Claudius, xvi
  Constantine I, 51
  Constantius II, 53
  Gratian, 19
  Justinian, 41
  Marcian, 51
  Maurice, 22
  Phocas, 22
  Theodosius I, 51
  Theodosius II, 51
Epicureans, 63, 65
Epiphanius, 39, 40n, 198, 314
Erasmus, xix, 93, 95 f., 240n, 243, 326 f.

Ethelred, 80
Eusebius of Caesarea, 24, 214n, 317
Eusebius Emissene, 317
Eutychianism, 167n

Faber Stapulensis, 25, 242
Faithful witnesses, 65, 83
Firth, 65
Fish, Simon, xviii
Flacius Illyricus, 82nn
Flemish Anabaptists, 64
Fox, George, 222
Foxe, John, 61 ff., 89, 149n, 221, 310 ff., 324, 326
Fredericus Barbarossa, 76
Frere, W. H., 223n
Froude, J. A., xvii
Fry, Francis, 94, 106
Fulgentius, 21n, 317
Fuller, Thomas, 103n, 323

Gardiner, xvii, 150, 186, 255 ff., 293, 301n, 303nn, 306n, 308n, 324
Gelasius Cyzicenus, 29n
Gelasius (Pseudo-), 28n
Gildas, 79
Giles, J. A., 79n
Gratian, 21n, 82n
Grecia, Greeks. See Eastern Church
Gregory of Nazianzus, 25
Griffiths, 257
Grindal, 150
Gualter, Rudolph, 222

Habsburg, 332n
Hall, Basil, 92
Haller, 68
Hanslik, R., 40n
Harding, Thomas, 7, 9 f., 19n, 21n, 22n, 41n, 54n
Harford, G., 147n
Hastings, 242n
Heinemann, L. de, 25n
Henry II, of France, 332n
Henry VIII, xv, 3
Heywood, J., 103n
Hierome. See Jerome
Hilary of Poitiers, 54, 265 f., 314
Hildebrand. See Pope Gregory VII
Hilles, Richard, 222
Hilsey, 148, 222
Homilies, First Book of, xv, 223, 225 f., 255 ff., 328
Hooper, 89, 185 ff., 222
Horace, 73n
Hosius, 37
Hostiens (Henry of Segusio, Card. of Ostia), 49n
Hus, 84

Injunctions, 1536, 223
Injunctions, 1538, 223, 225

NAMES

Irenaeus, 194, 214
Isidore of Seville, 242n

Jacob, W., 40n
Jacobs, 224n
Jelf, 38n
Jenkyns, 257
Jerome, 16n, 18, 22, 26, 39, 51, 55, 233, 314
Jewel, 3 ff.
Joachim of Fiore, 81
John Damascene, 201
Jonas, Justus, 148
Joye, George, 148
Justin Martyr, 4, 38

"Kalender" of believers, 65
Katherine of Aragon, 323
Kennedy, W. M., 223n
"King Henry's Primer," 148
King James's Version. See Authorized Version
Knox, D. B., 226
Knox, John, xx
Kuhn, S. M., 147n
Kurath, Hans, 147n

Lactantius, 313n
Latimer, 222, 323 ff.
Latomus, Jacobus, 25
Laziardus, 75
Lefèvre d'Étaples. See Faber Stapulensis
Lewis, C. S., 326, 327
Lightfoot, J. B., 93
Lily, George, 75
Luther, 67, 83, 92, 95 f., 147 f., 187, 328

Magdeburg "Centuries," 61
Maid of Ipswich, 68
Maid of Kent, 68
Marcion, 37
Marshall, William, 148
Martinus, 75
Martyr. See Peter Martyr
Martyrs of Alsace, 81
Mary Tudor, 3, 10
Massæus, 82
Matilda, Duchess, 79
Maurice, F. D., xix
Medieval enemies of Pope, 81 f.
Melanchthon, 89, 187, 261
Monophysitism, 167n
Montanus, 37
More, xvi, xx
Mozley, J. F., 63, 65, 94
Münster, Sebastian, 89, 327, 336
Musculus, 89
Mutius, 81

Nauclerus, 75
Nicene Creed, 194
Nicholas of Lyra, 242nn

Nicolaus Leonicus, 30n
Nicostratus, 55
Ninety-five Theses, 63
Norfolk rebellion, 332n
Northumberland, Duke of, xv, 185
Nowell, Alexander, 152, 257

Oecolampadius, 89
Œcumenius, 266
Olivétan, 92
Onuphrius, 75
Origen, 26, 28, 30, 39, 266
Osiander, 187
Oswald, 80

Packington, 67 f.
Palladius, 53
Panormitanus (Nicolo de Tudeschi), 25, 49n
Parker, Matthew, 7 ff.
Parker, T. M., xvi, 257, 258
Parker Society, 95, 222, 257
Parkhurst, John, 10
Paul of Samosata, 214
Pelagianism, 53, 328
Pellicanus, 89, 326 f.
Peter Martyr, 8 ff., 185, 222
Petilian, 18
Philpot, 149
Photius, 266
Pighius, 37n
Pilkington, 89
Platina, 26n, 75
Pliny, 75, 336
Plutarch, 336
Polycarp, 214
Polydore Vergil, 75
Ponet, 147 ff.
Popes
  Anacletus I, 27n
  Boniface VIII, 41n
  Clement I, 41
  Gelasius I, 42, 46
  Gregory I, 23, 57, 77, 243
  Gregory VII, 80
  Innocentius III, 80 f., 301 f., 307, 309
  Julius III, 16 f., 17n, 41
  Leo I, 41
  Martin V, 84
  Nicolas I, 40n
  Paul III, 25 f.
  Pius II. See also Aeneas Sylvius
  Pius IV, 16
Powicke, Sir Maurice, xvi f.
Poynet. See Ponet
Prayer Book. See Book of Common Prayer
Prosper of Aquitaine, 266

Ratramnus, 81, 314, 317
Ridley, Lancelot, 89 ff.
Ridley, Nicholas, 89, 150, 185, 289 ff.

352

INDEXES

Rosdell, Christopher, 189 f.
Rufinus, 16, 51
Rupp, 257

Sabellicus, 75
Sarcerius, 224
Saxon churchmen, 80
Saxon saints, 79
Secundus, 53
Seyton, 67 f.
Six Articles, 222, 225 f.
Smith, Maynard, xviii f.
Smith, R., 293, 310, 317 ff.
Socrates, 151, 155
Some, Thomas, 324 f.
Somerset, Duke of, 185 f., 255 ff.
Sozomen, 25, 40n
Spyridon (Spiridion), 25
Stevenson, J., 79n
Stevenson, M., 147
Strype, 9, 256
Suffolk, Duchess of, 323
Suffolk, Duke of, 323

Tanner, 90
Taverner, 221 ff., 255
Ten Articles, 223
Tertullian, 4, 14n, 24, 26, 38, 44, 52
Theodoret, 28
Theophylact, 28

Thirty-nine Articles, xx f.
Thomas Aquinas, 242n
Thomists, 6
Throckmorton, 8
Tolwyn, 67 f.
Trevelyan, G. M., xviin
Tyndale, xv, 89 ff.

Udalrichus (Pseudo-), 25n

Valois, 332n
Vatablus, 89, 327, 336
Vigilius Tapsensis, 21
Vincentian Canon, 44n
Vincentius, 75
Vulgate, 95 f., 263n, 264, 326 f., 336

Waldensians, 81 f.
Watson, 294 f.
Westcott, 94, 95n, 320
Weston, 149, 294, 318
Wolfe (Woulfe), Rainolde, 9
Wolsey, Cardinal, 115n
Wootten, 257
Wyatt's rebellion, 150
Wycliffe, 67, 84

"Zurich" Bible, 92
Zwenkfeldians, 37
Zwingli, 89, 185

Subjects

Adversity, 248–252
Antichrist, 118 ff.
Antinomianism, 200
Atonement, 163, 203, 235 ff., 257 f.

Baptism
  inward and outward, 210 f.
  need for faith, 241
  practice, 174
  and preaching, 240 f.
  profession of, 100, 102 f., 114
  remission of sins, 27
  washing, 27
Believer
  new life, 114
  sinful, 110 f.
  sinlessness, 142
Bible. *See also* Scripture
  commentaries, 89 ff.
  English, 94 ff.
  need for vernacular, 105
  vernacular, 47, 64

Catechising, 147
Catechism, 147 ff.

Celibacy, 334 f.
Chosen nation, 68
Christian prince, 6, 49 ff.
Christian religion, 156
Christianity, 151
Church
  always persecuted, 14
  apostolic norm, 214 f.
  apostolic succession, 55 ff., 65, 121, 214
  belief in, 169, 172
  body of Christ, 21
  catholic, 21
  communion, 247
  in early Church, 78
  under the Emperors, 78
  governed by God, 213
  marks of, 171, 213 f.
  mission of, 232 ff.
  and State, 40 f.
  traditions, 214
  the two churches, 77 f., 132
  unity, 6, 21
Church in England
  decay, 80 f.
  independence from Rome, 79

SUBJECTS

Church fathers, 38, 52
Church history, need for, 62, 64, 74 f., 76 f.
Civil order, 332
Common Prayer
 audibility, 41
 vernacular, 31, 41, 46
Communion
 with believers, 108 f.
 with God, 108
Community, 338 f., 345
Confession of sin, 23, 110
Councils of Church, 47 f., 52 ff.
Covenant with Abraham, 162 f.
Covetousness, 117 f.
Creation, 160
Creed
 exposition of, 151, 160 ff.
 symbol, 156

Education of children, 332 f.
Eschatology, 118, 168 f., 177
Eucharist, 5, 174 f., 289-320
 abuses, 30, 41 f.
 adoration of, 291, 298
 body and blood, 26, 208 f., 291, 293 f., 300, 302, 320
 in both kinds, 27, 307
 celebration of, 174, 207 f.
 communication, 293
 communion with believers, 27
 communion with Christ, 26 f., 313
 consecration, 301 ff.
 consubstantiation, 205
 corporal presence, 208, 291, 298, 300, 310 f.
 death or life, 291
 faithful reception, 29
 figurative, 295, 305 f., 315
 by grace, 294, 301
 Holy Spirit, 295
 mass, derivation of, 314 f.
 participation, 27
 practice, 46
 presence of Christ, 28 f., 299, 313, 318 f.
 presence by grace, 300, 314
 propitiation, 315
 reception by wicked, 291, 298, 313
 remembrance, 27, 290, 301, 313
 representation, 27
 sacramental nature, 320
 sacrifice, 207, 291, 298, 307, 314 ff.
 spiritual, 175, 208, 291 f., 294 f.
 thanksgiving, 27
 transubstantiation, 28 f., 46, 205, 208, 226, 291, 298, 308 ff., 312 ff., 315
 Trinity, 295
 and Word of God, 311
Evangelization of England, 222
Evil works, spring from unbelief, 116
Excommunication, 23

Faith, 203 ff., 231, 233, 235 f., 272-282
 assent and trust, 107, 113, 134 f., 272
 coercion to, 239
 confidence, 129
 dead, 269 f., 272
 freedom, 239
 fruits of, 271, 274 ff.
 historical, 135, 238, 269 f., 272
 life-giving, 283
 living, 124, 273
 and love, 273
 nature of, 137 f.
 object of, 259, 267
 personal, 238
 signs of, 128 f.
 trust, 270, 273
 victory, 116 f., 139
 and works, 204, 264, 266 f.
 works of, 275 f.
Fall, 161 f.
Farmers, 337 f.
Forgiveness, 111 f., 116, 178 f.
Fraud, 341

God, 20
 chastises his own, 249
 and devil, 127
 Fatherhood, 160 f., 176
 Fatherly love, 101, 124, 133
 justice and mercy, 263
 light and truth, 109
 nature of, 156
 omnipresence, 177
 power, 132
 protector, 179
 service of, 172 f.
 wrath of, 202 f.
Godliness, 180 ff., 199 ff.
 man's duty to God, 269
 springs from faith, 259, 271
Godly prince. *See* Christian prince
Good works, 32 f., 283-286
 follow faith, 283 f.
 necessary, 212
 signs of love, 138 f.
 spring from faith, 109 f., 114 ff., 123, 206, 345
Gospel, 221 f., 239
 key to Scripture, 102, 104 f.
 and Law, 156, 216 f.
 meaning of, 106
 power of keys, 102
Grace, 100, 206
 time of, 230

Heaven, 176 f.
Heresy, 6, 104
History and apocalypse, 62 f., 66 ff., 85 f.
Holy Spirit, 119, 163, 171 f., 196
 deity, 21
 giver of faith, 130
 indwelling, 125

Holy Spirit—*continued*
  inward witness, 140 f.
  office of, 21
  sanctifier, 170, 172

Idolatry, 143 f.
Image of God, 134, 161
  defaced, 159, 162
Images, 39, 201 f.

Jesus Christ
  anointed, 137
  Anointer, 119
  ascension, 20, 232–244
  ascension and session, 151 f., 163 ff., 317 f.
  crucifixion, 20, 163, 194 f.
  deity, 106 f., 143
  Emmanuel, 120
  eternal life, 143
  giver of grace, 143
  glorification, 21, 165 f.
  God-man, 194
  Head of Church, 5, 21, 54 f.
  humanity, 107, 131
  identity of being and name, 112, 120
  imitation of, 168
  incarnation, 20
  Intercessor, 200 ff.
  King, 112, 120, 187, 212–215
  life of believers, 107 f.
  loving kindness, 245
  Mediator, 31 f., 236
  merits of, 204
  office of, 187 f., 245 f.
  presence in world, 164 ff.
  Priest, 112, 186 f., 195–212, 316 f.
  Priest and King, 113
  Ransom, 264
  reconciliation in, 108
  Redeemer, 120, 137, 231, 246
  resurrection of, 20, 163 f., 235
  righteous, 112
  sanctifier, 119
  Sanctus, 120
  satisfaction for sin, 262
  second coming, 122 f., 124, 169
  session, 20, 299, 312
  Shepherd, 246
  triumphant, 237 f.
  unity with, 167 f., 243
  Word of God, 194
Judgment, 169
Justification, 257, 262–271
  action of God, 258, 267
  and atonement, 258
  by Christ alone, 101, 267 f.
  Christ's satisfaction, 264 f.
  by faith alone, 170, 203, 206, 246 f., 258, 264 f., 267 ff.
  free, 263
  grace and faith, 264 f.

ransom paid, 263
by works, 246 f.

Kingdom of Christ. *See also* Church
  defended by God, 213
  persecuted, 213
  spiritual, 213
Knowledge of God, 121
  in Christ, 116 f.

Law, 151, 204
  civil, 217
  convicts of sin, 159
  darkness, 231
  exposes sin, 107 f., 217
  exposition of, 156 ff.
  felt by believers, 217 f.
  fulfilled in love, 138, 158
  is faith and love, 125
  moral use, 218
  of nature, 151, 158 f.
  spiritual, 100
Lechery, 117
Lord's Supper. *See* Eucharist
Love
  charity, 339 f.
  for Christ and brethren, 128 f.
  confidence of, 135 f.
  for God, 133
  for God and neighbor, 136 ff.
  instrument of faith, 134
  for neighbor, 100 f., 115
  sign of faith, 135
  sign of Spirit, 134
  springs from faith, 115, 130, 132, 136, 170 f.
  for world, 117

Magistracy, 331
Man, 215–218. *See also* Image of God
  creation, 161
  self-knowledge, 215 f.
  sinner, 32, 215
  wretchedness, 216
Mariolatry, 32
Marriage, 333 f.
Martyrs, 62 f.
Ministry
  apostolate, 22
  episcopacy, 22 f.
  lawfully called, 23
  marriage of priests, 25, 39 ff.
  office, 5. *See also* Preaching
  papal system rejected, 21 ff.
  power of keys, 5, 23 f.
  priest, 311
  threefold order, 5, 21
Miracles, 242
  no longer necessary, 243
  testify to Word, 243
Monks, 40
Mortification, 126

Penance, life of, 101
Plurality, 42
Pope, 42 f.
 arbiter, 48
 not vicar of Christ, 197
Prayer, 175 ff., 179 f., 331–348
 asking, 141, 178
 confidence, 141
 after God's will, 177 f.
 and work, 342 f.
Preaching, 21, 23 ff., 42, 175, 221–226, 232 ff., 239, 247, 255–259, 331
 apostolic succession, 241
 by Holy Spirit, 119, 121 f.
 Latimer's, 323–328
 testing of, 130 f.
 world mission, 232, 239 f.
Providence, 63, 65 f., 160
Purgatory, 5, 30 f.

Reconciliation, 32, 131
 and satisfaction, 112 f.
Redemption, 262–271
Reformation
 anticlericalism, xvii f.
 correction of abuses, xviii f.
 heresy, 4, 15, 17 ff., 33
 meaning of, xv ff., 1 ff.
 novelty, 15, 17, 39, 61, 64, 83 ff.
 political, xvi f.
 schism, 15, 33 f., 44 f.
 theological, xix
 witness to Christ, xv ff., 221 ff.
Regeneration, 133
Repentance, 231, 247
Restitution, 344 f.
Resurrection, 6
 of flesh, 33
Revelation in creation, 202
Roman Church
 abuses, 6, 75 f.
 corruption by wealth, 79 f.
 decay, 80
 erring course, 34 ff.
 ineffectual Christology, 121
 schismatic, 45 f.
 taxes, 84

Sabbath, 173
Sacraments, 5, 173 ff.
 analogy, 312
 confirmation of faith, 26
 and Holy Spirit, 140
 nature of, 208, 212
 seals, 26
 signs, 26
 session of Christ, 312
 two, 27
 visible words, 26
Saints, invocation of, 200 f.
Sanctification, 210
 and baptism, 210
 knowledge of God, 209
 office of Christ, 209
 by Word, Spirit, and faith, 209 f.
Scripture, 5, 26, 39, 41
 criterion, 18, 26, 36 ff., 52, 134, 197 f.
 foundation, 197 f.
 interpretation, 198, 214 f.
 false, 102, 104
 figurative, 292, 305 f.
 mystical, 242n
 need for exposition, 106
 obedience to, 199
 oracles of God, 26
 and tradition, 122, 198 f.
 way of salvation, 26
Serpent in wilderness, type of Christ, 205
Servants, 335 ff.
Sin
 of believers, 127
 blamed on flesh, 234
 and curiosity, 123
 nature of, 125
 of unbelievers, 127
 the unforgivable, 141 f.
Stewardship, 347
Suffering of creation, 251 f.

Trinity, 5, 20 f.

War, 331 f.
Wealth, 338 ff.
Worship, ceremonies, 5, 31, 40

WORKS QUOTED IN TEXTS

Ælfric (10th–11th cent.)
   In die Sanctae Pascae   79
Aeneas Sylvius (15th cent.)
   Historia Bohemica, cap. XXI   79n
Ambrose (4th cent.)
   De fide, Lib. I, cap. vi.43   19n
   De Sacramentis
     Lib. IV, cap. iv   28n
     Lib. V, cap. iv   303n
Ambroisiaster (Pseudo-Ambrose; 4th cent.)
   Comm. in Ep. B. Pauli ad Corinthios Primam   266n
   De vocatione Gentium, Lib. I, cap. iii   285n
Anacletus (1st cent.)
   Epistola i   27n
Antoninus (15th cent.)
   Prima [-tertia] pars historialis   75n
Apostolic Canons   40n

356 INDEXES

Aristotle (4th cent. B.C.)
  Metaphysica Bk. Δ. 22   209n
  Oeconomica I. vi.3   336n
Arnoldus Carnotensis (12th cent.)
  De cardinalibus Christi operibus   29n
Augustine (4th–5th cent.)
  In Ps. XVIII.ii.1   31n
  In Ps. XXXI.ii.4   284n
  In Ps. LXXXIII   285n
  In Ps. LXXXV   31n
  In Ioan. Evang.
    I.4   30n
    XXX.1   21n, 319n
    XLV   277n
    LXXX.3   30n
  Contra Faustum xix.16   317n
  Contra Iulianum Pelagianum,
    Lib. IV   284n
  De bono viduitatis X.13   40n
  De civitate Dei, Lib. XIX, cap.
    xix   22n
  De doctrina Christiana III.16   306n
  De peccatorum meritis et remissione III.8   241n
  De Sermone Domini in Monte,
    Lib. II, cap. xiii   284n
  De unitate ecclesiae
    III.5   18n, 36n
    III.6   36n
    IV.7   36n
  Epistola ad Dardanum   313n
  Epistola
    LV.xix.35   31n, 40n
    CLIII.xx   344n
    clxxxv, cap. 1   317n
    CLXXXVII.iii.10   21n
  Sermo CCLXXII; *De nativitate*   28n
Pseudo-Augustine
  Hypomnesticon V.v   31n

Bale, John (16th cent.)
  Image of bothe churches, The   77n
Basil (4th cent.)
  Homilia de humilitate   266n
Bernard de Clairvaux (12th cent.)
  De consideratione II, cap. 6, 10,
    11   41n
Book of Common Prayer   31n
Bruschius (16th cent.)
  De omnibus Germaniae Episcopatibus   82n

Cassiodorus (6th cent.)
  Historia ecclesiastica tripartita   40n
Chrysostom (4th–5th cent.)
  In Matthaeum, Hom. II   39n
  Opus imperfectum in Matthaeum, Hom. XLIX   24n
  In Ioannem, Hom. XXXII   39n
  In Ep. I ad Corinthios, Hom.
    XXIV   29nn, 320n
  In Ep. ad Titum, Hom. II, cap. I   25n

  De fide et operibus, cap. xvi   275n
  De proditione Judae., Hom. i   303n
  In sermone de Eucharistia in Encaenis   303n
Pseudo-Chrysostom
  De fide et lege naturae   275n, 285n
  De Spiritu Sancto Homilia   38n
Cicero (1st cent. B.C.)
  Oratio 2   73n
  Pro Roscio, cap. XX   73n
Corpus Iuris Canonici
  De consecratione
    Dist. II, can. VII   41n
    Dist. II, can. XII   28n, 42n, 46n
    Dist. II, can. XLIV   21n
  De Poenitentia, Dist. I, can. LI   24n
  Extravagantes communes   82n
Corpus Iuris Civilis   41n
Crabbe, Peter (16th cent.)
  Concilia omnia   25n
Cranmer (16th cent.)
  A confutation of unwritten verities   197n
  Defensio verae et catholicae doctrinae, Lib. V   308n
  Notes on Justification   266n
Cyprian (3d cent.)
  De unitate ecclesiae   22nn
  Epistola IV   39n
Cyril of Alexandria (4th–5th cent.)
  Apologeticus . . . adversus Orientales Episcopos   29n

Decretalium Collectiones   81n
Didymus of Alexandria (4th cent.)
  Enarratio in Ep. B. Iacobi, cap.
    II, v. 26   273n
Duns Scotus (13th–14th cent.)
  Quaestiones in Lib. IV Sententiarum, Lib. IV, Dist. VIII,
    Quaest. II   308n

Egidius Viterbiensis (15th–16th cent.)
  Oratio Synodi Lateranensis   35n
Epiphanius (4th–5th cent.)
  Adversus Haereses, Lib. ii, tom.
    1, Haer. lxi   39n
Erasmus (16th cent.)
  Paraphrasis in . . . Novum Testamentum   240n
Eusebius (3d–4th cent.)
  Historia ecclesiastica V.xxviii   214n
Faber Stapulensis (15th–16th cent.)
  Epistolae D. Pauli . . . cum commentariis   25n
Flacius (Matthias), Illyricus (16th cent.)
  Catalogus testium veritatis   82nn
Fulgentius (5th–6th cent.)
  Libri tres, ad Trasim. Reg., Lib.
    II, cap. xvii   21n

WORKS QUOTED IN TEXTS 357

Gardiner (16th cent.)
  explication and assertion by   303nn,
                                  306n, 308n
  Confutatio cavillationum   301n
Gelasius Cyzicenus (5th cent.)
  *Epistola Maiorico et Iohanni
    episcopis*   28n
  Hist. Con. Nic., cap. xxx   29n
Pseudo-Gelasius
  De duabus naturis in Christo   28n
Gildas (6th cent.)
  Epistolae   79n
  Glossa ordinaria   242n
Gratian (12th cent.)
  See *Corpus Iuris Canonici* (*De
    consecratione*, Dist. II, can.
    XLIV)
Gregory the Great (6th–7th cent.)
  Epistola XXXIII   57n
  Moralium, XXVII.xviii   243n
Gregory of Nazianzus (4th cent.)
  Orationes xviii. 8   25n

Haereseologia   28n
Harding, Thomas (16th cent.)
  confutation by 19n, 21n, 22n, 41n, 54n
Heywood, John (16th cent.)
  *A dialogue conteinyng . . . all
    the proverbs . . .*   103n
Hilary of Poitiers (4th cent.)
  Tract. in Ps. CXXVI   54n
  Comm. in Matth., cap. VIII   265n
Horace (1st cent. B.C.)
  Epistola I.18   73n
Hosius (16th cent.)
  De expresso Dei verbo   37n
Hostiens (Henry of Segusio, Card.
  of Ostia, 13th cent.)
  *Lectura in quinque Decretalium
    Gregorianarum libros*   49n

Innocentius III (12th–13th cent.)
  De sacro altaris mysterio   307n
Irenaeus (2d cent.)
  Contra haereses III.xix.3   194n

Jerome (4th–5th cent.)
  In Aggaeum proph. I.11   19n
  Apologia adv. libros Rufini, Lib.
    II   51n
  Comm. in Evang. sec. Marc.
    XVI   233n
  Epistola
    LI   39n
    LXXXVI   51n
    XCVII, *ad Demetrium*   39n
    CXLVI   22n, 55n
John Damascene (8th cent.)
  De imaginibus, Oratio I. 17   201n
Julius Caesar (1st cent. B.C.)
  Commentarii de bello Gallico   272

Lacrymæ Ecclesiæ   82
Lactantius (3d–4th cent.)
  Divinae Institutiones, Lib. I,
    cap. ii   313n
Latomus, Jacobus (16th cent.)
  *Opera, quae praecipue adversus
    horum temporum haere-
    ses . . .*   25n
Laziardus (16th cent.)
  *Epitomata a primaeva mundi
    origene*   75n
Leo I (5th cent.)
  Epistola ix.2   41n
Lily, George (16th cent.)
  Chronicon   75n

Martinus, Polonus (13th cent.)
  Chronicon expeditissimum   75n
Massæus (16th cent.)
  *Chroniconum multiplicis histo-
    riae . . . libri viginti*   82n
Mutius (16th cent.)
  De Germanorum prima origine   81n

Nauclerus (15th–16th cent.)
  Chronica . . . usque ad 1564   75n
Nicholas of Lyra (14th cent.)
  Biblia   242nn
Nicolaus Leonicus (15th–16th
  cent.)
  De varia historia libri tres   30n

Opusculum tripartitum, Lib. III,
  cap. vii   25n
Origen (3d cent.)
  In Leviticum, Hom. ix.5   39n
  *In Matt., commentarium tomus
    xi.14*   29n
  In Ep. ad Rom., Lib. III.8   30n

Panormitanus (Nicolo de Tudes-
  chi, 15th cent.)
  In tertio libro Decretalium   25n, 49n
Panvinius (16th cent.)
  Chronicon ecclesiasticum   75n
Pighius (16th cent.)
  Explicationes Catholicae   37n
Platina (15th cent.)
  *Liber de vita Christi ac de vitis
    . . . 1479* (or under title
    *De vitis ac gestis summorum
    pontif, 1551*)   26n, 75n
Pliny (1st cent.)
  Historia naturalis, Lib. XXXV,
    cap. X   75n
  Pœnitentiarius Asini   82
Polydore Vergil (16th cent.)
  Anglicae historicae, Lib. XXVII   75n
Prosper of Aquitaine (5th cent.)
  *Liber sententiarum ex operibus
    S. Augustini delibatum*   284n

INDEXES

Rufinus Tyrannius (4th–5th cent.)
   In Hieron. invect., Lib. I   16n

Sabellicus (15th–16th cent.)
   Exempla virtutum et vitiorum   75n

Sozomen (5th cent.)
   Historia ecclesiastica, Lib. i, cap. xi   25n

Statutes of the Realm,   83n, 84n

Tertullian (2d–3d cent.)
   Adversus Marcionem
     IV.5   76n
     IV.27.9   24n
   Apologeticus
     I.2   14n
     XVIII.4   44n
     XXXIX.3   38n

Theodoret (5th cent.)
   Eranistes seu Polymorphus. Dialogus II. Inconfusus   28n

Theophylact (11th cent.)
   In Evang. Ioannis, cap. vi, v. 53, seq., *enarratio*   28n

Thomas Aquinas (13th cent.)
   In quatuor Euangelia enarrationes   242n

Pseudo-Udalrichus (11th cent.)
   Epistola de continentia clericorum   25n

Vigilius Tapsensis (5th cent.)
   Contra Eutychetem, Lib. I   21n

Vincentius (13th cent.)
   Speculum historiale   75n

Vitae Patrum
   Lib. III.130   333n
   Lib. VII, cap. xv.2   333n

Scripture References

Genesis
3:19 346
4:9 346
6 35
6:12 35
7 35
24:33 337
31:39 337
39:1-6 337

Exodus
20:4-5 201
20:15 341

Numbers
16 15
19 197
22 ff. 117
22:21 ff. 201

Deuteronomy
6:5 204
12:32 201
25:1 303

I Samuel
11:1 ff. 55

I Kings
8:11 72
9:30 72
18:41 ff. 348
19:10 36

Psalms
5:6 270
16:10 164
18:41 236
19:1 202
19:4 240
22 217
32:1 205
51:10-12 206
68:18 244
79 296
84:3 .... 284 f.
91:13 243
109:7 236
111:10 173
116 296
119:105 .... 109, 218
128:2 346
143:2 205
145:15-16 178

Proverbs
10:22 338
14:12 333
19:21 54
21:30 54

Ecclesiastes
9:1 343

Isaiah
1:6 36
1:21 36

Isaiah—*continued*
1:22 36
9:2 231
9:20 338
11:9 63
29:13 218
38:13 217
42:7-9 246
43:27 197
49:23 50
56:10 48
59:21 214
63:16 277
64:4 249
65:25 63
66:1 176

Jeremiah
2:28 32
7:4 34
11:13 32
17:7 ff. 275
23:23-24 177
23:24 176
48:10 336

Ezekiel
18:21 344
33:14 ff. 203
33:19-20 203

Daniel
6:4 337

SCRIPTURE REFERENCES 359

Micah
3:6 48
Habbakuk
1:5 239
2:4 275
Malachi
4:2 300
Ecclesiasticus
1:21 279
15:1 279
Matthew
3:17 195
5:13 48
5:14 109
5:20 247
5:45 343
6:9 ff. 176
6:23 284
6:33 342
7 191
7:7 141
7:12 181
7:20 281
9:15 312
10:1 243
10:7 196
11:14 29
11:27 121
13:31-32 235
16:17 135
16:18 213
17 203
17:5 195
19:29 347
21:13 36
22:19-21 202
22:37 ff. 100
23:8 ff. 119
24:23 312
24:28 312
25:46 279
26 291
26:26-30 290
28:18 ff. 213
28:19-20 196
28:20 196

Mark
7:7 218
12:30 & par. 158
13:14 & par. 34
14 291
14:22 ff. 300
14:22-25 290
14:25 & par. ... 29, 302
15:31 164
16:15 213
16:15 ff. 196
16:16 ff. & par. ... 214

Luke
2:10 109
6:38 347
10 (?) 196
11:1 ff. 176
11:13 343
11:52 24
12:48 346
16:15 ...... 247, 327, 333
19:1-10 344
19:8 345
19:10 246
22 291
22:19-20 290

John
1:1 .... 107, 194
1:4 107
1:5 104
1:9 109
1:12 137
1:13 300
1:14 .... 107, 194
1:17 206
1:29 .... 210, 268
3:5 172
3:14 205
3:16 205
3:36 ...... 108, 195, 278
4:34 337
5:23 168
5:29 270
6 .... 294, 313
6:29 285
6:35-36 208
6:45 119
6:47 278
6:52 ff. 292
6:53 306
6:63 107
8 .... 106, 109
8 f. 126
8:34, 39 34
8:40 f. 55
8:49 16
10:29 196
12:24 .... 190, 202
14:3 312
14:12 243
14:21 279
14:23 f. 279
14:26 213
15:1-11 196
15:4-5 283
15:14 136
16:5 ff. 208
16:7 312
16:13 201
16:22 312
16:23 ..... 141, 176, 236
16:33 249
17:14 213

John—continued
17:17 209
17:19 209
17:20 ff. (?) 208, 210
19:30 32

Acts
2:42 302
2:44 345
2:46 302
3:21 208
5:1-11 75
5:29 215
8:9 ff. 212
9:4 249
10:43 265
11 155
15:9 209
20:7 302
20:35 346
24:14 19

Romans
1:7 275
1:16 .... 38, 213
2:8 270
3:4-5 203
3:20 108
3:23 f. 263
3:24 204
5:1 131
5:8 ff. 133
5:20 193
6:1-11, 23 212
6:3 f. 126
7 191
7:7 217
7:9 .... 190, 218
7:9-11 217
7:11 216
7:13 .... 216, 217
7:14 216
7:18 218
7:24 218
8:3 f. 263
8:12 ff. 125, 206
8:13 206
8:16 138
10:4 263
10:9 238
11:32 218
12:13 315
12:21 179
13 89
13:10 100
14:23 283

I Corinthians
2:9 249
2:11 119
2:15 119
3:5 ff. 196

I Corinthians—continued

3:7	343
3:11	198
4:1	196
4:3	54
4:7	338
5:9 ff.	114
6:11	210
7:32	327
7:32 f.	335
10	302, 320
10:16	293, 302
11	291, 302
11:23 ff.	214, 300
11:23-25	174, 290
12:3	135
14:12 ff.	31
14:16	46
15:13 ff.	164
15:14	237
15:17	237
15:25	213
15:56	217

II Corinthians

1:22	122, 125
3:6	104
3:18	125
4:13 (?)	277
12:14	109

Galatians

1:6-9	196
1:8	38
1:11-12	196
2:16	263
2:21	265
3:11	107
3:11 (?)	262
3:16	162
3:21	265
3:24	217
5:4	265
5:6	273
5:19-21	128
6:1	234

Ephesians

1:10	66
1:21	20
2:3	108
2:4 ff.	133
2:8	206
2:9	265
2:10	33
2:13	231
2:20	36, 214
4:7 ff.	168
4:8	244
4:10	166
4:28	346
5:8	109

Philippians

2:5 ff.	165
2:12	33
4:13	249

Colossians

1:13	33
1:15	194
1:21-22	317
2:9	194
3:1 ff.	206
3:24	336

I Thessalonians

1:9	33
4:7	33
5:19	130

II Thessalonians

2:7	307
3:10	346

I Timothy

2:1	326
2:1-2	332
2:2	327
4:1	25
4:8	180
6:10	118

II Timothy

3:13	24
3:16	105
3:16-17	18
4:14	142

Titus

1:16	270, 272
2:12	212

Hebrews

1:3	194, 317
2:17	190
5:5-6	195
6:4 ff.	111, 142
7:24-25	200
7:25	112
7:27	207
9:12	207
9:22	207
9:26	316
10:10	207, 317
10:12	317
10:14	317
10:18	207, 315
10:26 ff.	111, 142
11:1	273
11:6	273, 283
12	207
13:4	335
14	207

James

1:7	180
1:27 (bis)	333

James—continued

2:14 ff.	270
2:18	281
2:19	272

I Peter

1:9	282
3:18-19	163
4:1	194

II Peter

1:5-7	281
1:10	281
3:10	169
3:13	168

I John

1:2	95
1:6	280
1:7	207
2:1-2	317
2:3-4	277
2:4	96, 280
2:5	278
2:7	95
2:9-11	280
2:12	96
2:18	95
2:21	96
2:25	95
2:26	94
2:28	96
3:2 f.	278
3:4	95
3:6	95
3:6-7	278
3:7	96
3:9	95, 142
3:10	95, 280
3:12	95
3:15	96
3:16	94
3:17	95, 340
3:18	96
3:19	96
3:19-22	278
4:6	96
4:17	94
4:20	280
5:1	95, 278
5:4	117
5:6	96
5:13	95, 278
5:18	95, 278
5:21	96

III John

11	278

Revelation

13	63
13:13	63
21:6-8	279

www.ingramcontent.com/pod-product-compliance
Lightning Source LLC
Chambersburg PA
CBHW031403290426
44110CB00011B/246